Parliaments and Politics during the Cromwellian Protectorate

This ground-breaking volume fills a major historiographical gap by providing the first detailed book-length study of the period of the Protectorate Parliaments from September 1654 to April 1659. The study is very broad in its scope, covering topics as diverse as the British and Irish dimensions of the Protectorate Parliaments, the political and social nature of factions, problems of management, the legal and judicial aspects of Parliament's functions, foreign policy, and the nature of the parliamentary franchise and elections in this period. In its wide-ranging analysis of Parliaments and politics throughout the Protectorate, the book also examines both Lord Protectors, all three Protectorate Parliaments, and the reasons why Oliver and Richard Cromwell were never able to achieve a stable working relationship with any Parliament. Its chronological coverage extends to the demise of the Third Protectorate Parliament in April 1659. This comprehensive account will appeal to historians of early modern British political history.

PATRICK LITTLE is Senior Research Fellow at the History of Parliament Trust, London.

DAVID L. SMITH is Fellow and Director of Studies in History at Selwyn College, Cambridge.

Cambridge Studies in Early Modern British History

Series editors

ANTHONY FLETCHER
Emeritus Professor of English Social History, University of London

JOHN GUY
Fellow, Clare College, Cambridge

JOHN MORRILL
*Professor of British and Irish History, University of Cambridge,
and Fellow of Selwyn College*

This is a series of monographs and studies covering many aspects of the history of the British Isles between the late fifteenth century and the early eighteenth century. It includes the work of established scholars and pioneering work by a new generation of scholars. It includes both reviews and revisions of major topics and books which open up new historical terrain or which reveal startling new perspectives on familiar subjects. All the volumes set detailed research into our broader perspectives, and the books are intended for the use of students as well as of their teachers.

For a list of titles in the series, see end of book.

PARLIAMENTS AND POLITICS DURING THE CROMWELLIAN PROTECTORATE

PATRICK LITTLE
History of Parliament Trust

AND

DAVID L. SMITH
University of Cambridge

CAMBRIDGE
UNIVERSITY PRESS

CAMBRIDGE UNIVERSITY PRESS
Cambridge, New York, Melbourne, Madrid, Cape Town, Singapore, São Paulo, Delhi

Cambridge University Press
The Edinburgh Building, Cambridge CB2 8RU, UK

Published in the United States of America by Cambridge University Press, New York

www.cambridge.org
Information on this title: www.cambridge.org/9780521838672

First published 2007

Printed in the United Kingdom at the University Press, Cambridge

A catalogue record for this publication is available from the British Library

ISBN 978-0-521-83867-2 hardback

For Barry Coward and John Morrill,
with gratitude

CONTENTS

PREFACE

In the course of planning, researching, and writing this book, we have incurred many debts. We are very grateful to John Morrill for his advice and assistance in planning the book and devising the chapter structure. He also gave us helpful comments on an early version of chapter 6, as did Barry Coward on drafts of chapters 5 and 11. We have benefited greatly from conversations with many other friends and colleagues, especially Phil Baker, Andrew Barclay, Alexander Courtney, Colin Davis, Tim Harris, Mark Kishlansky, Kirsteen MacKenzie, Jason Peacey, Stephen Roberts, David Scott, Graham Seel, David Underdown, and Blair Worden. Needless to say, none of the above bears any responsibility for the shortcomings of the finished book.

We are most grateful to Clive Holmes and to Jason Peacey for allowing us to read work prior to publication. We also wish to thank the History of Parliament Trust for permitting us to see draft constituency articles before publication, and to make use of this material in the chapter on elections. Thanks are due to His Grace the Duke of Northumberland for permission to consult the microfilm of the Alnwick Castle manuscripts in the British Library. An early version of chapter 5 was presented at a seminar at the Institute of Historical Research, London; early versions of chapter 6 were read at seminars at Cambridge, Sussex, Yale, and the University of Pennsylvania, and at the Protectorate symposium held at the History of Parliament Trust, London. We are indebted to all those who participated on these occasions for their helpful contributions and suggestions. We are also grateful to the editorial team at Cambridge University Press, and especially to Karen Anderson Howes, Rosina Di Marzo, and Michael Watson.

The dedication reflects our profound and longstanding debt to two of the pre-eminent historians of this period and, appropriately, the past and present presidents of the Cromwell Association: it is offered with gratitude for their unstinting friendship, support, and inspiration.

This book is the result of a collaborative endeavour. We jointly devised the overall shape and chapter structure, and then allocated each chapter to one of us to produce a working draft. We then swapped drafts, sent comments to each other, and rewrote in the light of them. DLS is principally responsible for chapters 1, 3, 4, 6, 7, 8, and 9, and appendix 1; PJSL for chapters 2, 5, 10, 11, 12, and 13, and appendix 2.

In the footnotes and bibliography, the place of publication is London unless otherwise stated. Spelling in quotations from primary sources has been modernised and the standard abbreviated forms have been expanded. Dates are given in old style, except that the year is taken to begin on 1 January rather than 25 March.

ABBREVIATIONS

A & O	C. H. Firth and R. S. Rait, eds., *Acts and Ordinances of the Interregnum, 1642–1660* (3 vols., 1911)
Abbott	W. C. Abbott, ed., *Writings and Speeches of Oliver Cromwell* (4 vols., Cambridge, Mass., 1937–47)
BL	British Library
Bodl.	Bodleian Library
Burton	J. T. Rutt, ed., *Diary of Thomas Burton, Esq.* (4 vols., 1828)
CJ	*Journals of the House of Commons*
Clarendon, *History*	Edward, Earl of Clarendon, *The History of the Rebellion and Civil Wars in England*, ed. W. Dunn Macray (6 vols., Oxford, 1888)
Clarendon SP	*State Papers Collected by Edward, Earl of Clarendon* (3 vols., Oxford, 1757)
Clarke Papers	C. H. Firth and Frances Henderson, eds., *The Clarke Papers* (5 vols., Camden Society, 2nd series, 49, 1891; 54, 1894; 61 [*recte* 60], 1899; 62, 1901; 5th series, 27, 2005)
CSPD	*Calendar of State Papers Domestic*
CSPI	*Calendar of State Papers Ireland*
CSPV	*Calendar of State Papers Venetian*
EHR	*English Historical Review*
Firth, *Last Years*	C. H. Firth, *The Last Years of the Protectorate, 1656–1658* (2 vols., 1909)
Gardiner, *Commonwealth and Protectorate*	S. R. Gardiner, *History of the Commonwealth and Protectorate, 1649–1656* (4 vols., 1903; reprinted 1989)
Gardiner, *Constitutional Documents*	S. R. Gardiner, ed., *Constitutional Documents of the Puritan Revolution, 1625–1660* (3rd edn, Oxford, 1906)

Guizot, *Richard Cromwell*	F. G. P. Guizot, *History of Richard Cromwell and the Restoration of Charles II*, trans. A. R. Scoble (2 vols., 1856)
HJ	*Historical Journal*
HMC	Historical Manuscripts Commission
HR	*Historical Research*
LJ	*Journals of the House of Lords*
Lomas–Carlyle	S. C. Lomas, ed., *The Letters and Speeches of Oliver Cromwell, with Elucidations by Thomas Carlyle* (3 vols., 1904)
Ludlow	C. H. Firth, ed., *The Memoirs of Edmund Ludlow* (2 vols., Oxford, 1894)
NAS	National Archives of Scotland
Nicholas Papers	G. F. Warner, ed., *The Nicholas Papers* (4 vols., Camden Society, 2nd series, 40, 1886; 50, 1893; 57, 1897; 3rd series, 31, 1920)
NLI	National Library of Ireland
NLS	National Library of Scotland
NRAS	National Register of Archives for Scotland
ODNB	*The Oxford Dictionary of National Biography* (Oxford, 2004)
OPH	[Various editors,] *The Parliamentary or Constitutional History of England* (often referred to as the 'Old Parliamentary History') (24 vols., 1751–61)
Parl. Hist.	*Parliamentary History*
Schilling	W. A. H. Schilling, 'The Parliamentary Diary of Sir John Gell, 5 February–21 March 1659' (MA thesis, Vanderbilt University, 1961)
Stephen	William Stephen, ed., *Register of the Consultations of the Ministers of Edinburgh and some other Brethren of the Ministry* (2 vols., Scottish History Society, 3rd series, 1, 1921; 16, 1930)
TNA	The National Archives (Public Record Office), Kew
TSP	Thomas Birch, ed., *A Collection of the State Papers of John Thurloe, Esq.* (7 vols., 1742)
Vaughan	Robert Vaughan, ed., *The Protectorate of Oliver Cromwell and the State of Europe during the Early Part of the Reign of Louis XIV* (2 vols., 1839)

Whitelocke, *Diary*   Ruth Spalding, ed., *The Diary of Bulstrode Whitelocke, 1605–1675* (British Academy, Records of Social and Economic History, new series, 13, Oxford, 1990)

Whitelocke, *Memorials*   Bulstrode Whitelocke, *Memorials of the English Affairs* (4 vols., Oxford, 1853)

The place of publication of printed works in the above list, and in the footnotes, is London unless otherwise indicated.

1

Introduction: historiography and sources

THE PROBLEM

Amidst the vast body of scholarly writing that has been published on seventeenth-century Britain in general, and on the revolutionary events of the 1640s and 1650s in particular, the period of the Cromwellian Protectorate from December 1653 to May 1659 remains relatively neglected. Several recent writers on Cromwell and the Interregnum have remarked on the lack of a detailed book-length study of the politics of the Protectorate, and specifically of the Protectorate Parliaments. Ivan Roots, for example, has observed that although 'biographies of Cromwell abound ... There is surprisingly little detailed work on the central government and politics of the Protectorate and less still specifically on the Protectorate Parliaments.'[1] Similarly, Barry Coward has commented that 'there is no full published account of parliamentary politics during the Protectorate',[2] while Peter Gaunt has written that 'the three Protectorate Parliaments ... have attracted no ... thorough investigation and remain sadly understudied. Moreover, most of the rather meagre attention has tended to focus on the second Protectorate Parliament, to the further neglect of the other two.'[3] A symposium on the Protectorate held in January 2004 at the History of Parliament Trust in London revealed both the limitations of the historiography to date and the remarkable potential for further research on this period.[4] At present, there is no detailed monograph, focused on

---

[1] Ivan Roots, ed., *'Into another Mould': Aspects of the Interregnum* (2nd edn, Exeter, 1998), p. 145.
[2] Barry Coward, *Oliver Cromwell* (1991), p. 190.
[3] Peter Gaunt, 'Cromwell's Purge? Exclusions and the First Protectorate Parliament', *Parl. Hist.*, 6 (1987), 1–2. Cf. his comment about the first two Protectorate Parliaments that 'a comprehensive and compelling full-length account of these Parliaments is badly needed': Peter Gaunt, 'Oliver Cromwell and his Protectorate Parliaments: Co-operation, Conflict and Control', in Roots, *'Into another Mould'*, p. 73.
[4] Revised versions of the papers presented at this symposium have recently been published in Patrick Little, ed., *The Cromwellian Protectorate* (Woodbridge, 2007).

parliamentary history, that spans the period between the end of 1653 (when the studies by Blair Worden and Austin Woolrych end)[5] and the autumn of 1658 (when that by Ronald Hutton begins).[6] There are a number of relevant unpublished doctoral theses, notably those by Sarah Jones, Peter Gaunt, Carol Egloff, and Paul Pinckney, but these are not readily available to a wide audience.[7] The present book is therefore intended to fill this major histor-iographical gap.

    Although the nature of parliamentary politics during the Protectorate is the book's central focus, this will be set within a broad context. The scope of this study includes the British and Irish dimensions of the Protectorate Parliaments, the political and social nature of factions, problems of manage-ment, the legal and judicial aspects of Parliament's functions, foreign policy, the reasons why Oliver and Richard Cromwell were never able to achieve a stable working relationship with any Parliament, and the nature of the parliamentary franchise and elections in this period. The aim is thus to construct a wide-ranging analysis of Parliaments and politics throughout the Protectorate. The volume examines both Lord Protectors and all three Protectorate Parliaments, and its chronological coverage extends to the demise of the Protectorate in May 1659. This opening chapter will briefly survey the existing historiography surrounding the Protectorate Parliaments, Oliver and Richard Cromwell's relations with them, and the politics of the Protectorate in general, and will indicate how the present study will add to or qualify that historiography. The chapter will also describe the principal categories of primary sources, both printed and in manuscript, on which the book is based.

HISTORIOGRAPHY

Historians in search of a really detailed narrative of the Protectorate and its Parliaments still have to go back to the works of S. R. Gardiner and

---

[5] Blair Worden, *The Rump Parliament, 1648–1653* (Cambridge, 1974); Austin Woolrych, *Commonwealth to Protectorate* (Oxford, 1982).
[6] Ronald Hutton, *The Restoration: A Political and Religious History of England and Wales, 1658–1667* (Oxford, 1985).
[7] Sarah E. Jones, 'The Composition and Activity of the Protectorate Parliaments' (Ph.D thesis, University of Exeter, 1988); Peter Gaunt, 'The Councils of the Protectorate, from December 1653 to September 1658' (Ph.D thesis, University of Exeter, 1983); Carol S. Egloff, 'Settlement and Kingship: The Army, the Gentry, and the Offer of the Crown to Oliver Cromwell' (Ph.D thesis, Yale University, 1990); Paul J. Pinckney, 'A Cromwellian Parliament: The Elections and Personnel of 1656' (Ph.D thesis, Vanderbilt University, 1962). Although not published in their entireties, parts of some of these works have nevertheless appeared in print, and are cited in the footnotes of this and other chapters.

Sir Charles Firth.[8] These provide a deeply researched and thorough account of the period that has not yet been superseded. The fullest recent study of the politics of the Protectorate, by Barry Coward, offers an excellent overview but makes no claim to analyse parliamentary proceedings in any great depth.[9] The more detailed historiography of particular aspects of the Protectorate Parliaments will be discussed more fully in the relevant chapters, but it is worth noting here that to date only three articles have focused specifically on the Protectorate Parliaments as a group, and all three largely confined their attention to the first two without more than a brief look at Richard Cromwell's Parliament.

In 1956, Hugh Trevor-Roper published a highly influential article on 'Oliver Cromwell and his Parliaments' in which he suggested that the main problem lay in Cromwell's failure to manage his Parliaments effectively. 'They failed', he wrote, 'through lack of that parliamentary management by the executive which, in the correct dosage, is the essential nourishment of any sound parliamentary life.' Taking Elizabeth I's handling of Parliaments as his yardstick, Trevor-Roper claimed that by comparison Cromwell was inept, inconsistent, and lacking in coherent purpose: he was 'a natural back-bencher'.[10] The article was compellingly written and elegantly sustained, and it was only in 1988 that it received significant criticism, from Roger Howell. Howell argued persuasively that the comparison with Elizabethan Parliaments was inappropriate, that the main problem was not one of management, and that the army 'both stood in the way of the legitimation of the government via the parliamentary route and heightened the level of the politics of frustration and confrontation within Parliament itself'.[11] Although Howell's untimely death in 1989 prevented him from developing these ideas further, subsequent work has generally underlined the validity of his criticisms. Sir Geoffrey Elton, Michael Graves, and others have challenged Sir John Neale's interpretation of Elizabethan Parliaments on which Trevor-Roper relied, thus making it even clearer that later sixteenth-century Parliaments cannot be treated as a model against which to judge the Protectorate

---

[8] Gardiner, *Commonwealth and Protectorate*, III–IV; Firth, *Last Years*. An account of the years 1658–60 is found in a somewhat less distinguished but still useful volume: Godfrey Davies, *The Restoration of Charles II, 1658–1660* (Oxford, 1955).

[9] Barry Coward, *The Cromwellian Protectorate* (Manchester, 2002).

[10] Hugh Trevor-Roper, 'Oliver Cromwell and his Parliaments', in Trevor-Roper, *Religion, the Reformation and Social Change* (3rd edn, 1984), p. 388. This article first appeared in Richard Pares and Alan J. P. Taylor, eds., *Essays Presented to Sir Lewis Namier* (1956), pp. 1–48.

[11] R. C. Richardson, ed., *Images of Oliver Cromwell: Essays for and by Roger Howell, Jr* (Manchester, 1993), p. 134.

Parliaments.[12] Most recently, Peter Gaunt has also revised the Trevor-Roper thesis by suggesting that Cromwell's failure to secure parliamentary co-operation owed most to his own and the members' inexperience, and to his ultimately unrealistic hope that they would share his pursuit of ideals such as liberty of conscience.[13] The present volume will offer a further refinement to this picture by drawing out the underlying tensions and contradictions within Cromwell's own vision of Parliaments. In particular, the book will explore the inherent difficulty that he faced in his attempts to use an institution intended as the 'representative of the whole realm' to promote a radical agenda that was never espoused by more than a minority of the nation.[14]

Thanks to Elton and Graves, the story of Elizabeth I's Parliaments now looks very different from when Trevor-Roper, drawing on Neale's work, used them as his point of comparison for the Protectorate Parliaments. This 'revisionism' has also characterised recent research on early seventeenth-century Parliaments, most notably by Conrad Russell.[15] One of the key features of the 'revisionist' history of late Tudor and early Stuart Parliaments has been to accentuate how much they were the successors of medieval Parliaments rather than the forerunners of modern Parliaments. By highlighting Parliament's significance as the monarch's Great Council and High Court, and the political implications of those functions, 'revisionism' has emphasised that Parliament remained what it had been in the Middle Ages: part of the machinery of royal government rather than a counterbalance to it. Indeed, Elton's account of Elizabethan Parliaments owed an explicit debt to F. W. Maitland's earlier work on the Parliament Roll of 1305.[16] The importance of this medieval context was similarly evident when Russell wrote that: 'it could still be said in the seventeenth century, as Fleta said in the thirteenth, that "the King has his court and council in his Parliaments"'.[17] These continuities in parliamentary history have likewise formed a central theme in David Smith's recent survey of Stuart Parliaments.[18]

---

[12] See in particular G. R. Elton, *The Parliament of England, 1559–1581* (Cambridge, 1986); David Dean, *Law-Making and Society in Late Elizabethan England: The Parliament of England, 1584–1601* (Cambridge, 1996); and Michael A. R. Graves, *Elizabethan Parliaments, 1559–1601* (2nd edn, Harlow, 1996). For a judicious blend of the revisionist and traditional interpretations, see T. E. Hartley, *Elizabeth's Parliaments: Queen, Lords and Commons, 1559–1601* (Manchester, 1992).

[13] Gaunt, 'Oliver Cromwell and his Protectorate Parliaments'.

[14] Cromwell's religious policies, and in particular his attempts to extend liberty of conscience more widely, are discussed in detail in chapters 6 and 9.

[15] See especially Conrad Russell, *Parliaments and English Politics, 1621–1629* (Oxford, 1979); and Russell, *Unrevolutionary England, 1603–1642* (1990), pp. 1–57.

[16] G. R. Elton, *F. W. Maitland* (1985), pp. 56–69.   [17] Russell, *Unrevolutionary England*, p. 7.

[18] David L. Smith, *The Stuart Parliaments, 1603–1689* (1999).

The 'revisionist' emphasis on Parliament as an institution of royal government raises interesting questions when applied to the Parliaments of the Interregnum, and in particular those of the Protectorate. What was the status and significance of the Parliaments that met while the monarchy was abolished? Sarah Jones recounts that, when she told Geoffrey Elton that she was doing doctoral research on the Protectorate Parliaments, he replied that there were no such Parliaments because there was no monarch to summon them.[19] The study of Parliaments in a republican setting necessarily involves adopting a different approach from the 'revisionist' account of Elizabethan and early Stuart Parliaments, so much of which rests on the assumption that parliamentary history can be fully understood only within a monarchical framework. Furthermore, the Protectorate Parliaments operated within a very different political and constitutional context from their sixteenth- and early seventeenth-century predecessors. Between 1642 and 1653, Parliament had assumed an unprecedented degree of executive power, and this created a legacy of administrative and legislative control with which the Protectorate Parliaments necessarily had to engage. The Protectorate Parliaments were also the only Parliaments in British history that met and conducted their business under the terms of a written constitution: first the Instrument of Government (1653) and then the Humble Petition and Advice (1657). This was very different from the web of unwritten custom and tradition that had provided the setting for earlier Parliaments. The role of the Lord Protector as head of state in relation to Parliaments was ambiguous: the paper constitutions granted him extensive but not unlimited powers, and he did not have complete freedom to determine when Parliament met, and for how long, in the way that the monarch had done prior to 1641. The Instrument of Government also gave the council much greater control over the membership of Parliament than ever before, although the Humble Petition and Advice later curtailed these powers. All these very significant contrasts surely justify taking a different approach from the one that historians have applied to Elizabethan and early Stuart Parliaments.

This book therefore seeks to place the Protectorate Parliaments within their wider political context in the Britain of the 1650s. It is a political rather than a procedural or institutional study. The book does not attempt to analyse in depth the social background of the members who sat in the Protectorate Parliaments. We felt that this would only anticipate the full-scale analysis that will in due course appear in the History of Parliament volumes for 1640–60, and that it would therefore be better to devote the present volume to other problems and issues. One of its chief priorities is to

---

[19] Jones, 'Composition and Activity of the Protectorate Parliaments', p. 1.

deepen our understanding of the nature of political groupings – such as the Presbyterians, the courtiers, and the army interest – and the tensions that existed between them.[20] It seeks to reconstruct as carefully as possible the motives of the leading political actors, especially the two Protectors, and among its conclusions will be that Richard Cromwell was more different from his father than has often been suggested, and that his fall in 1659 was by no means a foregone conclusion. This book analyses the range of activities that took place within these Parliaments, and the diversity of issues that preoccupied their members. This in turn reflected the Protectoral regime's relations with the social and political elite more broadly, and one of the insights that the book does absorb from 'revisionism' is Conrad Russell's seminal suggestion that the early Stuarts' problems were 'not difficulties with their Parliaments; they were difficulties which were reflected in their Parliaments'.[21] Much the same was true of the Cromwellian Protectors and their Parliaments.

Interestingly, despite the important contrasts between the Protectorate Parliaments and their Elizabethan and early Stuart predecessors, there is considerable evidence that they sought to follow established procedures and looked to 'ancient' precedents for guidance. For instance, one of the first actions of the first Protectorate Parliament was to follow the customary practice of establishing a committee for privileges.[22] In similar vein, members affirmed that 'the privilege of Parliament did begin from the very day of the election', and that the power of making war historically rested with Parliament.[23] It was not so much that members of the Protectorate Parliaments were indifferent to precedents as that they were often uncertain about how to apply them to new situations and in novel circumstances. During the trial of James Nayler in December 1656, for example, members disputed which precedents were relevant and how they related to the present case.[24] Equally, much of the ceremonial that attended the giving of Protectoral assent to bills was traditional in form.[25] Elizabeth Read Foster has likewise observed that when the Other House was established under the terms of the Humble Petition and Advice, the use of Black Rod as messenger was revived; the House adhered to 'a corpus of procedure' that had been 'firmly established' in the Lords in 'the years 1603–49'; and in January 1658 the committee for petitions in the Other House was chosen on the third day

[20] These political groupings, and relations between them, are discussed in detail in chapter 5.
[21] Russell, *Parliaments and English Politics*, p. 417.   [22] Burton, I, xxi.
[23] Burton, I, xliv–xlv, xlviii.
[24] See, for example, Burton, I, 30, 120–1, 163. This is discussed more fully in chapter 8.
[25] Burton, I, cxcii.

of the session, following the usual pre-1649 procedure.[26] The members of the Other House regularly asked for the records of the Lords to be examined for precedents that could be used to guide them in their deliberations.[27] The Other House was thus very conservative in outlook. Much the same can be said of the Commons, despite the radical political, religious, and constitutional upheaval of the Protectorate. It was thus possible to be conservative in form and radical in debate, and this paradox will form another theme of this book. This helps to nuance and extend recent work on the Cromwellian Protectorate, and to underline that we can do justice to the conservative aspects of the Protectorate, and the continuities that persisted within it, without simply depicting it as a slow trek back towards a Stuart restoration.[28]

SOURCES

Finally, it is worth briefly describing the main categories of primary sources on which this book is based. What follows cannot claim to be in any way an exhaustive list, even of materials cited in the footnotes, but it will at least give a rough sense of the surviving evidence and what this can reveal about the Protectorate Parliaments. It can broadly be divided into official and unofficial sources.

First of all, the institutional records generated by Parliament's conduct of business provide a vital foundation for any kind of parliamentary history, and they have been the starting-point for the present volume.[29] The printed *Commons' Journal* offers an authoritative record of matters discussed, decisions reached, committees appointed, orders and letters issued, and bills read and passed. The journal of the Other House in 1658–9 is a similar source and has also been printed, although historians have so far made very little use of it.[30] No legislation received the royal assent during the period 1642–60, and *Statutes of the Realm* therefore does not exist for these years, but Firth and Rait filled this gap in 1911 with three admirable volumes that contain the acts produced by the three Protectorate Parliaments.[31] Between them, these sources constitute the official records of the Parliaments.

---

[26] E. R. Foster, *The House of Lords, 1603–1649: Structure, Procedure and the Nature of its Business* (Chapel Hill, 1983), pp. 66, 209, 266, n. 158.

[27] For some examples, see HMC, *The Manuscripts of the House of Lords, 1699–1702* (1908), pp. 513, 526–7, 551.

[28] Cf. Little, *Cromwellian Protectorate*.

[29] Cf. Elton, *Parliament of England*, pp. 3–15; Elton, *Studies in Tudor and Stuart Politics and Government* (4 vols., Cambridge, 1974–92), III, 58–155.

[30] HMC, *MSS of the House of Lords, 1699–1702*, pp. 503–67.   [31] *A & O.*

The unofficial records include first of all the three private diaries that survive for this period, by Thomas Burton, Guybon Goddard, and Sir John Gell. Of these, only the first has been published in its entirety, in a four-volume edition by John Towill Rutt in 1828 that was reprinted in 1974.[32] Burton's diary covers only the second and third Protectorate Parliaments, and is rather fuller for 1659 than for 1656–8.[33] Rutt printed, as a preface to the first volume of Burton's diary, the diary of Guybon Goddard for the first Protectorate Parliament.[34] Goddard also sat in the third Protectorate Parliament, but his diary for that Parliament (which ends on 5 March 1659) so far remains unpublished.[35] Sir John Gell's diary only covers part of the third Protectorate Parliament, and is less full than that of Burton. W. A. H. Schilling edited the portion from 5 February to 21 March for his dissertation, but the complete diary continues up to 8 April 1659.[36] Gell's diary is less comprehensive and harder to follow than Burton's, not least because he was less careful to identify speakers, but his diary does sometimes add to Burton's, especially on occasions when the latter was absent from the House.[37] Scholars have generally used the diaries of Goddard and Gell much less than that of Burton, and here they are deployed wherever they add significantly to Burton's account.

Between them, these three diaries all throw useful light on proceedings in the Protectorate Parliaments. In recent years, there has been a lively debate over how far it is acceptable to quote directly from such seventeenth-century diaries given that they cannot be taken as verbatim transcripts of words actually spoken in Parliament.[38] In summarising and commenting in detail

---

[32] The manuscript of Burton's diary is BL, Add. MSS 15859–64.

[33] To illustrate this point, in the printed edition Burton's account of the first sitting of the second Protectorate Parliament takes up 739 pages, the second sitting 164 pages, and the third Protectorate Parliament 1,082 pages.

[34] Burton, I, i–cxcii. All page references to the first volume of Rutt's edition of Burton's diary that are cited with lower-case Roman pagination are to the diary of Guybon Goddard. This diary unfortunately breaks off in mid-sentence on 18 December 1654.

[35] The original manuscript is apparently lost, but a transcript of 1720 survives as BL, Add. MS 5138: pp. 105–283 cover the period from 19 January to 5 March 1659.

[36] W. A. H. Schilling, 'The Parliamentary Diary of Sir John Gell, 5 February–21 March 1659' (MA thesis, Vanderbilt University, 1961). The original manuscript is Derbyshire Record Office, MS D258.

[37] Ivan Roots offers a helpful assessment of these three diaries in his introduction to the reprint of Burton's diary (New York, 1974), and his lives of Burton and Goddard in the *ODNB* are valuable as well. Derek Hirst usefully discusses the three diaries' respective qualities in 'Concord and Discord in Richard Cromwell's House of Commons', *EHR*, 103 (1988), 339–58; and see also Schilling, pp. 1–2.

[38] The initial debate can be found in Elton, *Studies*, II, 3–18, the latter part of which is a reply to J. H. Hexter, 'Parliament under the Lens', *British Studies Monitor*, 3 (1972–3), 4–15. For Elton's views, see also Elton, *Parliament of England*, pp. 10–14. Hexter made a further contribution in 'Quoting the Commons, 1604–1642', in DeLoyd J. Guth and John W. McKenna, eds., *Tudor Rule and Revolution* (Cambridge, 1982), pp. 369–91. More

on this debate elsewhere, David Smith has suggested that there is no reason to avoid altogether quoting from members' private diaries, provided that one always bears in mind their limitations as sources and does not treat them like a seventeenth-century equivalent of *Hansard*.[39] It also seems important wherever feasible to try to choose the most reliable account rather than merely the most quotable, although the varying degrees of reliability among diarists are not always very easy to establish. In the present book, different accounts of speeches have been compared where possible, but often there are only unique accounts, and this needs to be borne in mind when quotations are given for what a speaker was reported as having said in one of the diaries.

With Cromwell's own words, scholars are on rather firmer – or at least more fully documented – ground. Throughout this book, the basic edition that has been chosen when quoting from Cromwell's surviving letters and speeches is that by Thomas Carlyle, as revised and extended by S. C. Lomas in 1904.[40] This has generally been preferred to W. C. Abbott's edition for the reasons that John Morrill has explored in an extended critique of Abbott, namely that Lomas–Carlyle is at least as reliable as Abbott, more readily available, and much easier to use.[41] For Cromwell's letters, Abbott adds virtually nothing to Lomas–Carlyle. For his speeches, the finest edition is that by Charles L. Stainer, and Ivan Roots took this as the basis of his Everyman edition.[42] For ease of reference and to assist checking, all quotations from Cromwell's speeches are here cited from Lomas–Carlyle – which remains the most widely available edition – but every extract has been compared with the text in Stainer/Roots and any significant variations are noted in the relevant footnote. The Stainer/Roots and Abbott editions have been quoted only on those (relatively rare) occasions where they add material not printed in Lomas–Carlyle.

Several collections of correspondence throw valuable light on parliamentary proceedings and help us to locate them within a wider political context. This is a large and diverse category of material, and here there is space only to indicate a cross-section of the most important examples. The voluminous papers of Cromwell's secretary John Thurloe, mostly published in a

recently, John Morrill has addressed these issues in three articles: 'Reconstructing the History of Early Stuart Parliaments', *Archives*, 21 (1994), 67–72; 'Paying One's D'Ewes', *Parl. Hist.*, 14 (1995), 179–86; and 'Getting Over D'Ewes', *Parl. Hist.*, 15 (1996), 221–30. The third of these papers is a reply to Maija Jansson, 'Dues Paid', *Parl. Hist.*, 15 (1996), 215–20.

[39] Smith, *Stuart Parliaments*, pp. 13–15, and Smith, 'Reconstructing the Opening Session of the Long Parliament', *HJ* (forthcoming).

[40] Cited throughout as Lomas–Carlyle.

[41] John Morrill, 'Textualizing and Contextualizing Cromwell', *HJ*, 33 (1990), 629–39.

[42] Charles L. Stainer, ed., *Speeches of Oliver Cromwell, 1644–1658* (1901); Ivan Roots, ed., *Speeches of Oliver Cromwell* (1989).

seven-volume edition by Thomas Birch in 1742, are crucial in enabling us to
reconstruct the government's perspective and the information on which it
was acting.[43] There is a wide variety of material, especially relating to the
council, in the State Papers Domestic.[44] The largely unpublished correspondence of Henry Cromwell also offers helpful sidelights on developments at
Westminster and again assists us in exploring the relationship between
conciliar and parliamentary politics.[45] The *Thurloe State Papers* contain
many dispatches from foreign ambassadors resident in London, especially
the French and Dutch, and these can be supplemented by further French
reports,[46] and by the extensive accounts of successive Venetian ambassadors
and secretaries.[47] Although they are not always reliable, and need to be
tested wherever possible against other sources, these diplomatic dispatches
can provide helpful information. The same is true of the various collections
of royalist correspondence in this period, especially the Clarendon State
Papers and the Carte Papers in the Bodleian Library, and the Nicholas
Papers.[48] Further useful newsletters and other documents survive in the
papers of William Clarke, who during the Protectorate was secretary to
General Monck and the commanders of the army in Scotland.[49] All this
and other correspondence helps to integrate parliamentary proceedings into
a broader account of Protectorate politics in general.

Contemporary memoirs present particular problems of their own. The
most voluminous and the best placed to comment on parliamentary politics
are those of Edmund Ludlow and Bulstrode Whitelocke. However, Blair
Worden has shown that both are extremely complex and problematic
sources.[50] Both Ludlow's *Memoirs* and Whitelocke's *Memorials* were extensively 'edited' during the later seventeenth century to help them to serve the
Whig cause, and readers even have to be alert to the retrospective element in

[43] *TSP*. The originals are mainly found in either Bodl., MSS Rawlinson A 9-64, or BL, Add. MSS 4156–8 (Thomas Birch collection: Thurloe Papers).
[44] *CSPD*. The originals are mostly found in TNA, SP 18 (State Papers Domestic, Interregnum), and SP 25 (Council papers, Interregnum).
[45] BL, Lansdowne MSS 821–3 (Henry Cromwell correspondence); BL, Add. MS 43724 (Henry Cromwell correspondence).
[46] TNA, PRO 31/3/95–103 (Baschet's transcripts); F. G. P. Guizot, *History of Oliver Cromwell and the English Commonwealth*, trans. A. R. Scoble (2 vols., 1854); Guizot, *Richard Cromwell*.
[47] *CSPV*. On this source, see John Morrill, 'Through a Venetian Glass, Darkly', *Parl. Hist.*, 17 (1998), 244–7.
[48] Bodl., MSS Clarendon (some of which were published in *Clarendon SP*); Bodl., MSS Carte; *Nicholas Papers*.
[49] *Clarke Papers*.
[50] On Whitelocke, see Blair Worden, 'The "Diary" of Bulstrode Whitelocke', *EHR*, 108 (1993), 122–34. On Ludlow, see Worden, *Roundhead Reputations: The English Civil Wars and the Passions of Posterity* (2001), chapters 1–4. These chapters draw on two more technical discussions: A. B. Worden, 'Introduction' to Edmund Ludlow, *A Voyce from the Watch*

Whitelocke's *Diary*, which he apparently did not compose until 1663 or later.[51] All these sources need to be handled with considerable caution, yet quoting from them has not been avoided entirely because as eyewitnesses to events they sometimes offer unique reports of important political developments.

Finally, a range of other printed material has been drawn upon. Officially authorised items can be readily identified from Sheila Lambert's listing of 'printing for Parliament'.[52] Much other printed matter, from a wide variety of political perspectives, has also been used, as have the newsbooks for these years. The only newsbook that ran continuously throughout the period of the three Protectorate Parliaments was *Mercurius Politicus*.[53] For the first Protectorate Parliament, roughly a dozen newsbooks were published each week: these were of very variable quality and some of them were clearly derivative from others. By the time of the second and third Protectorate Parliaments, this number had dwindled to about three or four, of which *Mercurius Politicus* was generally the fullest and most authoritative.[54]

The above discussion shows something of the range of primary sources that survive for the three Protectorate Parliaments and the problems that they present for historians. Although many of these sources have long been available in print, they have not always been fully integrated into accounts of the Protectorate Parliaments, and the fact that they have often not received the attention of modern historians makes them ripe for re-evaluation. It is now time to turn to the history that can be reconstructed from them, and the most appropriate place to begin is by considering the paper constitutions under which the Protectorate Parliaments met. These will form the subject of the next chapter.

Tower, Part Five: 1660–1662 (Camden Society, 4th series, 21, 1978), 1–80; and Blair Worden, 'Whig History and Puritan Politics: The *Memoirs of Edmund Ludlow* Revisited', *HR*, 75 (2002), 209–37.

[51] Ludlow; Whitelocke, *Memorials*; Whitelocke, *Diary*.

[52] Sheila Lambert, ed., *Printing for Parliament, 1641–1700* (List and Index Society, special series, 20, 1984), 191–4.

[53] *Mercurius Politicus* was at issue number 221 when the first Protectorate Parliament assembled, and had reached issue number 564 by the time of the dissolution of the third Protectorate Parliament.

[54] This information is derived from the listings in Carolyn Nelson and Matthew Seccombe, eds., *British Newspapers and Periodicals, 1641–1700: A Short-Title Catalogue of Serials Printed in England, Scotland, Ireland and British America* (New York, 1987).

2

Parliament and the paper constitutions

It is ironic that historians have tended to neglect the constitutions that framed the Protectorate, and dominated its Parliaments. There were in fact six different constitutional documents considered between 1653 and 1657: the Instrument of Government that established the Protectorate in December 1653; the failed Parliamentary Constitution (or 'government bill') of 1654–5; the monarchical Remonstrance introduced on 23 February 1657; the Humble Petition and Advice which replaced it on 31 March, and was itself turned into a Protectoral constitution on 25 May (which passed into law on 26 June); and finally the explanatory Additional Petition and Advice presented to Cromwell at the end of June, as a companion to the Humble Petition. Of these, only the Instrument has been thoroughly examined by modern historians,[1] and the most detailed studies of the Parliamentary Constitution and the Humble Petition remain those of S. R. Gardiner and C. H. Firth, published over a century ago,[2] as more recent students have concentrated on politics rather than constitutional affairs.[3] Even the most basic requirement for a study of these constitutions – the availability of definitive printed texts of the original proposals – has not been met in two of the six cases: those of the Remonstrance and the monarchical version of the Humble Petition. The resolution of this textual ambiguity is the first task of this chapter.

---

[1] G. D. Heath, 'Making the Instrument of Government', *Journal of British Studies*, 6 (1967), 15–34; Austin Woolrych, *Commonwealth to Protectorate* (Oxford, 1982), pp. 364–78.

[2] Gardiner, *Commonwealth and Protectorate*, III, 196–255; C. H. Firth, 'Cromwell and the Crown', *EHR*, 107 (1902), 429–42, and 108 (1903), 52–80.

[3] For partial exceptions, see David L. Smith, 'Oliver Cromwell, the First Protectorate Parliament and Religious Reform', *Parl. Hist.*, 19 (2000), 38–48; Peter Gaunt, 'Law-making in the First Protectorate Parliament', in Colin Jones, Malyn Newitt, and Stephen Roberts, eds., *Politics and People in Revolutionary England: Essays in Honour of Ivan Roots* (Oxford, 1986), pp. 163–86; and the brief, but useful, analyses in Austin Woolrych, 'Last Quests for a Settlement, 1657–1660', in G. E. Aylmer, ed., *The Interregnum: The Quest for Settlement, 1646–1660* (1972), pp. 184–5, and Barry Coward, *The Cromwellian Protectorate* (Manchester, 2002), pp. 41–7.

There is a general assumption that the Remonstrance of February 1657 was but an early draft of the Humble Petition and Advice, as presented to Cromwell on 31 March. The Remonstrance has been described as 'the embryo of the Humble Petition and Advice',[4] an early, rough-hewn version, perhaps, but in form and intention almost identical to the latter. This elision of the two constitutions is encouraged by the ready availability of the final, Protectoral, version of the Humble Petition in Gardiner's *Constitutional Documents* and other collections of constitutional material,[5] whereas the full text of the Remonstrance is available only in manuscript form. Firth knew of it, but included only the first article (as a comparison to the Humble Petition) in the third volume of the *Clarke Papers*,[6] and, with a few honourable exceptions, the existence of the manuscript has been studiously ignored. W. C. Abbott, in his monumental *Writings and Speeches of Oliver Cromwell* (1937–47), did not use the manuscript of the Remonstrance at all. He quoted instead the 'chief points' reported by the Venetian ambassador, and followed Ludlow in commenting (erroneously) that 'various sources' led him to believe that 'the place for the title was left blank in the original document'.[7] More recently, Peter Gaunt rediscovered two of the three surviving manuscripts of the Remonstrance while working on his doctoral thesis, and in his study of the constitutional powers of the Protectoral council contrasted the attitude of the Remonstrance with that of the Humble Petition,[8] but he did not develop his argument to cover areas other than the council. The Remonstrance is published in its entirety in appendix 2 of the present volume, and its contents are discussed in this chapter.

The second example of textual uncertainty concerns the monarchical version of the Humble Petition and Advice. This has become obscured behind the later Protectoral version, which was printed by order of Parliament of 26 June 1657, and has reappeared in collections of constitutional documents of the period ever since. Historians' assumptions have perhaps been swayed by Ludlow's assertion that the two versions were identical other than 'the sole alteration of the word king into that of Protector'.[9] Yet the changes between the two documents, although small, are of greater magnitude, and significance, than Ludlow allowed. The first article was naturally revised, as the title changed from king to Protector, and

[4] Barry Coward, *Oliver Cromwell* (1991), p. 149.
[5] Gardiner, *Constitutional Documents*; *A & O*; J. P. Kenyon, *The Stuart Constitution, 1603–1688: Documents and Commentary* (Cambridge, 1966), pp. 350–7; 2nd edn (Cambridge, 1986), pp. 324–30.
[6] *Clarke Papers*, III, 94n.   [7] Abbott, IV, 412.
[8] Peter Gaunt, 'The Councils of the Protectorate, from December 1653 to September 1658' (Ph.D thesis, University of Exeter, 1983), pp. 219–23.
[9] Ludlow, II, 28.

the powers ascribed to the 'single person' also differ, as we shall see. More serious is the omission, in the later version, of article 15, which stipulated that all acts passed under the name of the Protector would still have validity when the title was changed to king. In point of fact, this article remained in the Humble Petition and, despite complaints by members of Parliament that it needed 'expunging' at the end of May 1657, no action was taken. This may reflect the members' reluctance to reopen the bitter debate on the kingly title, but it led to a constitutional anomaly. The printed version (and presumably the version read out before Cromwell at his reinstallation on 26 June) silently passed over the fifteenth article, leading some historians to accuse the clerk of misnumbering the ensuing articles.[10]

With the rediscovery of the Remonstrance and the clarification of the differences between the monarchical and Protectoral versions of the Humble Petition, it is possible to attempt a detailed comparative analysis of the various constitutions proposed between 1653 and 1657.[11] The bulk of this chapter will conduct such an analysis, approaching the texts thematically, and each theme chronologically, to produce a 'genealogy' of constitutional ideas through the 1650s. In turn, it will consider the 'single person', the council, Parliament, royalists, and religion. Such an undertaking cannot concentrate on constitutional issues alone, and at each stage political and factional considerations will be referred to, although an in-depth analysis of the politics of the Protectorate Parliaments will be left until the fifth chapter. For the moment, it should be emphasised that the paper constitutions them-selves, as well as the evidence from correspondence, diaries, or the *Commons' Journals*, suggest that constitutional questions were highly politicised, with each main political faction – the army interest, the civilian 'court party', and the 'Presbyterian' and 'country gentry' interest – each having its distinct agenda.[12] This factional influence is fairly obvious in the Instrument of Government, which was created by a group of senior officers headed by General John Lambert (presumably with the consent of Cromwell himself), and in the Parliamentary Constitution of 1654–5, through which the

---

[10] For the details, see Patrick Little, 'Monarchy to Protectorate: Re-drafting the Humble Petition and Advice, March–June 1657', *HR*, 79 (2006), 144–9.

[11] The texts referred to in this chapter (apart from the Remonstrance and the monarchical Humble Petition) are printed in Gardiner, *Constitutional Documents*, pp. 405–17 (Instrument of Government), 427–47 (Parliamentary Constitution), 447–59 (Protectoral Humble Petition and Advice), and 459–64 (Additional Petition and Advice). References here are to the article and chapter numbers, not page numbers, to allow other editions to be used for cross-referencing. For completeness, it should be noted that Peter Gaunt (in 'Law-making', 166n) has identified a variant of the Parliamentary Constitution in the Clarke manuscripts at Worcester College, Oxford.

[12] The validity of this nomenclature, and their identification as distinct 'factions', will be examined in chapter 5.

Presbyterians challenged the Instrument. The latter certainly angered Cromwell, and was resisted in Parliament by the 'courtiers'. The civilian courtiers (possibly with Cromwell's approval) were responsible for drafting the Remonstrance in February 1657, which tried to re-establish the 'ancient constitution' of king and two Houses of Parliament; and the transition from Remonstrance to Humble Petition was just as controversial, relying as it did on an uneasy compromise being reached between the courtiers and the Presbyterian majority in the Commons, to ensure the safe passage of the new civilian constitution through Parliament. Even the Additional Petition, framed as a document to explain the ambiguities of the Humble Petition, was in reality a highly charged attempt to redirect the constitutional basis of the state. Each new proposal, with its political as well as constitutional significance, thus marked a further stage in the on-going struggle for the soul of the Protectorate, and the heart of the Protector.

THE 'SINGLE PERSON'

Although Edmund Ludlow and other disaffected officers thought the Instrument of Government 'tended to the sacrificing of all our labours to the lust and ambition of a single person',[13] it was, in constitutional terms, a rather conservative document, founded on the concept of the balance of powers.[14] Under article 1 of the Instrument, the 'supreme legislative authority' resided in 'one person' – styled Lord Protector – and Parliament, while under article 2 the 'chief magistracy' was shared between the Protector and his council. The system of checks and balances was underwritten by the Instrument itself, which formed an additional restriction on the powers of the Protector, as well as on the council and Parliament. Under article 3, the Protector was charged to 'govern the said countries and dominions in all things by the advice of the council, and according to these presents and the laws', thus establishing the Instrument as a yardstick of good governance. The oath to be taken by the Protector, outlined in article 41, again emphasised the role of the constitution as a restraint: he promised 'that he will not violate or infringe the matters and things contained in this writing' as well as to govern 'according to the laws, statutes and customs' of the three nations. A Protectoral veto over legislation was deemed unnecessary (and thus was not provided for), as the Instrument constituted a superior authority; this avoided the risk of charges of tyrannical, 'arbitrary' government being levelled against the single person. By this very Cromwellian arrangement, the Instrument rather than the Protector became the touchstone of the new

---

[13] Ludlow, I, 369. [14] Woolrych, *Commonwealth to Protectorate*, pp. 366–8.

government. Later debates certainly emphasised this, stating that under the Instrument the 'negative voice was said to be not a positive negative', but rather a way of ensuring 'co-ordination' (or interpretation) of the written constitution, by the single person. The Instrument itself was 'absolute ... in regard it was the very foundation, and foundations were not to be altered or removed'.[15] The buck would stop not at Cromwell, but at the Instrument of Government.

When it came to executive government, the individual powers of the Protector were bounded by council and Parliament. The council had the right to advise on the making of peace and war (article 5), the summoning of Parliament (article 23), and the election of future Protectors (article 25). Parliament's role in the executive was deliberately reduced, to avoid the perceived abuses of unbridled parliamentary government as seen under the Rump, although its legislative rights were safeguarded, and the Protector was not allowed to refuse to pass bills (under article 24) as long as the matter in question was included within the terms of the Instrument. Between sessions of Parliament, the council covered for it, and between them the two bodies had something of a joint role in restricting the Protector's freedom of action, at least in theory.

The Parliamentary Constitution, developed by the Presbyterian opposition during the Parliament of 1654–5, sought to overturn the constitutional arrangements so carefully crafted by the Instrument by attacking both the executive and legislative roles of the single person and his council, and by reducing the standing of the constitution itself. Instead it was claimed that Parliament was sovereign, and that executive as well as legislative powers were derived from it, although the former were 'communicable' to a single person, who could exercise power on Parliament's behalf.[16] It was this claim that prompted Cromwell to suspend the Parliament, and to harangue the members of Parliament in the Painted Chamber on 12 September: 'I thought it was understood that *I* was the Protector, and the authority that called you, and that *I* was in possession of the government by a good right from God and men.'[17] He proceeded to stipulate four things – government by single person and Parliament, restrictions on the duration of Parliaments, joint control of the armed forces, and the guarantee of religious liberty – that he considered 'fundamentals ... [which] may not be parted with, but will, I trust, be delivered over to posterity'.[18] To gain readmittance to the Commons, members were forced to sign a 'recognition' of the government under a single

[15] Burton, I, xxix.   [16] Burton, I, xxvi.
[17] Ivan Roots, ed., *Speeches of Oliver Cromwell* (1989), p. 50 (emphasis added); see Lomas–Carlyle, II, 379–80.
[18] Roots, *Speeches of Oliver Cromwell*, p. 51.

person and Parliament (in that order) but, even after Parliament reconvened, the Presbyterian critics of the Instrument continually tried to assert Parliament's authority over the Protector, as in the discussion of making war (on 2 October), which was said to be undertaken with 'arbitrary power' if conducted without Parliament's consent, as it remained one of its 'ancient' rights.[19] On 23 October it was argued that Parliament had 'an original, fundamental right' to elect a new Protector.[20] On 18 November control of the armed forces was also claimed as a right of Parliament, 'as a trust derived from them and reposed in them, for the good of the nation', and, although Cromwell might be accorded an 'equal share' of that trust, Parliament reserved the right to withhold it from his successors altogether. This last claim was made 'to the great dissatisfaction of the court' and, no doubt, of Cromwell himself, who had so recently identified control of the militia as one of his 'fundamentals' of government.[21]

Despite such criticism in debate, the more extreme claims of parliamentary sovereignty did not make a lasting impression on the final version of the Parliamentary Constitution drawn up in January 1655. Indeed, the chapters referring to the Protector and his executive powers generally repeat the wording, and thus presumably the intentions, of the Instrument of Government. Chapter 4, on the elective nature of the Protectorate, is similar to article 32 of the Instrument; chapters 23–5 on the calling of Parliament are an expansion of article 11; and, despite the claims of his enemies in Parliament, the rights of the Protector to control the armed forces under chapter 45 are the same as those in article 4. Changes *were* made, but these seem to have been designed to account for the shift in emphasis from the council to Parliament as the main balance to the single person, rather than constituting an all-out assault on the Protector's powers. Thus, chapter 5 stipulates that Parliament is to decide the conduct of the election of a new Protector, with the council playing a part only when Parliament is not sitting (cf. article 32). Chapter 7 says that the Protector's oath was to be taken before Parliament, not the council (contrary to article 41), and chapters 52–3, concerning the making of peace and war, again transfer the right of consent from the council to Parliament (cf. article 5 of the Instrument). Otherwise, the Parliamentary Constitution tended to explain the Protector's executive powers in greater detail, but without introducing further restrictions.

The Parliamentary Constitution was much more aggressive towards the legislative powers of the single person. Within days of the Parliament convening, the Presbyterian hardliners claimed 'legislative power . . . to be the

[19] Burton, I, xliv–xlvi.   [20] Burton, I, liii.   [21] Burton, I, lxxx–lxxxii, cviii.

right of the Parliament alone, without communicating the least part of it to any single person in the world'.[22] After a tense debate, on 11 September an uneasy compromise was reached, in which, although the 'truth' of Parliament's legislative supremacy was accepted, it was deemed 'convenient or expedient' to share this power with the Protector, to provide a 'check' against abuses.[23] Cromwell's closure of the Parliament the next day, and his insistence on the members' subscription of a 'recognition' of the government before they were readmitted, was provoked by such high-handedness, which raised fears that members sought to re-establish in Parliament the kind of sovereignty it had exercised during the Rump. Cromwell's intervention did not prevent further debates on the single person, however. The most explosive issue was the matter of his right to have a 'negative', or veto, over legislation. Whereas the Instrument allowed all parliamentary legislation to pass even without the Protector's consent, provided it accorded with the Instrument itself (article 24), the Parliamentary Constitution discarded the idea of a sacrosanct founding document, and instead introduced the notion of a limited Protectoral veto over 'such matters wherein the single person is hereby declared to have a negative' (chapter 1). Cromwell's list of 'fundamentals' had identified the issues which were to remain immutable, and thus subject to his veto. This was broadly accepted by the members, but the authority by which he possessed this power was not so easily conceded. The debate on 10 November was particularly ill tempered, with the Presbyterians declaring that the negatives were allowed only if the single person should 'receive them of the concession of the Parliament'. The horrified courtiers paraphrased this, saying that agreement on this would have placed 'the legislative power absolutely in Parliament, and left it at courtesy, whether the Parliament would after concede any negatives to him'.[24] The courtiers' protests did not prevent the proposed chapter 1 of the Parliamentary Constitution from making the provocative claim that Parliament was to 'give' the negative right to the single person – a word that caused the courtiers to howl that the measure had 'destroyed the government' and 'unmade the Protectorate'.[25] As it turned out, this provocative stance was more than many ordinary members could stomach. A swift change from 'give' to 'declare', and a final reordering of the clause ('wherein the single person is hereby declared to have a negative') had to be made before the resolution could gain sufficient support to pass as part of chapter 1 of the new constitution.[26]

Worse was to follow, as the Presbyterians sought to emphasise the temporary nature of the powers they were allowing the single person. On

---

[22] Burton, I, xxvi.   [23] Burton, I, xxviii, xxxii.   [24] Burton, I, lxiv.   [25] Burton, I, lxv–lxvi.
[26] Burton, I, lxvii, lxix, lxxiv–lxxv.

24 November, the right to alter the government from a single person and a Parliament was again raised, with some members arguing that to forbid discussion of this point was 'too comprehensive', requiring 'that it should not be in the power of future Parliaments to alter any part of it'.[27] This principle was also enshrined in chapter 59 of the Parliamentary Constitution (resolved on 12 January 1655), which refused to allow 'that the article herein contained, nor any of them, shall be altered, repealed or suspended without the consent of the Lord Protector and Parliament'. This was a far cry from the Instrument's status as 'the very foundation' of the Protectoral state. On 20 January a move against such temporary structures, in the form of a proviso 'that no future Lord Protector should consent to take away the negatives hereby declared to be in the Lord Protector', was rejected out of hand by the Parliament.[28] This added a constitutional dimension to the religious tension that was turning Cromwell against his first Protectorate Parliament.[29] Only two days later, in exasperation, he dissolved it.

The Remonstrance introduced by civilian 'courtiers' on 23 February 1657 was above all a monarchical document. It was 'a shoe fitted to the foot of a monarch', according to one critic.[30] The intention of reviving the full traditional powers of a king was plain from its very beginning. The first article called on Cromwell 'to assume the name, style, title, dignity and office of king ... with the rights, privileges and prerogatives justly, legally and rightly thereunto belonging'. As the first article hinted, the kingship on offer was not an absolute one. The preamble made this abundantly clear, asserting the benefits of a return to 'the ancient constitution of this nation, consisting of a king and two Houses of Parliament', which were deemed to be 'most agreeable to the temper and inclination of this people, and to conform to their laws, and the best means to preserve our nation and fundamental rights and privileges'. Beyond these bold statements, the provisions for the monarchy in the Remonstrance were sparse. For example, articles 3 and 5, which provided for the privilege of the two Houses of Parliament, assumed that the king's relationship with Parliament would be along traditional lines, with the monarch agreeing not to interfere in elections for the Commons, and summoning all members of the upper House unless exceptional circumstances intervened. These articles depended on article 6, which requested that 'your highness will be pleased that the laws of the land be observed and kept, and that no laws be altered, suspended, abrogated and repealed, or new ones made, but by act of Parliament'. A great deal hinged on an agreed definition of what these 'laws of the land' might consist, along with the 'prerogatives' and 'rights and privileges' which could legitimately be claimed

---

[27] Burton, I, xcvi. [28] *CJ*, VII, 421.
[29] See Smith, 'Religious Reform', 42–3, and chapter 9. [30] Ludlow, II, 21.

by the king and subjects, respectively. The omissions in the Remonstrance were, in this regard, as telling as the provisions. In particular, there was no mention of control of the armed forces or the making of treaties or declarations of peace and war, which were presumably the sole responsibility of the new king through his prerogative powers; likewise, the appointment of officers of state and the judiciary was unmentioned, the assumption being that such matters came under the king's traditional remit.[31]

The Remonstrance of February 1657 was a very different document from the Instrument or the Parliamentary Constitution, as it created a constitutional monarchy, rather than a Protectorate. Under the Instrument, the Protector, although enjoying a traditional title, had completely new powers. These were well defined, balanced by the council and Parliament, and underwritten by the terms of the constitution itself. Cromwell was required to uphold the articles of the Instrument under the terms of his oath, and the precedence of these articles effectively removed his right – or need – to veto legislation. The contrast between the newborn Protectorate of 1653 and the embryonic monarchy of 1657 could hardly be greater. The Remonstrance included no oath for the new king, and had no reference to its own provisions as forming a permanent restriction on his actions. Yet the whole document was couched as a plea that the new king would 'be pleased' to give his 'consent' to its provisions – terms repeated in various forms in articles 1, 2, 5, 6, 9, and 10. The monarchical right of veto over parliamentary legislation was thus implicitly revived, although there was no specific provision for one. Like the Parliamentary Constitution, the drafters of the Remonstrance did not intend it as a binding constitutional document; but in other respects their intentions were very different. They planned not to attack Cromwell but to promote him. By re-establishing a traditional form of government with the traditional lack of safeguards, they placed all their trust in Oliver and his successors to do the right thing by their subjects. Despite the lessons of recent history, and despite general calls for government within the established laws and customs of the 'ancient constitution', they deliberately chose to vest the new dynasty with ill-defined prerogative powers, similar to those enjoyed by Charles I before 1641–2.

The divisive nature of the kingship proposals was obvious from the very start of the parliamentary debates on the Remonstrance. Indeed, Parliament showed a marked reluctance to deal with the issue head-on. On 2 March 1657 the debate on the first clause of the first article, with its offer of the crown, was postponed until the other articles had been discussed.[32] When it

---

[31] These would be inserted into the Humble Petition, articles 8 and 9.

[32] *CJ*, VII, 497–8. The second clause, on hereditary succession was, by contrast, passed 'without division, or opposition' (BL, Lansdowne MS 821, fo. 316r).

came to it, the monarchical clause was retained in a vote of 25 March, which the supporters of kingship (known as the 'kinglings') won by the comfortable majority of 123 votes to 62.[33] Support for the offer of the crown may have increased during the debates, as restrictions were placed on what had been near-absolute powers proposed by the original Remonstrance. Its successor, the Humble Petition and Advice, omitted those sections of the preamble dealing with the personal responsibilities and providential mandate of the new king, and dropped any reference to the 'ancient constitution'. Clauses were also added to articles 1 and 2, elevating the new constitution to the status of the Instrument – demanding that the Protector 'govern according to this petition and advice in all things therein contained' – and replacing the wide-ranging 'rights, privileges, and prerogatives' of the king allowed by the Remonstrance with the much more restricted right 'to exercise the same according to the laws of these nations'.[34] During debate, there was an attempt to increase the role of the council to something approaching the position it had enjoyed under the Instrument, and the armed forces were formally placed in the Protector's hands, with the requirement that he act 'by consent' of Parliament, or (between sessions) 'by the advice' of the council (article 8). Equally, the officers of state were to be appointed with Parliament's approval (article 9). Article 17 also returned to the Instrument in making provision for an oath 'in such form as shall be agreed upon by your highness and this present Parliament, to govern these nations according to the law'. Thus the Humble Petition tried to reintroduce some of the controls over the single person which had been jettisoned by the Remonstrance, but there was still no mention of a right of veto, whether it was allowed (as, by implication, in the Remonstrance) or considered unnecessary (as in the Instrument).[35]

This attempt to limit the new king's powers under the Humble Petition was probably the result of Presbyterian pressure, although the lack of a diary for this crucial period obscures the precise factional line-up during the debates.[36] Some leading Presbyterians were certainly keen to prune the single person's freedom of action during April and early May 1657, when Lambert Godfrey claimed that Cromwell's interests and those of Parliament were incompatible, and questioned his right to nominate members of the Other House.[37] Cromwell's control of the revenue brought further questions from Thomas Bampfield and John Trevor, with Godfrey describing the voting of a

[33] *CJ*, VII, 511. [34] *CJ*, VII, 511 (this was altered on 24 March).
[35] A point made in Woolrych, 'Last Quests', p. 185.
[36] For discussion of this, see Patrick Little, *Lord Broghill and the Cromwellian Union with Ireland and Scotland* (Woodbridge, 2004), pp. 148–52.
[37] Burton, II, 22.

'constant revenue' without a time limit as 'a fair way to put it in the power of your chief magistrate never to have a Parliament'.[38] Bampfield called for army officers, as well as officers of state, to be approved by Parliament, not chosen by Cromwell alone – a proposal that left the Speaker speechless, and Thomas Burton concluded that he 'either did not or would not understand this motion'.[39] On 28 April there were further clashes, with Griffith Bodurda describing the confirmation of the approbation of preachers – which Cromwell, a week before, had described as one of his greatest achievements – as an attack on Parliament itself: 'either the single person must be trusted before the Parliament, or else the Parliament must be trusted'.[40] Such aggressive attempts to restrict the single person further were unsuccessful, but they reflected a trend which can be traced to the final terms of the Humble Petition and, beyond it, to the debates on the Parliamentary Constitution in 1654–5.

Despite Presbyterian pressure for further concessions, very few changes were made to the Humble Petition when it was turned from a monarchical to a Protectoral constitution after Cromwell's rejection of the crown in May. A committee was appointed to consider how the new title might be 'bounded',[41] but in this respect, as in many others, it was obvious that, although the Protectoral constitution passed on 25 May 1657 badly needed further clarification, no one was prepared to reopen old wounds by debating the matter in the House.[42] The Additional Petition and Advice tidied a few inconsistencies in articles 7 and 9, and instituted an oath, by which the Protector swore to 'endeavour ... the maintenance and preservation of the peace and safety, and of the just rights and privileges of the people thereof'. There was no oath to uphold the principles of the Humble Petition itself, but otherwise the office of Protector emerged from the acrimonious debates and constant constitutional amendments of 1657 in a form which closely resembled that established in December 1653. The main differences introduced by the Humble Petition affected not the Protector, but the relative importance of the council and Parliament in the 'new' Protectorate.

THE COUNCIL

The power of the council was central to the Protectorate established under the Instrument of Government. The Protector was to be 'assisted with a council' in the 'exercise of the chief magistracy' under article 2 of the Instrument, and further articles clarified, and magnified, its authority. The

---

[38] Burton, II, 28.   [39] Burton, II, 33–4.
[40] Burton, II, 51; see also Bampfield's comments (*ibid.*, 54).   [41] *CJ*, VII, 535.
[42] The most obvious example is the 'missing' article 15: see Little, 'Monarchy to Protectorate'.

ordering of the armed forces, the raising of revenue, the appointment of judges, and the conduct of foreign diplomacy were all to be shared between the Protector and his council. The councillors would elect a new Protector on the death of his predecessor, and during any interregnum 'the council shall take care of the government, and administer in all things as fully as the Lord Protector, or the Lord Protector and council are enabled to do'. The councillors were appointed for life, and complicated rules ensured that new members had to be nominated by Parliament, elected by the council, and then presented to the Protector, who was allowed to choose one of two candidates offered to him. Most controversially, the Protectoral council had the role (under article 21) of vetting the return of members of Parliament, who had to be 'approved of by the major part of the council' – a clause which led to exclusions of members of Parliament in 1654 and 1656. The historian of Cromwell's council, Peter Gaunt, has described it as 'a stable, permanent and very powerful body, almost entirely independent of the legislature', with powers greater even than a royal council, 'for where the king was free to ignore his council altogether or to disregard its advice, the Protector was often constitutionally bound to seek and obtain conciliar consent'. Even the appointment and dismissal of councillors was beyond the Protector's ken. As Gaunt asserts, the Instrument 'placed Cromwell under the tight supervision of a powerful and independent body of council-lors with wide powers to control and constrain the single person'.[43] This was the constitutional position, at least.

Although paying lip-service to the principle that the 'chief magistracy' was to be by a 'Lord Protector assisted with the council' (under chapter 10), the drafters of the Parliamentary Constitution of 1654–5 envisaged a drastic reduction in the power of the council, with most of its functions being assumed by a stronger Parliament. Matters such as the administration of the oath taken by the Protector (chapter 41) and the making of war and peace (chapter 52) were transferred from council to Parliament. The council's role in electing a Protector, as established under article 32 of the Instrument, was replaced by chapter 5, which allowed the election to be conducted 'as the Parliament shall see fit'. This was the result of a violent episode in the House in October 1654, when the 'original, fundamental right, inherent in the Parliament' to choose a new ruler was asserted, challenging both the council and the Protector in one go.[44] The council was still to assume Protectoral

---

[43] Gaunt, ' "The Single Person's Confidants and Dependents"? Oliver Cromwell and his Protectoral Councillors', *HJ*, 32 (1989), 547; whether this followed in practice has now been questioned: see Blair Worden, 'Oliver Cromwell and his Council', in Patrick Little, ed., *The Cromwellian Protectorate* (Woodbridge, 2007), pp. 82–104.
[44] Burton, I, liii–lvi.

power during an interregnum (ch. 11), but this too had been challenged in debate.[45] The nomination of councillors was also submitted to radical change.[46] Instead of the complicated arrangements under article 25 of the Instrument, councillors were now to be nominated by the Protector and then approved by Parliament alone (ch. 39). Again, this compromise masked the angry debates that preceded it, when the Parliament questioned the Protector's right even to nominate, arguing that 'it seems strange, that the council should nominate the Protector, and the Protector nominate the council', and claiming that the right of choice should be Parliament's.[47] On this occasion, however, the courtiers managed to force a compromise measure through by a narrow margin.[48] The Presbyterians were also keen to make sure, under chapter 40, that 'no person shall continue to be of the council longer than forty days after the meeting of each succeeding Parliament without a new approbation of the Parliament', and councillors were to take an oath in Parliament when approved. This oath had been shorn of all mention of 'power' being inherent in the councillors, making their limited, advisory role plain.[49]

Under the Parliamentary Constitution, members of Parliament also claimed the right to try councillors without the Protector being able to grant them pardons, under chapter 16 – a measure that replaced a system of investigation based on a commission of councillors, Parliamentarians, and officers of state under article 25 of the Instrument. The very survival of the council was put in question by chapter 38, which reiterated chapter 10 by saying that the Protector was to be assisted by a council, but stated, ominously, that this would be 'for the time being'. The Presbyterian members were not only eager to assert Parliament's authority over the council, but also to reduce the council's encroachment over Parliament's powers. Thus, chapter 50 made sure that the extra-parliamentary ordinances passed by the council earlier in 1654 would not survive the present session unless approved by the Parliament; and, when it came to exclusions of members, the council's role was reduced under chapter 34 to merely certifying the truth of allegations to Parliament, which would then suspend the accused 'until the House have adjudged the same'. The retention even of this limited role had been challenged in debate, as some members objected that it was 'dangerous to place a judicatory out of the House . . . for so the Parliament might be pinned at the girdle of other men', and it was proposed that a Scottish system be adopted, whereby a parliamentary committee would scrutinise members before other business began.[50] Overall, if the Presbyterians and their friends

---

[45] Burton, I, lxxx–lxxxiv.   [46] Gardiner, *Commonwealth and Protectorate*, III, 201–2.
[47] Burton, I, civ–cvii.   [48] *CJ*, VII, 394.   [49] *CJ*, VII, 394.   [50] Burton, I, ci.

had had their way, the council would have been emasculated, and Parliament's executive role re-established.

The terms of the Remonstrance of February 1657 also limited the role of the council, but there the similarity with the Parliamentary Constitution ends. Renamed the 'privy council', the new body was 'modelled quite closely on the old royal privy council, the members acting as general advisers to the single person but possessing few, if any, specific powers'.[51] The only significant role remaining for the privy council was that established under article 8, for the management of an interregnum, which provided that 'after your highness's death, the commander in chief under your successors of such army or armies, as shall be necessary to be kept in England, Scotland or Ireland, as also such field officers at land or general by sea (which often time shall be newly made and constituted by your successors) be but by the consent of the council and not otherwise'. Even this caretaker role was apparently restricted to the armed forces, rather than the wide-ranging powers accorded to the council in similar circumstances by the Instrument and even accepted by the Parliamentary Constitution. Other functions of the privy council were limited by yoking it firmly to Parliament. There is perhaps a hint of a blurring of distinction between their functions in article 2, which refers to Parliament itself as 'your great council' – a traditional phrase conspicuously absent from the Instrument. Article 4 gave the two bodies joint responsibility for exclusions from Parliament,[52] ordering that 'a committee of the House of Commons of every preceding Parliament consisting of [blank] in number, may with the privy council from time to time examine, whether the persons so elected, and returned be either disabled or not qualified ... to sit or serve in Parliament', although the privy council's role was more advisory than executive, as it was stipulated that the recommendations would be 'brought before the House (which shall be at their first meeting) and then determined'. Likewise, article 8 involved both Parliament and privy council in the choice of councillors,[53] allowing the nomination of members by the new king, but only with 'consent of the council, to be afterwards approved by both Houses of Parliament'. This reversed the order laid down in the Instrument, leaving the new king with a free hand in nominations, and the removal of councillors was apparently put entirely in his hands. Nor was there any limit to the number of councillors, which the Instrument had covered in some detail. The Remonstrance thus withdrew most of the powers of the council, whether over the armed forces, the revenue, the judicial system, or Parliament, and made the councillors themselves subservient to the new king, who could appoint or dismiss them almost

---

[51] Gaunt, 'Councils', 219.   [52] Gaunt, 'Councils', 222.   [53] Gaunt, 'Councils', 223.

without restriction, and take or leave their advice, much as earlier British monarchs had done. As Gaunt concludes, the Remonstrance 'all but abandoned the concept of the council as a restraint upon the single person'.[54]

The radical changes to the role of the council envisaged by the Remonstrance accorded with the desire of the civilian courtiers – with, perhaps, the backing of the Protector – to return to 'the ancient constitution of this nation'; but it also had profound political implications, not least for the existing councillors expected to support the Remonstrance in the Parliament. Perhaps as a consequence, the Humble Petition drew back from the radical approach of the Remonstrance, and returned to the council at least part of its role as an effective balance to the power of the single person along lines similar to those established by the Instrument. This was not uncontroversial. The Presbyterians were keen to reduce the role of the council as well as that of the single person, and they were probably behind a motion, voted down on 16 March 1657, that required councillors to submit to the same 'qualifications' as those imposed on members under article 4. They had some success in passing an amendment ensuring that the removal of councillors would be allowed only with Parliament's consent (under article 8).[55] Despite this, there was a return to the forms of the Instrument when the number of councillors was restricted to twenty-one and the quorum set at seven (as in articles 2 and 25 of the Instrument). Article 8 of the Humble Petition also restored the council's role of giving 'advice' on the control of the armed forces between Parliaments, and, more generally, stipulated that 'your highness and successors will be pleased to exercise your government over these nations by the advice of your council', in what appears to be a return to article 2 of the Instrument. In one crucial respect, however, the Humble Petition did reduce the power of the council, by removing altogether its authority to exclude members from sitting in Parliament, vesting it instead in a commission appointed by act of Parliament.

The passing of the monarchical version of the Humble Petition did not end the debate on the future role of the council. In April 1657, the Presbyterians insisted on a detailed scrutiny of the ordinances passed by the council in 1653–4, 'to revise them, and see what is fit to be repealed', rather than pass the extra-parliamentary legislation in a lump; this suggests their continued hostility to the council.[56] This determination to prevent any further involvement by the council in the legislative process was underlined in June, when the oath of the privy councillors was discussed, and the word 'consent' was replaced by 'advise', as 'they have not any power of legislature'.[57] The oath was to form part of the Additional Petition, which restored the council's

---

[54] Gaunt, 'Councils', 219.   [55] *CJ*, VII, 505.
[56] Burton, II, 45, 50–1, 58–9, and *passim*.   [57] Burton, II, 288.

powers to advise on the revenues, the army, the officers of state, and the judges (under article 9), and established the 'privy council' on a footing similar to that allowed by the Instrument of Government, three and a half years earlier. There was one crucial difference, however. The exclusion of members from Parliament remained outwith the council's powers, with the 'commissioners' scheme under article 4 of the Humble Petition being made 'void, frustrate, null, and of none effect', the system instead relying on a system of fines imposed on each 'unqualified member (being so adjudged) by the said House of Commons'. This change was prompted by Cromwell's criticism of the Humble Petition voiced in April, but the final form reflected the Presbyterian arguments that Parliament should rule its own membership, and their fears that any ambiguity would leave 'the chief magistrate to choose' the triers who would exclude members. This marked a return to issues raised in the debates on the Parliamentary Constitution in November 1654, when the opponents of the Instrument, referring to Scottish practice, proposed that each Parliament appoint its own committee to regulate membership at the start of business. The 'courtiers' were opposed to such self-regulation in 1657 as well as 1654, but warnings from Lord Broghill and others that 'it is not safe to ravel into any part of the Petition' were ignored, and the measure was voted in by the Presbyterian majority.[58] The removal of governmental control over the membership of the Commons would have profound consequences for Oliver in 1658 and Richard in 1659, as we shall see in later chapters.

PARLIAMENT

The question of Parliament's constitutional role was of crucial importance during the Protectorate, not least because the Rump and the Nominated Assembly had both been accused of exceeding their powers and threatening to establish arbitrary government, and dissolved by the military under the orders of Oliver Cromwell. This experience made Cromwell very wary of Parliament's involvement in politics, despite his continued commitment to the principles of Parliament's legislative sovereignty, and it also informed his later insistence on limits being placed on the duration of Parliaments and their involvement in the army in his four 'fundamentals' of government. This suspicion in which Parliament was held by Cromwell and his army allies is also evident in the Instrument of Government, which represented an ill-disguised attempt to fetter Parliament by ensuring the pre-eminence of the Protector and his council in the executive, although the first article

---

[58] Burton, II, 15–18, 21.

acknowledged that 'the supreme legislative authority' rested in the single person 'and the people assembled in Parliament'. The role of Parliament was set out clearly elsewhere in the Instrument, with great efforts being made to govern its composition and the conduct of elections (in articles 9–27). These were to be union Parliaments, with 30 members each from Ireland and Scotland, and 400 from England and Wales, and the distribution of seats was changed, to increase the numbers representing counties and reduce the borough members to a minority. The great pocket-borough county of Cornwall now had eight county members, and only four burgesses; Wiltshire had ten and four; Yorkshire fourteen and eight. Wales was allocated twenty-five members, all but one (for the borough of Cardiff) being elected by the counties. There were equally complicated arrangements to ensure that writs were issued and elections took place, as well as precise qualifications to ensure that voters and candidates would be 'persons of known integrity, fearing God, and of good conversation'. The franchise itself was extended to include all with 'real or personal' estates of at least £200. Parliaments were guaranteed to meet 'once in every third year' (under article 7) and their meeting had to last at least five months unless dissolved with the members' consent (article 8), although after that time their continuance was at the pleasure of the single person.

The privileges guaranteed by such measures were offset by the powerful role assigned to the council. The nature of the executive changed entirely when Parliament was not in session. Control of the armed forces (article 4), the nomination of new councillors and removal of corrupt ones (articles 25–6), regulation of the revenue (article 29), and the appointment of officers of state (article 34) were to be taken in hand by the Protector and his council alone in the intervals between Parliaments – which could be as much as thirty-one months in thirty-six. When according Parliament the principal legislative role, the Instrument in fact gave with one hand and took away with the other. Under article 24, Parliament had the right to pass legislation without the Protector's consent after a delay of twenty days, but only if 'such Bills contain nothing in them contrary to the matters contained in these presents', meaning the terms of the Instrument. Although there was no mention of who would decide this, there can be little doubt that the final right of interpretation rested with the single person.[59] Even the granting of taxes was made conditional. Under article 6, such matters were dependent on 'common consent in Parliament', but this was qualified by article 30, which allowed the Protector and council 'for preventing the disorders and dangers which might otherwise fall out ... [to] have power, until the meeting of the

---

[59] Gaunt, 'Law-making', p. 165; Heath, 'Instrument', 29–30.

first Parliament, to raise money for the purposes aforesaid; and also to make laws and ordinances ... which shall be binding and in force, until order shall be taken in Parliament concerning the same'. As Peter Gaunt has shown, in the nine months from the establishment of the Protectorate until the sitting of its first Parliament in September 1654, the council took full advantage of its right to pass such extra-parliamentary legislation, including the raising of revenue, traditionally considered the right of the Commons.[60] This exacerbated the situation created by the Instrument's 'constant yearly revenue' (article 27) to maintain the armed forces and to provide £200,000 for the civilian government. The alteration of this revenue needed Parliament's consent, but the initial arrangements, including the source of the money exacted from the people, was to be by 'such ways and means as shall be agreed upon by the Lord Protector and the council'. The poaching of Parliament's legislative functions by the council demonstrates the suspicion with which Parliament was held in 1653, and the reluctance to allow it anything like its former status in the government, even in the legislature. This view was reinforced by the 1654–5 session, which saw the Presbyterian critics of the regime mounting a concerted attack on the Instrument, while putting forward their own Parliamentary Constitution.

Under the 1654–5 proposals, Parliament's rights were vigorously asserted. The very first chapter restated Parliament's powers to pass legislation even without the Protector's consent. This had been included in the Instrument, but not until article 24, and the Parliamentary Constitution explicitly connected this right to Parliament's role as 'the supreme legislative authority', even though certain negatives, including the right to veto attempts to perpetuate Parliament's sitting, were allowed to the Protector to safeguard his cherished 'fundamentals'. In debate, the supporters of parliamentary authority were not afraid to assert Parliament's supremacy not only over the legislature but also over the executive, which they claimed to hold in 'trust ... for the good of the nation'.[61] The tensions that this created between the Parliament – championed by the Presbyterians – and the Protector and his council – represented by the 'court party' – have been examined earlier in this chapter. Many of the members' wilder proposals did not make their way into the final text, but even so the revised constitution marked a dramatic change from the Instrument. Under chapters 7 and 8, the Protector was to swear an oath (as article 41 of the Instrument had also laid down) but the Parliamentary Constitution stipulated that this oath should be taken before Parliament (if sitting) rather than the council, and it was worded to include

---

[60] Gaunt, ' "To create a little world out of chaos": The Protectoral Ordinances of 1653–1654 Reconsidered', in Little, *Cromwellian Protectorate*, pp. 105–26.
[61] Burton, I, xxviii, lxxxii.

an undertaking to call Parliaments and protect their liberties and privileges. Equally, the ban on the Protector pardoning murderers and traitors was imported from article 3 of the Instrument, but chapter 16 added further details: that no councillor or officer of state could be saved from being questioned and sentenced in Parliament, and no pardon could be given for breaching parliamentary privilege. This not only protected Parliament's good name, it also implied that the Commons had a judicial function, in a presaging of the 1656 Nayler case.

Other measures promoting Parliament in 1654–5 can be seen only as attacks on the Instrument, the council, and Cromwell personally. Chapter 5 boldly stated that 'the manner of electing the Protector, in the vacancy of a Protector (sitting the Parliament), shall be such as the Parliament thinks fit', with the council having a say only between sessions. By contrast, article 32 of the Instrument had left the entire process in the hands of the council. The appointment of new councillors was to be by the approval of Parliament, under chapter 39, and they were to take their oaths before Parliament (chapter 40), promising to follow instructions from Parliament as well as the council. Other officers of state, judges, and commissioners were all to be appointed with the 'approbation' of Parliament (chapters 55–7). Although much of the detail of the summoning of Parliaments and the conduct of elections was similar to that set down in the Instrument, there were also sideswipes at the existing arrangements, such as (in chapter 31) the resurrection of earlier laws banning those in holy orders from sitting, and excluding blasphemers and loose-livers, which reflected the conservatism of the Presbyterian majority in the House. The franchise reverted to all those with 'an estate in freehold to the yearly value of forty shillings' (chapter 32), and this again seems to have been a Presbyterian motion, which overturned the innovations to the franchise included in the Instrument, and snubbed the army, 'which was particularly attached to the new mode of voting'.[62]

When it came to the revenue, the Parliamentary Constitution demanded widespread changes. Chapter 18 retained the yearly revenue of £200,000 for civilian government, as set under the Instrument, and also continued Parliament's right to give its consent to changes, but military expenses were separated from civilian, and were dealt with under chapters 48–50. These chapters allowed Parliament and the Protector the right of determining the size of the armed forces, and (under chapter 49) laid down a fixed sum of £1,100,000 for this purpose, to be raised from 'excise or other public receipts' – and not, therefore, from an unpopular land tax. Crucially, the new measures

---

[62] Gardiner, *Commonwealth and Protectorate*, III, 235; Woolrych, *Commonwealth to Protectorate*, pp. 372, 376. For the factional nature of the divisions on this, see *CJ*, VII, 391–2, 410–11.

also limited the duration of the grant until 25 December 1659, 'unless the Lord Protector and the Parliament shall agree to lessen the same sum before that time'. For good measure, chapter 50 also demanded that all monetary ordinances passed by the Protector and council before September 1654 should cease to have effect after the end of the present Parliament, unless the members voted otherwise. The Parliamentary Constitution thus wrested control of the revenues back from the council, and tied the 'constant revenue' to parliamentary consent. Worse still (from the government's point of view), under chapter 45 the Protector was required to control the army 'by consent of Parliament, and not otherwise', while Parliament was in session, and the size of the armed forces would be 'no more than shall be agreed upon from time to time by the said Lord Protector and the Parliament' (chapter 48). This cut out the council's advisory role, elevated parliamentary 'consent' far beyond what had been allowed by article 4 of the Instrument, and challenged Cromwell's insistence on a reduction of parliamentary influence over the army, which formed one of his four 'fundamentals'. Chapter 52 was the shortest, and most provocative, measure of this kind, stating that 'the power of making war is only in the Lord Protector and the Parliament'. Its counterpart, chapter 53, ensured that 'no peace shall be concluded but by consent of Parliament'. At a stroke, the provisions of article 5 of the Instrument, which vested such powers in the Protector, with the consent of the council, were overturned. Yet Parliament's claim to a direct involvement in policy was bound to prove unacceptable, not least because it threatened to revive the sort of parliamentary tyranny which was one of Cromwell's greatest bugbears.

The Remonstrance of February 1657 was framed as a parliamentary constitution, addressed to the Protector as 'the humble Remonstrance of the knights, citizens and burgesses now assembled in the Parliament of this commonwealth'. Article 2 required the establishment of triennial Parliaments ('or oftener as the affairs of the nation shall require'), arguing that this was 'your great council, in whose affection and advice yourself and this people will be most safe and happy'. This amicable tone was continued in article 3, which asked for the preservation of 'the ancient and undoubted liberties and privileges of Parliament', although there was no attempt to define what these might be. There was also an assertion of the rights of those 'legally chosen' as members not to be excluded from Parliament, although there were qualifications for those voting and being elected, and provisions for exclusions of the guilty through a commission made up of members of Parliament and council members. This last measure suggests the promotion of Parliament at the expense of the council, and this can also be seen in article 6, which ensured that the council played no role in legislation, 'that no laws be altered, suspended, abrogated and repealed, or new ones made, but by act of Parliament'. The right of the Commons to determine taxation was also acknowledged. The fixed revenue for the new king could not be 'diminished', or 'temporary supplies' raised, without 'common consent by act of Parliament, which is a freedom the people of this nation ought by the laws to inherit', although, in the absence of any specific provision, the 'necessity' for such extraordinary taxes was presumably to be established by the government alone, and there was no mention of where the funding for 'constant' or 'temporary' revenues would come from – leaving open the possibility of an increase in the land tax. Parliament's right to have a vote on whether or not the constant revenue was 'diminished' was in fact a weaker provision than that allowed in the Instrument, which had given the Commons a say in the 'variation, removal and changes to the method of collection' (article 27). The Remonstrance did not see a reassertion of the rights of Parliament as had been proposed by the Parliamentary Constitution – rather a degree of parity between Parliament and the council as subordinate institutions beneath the king. It is telling that just as the council shared a role in exclusions from the Commons, so Parliament had a part in the approval of new councillors chosen by the king.

The vagueness of the Remonstrance when discussing some of the details of Parliament was no doubt designed to work in the new monarch's favour. Unlike the Instrument, there was no mention of how the calling of triennial Parliaments was to be enforced; nor was there mention of national and local safeguards for the proper conduct of elections. The summoning of Parliament was not raised, presumably being part of the prerogative rights to be enjoyed by the king; nor was there any mention of restrictions on the king's veto – presumably because there were none. A list of seats and numbers of members, as provided in the Instrument, was eschewed in favour of a promise that 'the number of persons to be elected and chosen to sit and serve ... and the distribution of persons so chosen ... may be according to such proportion, as shall be agreed and declared in this present Parliament' (article 4). Similarly, the rehabilitation of former royalists was to be by act of Parliament, with an oath of loyalty, 'the form of which to be agreed on in Parliament'. This sense of imprecision can also be seen in the Remonstrance's single greatest parliamentary innovation, the establishment of the Other House. In the preamble, the 'ancient constitution' is defined as 'a king, and two Houses of Parliament'. The Other House is again mentioned in article 2, and dealt with, briefly, in article 5. The membership of the new chamber was not to exceed seventy or fall below forty, and replacement of those who died or were 'legally removed' was to be 'by consent of the House itself'. There was no mention of how the members were to be summoned (again, this was presumably a prerogative matter) and there was no discussion of the judicial role of the new House, despite the recent fuss over Parliament's judicial function during the Nayler case.

The brevity of the article establishing the Other House is striking. As with the measures concerning the Commons, this vagueness seems to have stemmed from two assumptions. First, that the 'laws of the land', including Parliament's privileges and the monarch's prerogatives, were self-evident under the 'ancient constitution', and that they would automatically be observed by both king and subject. Secondly, that there was plenty of time to fill in the missing details at a later stage. Nowhere is this clearer than in the catch-all article 6: 'That in all other particulars which concern the calling and holding of Parliaments your highness will be pleased, that the laws of the land be observed and kept.' This may have resulted from a misplaced confidence that the old way was well known (and had, after all, never been codified in this way before), or a naïve optimism that King Oliver's good intentions (and those of his successors), and his subsequent popularity with his subjects, would be sufficient to maintain decent order in Parliament. The result (perhaps the result intended all along by those around Cromwell) was to give the new king enormous prerogative powers, and to ensure that Parliament returned to its subservient, pre-Civil War, incarnation.

Superficially, the Humble Petition followed the Remonstrance in its handling of Parliament. Even though the 'ancient constitution' had disappeared from the preamble, the Humble Petition still emphasised that the representative was to return to its traditional form. Parliaments were to be triennial and bicameral; and the distribution of seats, although left to a further act of Parliament, was understood to revert to its pre-1653 arrangement. The property qualification, though unspecified, was also assumed to have returned to its pre-Instrument form. Articles 2, 3, and 6 of the Humble Petition were essentially the same as those in the Remonstrance. Yet behind this similarity lay a fundamental difference, as in its original form the Humble Petition greatly increased the power of Parliament in relation not only to the privy council, but also to the king or (in the later version) to the Protector himself. The undermining of the council can be seen in the provisions for exclusion of members of Parliament, which were no longer to be considered by a joint committee of members and councillors, but by forty-one commissioners 'appointed by act of Parliament', and the matter of their final exclusion or readmittance to the House was in the hands of the Commons alone. Within Parliament, the Commons asserted its right to exert influence over the Protector's cronies in the Other House. In the debate on 6 March, consideration of the third article was interrupted by members concerned by the terms of article 5, who demanded to know 'by whom and how the persons of that House shall be chosen; and likewise the powers and authorities of the Other House'.[63] It was decided that new peers were to be nominated by the king and 'approved by this House', rather than appointed

---

[63] *CJ*, VII, 499.

by Cromwell without restriction (as the Remonstrance had allowed). This measure was passed *nemine contradicente* in a House of at least 149 members, and the government's management of the Other House was further restricted by a resolution 'that the votes of the persons to be of the Other House shall not be by proxies'.[64] The judicial role of the Other House, left undetermined before, was now more fully defined, and restricted to 'cases adjourned from inferior courts', and criminal proceedings could be considered only 'upon an impeachment of the Commons assembled in Parliament, and by their consent'.

The government also came under increasing parliamentary scrutiny. In article 7, the rights of the Commons over revenues were pushed forward. The amount granted as 'constant revenue' was £1,300,000, of which £300,000 would be for the civilian administration and the remainder for the armed forces – a generous allowance pushed through despite opposition from the Presbyterians led by Thomas Bampfield and Thomas Grove.[65] Such opposition probably lay behind attempts to reach a compromise. Whereas the Remonstrance stated that the constant revenue could not be 'diminished' without consent, in the Humble Petition the word was changed to 'altered', requiring the increase of spending to be curtailed by Parliament. Crucially, 'no part thereof [is] to be raised by a land tax' – a measure that removed the government's control over the source of funding, and lay the burden on indirect taxation. Again, this seems to have originated with the Presbyterians, as land taxes were notoriously unpopular in the counties.[66] Similarly, it was decided that 'temporary supplies' would be raised with consent as before, but with the restriction that 'the Commons in Parliament' would 'adjudge the necessities of these nations to require' such advances of money. This may have been a sop to the Commons' traditional right to vote taxes, and it also allowed members a degree of direct control over policy that went far beyond even the terms of the Parliamentary Constitution of 1654–5.

In other areas, the government and increasingly the Protector himself were put under greater parliamentary restriction than had been envisaged under the Remonstrance. In article 8, a clause was inserted stating that councillors not only were to be approved by Parliament, but also that they 'shall not afterwards be removed but by consent of Parliament'. The control of the army, assumed to be part of the monarchical prerogative in the Remonstrance, was now deemed to be 'by consent of both Houses of Parliament' when in session, and the officers of state also had to be 'approved by both Houses' (article 9). Controversially, the rules on religion, which the Remonstrance had left to the discretion of the new king, were also brought within Parliament's remit, with

---

[64] *CJ*, VII, 501–2.   [65] *CJ*, VII, 502.   [66] Burton, II, 24, 32–3.

a new section in article 11 (article 10 of the Remonstrance) requiring that the confession of faith was 'to be agreed by your highness and the Parliament'. The new oath for the Protector was also to take 'such form as shall be agreed upon by your highness and this present Parliament' (article 17), and articles 14 and 15 tried to extend (if not perpetuate) the present Parliament, asserting that the present body would not dissolve automatically once the Humble Petition was enacted, and stating that all previous legislation 'not contrary' to the constitution would 'remain in force'. Such measures made it plain that Parliament was now expected to be a permanent, and potent, part of any new regime.

The Humble Petition witnessed an unprecedented assertion of Parliament's powers within a written constitution. Where the Instrument had subordinated Parliament to the council (which even acquired its own legislative role) and the Remonstrance had re-established royal control over Parliament (largely through omissions that would allow the return of full prerogative powers), the Humble Petition had put Parliament above the council, and had even given it the right to limit the role of the Protector. Small wonder that the Additional Petition and Advice (prompted by Cromwell's criticism of the Humble Petition in April) tried to redress the balance, reasserting the Protector's right to appoint members of the Other House without parliamentary approval (article 5) and putting the council, rather than Parliament, in the pivotal role of giving advice and consent on revenues and state officers (articles 7 and 9). Article 7's blanket provision that 'monies directed to be for the supply of the sea and land forces' would henceforth 'be issued by advice of the council', with the treasury giving an account to Parliament later, seemed designed to stymie Parliament's claim to influence the raising of revenue and the conduct of policy. In all these measures, the Additional Petition deliberately toned down the ideas introduced by the Presbyterians in the discussions that followed Cromwell's criticisms of the Humble Petition in April 1657. The Presbyterians had tried to limit the power of the Protector by promoting Parliament's role still further, calling for Parliament to nominate members of the Other House, questioning the 'constant revenue', which was seen as a threat to the very existence of Parliament, and even arguing for parliamentary approval of military as well as civilian officers.[67] The only surviving measure successfully promoted by the Presbyterians was the one vesting the power of exclusion in Parliament itself, rather than a commission of members and councillors. Overall, the Additional Petition served to create uncertainty as to the balance of power under the new constitution. While the Protector's

[67] Burton, II, 22, 28, 33–4.

function had remained more or less the same, from the summer of 1657 Parliament's powers had been significantly increased, the government's right to exclude members had been effectively destroyed, and crucial questions, including the exact nature of the franchise and the distribution of seats, the status of the Other House, and the legality of Irish and Scottish members sitting at Westminster, were left unresolved. These chickens would come home to roost in 1659.

ROYALISTS

The different constitutions agreed that royalists and other enemies of the state needed to be kept out of positions of authority – and above all excluded from Parliament – but they differed markedly in the way this was to be achieved. The Instrument of Government included certain principles which were followed almost word for word in the later constitutions. Under article 16, the penalty for seeking to vote or sit if disabled was the loss of one year's income from real estate and a third of the total personal estate, and this was duly copied by chapter 30 of the Parliamentary Constitution, and article 4 of the Humble Petition and Advice (although omitted, unaccountably, in the Remonstrance). Similarly, article 39 of the Instrument, concerning the permanence of the confiscation of crown and ecclesiastical lands was uncontroversial enough to reappear, almost verbatim, in the Parliamentary Constitution (chapter 58), the Remonstrance (article 11), and the Humble Petition (article 12). Such agreements were, however, the exception. The methods by which parliamentary exclusions were to be organised differed greatly from constitution to constitution, as we have seen. But the greatest source of friction seems to have been the qualification criteria themselves, and the attitude towards malignants that lay behind them. In short, were enemies to be reconciled to the regime, or excluded forever?

As usual, the Instrument set the terms of the debate. Under article 14, all who had aided or abetted the war against Parliament since 1 January 1642 were deemed to be disabled, unless they 'have been since in the service of Parliament, and given signal testimony of their good affection thereunto'. The definition of these terms was not given, although the Instrument made a clear distinction between Irish rebels and papists, who were disabled 'for ever' (under article 15), and the ordinary kind of royalist, who was prevented from electing or serving as a member 'in the next Parliament, or in the three succeeding Triennial Parliaments' (article 14) – in effect, for the next twelve years.[68] When it came to the majority of English royalists, the strictures of

---

[68] Woolrych, *Commonwealth to Protectorate*, p. 372.

the Instrument were therefore temporary, rather than permanent, and this was acknowledged in debate in the first Protectorate Parliament, when members worried that 'in future times, when all parties are returned to freedom of elections', they might end up with 'a Cavalier Parliament'.[69] The Parliamentary Constitution of 1654–5 was much less forgiving. Under chapter 29, all royalists who had been in arms since 1 October 1641 (rather than 1 January 1642)[70] were deemed to be disabled unless they had been in Parliament's service or given 'signal testimony', and were lumped together with the Irish rebels and papists in having this incapacity imposed 'during their lives'. Chapter 31 also reintroduced two older acts of Parliament to exclude from Parliament all in holy orders and those of 'atheistical, blasphemous, and execrable opinions'. The latter was a Presbyterian device to ensure a bar against religious radicals, who were considered as dangerous as royalists.

The Remonstrance of February 1657 also acknowledged the threat from radicals, but in a more oblique way. Its preamble included mentions of the 'discontented party' (who had recently been involved in plots against Cromwell's person) as well as the 'King's party' as serious threats to the regime, but there was no attempt to revive earlier laws that might have been used against them. Instead, the Remonstrance concentrated on reintegrating former royalists. Under article 4, Irish rebels and papists were disabled as in the Instrument, but article 12 allowed other royalists to be appointed to offices if restored by act of Parliament and having taken an oath abjuring Charles Stuart. This allowed royalists back into the political fold without a fixed time limit, and perhaps reflects the desire of the courtiers who drafted the Remonstrance to establish a broadly based, moderate government, as an alternative to military rule exemplified by the major-generals and their decimation tax. Oddly, the Remonstrance also seems to offer 'the like law for Papists', although presumably this was a drafting error, as it flatly contradicts article 4.

In dealing with malignants, the Humble Petition and Advice retreated from the relatively lenient approach taken in the Remonstrance. Its own article 13 made them incapable of any office or public trust, but made no provision for an act of Parliament and oath to absolve them – the last clause being summarily removed by the House.[71] Instead, the terms of exclusion and inclusion were precisely defined, in the lengthy article 4, which repeated the Instrument's proscription of Irish rebels, papists, and English royalists in arms since 1 January 1642, but restricted its exceptions to those who had

---

[69] Burton, I, lvi.
[70] This change was not disputed (see *CJ*, VII, 410), but the reasons for it are uncertain.
[71] *CJ*, VII, 508.

actively 'borne arms' (rather than merely 'served') in Parliament's cause thereafter. The Humble Petition also encompassed those who had joined rebellions and conspiracies against the regime since 16 December 1653, who were also considered disabled, and, following the Parliamentary Constitution (but not the Instrument or the Remonstrance), the Humble Petition also reintroduced the acts preventing the ministers and religious radicals from sitting in Parliament. This last, controversial, measure was adopted only after a paper to this effect was presented to the House by the leading Presbyterian, Joachim Matthews. Two prominent courtiers, Broghill and Wolseley, intervened in person to try to prevent this paper being read, but the motion was carried on the speaker's casting vote, after a tied division.[72] A new departure was the detailed provision made for the status of voters and members from Scotland and Ireland, which was referred to a committee and reported by Henry Cromwell's agent, William Aston, on 9 March.[73] The measures concerning Scotland were messy. The majority who had been covenanters before the spring of 1648 but had then joined the Duke of Hamilton's royalist Engagement were allowed to be involved in the Protectoral government if they had not supported the king thereafter; and, even then, Scottish royalists who had lived peaceably since 1 March 1652 (and had not been implicated in the Earl of Glencairn's highland rebellion of 1653–4) were also accepted. Such provisions may have been an attempt to appease Scots close to the government, such as William Lockhart and Lord Cochrane, who had supported Charles I earlier in their careers. The Irish situation was also clarified. Irish Protestants who had served Parliament before 1 March 1650 were also deemed politically acceptable, thereby preserving the rights of most of those who had defected from the Marquess of Ormond and Lord Inchiquin during the early stages of the Cromwellian invasion. In its attitude towards royalists, the Humble Petition once again betrays its origins as a compromise agreement. The inclusion of measures from the Parliamentary Constitution no doubt pleased the Presbyterians in the House; and the Scottish and Irish provisions were clearly made with the members from both nations in mind. The emphasis on loyalty after the early 1650s suggests an attempt by courtiers to make the new constitution as inclusive as possible, in pursuit of the elusive goal of healing and settling.

As the linchpin of the alliance that created the Humble Petition, the fourth article soon became a target for those who opposed civilian rule. This was apparent in the Additional Petition and Advice, which, in this instance, seems

---

[72] *CJ*, VII, 500; the order of the debate and the subsequent articles (Gardiner, *Constitutional Documents*, p. 450) confirms the contents of this paper. We are grateful to Dr Andrew Barclay for information concerning Matthews.

[73] *CJ*, VII, 499, 500.

to have been guided by the army interest. The chosen battleground was the overcomplicated measure concerning Scotland. Despite protests from one Scottish councillor that 'such as are your friends should be restored',[74] the Additional Petition summarily reversed the inclusive measures allowed in the Humble Petition. In the revised articles 4 and 13, the Hamiltonians were now deemed incapable of election or taking office, with the exception of those who had borne arms or shown 'signal testimony'. These terms were still not defined, but, crucially, it was stipulated that a definition was to be decided not by Parliament, but by the Protector and council. This was in keeping with the other measures in the Additional Petition, which sought to turn back the clock, to re-establish the conciliar government enshrined in the Instrument, and signalled an end to the more moderate policies towards royalists envisaged by the Remonstrance and (to a lesser extent) the Humble Petition.

RELIGION

Religion was the most controversial, and divisive, of issues during the 1650s, and it is hardly surprising that the religious articles in the various constitutions were hotly contested when debated in Parliament. In November 1654 the diarist Guybon Goddard said that the debate on the religious articles of the Instrument was 'more difficult than any thing that had been formerly propounded';[75] a month later John Fitzjames reported that 'nothing hesitates with us more than the debates of religion';[76] and in March 1657 William Jephson described the main religious article of the Remonstrance as the 'difficultest point' they had to deal with.[77] The key problem was the extent to which a 'national church' should be established and how those who disagreed with its tenets should be treated. In the Instrument of Government, article 35 defined the religious settlement in deliberately broad terms, requiring that 'the Christian religion, as contained in the scriptures, be held forth and recommended as the public profession of these nations'. As the wording suggested, this 'public profession' was not to be imposed, rather put forward as a guideline. Articles 36–7 laid down the principle of religious toleration, saying that 'none shall be compelled by penalties or otherwise' to observe this profession, and all those who 'profess faith in God by Jesus Christ' in ways 'differing in judgement' from the majority would be protected in their way of life and worship if their practices did not create disturbance or

---

[74] Burton, II, 11.   [75] Burton, I, lx.
[76] Alnwick Castle, Northumberland MS 551 (Fitzjames letterbook), fo. 13r.
[77] BL, Lansdowne MS 821, fo. 350r (17 March 1657).

scandal.[78] Toleration was thus enshrined in the Instrument itself, and (under article 38) all existing laws, statutes, or ordinances contrary to religious 'liberty' were deemed 'null and void'. Apart from this guarantee for the radical sects, the Instrument did little to set up a true religious settlement. Article 35 did not say how the public profession was to be defined, nor by whom; and it was unclear whether all ministers and preachers or only those conforming to the 'public profession' were to be paid by the state, although the existing funding arrangements were to continue until something 'less subject to scruple and contention' could be decided.

The Presbyterians used the Parliamentary Constitution to challenge the Instrument's tolerationist line head-on,[79] despite religious liberty being one of Cromwell's four 'fundamentals' of government. The Presbyterian attitude to liberty was summarised by John Fitzjames, in a letter to Robert Shapcote of 8 November 1654, who quipped: 'whether a religion that pleases *all* interests can please *one* God, there's the question'.[80] The effect of such hostility can be seen in the final draft of the Parliamentary Constitution. Chapter 41 demolished the Instrument's broad-based article 35, demanding that 'the true reformed protestant Christian religion as it is contained in the Holy Scriptures of the Old and New Testaments, and no other, shall be asserted and maintained as the public profession of these nations'. The profession of this 'Protestant' (rather than merely 'Christian') faith was now 'asserted' rather than 'recommended', and 'no other' forms were officially sanctioned. Toleration outside this official church was granted grudgingly under chapters 42 and 43. Although this kept in line with Cromwell's 'fundamentals', the Protector's veto over religious legislation was strictly limited. The Protector was allowed to veto any bill compelling observance of the profession of faith or any measure attacking tender consciences, but this was not to extend to bills forcing the 'submission and conformity to the public profession' of those ministers receiving money from the state, and Parliament retained the right to pass legislation against 'damnable heresies' and to discipline those who 'publicly maintain anything contrary to the fundamental principles of doctrines held within the public profession'. The radicals were not to be penalised without reason, but nor were they to be allowed to join the stipendiary ministry or voice their criticisms of the state church in public. When this was decided in early December 1654, it caused a storm of protest from the courtiers, who saw the Protector's own authority,

---

[78] Although 'faith in God by Jesus Christ' was later found sufficiently ambiguous to invite a gloss that penalised dissenters, the intention of the Instrument was surely the reverse. See Blair Worden, 'Toleration and the Cromwellian Protectorate' in W. J. Sheils, ed., *Persecution and Toleration* (Studies in Church History 21; Oxford, 1984), p. 217.

[79] For religious controversy in this Parliament, see Smith, 'Religious Reform'.

[80] Alnwick, Northumberland MS 551, fo. 8v.

as well as the status of religious liberty as a 'fundamental' of the constitution, under attack. Any such restriction of the veto, they claimed, 'would, in a manner, disable him from being what they had voted him, that is, a Protector'.[81] Alongside the Protector and the court, the move also raised the hackles of the army, which publicly asserted its support for toleration.[82] The soldiers' fears were apparently confirmed in late December and early January, when votes were passed to leave the exercise of the negative to the 'absolute discretion' of Parliament, and requiring that 'the limits of toleration should be settled by Parliament alone'.[83] The Presbyterians had already made sure the rules on toleration were closely defined. Chapter 31 reintroduced earlier religious restrictions on those standing as members of Parliament, banning men in holy orders (under an act passed in 1641) or with atheists and blasphemers, who denied 'the sacraments, prayer, magistracy, and ministry to be the ordinances of God'. Again, this was a snare laid against the radical sectaries. The Protector himself had to subscribe an overtly religious oath of office (chapter 8), promising to uphold 'the true reformed Protestant Christian religion' – which was so narrowly defined in the other articles. The bitterness of the courtiers confronted with these changes can be seen in a sarcastic proposal raised in mid-December, to add 'Presbytery' to 'popery' and 'prelacy' as one of the creeds not to be accorded any toleration.[84] And the religious changes proposed in the Parliamentary Constitution were high on Cromwell's list of grievances when he dissolved Parliament in January 1655.[85]

The Remonstrance was a very different document from what had gone before. Its lengthy preamble was full of religious language, beginning with an acknowledgement of 'the wonderful mercy of almighty God in delivering us . . . [from] the late king and his party' and God's decision 'to preserve' Cromwell's person 'in many battles'. The preamble also made direct reference to providence – the only such reference in any of the Protectoral constitutions – urging Cromwell to accept the crown, as 'God who puts down one and sets up another and giveth the kingdoms of the world to whomsoever he pleaseth, having by a series of providences raised you to be a deliverer of these nations' had preordained it. Article 10 laid down the form of the religious settlement, in what reads like a curious hybrid between the Instrument and the Parliamentary Constitution: 'that the true Protestant reformed religion, and no other, be asserted and recommended for the public profession of these nations'. Words like 'asserted' and 'recommended' sit awkwardly together, even without reference to article 35 of the Instrument

---

[81] Burton, I, cxvi.   [82] Worden, 'Toleration', p. 219.
[83] Gardiner, *Commonwealth and Protectorate*, III, 239.   [84] Burton, I, cxviii.
[85] Gaunt, 'Law-making', p. 182; Roots, *Speeches of Oliver Cromwell*, pp. 66–7.

and chapter 41 of the Parliamentary Constitution, where they are clearly at odds. Toleration was allowed under article 10 of the Remonstrance, in terms similar to those used by the Instrument, allowing liberty to those who 'profess faith in Jesus Christ his eternal son … [but] differ in doctrine, discipline or worship from the public profession held forth'. The courtiers were evidently well pleased with this provision. As Secretary Thurloe commented, the new constitution had 'full liberty of conscience … contained in it'.[86] The confidence of supporters of liberty was apparently increased by the fact that the final shape of the national church was left largely in the hands of the Protector. Under the new monarchy, Cromwell was not required to take an oath, nor was he restricted in his use of a veto over parliamentary legislation. Article 9 therefore expressed a desire that the 'Godly ministry' would be encouraged, and that 'such as openly revile them or disturb their assemblies to the dishonour of God … may be punished according to law', but Parliament could not enforce this alone, being reliant instead on the hope that 'your highness will give your consent to such laws as shall be made in that behalf'. Similarly, the granting of toleration under article 10 was balanced by the hope (which may be a deliberate echo of chapter 31 of the Parliamentary Constitution) that 'this liberty be not extended … [to] such, who publish horrible blasphemies or practice, or hold forth licentiousness or profaneness under the profession of Christ', but this was a measure dependent on Cromwell's pleasure, without teeth of its own. As in the secular articles, the religious reforms of the Remonstrance showed a remarkable willingness to trust Cromwell and his successors, rather than Parliament.

The Humble Petition and Advice grew from the Remonstrance, but its religious articles are much closer, in both wording and intention, to the rigid provisions put forward in the Presbyterian-dominated Parliamentary Constitution. The preamble dropped the providential language of the Remonstrance while retaining the more general references to God's preservation of the nation and the Protector's person. Article 10, on the prevention of disturbance of ministers, echoed article 9 of the Remonstrance, but article 4 imported a measure directly from the Parliamentary Constitution (chapter 31), confirming the 1641 act on holy orders and the 1650 act against atheists and blasphemers sitting in Parliament. It comes as no surprise that this clause was included on the motion of a leading Presbyterian in 1657 (and a veteran from 1654), Joachim Matthews.[87] The first sentence of article 11 is also an amalgamation, mixing terms used in article 10 of the Remonstrance and chapter 41 of the Parliamentary Constitution ('that the true protestant Christian religion'), continuing with a direct quote from the latter ('as it is

[86] *TSP*, VI, 74.   [87] *CJ*, VII, 500.

contained in the holy Scriptures of the Old and New Testaments, and
no other') and ending with a further hybrid ('be held forth and asserted
for the public professions of these nations'), which seems to be a cross
between chapter 41 of the Parliamentary Constitution (via article 10 of the
Remonstrance?) and article 35 of the Instrument. This revised wording was
introduced in a paper submitted by another key Presbyterian, Sir Richard
Onslow.[88] The complications caused by the Remonstrance were again
reflected in article 11 of the Humble Petition, where the 'confession of
faith' is to be 'asserted, held forth and recommended', in a mishmash of
wording taken from all three constitutional predecessors, which was voted in
by a majority of only three.[89]

When it came to liberty of conscience, the Humble Petition was more
restrictive than the Instrument or the Remonstrance, laying down that 'none
may be suffered ... to revile or reproach the confession of faith'. Although
this was less aggressive in tone than chapter 43 of the Parliamentary
Constitution, there is no doubt that the measure was a Presbyterian-backed
attempt to strengthen conformity. Indeed, during the debate, members
resolved that this stricture should apply to private as well as public criticism
of the confession.[90] This can also be seen in measures to ensure that those
who 'agree not ... [with] the public profession aforesaid' were excluded from
public maintenance, which are very similar to the stance taken in chapter 42
of the Parliamentary Constitution. Crucially, article 11 was less restrictive of
religious liberty. Although this would be allowed only to those who believed
in the Trinity ('such as profess faith in God the Father, and in Jesus Christ His
eternal son, the true God, and in the Holy Spirit, God co-equal with the
father and the son'), thus excluding the more extreme sects, such as Quakers
and Unitarians, it was not as severe as the Presbyterians would have liked,
and was the focus of a great deal of controversy. This clause was carefully
worded by a small group of courtiers led by Lord Broghill, who reputedly
framed it so that 'any man might believe it, and never hurt his conscience'.[91]
Despite this, the clause was pored over, word for word, on 19 March, and
when it came to a vote on the whole article on the next day, it was pushed
through by only one vote, with the tellers against the motion being John
Fitzjames and Henry Markham – men whose close links to Broghill did not
override their loyalty to the Presbyterians, especially over religion.[92] This

[88] CJ, VII, 506.
[89] See the Parliamentary Constitution, chapter 41; Remonstrance, article 10; Instrument, article 35; CJ, VII, 506–7.
[90] CJ, VII, 509–10.
[91] Little, *Broghill*, p. 150, quoting Whitelocke, *Diary*, p. 459, and BL, Harleian MS 6848, fo. 146r.
[92] CJ, VII, 507–9.

was the narrowest of victories, but one of the utmost importance, as it promised to secure not only the religious settlement but also Cromwell's acceptance of the new constitution as a whole. Indeed, the religious compromise was something that Cromwell could embrace whole-heartedly. As Blair Worden puts it, Parliament's articles on religious liberty 'which gave statutory protection to the people of God, and which at the same time would have trapped both Biddle and Nayler, delighted Cromwell'.[93] The religious provisions also satisfied – if they did not exactly 'delight' – the army. Even if they were still unhappy about the implications of a civilian constitution, the officers were now reported to 'think the other things in the Petition and Advice are very honest'.[94]

As it turned out, the problem of acceptance lay not with Cromwell and the army, but with the hardline Presbyterians in Parliament, who were unwilling to let the matter rest, even when the religious articles had been passed and the monarchical form of the Humble Petition drafted. Robert Beake recognised that the task was incomplete, but was optimistic of further gains on 28 March, reporting back to a friend that 'I would not have too much prejudice conceived against it [the Humble Petition] upon the account of religion, for though it be not provided for as it ought, yet the provision is better than what we yet have had', and saying that he remained hopeful of 'after laws to comment upon this text, and then it will appear narrower'.[95] Beake was not alone. In April, when the confirmation of acts and ordinances was considered, the opportunity was taken to review earlier religious legislation. On 28 April, the ordinance for the approbation of preachers of March 1654 was attacked, despite being commended by Cromwell only a week before,[96] with Alexander Thistlethwaite arguing that, 'if the supreme magistrate should be a papist or a fifth monarchist, he might change but six names of the approvers, and turn out all the godly ministers in the nation'. Lambert Godfrey called for it to be continued for a limited period only. This was dangerous talk: to 'have this ordinance singled out for a particular dislike' threatened Cromwell as well as toleration, as Secretary Thurloe well knew. But Griffith Bodurda, Thomas Bampfield, and their friends seemed intent on broadening the attack still further, turning the debate into a question of whether Parliament or the single person 'must be trusted'.[97] The ordinance for ejecting ministers was also targeted (again on 28 April), with Bampfield, backed by Godfrey, Sir John Hobart, and others, calling for it to be limited to

[93] Worden, 'Toleration', p. 227.   [94] *TSP*, VI, 219, 281.

[95] Coventry City Archives, BA/H/Q/A79/302: Robert Beake to Leonard Piddock, 28 March 1657; this is printed in Carol Egloff, 'Robert Beake and a Letter Concerning the Humble Petition and Advice', *HR*, 68 (1995), 233–9.

[96] William Goffe pointed this out during the debate (Burton, II, 52).

[97] Burton, II, 51, 53–4.

six months.[98] In essence, the assaults on the ordinances were a rerun of Presbyterian attempts to undermine them in 1654–5.[99] The religious controversy contrasts with the smooth passage of most of the secular ordinances included in the bill, which (in Burton's words) 'went off cleverly, without any debate'.[100] Bampfield, always happy to court controversy, reopened the question of religious liberty on 5 May. His proposed bill against Quakers was opposed by courtiers unhappy about the acrimonious debate that it might provoke, but was read after a division won by 90 votes to 51.[101] This revival of the Nayler question, with its obvious implications for tender consciences, came only two days before Cromwell's final rejection of the crown, and demonstrated that there still remained significant religious differences between the Cromwellians and the Presbyterians, despite their alliance over secular issues.

The divisiveness of the religious situation in the summer of 1657 is nowhere more apparent than in the Additional Petition and Advice. This sought to clarify the terms of the Humble Petition, as in the clause on article 4, where it was 'explained and declared' that the 1641 act preventing those in holy orders from sitting as MPs applied only to ministers maintained by the public. This prevented any attempt to exclude 'colonels that preach' or those who 'speak in their turns' in congregations, and marks a further victory over the rigidity of the more extreme Presbyterians.[102] A similar attempt at 'explanation' had quite the opposite effect. The wording of the oath to be taken by the Protector, as now specified, was to begin with a religious section, promising 'to the uttermost of my power I will uphold and maintain the true reformed protestant Christian religion in the purity thereof, as it is contained in the Holy Scriptures of the Old and New Testament, *to the uttermost of my power and understanding*, and encourage the profession and professors of the same'. The words we have highlighted here, although repetitive, were inserted on 25 June at the request of the Protector.[103] Otherwise, this section of the oath is identical to that drafted under article 8 of the Parliamentary Constitution, which Cromwell rejected so scornfully in January 1655. This was no accident. The clause was added to the oath on the motion of the leading Presbyterian, Thomas Bampfield, on 24 June.[104] Indeed, this return to the forms of the discredited Parliamentary Constitution in the oath, although apparently unnoticed at the time, is highly symbolic of how far the Presbyterians and their views would soon become mainstream within the Cromwellian Protectorate.

---

[98] Burton, II, 58–9.   [99] See Smith, 'Religious Reform', 41.   [100] Burton, II, 60.
[101] Burton, II, 113–14.   [102] Burton, II, 13–14.   [103] *CJ*, VII, 574.   [104] Burton, II, 284–5.

CONCLUSION

The different paper constitutions presented competing solutions to the problems of Protectoral government. The Instrument of Government of December 1653 had placed the greatest power in the hands of the single person and the council, with Parliament largely confined to a legislative function – and even this was subject to encroachment by the executive. Royalists were kept out of official positions and excluded from parliamentary elections for a limited period, and religious liberty was guaranteed, but not in strident terms, under a broad settlement designed to accommodate all opinions, avoid friction, and promote healing and settling. Despite its weaknesses – not least its inherent unpopularity as a document issued by the army – the Instrument at least represented a coherent, and workable, system of government. That was more than could be said about the Parliamentary Constitution of 1654–5, which was an attempt to force the Instrument into a Presbyterian mould. Under its terms, Parliament was elevated above the council in the executive as well as the legislature, and in debate (if not in the final proposals) the supremacy of the single person was also attacked. The Presbyterians ensured that the document was much less tolerant, politically and religiously. Rules against royalists were tightened, and religious radicals were included in penal measures; at the same time, religious liberty was curtailed, and a 'public profession' promoted and protected from criticism. Faced with measures that more or less observed the letter, but certainly not the spirit, of his four 'fundamentals', Cromwell brought the whole scheme to a sudden halt by dissolving Parliament on 22 January 1655.

If the Instrument was the army's constitution, and the Parliamentary Constitution was the organ of the Presbyterians, the Remonstrance of February 1657 was the darling of the civilian courtiers. In seeking to re-establish the 'ancient constitution', the Remonstrance offered the crown to Cromwell with full prerogative powers, stripped the 'privy council' of most of its executive authority, and, despite the restoration of an upper House, returned Parliament to its legislative role, limited by an unconditional royal veto. Royalists were to be rehabilitated on easier terms, and exclusions from Parliament managed by a commission of members of Parliament and councillors. In a return to ideas encapsulated in the Instrument, religion was left relatively open, with a voluntary 'confession' and general toleration, but, unlike in the Instrument, final responsibility lay with the new king, with his unfettered right to consent to all laws, including the Remonstrance itself. The Humble Petition and Advice, whether in its monarchical or Protectoral forms, was to the Remonstrance what the Parliamentary Constitution had been to the Instrument. It was less of a dialogue with its predecessor than a tense argument with it – an attempt to force the existing arrangements into a more obviously Presbyterian form. The courtiers, aware of the need for broader support for a civilian constitution, were left to try to accommodate the wishes of the Presbyterian interest, which demanded radical changes. These included attempts to reintroduce the wording, as well as the general ideas, served up under the Parliamentary Constitution. The Humble Petition thus retreated from the generous terms allowed under the Remonstrance, placing restrictions on the single person, and insisting that the constitution itself would be a check on his activities. The council's role was again increased, but the main beneficiary would be Parliament, which took a greater executive role, and was allowed to choose its own commissioners to decide on the exclusion of its members. Royalists and other subversives were considered in great detail, to the benefit of the Irish and Scots and the detriment of the English. Predictably, the greatest struggle was over the religious articles, which saw toleration restricted (although not eliminated) and stricter public compliance with the 'profession' of faith. Only a rearguard action by the courtiers prevented the Presbyterians from overturning toleration altogether, and salvaged a set of terms that they hoped would be broadly acceptable. The resulting document was an uneasy compromise, in which the 'civilian' elements were unacceptable to the army and the religious clauses unpalatable to the Presbyterian majority in Parliament.

The Additional Petition, intended to clarify the Humble Petition and Advice in light of Cromwell's personal objections, reflected this compromise, but also signalled a retreat from it. This was a mixture of proposals, some apparently coming from the army interest, others from the Presbyterians, others from Cromwell himself. Under its terms, the council's powers increased and restrictions were placed on Scottish royalists (probably at the behest of the army); the government's right to exclude members was eroded further, and a system of self-regulation put in place (to the delight of the Presbyterians). The ambiguities of the Additional Petition are most obvious in the Protector's oath, which incorporated religious clauses from the loathed Parliamentary Constitution, apparently without a murmur. With Cromwell's rejection of the crown in May, the strong direction provided earlier in the session by the civilian courtiers had dissipated, to be replaced by competing smaller groups intent on elevating smaller issues. It was this failure of leadership in the last weeks of the second Protectorate Parliament that lay behind the muddled, unfinished nature of the Humble Petition as it was passed on 26 June 1657.

The problems of the new Protectoral Constitution established in the summer of 1657 were raked over endlessly in the third Protectorate Parliament in 1659. There was a genuine sense of confusion at the constitutional implications of the Humble Petition and the Additional Petition, and still more concern at the absence of the supporting legislation caused by the collapse of the second sitting in February 1658. This raised concerns from supporters and critics of the Protectorate alike. Jason Peacey, in a survey of the constitutional debates in the 1659 Parliament, has argued that 'the government's critics were less concerned with undermining the Protectorate than with exposing the weakness and incoherence of the constitution, and its dictatorial implications, in order to place the Protectorate on a more secure footing',[105] but this shared sense of concern should not mask the very different agendas that were being pursued during this period. Underlying the constitutional confusion was a deepening factional rift between the civilian courtiers and the Presbyterians who supported Richard Cromwell, on the one hand, and the army interest and their new allies, the republican commonwealthsmen, on the other. This rift, which did so much to destabilise and eventually destroy the Protectorate, will be examined in detail in the fifth chapter. First, however, we will turn to consider the elections that returned members to the three Protectorate Parliaments and then, in chapter 4, the ways in which some of those members found themselves excluded.

---

[105] Jason Peacey, 'The Protector Humbled: Richard Cromwell and the Constitution', in Little, *Cromwellian Protectorate*, pp. 32–52; see also Derek Hirst, 'Concord and Discord in Richard Cromwell's House of Commons', *EHR*, 103 (1988), 339–58.

3

Elections

The first two Protectorate Parliaments were elected under the terms of the Instrument of Government which, by reapportioning seats and revising the franchise, ensured that the composition of these Parliaments departed significantly from earlier practice. The Instrument also provided for Scotland and Ireland to be represented as well as England and Wales, and these were thus the only fully British and Irish Parliaments ever to meet at Westminster other than between 1801 and 1922.[1] The third Protectorate Parliament saw a return to the position of 1640, and thereby generated intense controversy over the status and eligibility of the Scottish and Irish members. This chapter will examine the nature of the franchise, the distribution of seats, the ways in which members were chosen, and the workings of electoral patronage and influence. Throughout, a complex mixture of continuity and change will become evident. Electoral choice gradually became more ideologically driven and even polarised in the revolutionary decades than it had been prior to the Civil Wars, and this trend persisted after 1660; yet by 1659 the distribution of constituencies and the franchise were steadily coming to look more like they had in 1640.

THE REFORM OF THE FRANCHISE

The Instrument of Government not only introduced a major redistribution of seats from the boroughs in favour of the counties but also reformed the county franchise. It represented a compromise between the old system that had evolved up to 1640, and the radical schemes for parliamentary reapportionment that the Levellers had advanced in the second *Agreement of the People* (December 1648), and that the army officers had modified in

---

[1] There had been Scottish and Irish members in Barebone's Parliament, but these had been nominated rather than elected and thus were not representative in the way that the Scottish and Irish members of the Protectorate Parliaments were: Austin Woolrych, *Commonwealth to Protectorate* (Oxford, 1982), pp. 176–83.

49

January 1649. By 1640, the lower house of the Parliament of England and Wales contained 507 seats. Of the 483 English seats, no fewer than 401 were for boroughs, 78 for the counties, and 4 for the two universities. The 24 Welsh seats were divided equally into 12 for the counties and 12 for the boroughs. There was no representation of Ireland and Scotland, each of which had its own Parliament in Dublin and Edinburgh respectively. The Instrument reduced the total number of seats from 507 to 460. Thirty seats each were allocated to Scotland and to Ireland, and Wales was given twenty-five seats, all but two of them for the counties. The remaining 375 seats were English: 236 for the counties, 137 for boroughs and 1 each for the Universities of Oxford and Cambridge.[2]

This reapportionment was less radical than the proposals of 1648 and 1649 had envisaged. For example, the Leveller scheme in the second *Agreement of the People* proposed 300 seats: 16 for Wales and 284 for England (243 for counties, 41 for boroughs). The army officers' scheme of 1649 suggested 400 seats: 31 for Wales and 369 for England (297 for counties, 72 for boroughs). Since both these schemes predated the Cromwellian conquests of Ireland and Scotland and their incorporation into a single commonwealth with England and Wales, neither of them planned for Scottish or Irish representation at Westminster.[3] These figures show that, although the Instrument greatly reduced the number of borough constituencies by comparison with the pre-Civil War arrangements (401 down to 137), the reduction was significantly less drastic than that envisaged by the schemes of 1648 (forty-one) and 1649 (seventy-two).[4] Indeed, fifty-eight of the boroughs listed in the Instrument had been excluded in those earlier schemes.[5] The Instrument nevertheless implemented the biggest pruning of 'decayed boroughs' until the Great Reform Act of 1832.

The Instrument's redistribution of constituencies gave representation for the first time to several rapidly growing towns and cities, including Manchester, Durham, Leeds, and Halifax. It also helped to redress the marked imbalance in the regional distribution of seats. Whereas in 1640 the 10 south-western, central southern, and south-eastern counties accounted for 226 (45 per cent) of all seats, under the Instrument they were allocated only

---

[2] For these figures, and for comparisons with the earlier proposals, see Vernon F. Snow, 'Parliamentary Reapportionment Proposals in the Puritan Revolution', *EHR*, 74 (1959), 409–42. The full list of constituencies (except for those in Scotland and Ireland) is set out in article 10 of the Instrument: Gardiner, *Constitutional Documents*, pp. 407–8.

[3] For the 1648 plan, see Don M. Wolfe, ed., *Leveller Manifestoes of the Puritan Revolution* (1944), pp. 295–7; for the 1649 plan, see Gardiner, *Constitutional Documents*, pp. 359–63. These texts are discussed in detail in Keith Thomas, 'The Levellers and the Franchise', in G. E. Aylmer, ed., *The Interregnum: The Quest for Settlement, 1646–1660* (1972), pp. 57–78.

[4] Snow, 'Parliamentary Reapportionment Proposals', 414–21.

[5] These boroughs are listed in Snow, 'Parliamentary Reapportionment Proposals', 422–3, n. 3.

128 (28 per cent). By contrast, the 25 eastern, western, and midlands counties that in 1640 had 195 (38 per cent) of all seats were now accorded 204 (44 per cent). This still did not fully reflect the relative balance of wealth and population within and between these regions, nor was it as radical as the shifts envisaged in the schemes of 1648 and 1649, which would have changed the relative percentages of seats to 25 and 59 per cent for the earlier scheme and 28 and 44 per cent for the later one. But it was certainly a significant step towards a more proportionate distribution of seats.[6]

The same desire to give greater electoral strength to property-owners was reflected also in the franchise, even though this was not extended as widely as proposed in the schemes of 1648 or 1649. The second *Agreement of the People* enfranchised all adult males except servants, beggars, royalists, and those who did not sign the *Agreement*.[7] The army officers' scheme in January 1649 reflected Henry Ireton's concern (as expressed in the Putney Debates) that the franchise should not be extended beyond 'the people that are possessed of the permanent interest in the land'.[8] Both the electors and those elected had to be 'natives or denizens of England; not persons receiving alms, but such as are assessed ordinarily towards the relief of the poor; no servants to, and receiving wages from, any particular person'. Electors had to be aged at least twenty-one (except in the universities), and be 'housekeepers, dwelling within the division for which the election is'. Those elected were to 'be men of courage, fearing God and hating covetousness', and any who were unable to provide evidence of actively supporting Parliament during the 1640s would be excluded.[9]

The Instrument established a franchise that was narrower than either of these schemes had proposed, but still broader than that of 1640. The county franchise was vested in all those who possessed 'any estate, real or personal', to the capital value of £200 or more, but no attempt was made to address the immensely varied borough franchises for those towns and cities that still retained parliamentary seats.[10] Roman Catholics, royalists, and any who had 'advised, assisted or abetted the rebellion in Ireland' or 'any war against the Parliament' since 1 January 1642 were debarred from being either electors or elected. Those elected were required to be aged at least twenty-one and to be 'persons of known integrity, fearing God, and of good conversation'.[11] The council was empowered to vet election returns and exclude those who failed to meet these criteria: this procedure and its implementation

---

[6] Snow, 'Parliamentary Reapportionment Proposals', 428–30; this analysis is based on the table at 426–7, which names the counties placed in each category.
[7] Wolfe, *Leveller Manifestoes*, pp. 291–303.   [8] *Clarke Papers*, I, 319.
[9] Gardiner, *Constitutional Documents*, pp. 363–4.
[10] Gardiner, *Constitutional Documents*, p. 411 (Instrument, article 18).
[11] Gardiner, *Constitutional Documents*, pp. 410–11 (Instrument, articles 14, 15, 17).

will be examined in the next chapter. The Instrument also stipulated that Parliament should meet triennially, and sit for a minimum of five months (it did not stipulate whether lunar or calendar months, thereby creating an ambiguity that Cromwell was able to exploit).[12] Writs of summons for the first Parliament under these constitutional arrangements were to be issued by 1 June 1654, and the Parliament was to meet on 3 September following.[13]

The impact of the franchise reforms introduced by the Instrument of Government upon the electorate has generated controversy among historians. In his work on the elections in Suffolk and Cheshire, Paul Pinckney has suggested that the replacement of the forty-shilling-freehold qualification with one based on the ownership of real or personal estate worth £200 or more had the effect of expanding the county electorate, possibly by as much as 50 per cent.[14] By contrast, John Morrill has argued that the reforms almost certainly 'reduced the size of the electorate substantially'.[15] Derek Hirst has likewise concluded that 'the Instrument narrowed the electorate'.[16] Hirst has further suggested that, by eliminating many rotten boroughs and raising the property qualification, the Instrument's reformed franchise excluded significant numbers of poorer voters and produced an electorate that was 'as a whole less easily influenced' and 'more solidly composed of those substantial people who had little cause by 1653 to love much of what Cromwell aspired towards'.[17] John Cannon similarly believes that, 'though the new definition allowed property other than land to be represented, giving the vote to merchants, the qualification was fixed so high that it must have curtailed dramatically the county electorate'.[18] A recent local study by Stephen Roberts has also revealed that 'the Warwickshire evidence provides no support for Pinckney's view of an expanded electorate', and that the Warwickshire poll book for 1656 'suggests an electorate reduced in size from that common under the old constitution'.[19]

---

[12] See pp. 134–5.
[13] Gardiner, *Constitutional Documents*, pp. 406, 409 (Instrument, articles 7, 8, 11); Vaughan, I, 12.
[14] Paul J. Pinckney, 'The Cheshire Election of 1656', *Bulletin of the John Rylands Library*, 49 (1966–7), 418–19; Pinckney, 'The Suffolk Elections to the Protectorate Parliaments', in Colin Jones, Malyn Newitt, and Stephen Roberts, eds., *Politics and People in Revolutionary England: Essays in Honour of Ivan Roots* (Oxford and New York, 1986), pp. 207–8.
[15] J. S. Morrill, 'Parliamentary Representation, 1543–1974', in B. E. Harris, ed., *Victoria History of the County of Chester, Volume II* (Oxford, 1979), p. 109.
[16] Derek Hirst, *England in Conflict, 1603–1660: Kingdom, Community, Commonwealth* (1999), p. 293.
[17] Derek Hirst, *The Representative of the People? Voters and Voting in England under the Early Stuarts* (Cambridge, 1975), p. 3.
[18] John Cannon, *Parliamentary Reform, 1640–1832* (Cambridge, 1973), p. 17.
[19] Stephen K. Roberts, 'The 1656 Election, Polling and Public Opinion: A Warwickshire Case Study', *Parl. Hist.*, 23 (2004), 366, 374.

It thus seems probable that the Instrument's franchise reforms disenfran-chised some people (especially those in rotten boroughs and some of the poorest voters) while enfranchising others (particularly those whose wealth met the £200 qualification but was not necessarily in the form of freehold). This would help to explain why Pinckney detected the presence of 'a newly enfranchised group which had profited from the election', but this need not necessarily justify his conclusion that 'the electorate had been noticeably increased'.[20] The Instrument had the effect of enfranchising some people while disenfranchising others, but the net result seems to have been an overall decrease in the size of the electorate. William Prynne lamented in 1656 that the Instrument has 'disabled many thousands of their votes in elections'.[21] Furthermore, by granting so many more seats to the counties, and basing the county franchise on the £200 qualification, the Instrument ensured that a greater proportion of voters than hitherto were people of some substance. This necessarily gave them greater economic and political independence, and thus made them less susceptible to influence and less likely to defer meekly to pressure from the Protectoral regime. As Derek Hirst has written, the 'Instrument strengthened the backwoods'.[22] The consequences of this for the elections of 1654 and especially 1656 will become apparent in the sections that follow.

A further, related, issue concerns the number of votes that electors could cast in county elections. In previous elections, county electors had two votes with which to choose the members who would sit for two seats. The Instrument greatly increased the number of county seats, but it did not specify whether electors still possessed only two votes, as before, or whether they could now cast as many votes as there were seats available. Paul Pinckney has claimed, in relation to the elections in Cheshire and Suffolk, that electors still possessed only two votes, regardless of how many members were to be returned for the county.[23] By contrast, John Morrill has argued that electors surely possessed as many votes as there were members to be returned.[24] Clive Holmes has reached a similar conclusion on the basis of the Lincolnshire evidence, as have Anthony Fletcher and Stephen Roberts in their studies of Sussex and Warwickshire respectively.[25]

---

[20] Pinckney, 'Cheshire Election', 419.
[21] William Prynne, *A summary collection of the principal fundamental rights, liberties, propri-eties of all English freemen* (1656), quoted in Cannon, *Parliamentary Reform*, p. 18.
[22] Hirst, *England in Conflict*, p. 293.
[23] Pinckney, 'Cheshire Election'; Pinckney, 'Suffolk Elections'.
[24] J. S. Morrill, *Cheshire, 1630–1660: County Government and Society during the English Revolution* (Oxford, 1974), pp. 287–99; Morrill, 'Parliamentary Representation', 108–9.
[25] Clive Holmes, *Seventeenth-Century Lincolnshire* (Lincoln, 1980), pp. 213–16; Anthony Fletcher, *Sussex, 1600–1660: A County Community in Peace and War* (1975), pp. 301–2, 310–11; Stephen Roberts, 'The 1656 Election', 366–73.

It is possible that both arguments are plausible reconstructions based on the evidence that they use. It may be that the Instrument's silence on this point allowed a diversity of practice in which individual sheriffs could determine the procedure in their own county. However, it seems more likely that the evidence adduced by Pinckney can actually be read in a way that tells against his argument and suggests instead that electors possessed more than two votes. This would perhaps offer a more convincing explanation of the rise in the total number of votes cast than his hypothesis of a significant expansion of the county electorate. Given the evidence offered above in support of an overall decrease in the number of county voters, the most probable scenario would seem to be one in which a smaller number of voters possessed as many votes as there were seats available, thus explaining why the number of votes cast increased while the number of voters diminished. The surviving evidence may not permit a definitive answer to this problem, but a solution along these lines would both be consistent with what is known and also help to resolve the apparent contradictions between the different arguments that historians have put forward on this question.

THE FIRST PROTECTORATE PARLIAMENT

In most counties in England and Wales, the elections to the first Protectorate Parliament took place on 12 July 1654, while borough elections were generally held at some time between mid-June and mid-July. Irish and Scottish elections followed in late July and August.[26] As the next section will show, the major-generals experiment produced a much higher political temperature in the 1656 elections, and there was widespread local resentment of 'swordsmen' and 'decimators'. In 1654, by contrast, the atmosphere was somewhat less controversial, and Secretary Thurloe was able to report on 4 August that 'very great multitudes appeared at the election everywhere; yet all things carried with great quiet, and very good elections are made, for the most part, in all places'.[27] The relationship between local choice and national political and religious issues was often less direct than in 1656, and a gradual trend back towards the return of traditional county gentry is also evident in a number of constituencies.

There were about twenty cases in 1654 in which defeated candidates or dissatisfied electors submitted petitions to the council complaining of malpractice in county or borough elections. In most cases, electors alleged that a candidate failed to meet the qualifications laid down in the Instrument. The introduction of political, religious, and moral criteria thus created an

[26] *Return of Members of Parliaments of England, 1213–1702* (2 vols., 1878), I, 499–503.
[27] Vaughan, I, 12.

opportunity for challenges to a candidate's eligibility that had not existed before. For example, on 1 August the 'well-affected' inhabitants of Tiverton (Devon) complained of being outnumbered by many who were not eligible to vote, having acted against Parliament since 1641, and as a result the Presbyterian Robert Shapcote had been returned instead of the government candidate, Major John Blackmore. These 'well-affected' inhabitants claimed that Shapcote had formerly been a field officer under Charles I, and had only joined Essex's army in 1644.[28] A similar case was that of Charles Staynings, returned for Somerset, who was alleged to be a malignant who despised Cromwell and Parliament, and composed anti-government verses that included lines such as:

> A Cromwell makes all people take an oath,
> T'were pity two houses should hold them both . . .
> The thing which Parliament did first intend
> The General has brought unto an end . . .
> Who votes for Commons I will vote a fool.[29]

However, after examining these cases, the council decided against excluding either Shapcote or Staynings, and both duly sat in the Parliament. Likewise, various Bristol burgesses complained that the sheriffs had permitted former royalists to vote, and that two aldermen of a similar persuasion, Robert Aldworth and Miles Jackson, had consequently been returned. Yet here again the council upheld the original returns and the aldermen took their seats.[30] Councillors reached the same verdict in the case of Robert Wood of Surrey, which appears to have been partly an extension of the increasingly bitter factional infighting within the Kingston corporation, where the radicals had gained the upper hand. Wood successfully responded to complaints that he was 'a derider of the ways, worship and people of God', 'a profane swearer and of bad life and conversation', and a former royalist, by producing evidence that he had actively supported the Parliamentarian cause, and that he did not oppose godly ministers.[31] The council thus appears to have used its powers of exclusion very sparingly in 1654, and the relatively rare instances where it did employ them will be examined in the next chapter.

Such complaints were very much in the minority, and it was far more common for there to be no disputes at all or for any such to be resolved at local level. There is evidence of disputes in Reading, Buckinghamshire,

[28] TNA, SP 18/74/1–2. See also Stephen K. Roberts, *Recovery and Restoration in an English County: Devon Local Administration, 1646–1670* (Exeter, 1985), pp. 81–2.
[29] TNA, SP 18/74/4.   [30] TNA, SP 18/74/24.
[31] TNA, SP 18/74/93–4; History of Parliament Trust, London, unpublished article on Surrey for the 1640–60 section by Eleanor Reid.

Gloucestershire, and Wiltshire, but these were apparently sorted out without recourse to the council.[32] They suggest that local rivalries sometimes reflected ideological differences, and that these could become polarised for polemical purposes as competing individuals or interests tried to discredit their opponents as, for example, Presbyterians or Independents. The election dispute in Wiltshire provides a good illustration of this process. Two groups of candidates clashed, and each alleged that the other had derived support from unqualified voters. One group was led by Sir Anthony Ashley Cooper, and the Presbyterian sympathies of some of his supporters caused them to be labelled the 'Scottish interest'. Their opponents, led by Edmund Ludlow, were branded as 'Anabaptists' and 'Levellers'.[33] Although both sides vigorously defended themselves against these charges, such polemical attacks indicate that ideological differences could infect and aggravate local politics. In the end, the dispute appears to have been resolved in favour of Anthony Ashley Cooper and his allies, who enjoyed the council's support, but without any direct conciliar involvement.[34]

In some other election disputes, there was much less of an ideological dimension. Sometimes they arose from longstanding local controversies or uncertainties. For example, in Reading there had been a lack of consistency over how broadly the franchise had been defined since the 1620s. The mayor took advantage of this uncertainty to announce that the corporation had returned Cromwell's cousin, Colonel Robert Hammond. When the townsmen protested, they were permitted to vote, but members of the corporation allegedly intimidated the less wealthy by claiming that those with an estate worth less than £200 could not vote, even though this property qualification did not apply in the boroughs. In the end, however, Hammond was returned anyway, without the council becoming involved.[35] There was a similar dispute at Great Yarmouth, where the common council and the freemen of the town had vied for years over which body had the right to elect the borough's members of Parliament. The common councilmen submitted a petition to the council who, while promising 'to preserve their just right and the interest of honest men', immediately referred the

---

[32] Peter Gaunt, 'Cromwell's Purge? Exclusions and the First Protectorate Parliament', *Parl. Hist.*, 6 (1987), 7.

[33] *The Copy of a Letter sent out of Wiltshire, to a Gentleman in London* ([13 July] 1654), quotations at p. 1. The other side replied in *An Apology for the Ministers of the County of Wilts, in their Actings at the election of Members for the approaching Parliament* ([12 August] 1654).

[34] Ludlow, I, 388–90.

[35] [Henry Frewen,] *An Admirable Speech made by the Maior of Reading, upon the occasion of the late choice of a burgess for that Town, June 28, 1654* (1654).

matter to Parliament.[36] The House subsequently upheld the claims of the common councilmen.[37]

As Mark Kishlansky has argued, those elections that appear in the historical record are often the exceptional cases in which more harmonious procedures for selecting candidates broke down.[38] In 1654, there were many constituencies for which very little evidence survives, and the likelihood in those cases is that candidates were chosen without serious controversy. The members of the first Protectorate Parliament were, by the standards of seventeenth-century English Parliaments, relatively inexperienced. Peter Gaunt has estimated that 'fewer than thirty MPs seem to have sat prior to 1640 and almost two-thirds of the members had no prior parliamentary experience of any kind'.[39] Equally, there are signs in some counties of moves back towards traditional gentry families. In Somerset, the majority of county members 'were country gentlemen, although some were of lower status than the pre-war knights of the shire'.[40] Likewise, in Sussex, 'the gentry turned to their natural leaders' and returned 'honest, sound country gentry'.[41] Ann Hughes regards Warwickshire as 'unusual in 1654' precisely because in that county 'politically moderate members of the social elite were not yet willing to enter a Cromwellian Parliament themselves'.[42]

No complaints reached the council from either Ireland or Scotland, and this may reflect the degree of control that the Protectoral regime was able to exert over the choice of members. Each kingdom was allocated thirty members, although the numbers who actually attended Parliament were significantly lower than this. A Protectoral ordinance of 27 June divided Scotland into twenty-nine constituencies, each represented by one member, except for Edinburgh, which was given two members.[43] The disenfranchisement of malignants and the continuation of Glencairn's royalist rebellion in the north of Scotland led to a dearth of qualified candidates in some constituencies, with the result that in the end only twenty-two Scottish members (two for Edinburgh and twenty others) were returned. Nine of these

[36] TNA, SP 18/74/8; History of Parliament Trust, London, unpublished article on Great Yarmouth for the 1640–60 section by Eleanor Reid.
[37] *CJ*, VII, 369.
[38] Mark A. Kishlansky, *Parliamentary Selection: Social and Political Choice in Early Modern England* (Cambridge, 1986), esp. chaps. 1–5.
[39] Peter Gaunt, 'Oliver Cromwell and his Protectorate Parliaments: Co-operation, Conflict and Control', in Ivan Roots, ed., *'Into another Mould': Aspects of the Interregnum* (2nd edn, Exeter, 1998), p. 91.
[40] David Underdown, *Somerset in the Civil War and Interregnum* (Newton Abbot, 1973), p. 177.
[41] Fletcher, *Sussex*, pp. 301–2.
[42] Ann Hughes, *Politics, Society and Civil War in Warwickshire, 1620–1660* (Cambridge, 1987), p. 296 and n. 16.
[43] Gardiner, *Constitutional Documents*, pp. 422–5.

members were English, and of the thirteen remaining Scots the vast majority had close connections with the regime: six had served as commissioners to the English Parliament in 1652, and five held some public office. Thus, as Frances Dow has written, virtually all the members who sat for Scottish constituencies 'had some tie with the English interest'.[44] In the event, however, only twelve or thirteen of the Scottish members are known to have taken their seats, although the actual number is impossible to establish precisely and may have been higher than this.[45]

A somewhat similar pattern was evident in Ireland. As with Scotland, a Protectoral ordinance of 27 June set out the distribution of members among the constituencies.[46] It seems that the council based this on proposals drawn up by the Irish sub-committee and presented by John Lambert, an ally of the Lord Deputy, Charles Fleetwood. Some of the parliamentary commissioners in Ireland initially suggested that Cromwell and the council might nominate members directly, probably to thwart the Old Protestant interest that they perceived as pro-royalist. However, others including Ludlow successfully advised against this.[47] Elections were duly held in late July and early August. Of the twenty-nine members returned, twelve were English army officers: only five of these were close allies of Fleetwood, and three were associated with the Old Protestant interest. The Old Protestants won a further sixteen seats. As many as twelve army officers could not easily be spared, and Cromwell advised the Lord Deputy, Charles Fleetwood, to retain at least six of them in Ireland. Another five or so apparently stayed as well, with the result that those Irish members who sat at Westminster probably numbered no more than eighteen.[48] In practice, Fleetwood's suspicions of the Old Protestants proved unfounded. They were generally firm supporters of the Protectorate, and the upshot was thus that for Ireland, as for Scotland, the majority of members either were directly drawn from or were at any rate sympathetic to the Protectoral regime.[49]

That a majority of members of the first Protectorate Parliament were dissatisfied with the arrangements for the franchise contained in the Instrument of Government is evident from the changes proposed in the draft constitutional bill on which this Parliament laboured. The overall

---

[44] Frances Dow, *Cromwellian Scotland, 1651–1660* (Edinburgh, 1979), pp. 148–54 (quotation at p. 153).
[45] Gaunt, 'Cromwell's Purge?', 9 and n. 45. The number attending cannot be worked out more precisely than this because evidence of attendance relies very largely on committee lists, and where two or more members shared the same surname it is impossible to be certain who was being nominated.
[46] Gardiner, *Constitutional Documents*, pp. 425–7.   [47] Ludlow, I, 386–8.
[48] *TSP*, II, 445–6, 530, 558; Gaunt, 'Cromwell's Purge?', 9–10.
[49] This paragraph is based on Patrick Little, 'Irish Representation in the Protectorate Parliaments', *Parl. Hist.*, 23 (2004), 336–56.

distribution of seats – 400 for England and Wales plus 30 each for Scotland and Ireland – was retained with only minor adjustments.[50] The franchise, however, was subjected to more significant revision. On 27 November, the House voted to restore the county franchise to the forty-shilling freeholders while retaining it for those new voters who, although not freeholders, possessed real or personal property worth at least £200.[51] Then, on 1 January 1655, the House abolished the new qualification entirely, leaving just the old forty-shilling franchise in place.[52] Like the Instrument, the draft bill made no attempt to alter the wide variety of borough franchises, but its return to the forty-shilling franchise in the counties suggests a desire – understandable enough in a Parliament comprised predominantly of landed gentry – to curtail the new-found influence of urban fortunes in a way that ran counter to the army's preferences.

THE SECOND PROTECTORATE PARLIAMENT

Any hopes for such reforms died along with the draft bill when the Parliament was dissolved on 22 January 1655. Under the terms of the Instrument, Cromwell was not obliged to summon another Parliament for three years. However, by the early summer of 1656, most members of the council and the major-generals were urging him to call a new Parliament. Sir Edward Hyde wrote on 21 June that 'Cromwell is in great irresolution whether he shall speedily call another Parliament, to which not only the army but his council pressed him'.[53] However, on 26 June Thurloe was able to inform John Pell that it had been announced that day that writs would shortly be issued for the election of a Parliament to meet the following September; the exact date was soon afterwards fixed for 17 September.[54] Thurloe told Henry Cromwell a few days later that 'the chief end of calling this Parliament is to have their advice in the war with Spain, and to settle such other things, as may be for the peace and good of the nation'.[55] The major-generals appear to have played an important role in pressing for another Parliament, and on 27 February 1657 Cromwell accused them and other army officers of being 'impatient … till a Parliament was called'. He added bitterly: 'I gave my vote against it, but you [were] confident by your own strength and interest to get men chosen to your heart's desire. How you

---

[50] These adjustments were that, in Kent, Hythe gained a seat instead of Queenborough; one seat was transferred from the city of Leicester to Leicestershire; in Oxfordshire, Banbury gained a seat instead of Woodstock; and in Wales Carmarthenshire lost one member to the borough of Carmarthen: Gardiner, *Constitutional Documents*, p. 441.
[51] *CJ*, VII, 391–2. [52] *CJ*, VII, 410–11; Gardiner, *Constitutional Documents*, pp. 436–7.
[53] Bodl., MS Clarendon 52, fo. 39r. [54] Vaughan, I, 433, 439. [55] *TSP*, V, 176.

have failed therein, and how much the country has been disobliged, is well known.'[56]

The elections to the second Protectorate Parliament were much more divisive than those to the first, and Thurloe's initial optimism soon gave way to considerable anxiety. On 15 July he wrote to Henry Cromwell: 'The peace and welfare of the nation will be much concerned in the temper of this Parliament. We hope for good from it; and that we shall have none of those, who during the last Parliament were continuing very bloody designs against the Protector and peace of the nation.' However, on 12 August Thurloe told Henry Cromwell that 'the day of election now draws near; and here is the greatest striving to get into Parliament that ever was known. All sorts of discontented people are incessant in their endeavours.' Many of the elections took place on 20 August, and six days later Thurloe reported: 'much ado there has been about the elections here; every faction has bestirred themselves with all their might'.[57] All over England, many electors showed deep hostility towards candidates associated with the Protectoral regime in general, and with the rule of the major-generals in particular. Many of the county gentry especially deplored the rule of 'swordsmen', the imposition of the decimation tax upon former royalists, and the creation of 'commissioners to secure the peace', which appeared to undermine the status of the traditional commission of the peace. Indeed, Chris Durston has argued convincingly that 'the election quickly came to be seen as a referendum on the rule of the major-generals'.[58]

A good insight into the views of those opposed to the regime may be found in an anonymous pamphlet that according to Thomason was 'scattered about the streets' of London on 1 August 1656 and subsequently dispersed as widely as possible in the provinces. The author is unknown, but the Fifth Monarchist Thomas Venner was implicated in the distribution of the pamphlet.[59] Entitled *Englands Remembrancers. or, A word in season to all English men about their elections of the members for the approaching Parliament*, it began with a series of questions including 'how are all our rights, liberties and properties invaded and subverted by arbitrary powers and force of arms?'[60] The author urged readers to regard 'the present writs for election

---

[56] Lomas–Carlyle, III, 488.
[57] *Return of Members of Parliaments*, I, 504–6; TSP, V, 213, 303, 349. See also Vaughan, II, 8–9.
[58] Christopher Durston, *Cromwell's Major-Generals: Godly Government during the English Revolution* (Manchester, 2001), p. 190.
[59] TSP, V, 272–3. Venner had been summoned before the council on 29 July: TNA, SP 25/114, p. 21.
[60] *Englands Remembrancers. or, A word in season to all English men about their elections of the members for the approaching Parliament* (1656), p. 1. This pamphlet is printed in TSP, V, 268–71.

of our representatives' as ' the product of divine providence', and not to be 'afraid to vote in the choice of your deputies lest you should seem to approve [the Protector's] power, because the choice is appointed by his writs'. The pamphlet went on to stress the great importance of Parliament: 'an assembly of the people's deputies is the only visible means to settle justice, right and peace in the nation . . . no fear . . . can warrant the omission or neglect of using the last or only visible means of common right and safety, when there was no other visible means left to preserve her country from ruin'.[61] It was therefore the duty of all 'honest men' to 'choose their deputies for the approaching Parliament' and not to regard it as 'indifferent with you whether you go to the elections or not'. The pamphlet concluded by asking passionately: 'do not your infringed rights speak? Do not your invaded properties speak? Do not your gasping liberties speak? Do not your often affronted representatives (which have been trod upon with scorn) speak? Do not your encumbered estates speak? . . . Help, help, or England perishes.'[62]

Packets of *Englands Remembrancers* were seized wherever they were found, but otherwise there is no evidence to suggest that the regime conducted a co-ordinated election strategy to counter such opposition from the centre. Instead, it was largely left to the initiative of individual major-generals to support preferred candidates and to inform the government of its opponents' activities.[63] Thurloe acted, in Mark Kishlansky's phrase, 'as a clearinghouse for electoral information'.[64] The major-generals' regular reports throughout July and August enabled him to monitor local developments very carefully, and they suggest growing panic as the extent of anti-military feelings became ever more apparent. It seems that some major-generals, such as Hezekiah Haynes, William Goffe, Thomas Kelsey, and Edward Whalley, encountered greater difficulty in securing the return of acceptable candidates than others, including John Disbrowe, James Berry, and Tobias Bridge. It is worth examining the activities of each of these officers in turn as case studies of the electoral politics of 1656.

Haynes's concerns within his association (Essex, Cambridgeshire, the Isle of Ely, Suffolk, and Norfolk) were focused primarily on the last two named counties.[65] In mid-July he reported to Thurloe that the lack of a declaration

---

[61] *Englands Remembrancers*, pp. 1, 2, 4.   [62] *Englands Remembrancers*, pp. 5, 8.
[63] Gardiner, *Commonwealth and Protectorate*, IV, 267–71; Durston, *Cromwell's Major-Generals*, chapter 9.
[64] Kishlansky, *Parliamentary Selection*, p. 125.
[65] Haynes was generally thought of as a major-general in his own right, but technically he was a deputy to General Fleetwood. However, Fleetwood was a member of the council and generally resided in London, leaving provincial affairs to his deputy: Pinckney, 'Suffolk Elections', pp. 214–15. There is a helpful account of Haynes's life and career in W. L. F. Nuttall, 'Hezekiah Haynes: Oliver Cromwell's Major-General for the Eastern Counties', *Transactions of the Essex Archaeological Society*, 1, part 3 (1964), 196–209.

from Cromwell and the council 'has exceedingly heightened the spirits of the ill affected, and put great discouragement upon your friends', and he particularly feared the return of the crypto-royalist and episcopalian John Hobart for Norwich.[66] He requested greater resourcing of the militia as a precaution, and asked for 'but one hint, that some care will be taken as to the encouragement of honest men in their choice of parliament before and after the election'. By 19 July, he was beginning 'to fear Suffolk, finding so malignant a grand jury, who will have a great advantage to possess the country, and all occasioned by a malignant simple high sheriff'. He felt that 'honest men' would 'do their utmost ... but as the case stands, will be compelled to take in with the Presbyterian to keep out the malignant'.[67] Haynes was alarmed to learn that John Boatman, the ejected Presbyterian-turned-royalist pastor of St Peter Mancroft, Norwich, had returned to the city from London and was preaching in support of Hobart. But his attempts to ban Boatman from Norwich only led the preacher to condemn Haynes's 'tyrannical and unheard of persecution' and to move to a church 'about two miles [out] of the city, and [draw] multitudes after him'.[68] Haynes's troubles mounted in early August. In Ipswich, when the election indentures for Suffolk were read, one Robert Manning objected to the words 'his highness's parliament' on the grounds that 'the king never called it his parliament'. Boatman continued to support Hobart, whom Haynes described on 10 August as 'a person as closely maligning the government and good men, as any other in Norfolk'.[69] On 15 August, Haynes complained to Thurloe of the 'potency of the adverse party', and that same day he wrote despairingly to Cromwell that 'such is the prevalence of that spirit, which opposes itself to the work of God upon the [common] wheel, that the spirits of those, that are otherwise minded, have been much perplexed and discouraged from almost appearing at the election, seeing no visible way of balancing that interest'. He suggested that if the militia 'were but paid and exercised', that would be 'a sufficient strength to secure the interest of those counties'.[70]

When the elections were held in Norfolk on 20 August, the results confirmed all Haynes's worst fears. Hobart was returned for Norwich, despite Haynes's best efforts. By contrast, Cromwell's son-in-law, General Charles Fleetwood, gained a thousand fewer votes than Hobart, which only just secured him election for Norfolk, and the fact that he was returned at all

---

[66] *TSP*, V, 220. For a detailed examination of Hobart's career, and Haynes's dealings with him, see Carol S. Egloff, 'John Hobart of Norwich and the Politics of the Cromwellian Protectorate', *Norfolk Archaeology*, 42 (1994), 38–56. Hobart's role in the 1656 elections is discussed at 46–8.
[67] *TSP*, V, 230.   [68] *TSP*, V, 289, 297. See also Egloff, 'John Hobart', 46.
[69] *TSP*, V, 187–8.   [70] *TSP*, V, 311, 312–13.

probably owed much to Haynes's personal influence with the sheriff.[71] That evening Haynes wrote to Thurloe: 'There was such a clear combination, as never was known before, to bring in persons of apparent contrary principles to the government, and but few of them such as continued to own the parliament interest, by which choice the profane, malignant, and disaffected party and scandalous ministry are only gratified.' The election was, he continued, 'as bad as it could well have been made', and he warned that:

If other counties should do as this, it would be a sufficient alarm to stand upon our guard, the spirits of people being most strangely heightened and moulded into a very great aptness to take the first hint for an insurrection; and the county especially so disposed, may most probably begin the scene. Wherefore I most humbly beg, that a speedy order may be taken for the paying and mustering of militia horses, for as yet they have not been called together.

He concluded by hoping for 'the preservation of that interest that fear God in the nation and desire the settlement and peace with you'.[72]

Haynes's deep anxieties about Hobart were apparently well grounded. Major John Balleston reported that when he met Hobart after the election he 'perceived him extreme heightened'. According to Balleston, Hobart declared 'that we were ruled by an arbitrary power, and not by any known law; and that he had suffered himself to be distrained for taxes; and that Major-Generals, and such new raised forces, were needless people, the army being too great before'. When Balleston 'told him, that if his judgment was such, he had better forbear the House than to act, saying that he could not expect the power of the sword would be put into his or such hands', Hobart allegedly replied that 'it mattered not, the more long it was, the greater expectation of roving; intimating the Danes, and others who tyrannically acted'. Balleston regretted that 'we may perceive by the appearance at the elections the affections of the people, and I much grieve to see what a poor number appeared heartily for our friends ... Many of our seeming friends proved very faint.'[73]

Haynes found the results in Suffolk, where there were twenty-two candidates for the ten seats, similarly disappointing. Even Sir Thomas Barnardiston, although a prominent member of a long-established Suffolk gentry family, only just scraped into the tenth and last place on the list of successful candidates, almost certainly because his work as a commissioner for securing the peace led him to be perceived as closely associated with the major-generals' regime, an impression that his alliance with Haynes could only have reinforced. Paul Pinckney has plausibly attributed Barnardiston's loss of electoral favour to his support for 'a continuing Puritan reformation

[71] Pinckney, 'Suffolk Elections', p. 215.   [72] *TSP*, V, 328.
[73] *TSP*, V, 370. See also Egloff, 'John Hobart', 47.

through the major-generals, the decimation tax, and all the other activities that would be so offensive to the conservative gentry in the 1656 election'.[74] It seems that the Suffolk gentry wished to send a clear signal that they were deeply unhappy with the rule of the major-generals, and that of Haynes in particular.[75]

The experiences of William Goffe (Berkshire, Hampshire, and Sussex) were broadly similar. On 8 August, he wrote from Winchester that 'the unquiet spirit of discontented men doth begin to show itself'.[76] He managed to gain election for Hampshire, and reported that 'considering the great endeavours, that were used against my being elected, ... I have much cause to look upon my being chosen as a special providence of God'. Although Goffe secured the election of one of the captains of the county militia and several county commissioners, those returned also included open critics of the regime such as Richard Norton, Robert Wallop, John Bulkeley, and Edward Hooper.[77] Prominent on the list of those elected in Sussex were members of traditional gentry families like Herbert Morley, Sir John Pelham, Sir John Fagge, John Stapley, and Anthony Shirley.[78] On 23 August, Goffe informed Thurloe: 'I perceive that in Sussex Colonel Morley ruled the roost, by the help of a disaffected party, ... and that it was their design to have no soldier, decimator, or any man that has salary.' The list also included one George Courthop, a reputed royalist, and a newcomer to Westminster. The self-styled 'honest party of the county' complained that Courthop 'was formerly put out of the commission for the peace for malignancy and drunkenness'.[79] The attempt to dislodge Courthop failed, however, and he was duly returned. Goffe put a brave face on the results and told Thurloe: 'In reference to the elections, concerning which I hope it may be said, that though they be not so good as we could have wished them, yet they are not so bad as our enemies would have had them.'[80] Nevertheless, many of the returns within his association represented a pointed rebuff to the regime.

Thomas Kelsey (Kent, Surrey, and the Cinque Ports) expressed his deep concerns, especially in relation to Kent, to Cromwell on 26 August. He reported that at the Maidstone elections there was 'such a sad spirit appearing in the county against what good soever' that Cromwell had 'endeavoured to do, most of the Cavaliers falling in with the Presbyterians against all those persons owned' by the 'present Government'. Kelsey encountered a 'bitter spirit against swordsmen, decimators, courtiers, &c.', and 'most of those

[74] Pinckney, 'Suffolk Elections', pp. 214–24, quotation at p. 222.
[75] History of Parliament Trust, London, unpublished article on Suffolk for the 1640–60 section by Andrew Barclay.
[76] *TSP*, V, 287.   [77] *TSP*, V, 329; Durston, *Cromwell's Major-Generals*, p. 192.
[78] Fletcher, *Sussex*, p. 310.   [79] *TSP*, V, 341.   [80] *TSP*, V, 365.

that are chosen to sit in the ensuing Parliament' were 'of the same spirit'. He warned that there was 'such a perverseness in the spirits of those that are chosen that, without resolution of spirit in your highness and council to maintain the interest of God's people (which is to be preferred before 1,000 Parliaments) against all opposition whatsoever, we shall return again to our Egyptian taskmasters'.[81] Just over a week later, on 5 September, Kelsey told Thurloe that he found 'all the honest people in these parts full of fears of what the event of this parliament will be'. He suggested that 'all that sit in the House, may be put to sign a recognition to own the government, as it is in the Instrument'.[82] In the end, Kelsey failed to secure the return of candidates sympathetic to the regime, and his fears about Kent in particular seem to have been thoroughly borne out: the fact that no county had a larger number of its members excluded from the Parliament clearly indicates how unsuitable the council perceived most of those returned to be.[83]

The only other county that had as many of its members excluded as Kent was Lincolnshire, which fell within the association of Edward Whalley (along with Derbyshire, Leicestershire, Nottinghamshire, and Warwickshire). On 9 August, Whalley reported to Thurloe that 'truly I am confident that a man would not be chosen but upon apprehensions that they would not change the government'.[84] Two days later, he wrote to Cromwell from Nottingham to express his confidence that 'not a man from hence would be chosen to sit in this parliament, in whom they conceived a spirit of opposition to this present government'. He predicted, correctly, that Sir Henry Vane would not be elected at Boston, and Lincolnshire saw the defeat of such radical candidates.[85] As Clive Holmes has written, 'in the 1656 election Lincolnshire voters expressed their unease, their suspicions engendered by the protectorate, but not their outright opposition to Cromwellian government ... Perhaps the moderate oppositionists were preferred because Vane was believed to be too radical, to pose too direct a threat to the stability that Cromwell's government had achieved.'[86] Nevertheless, the high number of conciliar exclusions for Lincolnshire (eight of sixteen members returned) indicates that the outcome was less favourable than Whalley hoped or believed, and in his other counties the situation was only slightly more encouraging. He told Cromwell that 'Sir Arthur Hesilrige, if chosen' – which he duly was – 'will most blemish their choice in Leicestershire.' Whalley successfully headed off an attempt to make another of Cromwell's leading critics, Colonel Hutchinson, a candidate for Nottinghamshire, and he wrote confidently that 'for the town of Nottingham, I have a great influence upon it: they will not choose any without my advice'. His position

[81] TNA, SP 18/129/156. [82] *TSP*, V, 384. [83] See chapter 4. [84] *TSP*, V, 296.
[85] *TSP*, V, 299. [86] Holmes, *Seventeenth-Century Lincolnshire*, pp. 214–15.

there was probably strengthened by the fact that he was a 'native country-man' of Nottinghamshire.[87] Whalley hoped that the choice in Warwickshire would be 'so good' and, although – in contrast to 1654 – that county saw the return of some more traditional gentry such as Clement Throckmorton (for Warwick), and Edward Peyto and Sir Roger Burgoyne (for Warwickshire),[88] it appears that the overall outcome was, in Stephen Roberts's words, 'broadly supportive of the Protectoral regime'.[89]

Although the above discussion includes some of the most striking examples, such problems could be found in varying degrees in many more parts of England. There were, on the other hand, instances either where critics of the government did not command such strong support, or where the major-generals appear to have been rather more effective in securing the election of supporters of the regime and in preventing that of opponents. This task was sometimes a challenging one, as John Disbrowe found in his West Country association (Cornwall, Devon, Dorset, Gloucestershire, Somerset, and Wiltshire). On 12 August, he wrote to Cromwell from Launceston that there were 'designs on foot, in order to the subversion of what has been done for the nation's peace and safety', and that 'the honest people' were 'like to meet with great opposition'. He promised to 'make it my business to encourage the honest sober people, and strengthen their hands, as much as in me lies'. But on the basis of 'the elections that hitherto have been made in corporations hereabout', he could 'not apprehend any great danger', and he was pleased to report the return of himself for Bridgewater (although he subsequently sat for Somerset), Major John Jenkins for Wells, James Ashe for Bath, General Robert Blake and Colonel Thomas Gorges for Taunton, Sir John Coplestone for Barnstaple, Major Samuel Searle for Honiton, and John Buller for Looe.[90]

Commenting on these results in a letter that same day to Thurloe, Disbrowe wrote: 'By the elections already made in corporations we may give some judgment, that that spirit of opposition to the present government bears not that sway, that some men fancy.' He then reported: 'I have consulted with the honest people of every county, as I came along, and with them agreed upon names, and have set them at work for the improvement of their interest to elect sober and good men. I must confess in every county I yet came in, I hear of their making parties; and undoubtedly their designs are to overthrow all.' He therefore promised to make every effort to 'prevent and break all such contrivances'.[91] In the event, the county election

[87] P. R. Seddon, 'The Nottingham Elections to the Protectorate Parliaments of 1654 and 1656', *Transactions of the Thoroton Society of Nottinghamshire*, 102 (1998), 93–8, especially 96.
[88] TSP, V, 299–300; Hughes, *Warwickshire*, p. 296; Stephen Roberts, 'The 1656 Election'.
[89] Stephen Roberts, 'The 1656 Election', 373.   [90] TSP, V, 302.   [91] TSP, V, 303.

in Somerset returned neither overt opponents of the regime nor military men, apart from Disbrowe himself. Rather, the winners were generally from traditional county gentry families, such as John Buckland, Sir Alexander Popham, and Francis Luttrell.[92] Disbrowe's forceful personality was sometimes decisive, as for example in Gloucester, where he intervened on the eve of the poll to thwart the election of Christopher Guise, a county commissioner who had attempted to secure exemptions from the decimation tax for his royalist friends.[93]

On the Welsh borders and in Wales, Major-General James Berry (Herefordshire, Shropshire, Worcestershire, and Wales) apparently encountered fewer problems than some of his colleagues. He reported to Cromwell on 12 August that 'some dissatisfied persons attempt to be chosen, but they pretend they have received some late satisfaction, and want nothing but the seal of a parliament to all proceedings; and if you would but make them lords, they would give you leave to be king'.[94] In Wales, according to Geraint Jenkins, 'the elections for the second Protectorate Parliament during the summer of 1656 seemed to confirm that the power of the sword during the brief reign of the Major-Generals had bred loyalty and obedience to Cromwellian rule'.[95] Fourteen of the twenty-five members elected for Wales in 1654 were returned again, and most of those who joined them were supportive of the regime. Sometimes Berry and his supporters may have resorted to dubious methods to secure the outcome they desired. For example, the Presbyterian Edward Harley alleged that at Hereford the sheriff obtained the return of Berry's preferred candidate Benjamin Mason, the local militia lieutenant, by sending those who opposed him to a nearby field and thus away from the voting location.[96] But there is no evidence that Berry faced the kind of uphill struggle reported by Haynes, Goffe, Kelsey, or Whalley.

The same is broadly true of Tobias Bridge, who succeeded Charles Worsley as major-general of Cheshire, Lancashire, and Staffordshire following the latter's death in June 1656. Bridge reported to Cromwell on 15 August that in Cheshire, after 'much debate and arguing with' the commissioners for securing the peace, he had managed to persuade them to leave

---

[92] Underdown, *Somerset*, pp. 182–5.
[93] Durston, *Cromwell's Major-Generals*, p. 192; A. R. Williams, 'John Desborough: Gloucestershire's Major-General', *Transactions of the Bristol and Gloucestershire Archaeological Society*, 89 (1970), 123–9, especially 127–8; A. R. Warmington, *Civil War, Interregnum and Restoration in Gloucestershire, 1640–1672* (Woodbridge, 1997), pp. 123–5.
[94] *TSP*, V, 303.
[95] Geraint H. Jenkins, *The Foundations of Modern Wales: Wales, 1642–1780* (Oxford, 1987), p. 35.
[96] Durston, *Cromwell's Major-Generals*, p. 195.

out John Bradshaw, a prominent opponent of the Protectorate and an anti-militarist. 'With the advice of some honest friends', Bridge went on, 'I have taken the best course we could think of, to engage the gentlemen to bestir themselves to procure the election of persons of the most sober and suitable spirit to the present work.' He thought that another opponent of the regime, Sir William Brereton, commanded only 'very little' 'interest amongst the gentlemen', and he pushed instead for the election of Thomas Marbury, Thomas Croxton, Thomas Mainwaring, and Edward Hyde.[97] In the event, however, only Marbury was returned, along with Sir George Booth, Richard Legh, and Peter Brooke, who were all the sheriff's candidates. Bridge agreed to withdraw his other candidates in return for the omission of Bradshaw.[98] Bridge also expected to find 'much thwarting' in Lancashire, 'through the peevishness of some, and disaffection of others', although only two of its returned members were subsequently excluded.[99] Much the same was apparently true of Staffordshire, where at least three of the commissioners for securing the peace managed to secure election, along with Sir Charles Wolseley, a member of the council.[100]

The examples of Disbrowe, Berry, and Bridge are a reminder that the setbacks for the major-generals, and for the Protectoral regime in general, while considerable, were not uniform or universal. After all, of the eighteen major-generals and their deputies, all except George Fleetwood were returned to Parliament. Of the fifteen members of the council, four were major-generals (Disbrowe, Charles Fleetwood, Lambert, and Skippon), and, of the remaining eleven, all were returned except for Lord Lisle and the Earl of Mulgrave, who probably did not stand. Other high-ranking officials or supporters of the regime who were elected included John Thurloe, Bulstrode Whitelocke, William Lenthall, John Lisle, John Maidstone, and Richard Cromwell.[101] Nevertheless, a significant number of prominent critics of the regime were also returned. These included staunch commonwealthsmen such as Sir Arthur Hesilrige, Thomas Saunders, Thomas Scott, and John Weaver; and also crypto-royalists such as Thomas Adams, James Clavering, Sir John Gore, John Hobart, John Stanhope, Sir Horatio Townshend, and

---

[97] *TSP*, V, 313–14. On Bradshaw, see also Paul J. Pinckney, 'Bradshaw and Cromwell in 1656', *Huntington Library Quarterly*, 30 (1966–7), 233–40.

[98] For accounts of the 1656 elections in Cheshire, see Pinckney, 'Cheshire Election'; Morrill, *Cheshire*, pp. 287–93; and Morrill, 'Parliamentary Representation', p. 109.

[99] *TSP*, V, 314.

[100] John Sutton, 'Cromwell's Commissioners for Preserving the Peace of the Commonwealth: A Staffordshire Case Study', in Ian Gentles, John Morrill, and Blair Worden, eds., *Soldiers, Writers and Statesmen of the English Revolution* (Cambridge, 1998), pp. 151–82, especially p. 168.

[101] Gardiner, *Commonwealth and Protectorate*, III, 269–70. For Richard Cromwell's election, see pp. 151–2.

Peniston Whalley, as well as anti-Puritans such as John Buxton and Sir William D'Oiley. Then there were a large number of moderate or uncommitted individuals whose loyalty to the regime was at best lukewarm. These included John Bowyer, Richard Browne, Bernard Church, George Courthop, Sir John Fagge, Samuel Gott, Sir Ralph Hare, Herbert Morley, Sir Thomas Rivers, Thomas Sotherton, and Philip Woodhouse. As the next chapter will show, the council excluded all these figures before the Parliament assembled.[102]

Insofar as any regional pattern can be discerned in the results of the 1656 elections, it seems that the government faced its greatest problems in those areas that had been most strongly Parliamentarian during the Civil War. Although this might seem paradoxical, it can be explained by the fact that in those regions where royalist sympathies remained strongest, in particular towards the north and west of England and in Wales, Parliamentarians looked less critically upon the Cromwellian regime and were keener to submit to the protection of the major-generals. On the other hand, in those areas where they were more firmly established, and where royalism posed less of a threat – especially in the south and east of England – they felt secure enough to express concerns about the direction in which the regime was moving. More specifically, the moderate Parliamentarian or Presbyterian gentry in such areas felt confident that they could reassert themselves against the major-generals without risking bringing the republic down and provoking a resurgence of royalism. That such moderate or conservative opponents of the regime could on occasion make common cause with a range of allies, from commonwealthsmen to defeated crypto-royalists, in their assault upon 'swordsmen' and 'decimators' only served to strengthen their position.

In Scotland, sixteen of the thirty members returned in August 1656 were English, and the remaining fourteen were Scots.[103] The English contingent included four serving army officers and at least five others who held major public offices. Many of them were closely connected by kinship or influence to prominent individuals in England – for example, the brothers of Disbrowe, Whalley, and Wolseley were all elected for Scotland, as was Cromwell's cousin Robert Steward – and such connections enhanced their capacity to represent Scottish interests at Westminster. The fourteen Scots elected were all men of political and social substance, and this indicated a

---

[102] Durston, *Cromwell's Major-Generals*, p. 197; Carol S. Egloff, 'The Search for a Cromwellian Settlement: Exclusions from the Second Protectorate Parliament', *Parl. Hist.*, 17 (1998), 178–97, 301–21.

[103] This paragraph is based on the excellent discussions in Dow, *Cromwellian Scotland*, pp. 185–7; Paul J. Pinckney, 'The Scottish Representation in the Cromwellian Parliament of 1656', *Scottish Historical Review*, 46 (1967), 95–114; and Ellen D. Goldwater, 'The Scottish Franchise: Lobbying during the Cromwellian Protectorate', *HJ*, 21 (1978), 27–42.

trend towards the return of members of traditional local families similar to that already apparent in England. Paul Pinckney has suggested that in both England and Scotland the regime was keen to 'rely in the shires on the wealthiest and most traditional families who were willing to accept the protectorate'.[104] At least eight of the Scots elected were appointed justices of the peace in 1656 and six either held, or had held, some further public office. Thus, as in 1654, it would be misleading to regard the Scottish members as tame servants of the Protectoral regime. Even the Englishmen who were returned for Scotland were capable of representing Scottish interests, while the presence of the Scots, although they were known to be sympathetic to the Protectorate, reflected the regime's wish to conciliate traditional families.

In Ireland, the 1656 elections were marked by growing tension between the army officers and Henry Cromwell, who had taken over as acting governor following Fleetwood's departure in the summer of 1655.[105] There appears to have been considerable co-operation between the government and the Old Protestant interest, and the latter secured nineteen seats, the same number as in 1654. Indeed, eleven of these nineteen members had also been elected to the first Protectorate Parliament. The number of Old Protestants who were returned suggests the relative freedom of the elections and a willingness, as in England and Scotland, to accept candidates who were already well established in their localities. A further eight of the elections saw the return of Englishmen closely associated with Henry Cromwell. As in Scotland, representation was in effect shared between Englishmen who could be effective representatives at Westminster, and locals who were broadly sympathetic towards, or at any rate willing to work with, the Protectoral regime. The army interest in Ireland was reduced to just three members. Their presence diminished still further when Henry Cromwell followed the pattern of 1656 and chose six of the members (including two of the three from the army interest) to remain in Ireland rather than travel to Westminster. The army's unhappiness at being thus outnumbered probably explains the attempts to exclude some of the civilian members that will be examined in the next chapter. All in all, it is likely that at least twenty of the Irish members actually attended the second Protectorate Parliament.

This Parliament addressed the arrangements for elections and the franchise in the Humble Petition and Advice, which spelled out far more fully than either the Remonstrance or the Instrument of Government the moral and religious failings that would disqualify a person from sitting in

---

[104] Pinckney, 'Scottish Representation', 113.
[105] This paragraph is based on Little, 'Irish Representation'.

Parliament. Anyone convicted under the Blasphemy Act (9 August 1650) was automatically debarred. Further categories of excluded persons were: anyone who was a 'common scoffer or reviler of religion'; anyone who married a papist, or brought up any of their children as papists, or allowed any of their children to marry papists; anyone who denied 'the Scriptures to be the Word of God, or the sacraments, prayer, magistracy, and ministry to be the Ordinances of God'; and any 'common profaner of the Lord's day', or 'profane swearer or curser', drunkard or 'common haunter of taverns or alehouses'.[106] These qualifications, adopted by the House on 23 March 1657,[107] clearly reflected the desire of a majority of members to prevent liberty of conscience from running to licence. They may also have been inspired by some of the specific problems that had been encountered in the elections of 1654 and 1656. For example, the disqualification of swearers and drunkards may well have owed something to cases such as that of George Glapthorne, which will be examined in chapter 4. The Additional Petition and Advice further extended these stipulations by excluding all those who had assisted or participated in Hamilton's invasion of England in the summer of 1648, other than those who had borne arms for Parliament, or sat in Parliament, 'and are of good life and conversation', or whom Cromwell with the council's advice had declared to 'have given some signal testimony of their good affection and continuance in the same'. In addition, all members of Parliament were required to swear an oath promising to 'uphold and maintain the true reformed Protestant religion, in the purity thereof, as it is contained in the Holy Scriptures of the Old and New Testament', to 'be true and faithful to the Lord Protector', and to endeavour to preserve 'the rights and liberties of the people'.[108] That the Humble and Additional Petitions took the trouble to set out the disqualifications from membership of Parliament in such detail probably reflected widespread anxiety that the definitions stated in the Instrument had been too vague, and had thereby allowed the large-scale conciliar exclusions that took place before the second Protectorate Parliament assembled. By defining as clearly and fully as possible the failings that disqualified someone from sitting in Parliament, members hoped that similar exclusions would either not occur in future, or at least would be conducted on the basis of much more precisely defined criteria. They were also keen to place responsibility for such exclusions firmly in the hands of Parliament rather than the council, and how they did this will be examined in the next chapter.

---

[106] Gardiner, *Constitutional Documents*, pp. 450–1. [107] *CJ*, VII, 509–10.
[108] Gardiner, *Constitutional Documents*, p. 463.

We saw earlier that the second Protectorate Parliament did not agree arrangements for the number and distribution of seats prior to its dissolution in February 1658. When, on 29 November 1658, Richard Cromwell and his council agreed informally to call another Parliament, and confirmed this decision on 3 December, they decided to revert to the franchise and distribution of seats as they had been in 1640. According to one royalist observer, this reversion 'to the old laws' was 'much opposed by divers of the grandees of the council and army'.[109] Ludlow believed that the decision was taken 'principally because it was well understood that mean and decayed boroughs might be much more easily corrupted than the numerous counties and considerable cities'.[110] The French ambassador, Bordeaux, likewise wrote that 'the hope that is entertained that small communities will be more easy to manage than large assemblies, has led to the substitution of this arrangement in the place of that which was observed at the convocation of the last few Parliaments'.[111] There may be some justice in this charge: certainly we will see in the next chapter that over seventy of the hundred or more members whom the council excluded before the opening of the second Protectorate Parliament represented county seats. A reversion to the old franchise, which reduced the number of county seats from 236 to 78 at a stroke, may have been motivated partly by a wish to prevent such large numbers of troublesome county members from being returned. There may also have been a feeling that such a restoration of old established procedures would be more likely to generate support for the regime than persisting with the new arrangements associated with the controversial elections of 1654 and 1656.[112]

Clive Holmes has, however, suggested recently that the government's relatively limited efforts to manage the elections or to secure the return of members sympathetic to it might suggest that this was not the only consideration, and that there may have been other reasons for the decision.[113] First, a return to a Parliament composed along traditional lines was consistent with the rumours that had circulated in the spring and summer of 1658 about Cromwell's possible plans for calling another Parliament.[114] For example, as

---

[109] Bodl., MS Clarendon 59, fo. 279r.   [110] Ludlow, II, 48.
[111] Guizot, *Richard Cromwell*, I, 274.
[112] Cf. Ronald Hutton, *The Restoration: A Political and Religious History of England and Wales, 1658–1667* (Oxford, 1985), p. 27.
[113] Clive Holmes, 'John Lisle, Lord Commissioner of the Great Seal, and the Last Months of the Cromwellian Protectorate', *EHR*, 122 (forthcoming, 2007). We are most grateful to Clive Holmes for allowing us to read a copy of this paper prior to publication.
[114] Cf. Firth, *Last Years*, II, 271–80.

early as 19 February 1658, James Waynwright had thought it likely there
would be 'a Parliament once within nine months, called and constituted
according to the ancient rights of the nation in the late King's time ... The
ancient boroughs and cities their ancient number, and the peers of the nation
that have not forfeited their rights.'[115] Secondly, the council may have
wished not to grant continued legitimacy to the electoral arrangements
embodied in the Instrument of Government given that the Humble Petition
and Advice had now in other respects superseded the Instrument. This would
be consistent with the 'meticulous concern for proper form' that appears to
have characterised the government's approach to these elections.[116]

In the event, the results were so variegated as to defy easy generalisation.
Mark Kishlansky has written that 'the 1659 elections were a hodgepodge of
old and new'.[117] There was considerable competition to secure election, and
the commonwealthsmen actively co-ordinated their efforts to win as many
seats as possible. Thurloe told Henry Cromwell on 30 November 1658 that
'great strivings there will be to get in, and the commonwealthsmen have their
daily meetings, disputing what kind of commonwealth they shall have,
taking it for granted, they may pick and choose'.[118] A few days later he
reported that 'the several parties, who are enemies to the present government, go on very vigorously. There was a meeting the other day of several
commonwealthsmen, to wit, Scott, Weaver, Neville, Ludlow, Cole, Black,
Birch, etc., where resolutions were taken, how the business should be managed in Parliament ... What these men will be able to effect in the House,
I know not; but certainly no endeavours will be wanting to put us into
trouble.'[119] All these individuals, with the possible exceptions of Cole and
Black, were subsequently returned.[120] Bordeaux likewise wrote in mid-
December that 'a body composed of five hundred persons cannot fail to be
very difficult to govern, and the republicans promise themselves great
authority among its members'.[121] In some counties, on the other hand, the
principal impression is of the strength of conservative opinion. Somerset,
where only one commonwealthsman was successful in the sixteen borough
seats (John Barker at Ilchester), affords a good example of this, as it had in

---

[115] HMC, *Sixth Report* (1877–8), p. 442.
[116] Holmes, 'John Lisle, Lord Commissioner of the Great Seal'.
[117] Kishlansky, *Parliamentary Selection*, p. 128. For an overview of the 1659 elections, see
Godfrey Davies, 'The Election of Richard Cromwell's Parliament, 1658–9', *EHR*, 63
(1948), 488–501.
[118] *TSP*, VII, 541.   [119] *TSP*, VII, 550.
[120] *OPH*, XXI, 246–62; *TSP*, VII, 588, 590; Ludlow, II, 50–1. Nobody named Black appears in
the list of members of the third Protectorate Parliament, but Edward Blake was returned for
Shoreham (Sussex); similarly, there is no Cole, but William Coles was returned for Downton
(Wiltshire).
[121] Guizot, *Richard Cromwell*, I, 276.

the two previous elections.[122] Elsewhere, the government had reason to feel pleased with the outcome. In the Hampshire constituencies, for instance, more than half the members returned were office-holders, relations of Cromwell, or supporters of the regime. This result was almost certainly assisted by the influence of some of Cromwell's powerful local allies, such as John Dunch.[123]

Other areas saw much greater division and controversy. In Devon, the members were extraordinarily varied and included examples of crypto-royalists (Coplestone Bampfield), Presbyterian grandees (Sir John Northcote), Presbyterian lawyers (Thomas Bampfield, John Maynard), traditional gentry (Sir John Coplestone), and army officers (Samuel Searle, Thomas Gibbons).[124] Another deeply divided county was Cheshire where, 'far more than in 1640 or 1656, strong passions and bitter partisanship marked this election': 'certainly it was the most violent contest ever held in the county'.[125] This time, John Bradshaw was returned despite the vigorous efforts of the pro-royalist interest that was rapidly developing in the county by 1659. The Cheshire case may have been unusually divisive, but there is evidence of electoral contests in other parts of the country as well. Whereas the council had handled virtually all cases of disputed elections in 1654 and 1656, leaving only two and one respectively to be adjudicated by the Commons,[126] in 1659 the House was confronted by no fewer than nineteen disputes within England and Wales that needed to be resolved.[127] The *Commons' Journal* also reveals more instances of members being returned for more than one constituency than in the first two Protectorate Parliaments: eighteen compared with ten and fourteen respectively. This reinforces the impression of greater divisiveness and more vigorous competition to secure election than in 1654 or 1656. It was in this context that Thomas Clarges reported to Henry Cromwell in late December 1658 that 'I believe there was never more care taken in the elections for members to sit in Parliament than at this time, to have such chosen as are of peaceable and healing spirits.'[128]

In the Irish elections too, deeper divisions were apparent in 1659 than earlier.[129] Although the Old Protestant interest again secured the majority of

---

[122] Underdown, *Somerset*, p. 189.
[123] Andrew M. Coleby, *Central Government and the Localities: Hampshire, 1649–1689* (Cambridge, 1987), p. 72.
[124] Stephen Roberts, *Recovery and Restoration*, p. 60.
[125] Morrill, *Cheshire*, p. 297; Morrill, 'Parliamentary Representation', p. 109.
[126] *CJ*, VII, 369, 370, 441–2.
[127] *CJ*, VII, 595, 596, 598, 601, 605, 608, 611, 612, 616, 617, 618, 619, 620, 622, 624, 626, 632, 638.
[128] *TSP*, VII, 581.   [129] This paragraph is based on Little, 'Irish Representation'.

seats – twenty, compared with nineteen in 1654 and 1656 – no fewer than thirteen of these were newcomers to Parliament, due in part to the death or retirement of at least four key figures in 1657–8. The Old Protestants continued to work closely with the Cromwellian regime, but there were signs that the government's attempts to manage the elections, motivated by the recent loss of some of its most valuable supporters, caused division and discontent in the constituencies. In contrast to the earlier elections, tensions became evident within the Old Protestant interest, most spectacularly at the elections for the three county and borough seats of Cork on 20 January 1659, which saw a bitter conflict between two former allies, Lord Broghill and Vincent Gookin. Both claimed to have Henry Cromwell's support, and in the end the outcome was a draw.[130] Such divisions boded ill for the effectiveness of the Irish members as a group when they arrived at Westminster.[131] In addition to the twenty Old Protestants, there were seven Cromwellians and three members of the army interest, although the loss of two who opted to sit for English or Scottish constituencies for which they had also been returned (Thomas Waller and Jerome Sankey) brought the final total down to twenty-eight.

Likewise, there were signs that Scotland was more restive in 1659 than it had been in 1654 and 1656. Monck informed Thurloe on 28 December that 'there are some Scotchmen which endeavour to write to their friends in Scotland, to choose Scotchmen, and not Englishmen'; again, two days later, he wrote that 'my Lord of Argyll, and some others, … have endeavoured all they can, to get all Scotchmen chosen'.[132] Despite the regime's best efforts, Argyll was elected, along with ten other Scotsmen: this marked a drop from fourteen in 1656. Apart from the maverick Argyll, the other Scots all had some record of service to the Protectorate and were regarded as sympathetic towards it. The remaining fifteen members were all English: returns of individuals who chose to sit elsewhere explain why the overall total of those returned for Scotland was twenty-six rather than the allotted thirty. Of these Englishmen, four were serving army officers, and at least five more had close connections with the civil administration in Scotland. The pattern of Scottish returns thus remained broadly similar to the first two Protectorate Parliaments in that the members either were

---

[130] On this election, see T. C. Barnard, 'Lord Broghill, Vincent Gookin and the Cork Elections of 1659', *EHR*, 88 (1973), 352–65; and Patrick Little, *Lord Broghill and the Cromwellian Union with Ireland and Scotland* (Woodbridge, 2004), pp. 165–6.
[131] This is discussed more fully in chapter 12.
[132] *TSP*, VII, 583, 584. This comment about Argyll seeking the return of 'Scotchmen' may need to be treated with some caution, however, because it may refer to those who agreed with him rather than necessarily to ethnic Scots. See chapter 12 in the present book.

Englishmen or were Scots associated with, or sympathetic to, the Protectoral regime.[133]

Several weeks into the Parliament, on 8 March, a heated debate arose over the constitutional status of the Scottish and Irish members. Whereas in England and Wales there had been a return to the old franchise of 1640, the provision of thirty members each for Scotland and Ireland had been retained from the Instrument of Government. Thurloe reported that the council reached this decision 'with much to do'.[134] According to John Lisle, one of the commissioners of the Great Seal, the writs for Scotland and Ireland were written by Nathaniel Fiennes, the other commissioner, but were destroyed when objections were raised. The writs were then reissued and sealed by both commissioners 'in the presence of the Protector, those writs being of an extraordinary nature'.[135] When the Parliament assembled, the fact that the Instrument had been abandoned in other respects led some members to question whether the Scottish and Irish representatives could legitimately sit at Westminster at all. This debate dragged on for about two weeks and ended only with the recognition of the Scottish and Irish members' right to be present on 21 and 23 March respectively.[136] As we saw above, the Humble Petition and Advice stated simply that 'the number of persons to be elected and chosen to sit and serve in Parliament for England, Scotland and Ireland, and the distribution of the persons so chosen within the counties, cities and boroughs of them respectively, may be according to such proportions as shall be agreed upon and declared in this present Parliament'.[137] The second Protectorate Parliament had failed to make such arrangements before its dissolution, and the council had issued writs for Scottish and Irish constituencies on the basis of the distribution of seats contained in the Instrument.[138] Thurloe defended this decision on the grounds that 'this Parliament, of necessity, must consist of members sent from each nation. The means are as suitable to the Petition and Advice as could be. The protector was bound to call a Parliament out of the three nations. He was guided by the Act of Union as to the number, and by former distributions as to the distribution.'[139] Against this, a range of members objected that there

---

[133] On the Scottish elections to the third Protectorate Parliament, see Dow, *Cromwellian Scotland*, pp. 237–40; James A. Casada, 'The Scottish Representatives in Richard Cromwell's Parliament', *Scottish Historical Review*, 51 (1972), 124–47; and Little, *Broghill*, pp. 166–7.
[134] *TSP*, VII, 541.
[135] Holmes, 'John Lisle, Lord Commissioner of the Great Seal'.
[136] Burton, IV, 87–119, 122–39, 143–7, 163–91, 193–202, 204–23, 225–34, 237–43; *CJ*, VII, 613–16, 618–19; Schilling, pp. 182–260; Derbyshire Record Office, MS D258/10/9/2 (diary of Sir John Gell), fos. 3r–6r; BL, Lansdowne MS 823, fo. 259r; *TSP*, VII, 636, 637.
[137] Gardiner, *Constitutional Documents*, p. 452.   [138] TNA, SP 18/184/63.
[139] Burton, IV, 128. Cf. Schilling, pp. 208–9.

was no current legal basis for the inclusion of Irish and Scottish members. Commonwealthsmen such as Hesilrige, Scott, Weaver, Vane, and Neville all expressed this objection, as did Thomas Gewen, later to become a crypto-royalist; Lambert was another powerful voice against inclusion.[140] The very most that some of those who attacked the presence of Irish and Scottish members would concede was that there was 'an intimation' (Scott) or 'a kind of implication' (Sir Richard Temple) in the Humble Petition to this effect.[141] The most eloquent of the eleven Scottish members who spoke in these debates was Dr Thomas Clarges, who declared robustly: 'We have a statute for sending 30 members hither. You have no statute to call 400 members for England.'[142] In the end, on 21 March, the House resolved that 'the members returned to serve for Scotland shall continue to sit as members during the present Parliament'.[143] This strengthened the hand of the Irish members, of whom the most effective speakers were William Aston and Thomas Stanley. The latter argued simply that 'it is impossible to make any addition to what has been said in the case of Scotland', and on 23 March the House passed a similar resolution allowing the Irish members to 'continue to sit as members during the present Parliament'.[144] The third Protectorate Parliament, like the first two, was thus a fully British and Irish Parliament, and these debates in March 1659 generated some interesting explorations of the nature and implications of the Cromwellian Union of the three kingdoms, which will be analysed more fully in chapter 12.

In the end, the 1659 elections produced the largest House of Commons that had ever assembled up to that date. Potentially it might have contained a total of 567 members: 483 for England, 24 for Wales, and 30 each for Scotland and Ireland. In fact, it seems that only 558 of the seats were actually filled: 480 for England, 24 for Wales, 26 for Scotland, and 28 for Ireland. The House was apparently dissatisfied with these arrangements: on 31 March it resolved 'to take into consideration the business of an equal representative for this nation' on 22 April, but in the event the Parliament was dissolved on that very day.[145] Fewer than half the members (perhaps no

---

[140] Burton, IV, 94–5, 130, 164–5, 174–6, 179–81, 188, 195–8; Schilling, pp. 188–252. For Lambert's election to this Parliament, see BL, Add. MS 21425 (Baynes correspondence), fo. 5r.

[141] Burton, IV, 94, 132; Schilling, pp. 189, 214.

[142] Burton, IV, 113. Cf. Schilling, p. 197. Clarges referred here to the Protectoral ordinance of 12 April 1654 which stated that 'in every Parliament to be held successively for the said Commonwealth, 30 persons shall be called from and serve for Scotland': Gardiner, *Constitutional Documents*, p. 418.

[143] *CJ*, VII, 616; *Clarke Papers*, III, 185; BL, Lansdowne MS 823, fo. 261r.

[144] Burton, IV, 237–40 (quotation at 239); Derbyshire Record Office, MS D258/10/9/2, fo. 6r; *CJ*, VII, 619.

[145] Burton, IV, 312; *CJ*, VII, 622; *Clarke Papers*, III, 187.

more than 262) had previous parliamentary experience.[146] On 3 February, Henry Cromwell II took exception that Hesilrige 'should so often take notice that so many young men were in this House', and two days later Thomas Chaloner even questioned 'whether some are old enough to take an oath'.[147] From the government's perspective, the problem was not only the size and inexperience of the House but also its diversity. Thurloe wrote to Henry Cromwell on 18 January that: 'The Parliament now approaches. There is so great a mixture in the House of Commons that no man knows which way the major part will incline.'[148] Furthermore, Richard Cromwell preserved the existing composition of the Other House, thinking it 'not advisable to make any alterations in' it,[149] and he thereby removed some of his ablest allies from the Commons.[150] The government's difficulties of leadership and management were also exacerbated by the fact that the council no longer possessed the power to exclude members from Parliament. That power, conferred by the Instrument of Government, was of considerable significance in 1654 and especially in 1656, and this will be examined in the next chapter.

In essence, the story of the elections to the three Protectorate Parliaments reflected two parallel but connected trends: a growing political and ideological polarisation that meant that the elections became more divisive and contentious in 1656 and 1658–9 than in 1654; and a gradual drift back towards the return of members from traditional county families. Both these developments were symptomatic of a reaction within the political and social elite against the army, and in some quarters against the Protectorate itself. In the process, older constitutional arrangements increasingly came to be seen as a way of protecting parliamentary liberties against the rule of the 'swordsmen'. In the first Protectorate Parliament, the draft constitutional bill envisaged a return to the old franchise, and this became a reality in 1658–9. Many members feared and resented the power of exclusion that the Instrument of Government had vested in the council, and the vagueness of the grounds on which a member could be excluded. As a result, in 1657 the Humble and Additional Petitions defined the criteria for exclusion much more explicitly than the Instrument had done, and entrusted the power to exclude a member solely to Parliament rather than the council. This once again marked a return to pre-Civil War practice.

The growing animus against the army leaders was most dramatically evident in the 1656 elections. The case studies examined earlier suggest that the major-generals encountered widespread but by no means universal

---

[146] G. B. Nourse, 'Richard Cromwell's House of Commons', *Bulletin of the John Rylands Library*, 60 (1977), 98.
[147] Burton, III, 49, 76.   [148] *TSP*, VII, 594.   [149] *TSP*, VII, 578.   [150] See pp. 98, 108, 111.

opposition, and that the areas of greatest hostility were often those that had been controlled by Parliament since 1642. It seems likely that in those regions where the Parliamentarian cause was most firmly established, and where royalism had been most effectively defeated, such as in the south and east of England, members of the local elite felt secure enough to express concerns about the Protectorate and the rule of the major-generals. In such areas, the Presbyterian or 'country' gentry were sufficiently confident that they could reassert themselves against the major-generals without risking bringing the republic down and provoking a resurgence of royalism. By contrast, in those parts of the country where royalism retained greatest residual strength, it seemed more important to close ranks behind the Protectoral regime. Furthermore, in the 1656 elections, like those of 1654, the council always possessed the trump card that it could if necessary exclude from Parliament those whom it deemed to fail certain criteria. The loss of that conciliar power of exclusion in 1657 permitted the readmission of a significant number of previously excluded members, and their return added considerably to the turbulence of the second sitting of the second Protectorate Parliament and the third Protectorate Parliament. The story of elections thus needs to be closely associated with that of exclusions, and it is to this that we now turn.

4

Exclusions

Among the most revolutionary aspects of parliamentary history during the Protectorate was the Instrument of Government's empowering of the council to scrutinise election returns and to exclude any members whom it deemed to fail certain political, religious, and moral criteria. As we shall see, these qualifications were defined sufficiently vaguely – for example, members had to be 'of known integrity, fearing God, and of good conversation' – as to leave wide open the possibility of very extensive use and even abuse. In the event, somewhere between seven and eleven members of the first Protectorate Parliament were excluded before it met, and perhaps another fifty to eighty absented themselves rather than take the Recognition that Cromwell imposed as a condition of re-entering the House on 12 September 1654. The exclusions that preceded the second Protectorate Parliament were on a far larger scale and removed just over a hundred elected members, while a further fifty or sixty promptly withdrew in protest. This chapter will examine these exclusions of members from the first two Protectorate Parliaments, where responsibility for them lay, and what their impact was on those Parliaments. It will also consider the fact that the second sitting of the second Protectorate Parliament (1658) and the third Protectorate Parliament (1659) saw no such exclusions, and will assess what implications this had for parliamentary proceedings during those sittings.

EXCLUSIONS BEFORE THE FIRST PROTECTORATE PARLIAMENT

Under Article 21 of the Instrument, the Clerk of the Commonwealth in Chancery was instructed to pass to the council the names of all those who were returned for Parliament. The council would then 'peruse the said returns, and examine whether the persons so elected and returned be such as is agreeable to the qualifications, and not disabled to be elected'.[1] This power was explicitly vested in the council rather than the Lord Protector, and

---

[1] Gardiner, *Constitutional Documents*, p. 412.

we shall see that Cromwell carefully stood aloof from the conciliar exclusions from both the first and second Protectorate Parliaments.

In 1654, the majority of English and Welsh seats had been filled by mid-July and, on 17 July, the Clerk of the Commonwealth forwarded to the council the election returns to date. From then until the Parliament opened on 3 September, the council met daily from Monday to Friday, except during the second week of August. As Peter Gaunt has shown, little is known of their deliberations, although it is probable that they began to give serious consideration to various local petitions against certain elected individuals on 10 August.[2] The council soon delegated the bulk of the work of sifting through these disputes to a committee, and this body apparently met fifteen times from 11 August until 1 September, when it submitted its final report to the council. Once the council had approved members, it forwarded their names to the Clerk of the Commonwealth in Chancery, who issued each member with a ticket of approbation and admission granting him entry to Parliament.

The number of those whom the council excluded in 1654 was very small. There is no evidence that any members for Ireland or Scotland were debarred: it seems likely that the regime's influence had already secured the return mainly of English or pro-English members, and that further exclusions were therefore thought unnecessary.[3] Conciliar exclusions before the opening of the first Protectorate Parliament were thus confined to English and Welsh constituencies. There is reliable evidence that at least seven members were excluded in this way, and possibly as many as four more; but the maximum final figure still appears to be less than a dozen.[4]

The council excluded only three members under Article 17 of the Instrument, which required members of Parliament to be aged at least twenty-one and to be 'persons of known integrity, fearing God, and of good conversation'.[5] Sir Richard Temple was elected for Warwickshire on 12 July, but fell foul of the age qualification because he was then nine months short of his twenty-first birthday. Some of the local inhabitants petitioned the council, producing evidence of Temple's date of birth, and he was declared ineligible to sit in Parliament.[6] John Wildman was excluded under the same article on the basis of his previous record of leading violent protests against drainage operations

[2] Peter Gaunt, 'Cromwell's Purge? Exclusions and the First Protectorate Parliament', *Parl. Hist.*, 6 (1987), 4–5; *Severall Proceedings of State Affairs*, no. 255 (10–17 August 1654), pp. 4033, 4036, 4041, 4044, 4048.
[3] See chapter 3.
[4] This is based on the evidence convincingly presented in Gaunt, 'Cromwell's Purge?'
[5] Gardiner, *Constitutional Documents*, pp. 410–11 (Instrument, articles 14, 15, 17).
[6] TNA, SP 18/74/71, 72; *To the High Court of Parliament of the Common-wealth of England, &c. The humble petition of John Wagstaff, gent. Inhabitant of the county of Warwick* (1655); Gaunt, 'Cromwell's Purge?', 10–11.

around the Isle of Axholme and Hatfield Chase in 1650–1. Wildman had been excluded from the Rump's Act of General Pardon and Oblivion (24 February 1652) and had perjured himself before a parliamentary sub-committee. The inhabitants of Hatfield Chase called for his exclusion as someone not fit to sit in Parliament, and the council, possibly also swayed by Wildman's Leveller past, agreed to his exclusion.[7] Finally, George Glapthorne, chief bailiff of Ely, was denounced by the 'well-affected' of the Isle of Ely as 'a common swearer, a common curser, a frequenter of alehouses and an upholder of those of evil fame, [and] . . . famed to be a companion of lewd women'. He was therefore, they claimed, 'not fit to be a law maker or Parliament man for them'.[8] Witnesses were produced who gave evidence of Glapthorne's frequenting of alehouses, his gaming on the Lord's Day, and his cursing and swearing, sometimes at the rate of forty oaths an hour. The council duly excluded him as unfit to sit in Parliament.[9] These three individuals were the only cases of pre-sessional exclusions from the first Protectorate Parliament under Article 17.

Four others were apparently excluded under Article 14 on the grounds of their royalism. Sir John Price of Montgomeryshire had been a member of the Long Parliament from 1640 until 1645, but had then been expelled for deserting to the King. His subsequent return to Parliament was half-hearted, and, although the Rump had pardoned him in March 1652, the council excluded him from the first Protectorate Parliament.[10] The two members elected for the City of London, Thomas Adams and John Langham, were widely suspected of royalism. In August 1654, a group of London citizens protested to the council that they were 'not capable by the Instrument' because of their former 'disaffections to the said army, Parliament and good people'. The council committee for elections examined their cases and they were duly excluded.[11] Fourthly, it is probable (though slightly less certain than in the previous three cases) that Edward Pitt of Worcestershire was excluded. He had long been regarded as a royalist, and allegedly declared that he would be hanged rather than obey the Instrument. Although he was subsequently listed among nominees to certain parliamentary committees, the other surviving evidence suggests that he had been excluded.[12]

---

[7] TNA, SP 18/74/78, 79; CJ, VII, 87; A & O, II, 575; Gaunt, 'Cromwell's Purge?', 11.
[8] *A brief relation of the proceedings before his Highness Councel concerning the petitioners of the Isle of Ely, against George Glapthorne Esquire; to take away the false report that is made touching the same, and that the truth may plainly appear* ([4 November] 1654), quoted in Gaunt, 'Cromwell's Purge?', 11.
[9] Gaunt, 'Cromwell's Purge?', 11–13; TNA, SP 18/75/6, 7.
[10] Gaunt, 'Cromwell's Purge?', 13; CJ, VII, 112; TNA, SP 18/75/37.
[11] Gaunt, 'Cromwell's Purge?', 13–14; TNA, SP 18/75/8.
[12] Gaunt, 'Cromwell's Purge?', 14; TNA, SP 18/74/41.

There are four further cases of members who may have been excluded, but where the sources are either incomplete or contradictory. The members for Southwark, Samuel Highland and Robert Warcupp, were accused of electoral malpractice, political disaffection, and various moral offences, but their fate remains uncertain.[13] Thomas Lathom, member for Westminster, had no record of political disaffection or moral failings, and was apparently not the subject of any petition or complaint, but his name does not appear on the list of approved members and there is no record of his having taken part in the Parliament. His fate is unknown, as is that of Lord Grey of Groby, whose father, the Earl of Stamford, was accused of royalism but was apparently allowed to enter the Parliament. For Groby, however, there is no evidence that he was present during the session.[14] In sum, the surviving records suggest that those excluded from this Parliament before it met numbered at least seven but not more than eleven.

It also seems that Cromwell's personal involvement in these exclusions was at most slight. The Instrument gave the Protector no constitutional role in this process and he appears to have kept his distance from it. He attended only five of the twenty-five council meetings in the period from mid-August to 2 September when discussion of the election returns was at its peak. Two of the cases illustrate his desire to remain aloof and to leave such matters to the council. The Ely petitioners who complained about George Glapthorne made a direct approach to Cromwell, who indicated in general terms that he was sympathetic to their cause. However, the petitioners had to submit a second petition to the council in order to secure Glapthorne's exclusion. Similarly, when the free burgesses of Bristol attempted, unsuccessfully, to have their two members excluded, they likewise approached Cromwell personally after first petitioning the council. But, 'understanding from his highness that these matters judicially lay before your Honours', they were obliged to address a second petition to the council.[15] As Peter Gaunt has written: 'Cromwell, it seems, was taking no part in the exclusion process and was anxious that others should know it.'[16]

EXCLUSIONS DURING THE FIRST PROTECTORATE PARLIAMENT

It was an entirely different story with the large-scale exclusion of members that took place just over a week after the first Protectorate Parliament had assembled. This was the result of a direct personal intervention by Cromwell.

---

[13] Gaunt, 'Cromwell's Purge?', 14; TNA, SP 18/74/66–9.
[14] Gaunt, 'Cromwell's Purge?', 15; *Clarke Papers*, V, 207.
[15] Gaunt, 'Cromwell's Purge?', 17–18; TNA, SP 18/75/14.IV.
[16] Gaunt, 'Cromwell's Purge?', 18.

During that first week, instead of adopting the Instrument with a single vote as Cromwell had hoped, the House resolved to debate in Committee of the Whole House whether the government should be 'in a single person and a Parliament'. They soon embarked on a lengthy discussion of the relationship between the executive and the legislature; and the House also established an Assembly of Divines to advise them on religious reforms and possible measures to suppress the sects. On 11 September, they agreed to vote the following day on Matthew Hale's motion that government should be 'in a Parliament and single person limited and restrained as the Parliament should think fit'. It was at this point that Cromwell decided to act.[17]

On the morning of Tuesday, 12 September 1654, members arrived to find the doors of the House locked and guarded by soldiers, who informed them that the Protector would meet them shortly in the Painted Chamber. According to Guybon Goddard, Cromwell arrived at about 10 o'clock and spoke for around an hour and a half. He began apologetically – 'I could have wished with all my heart there had been no cause of it' – but went on: 'I see it will be necessary for me now a little to magnify my office, which I have not been apt to do.'[18] Cromwell then turned to consider four 'fundamentals': first, that no Parliament should sit perpetually, and that new Parliaments should be elected at regular intervals; secondly, 'government by one single person and a Parliament'; thirdly, 'liberty of conscience' in religion; and, finally, shared control of the militia between Parliament and the Lord Protector.[19] He then suggested that it would not have been 'dishonest nor dishonourable, nor against true liberty, no not the liberty of Parliaments' if 'an owning of your call and of the authority bringing you hither might have been required before your entrance into the House'. He had not chosen to implement this earlier, but he now felt necessitated to do so. With lavish apologies – 'I am sorry, I am sorry, and I could be sorry to the death, that there is cause for this' – he informed members that he had 'caused a stop to be put to your entrance into the Parliament House'. There was 'somewhat to be offered to you', assent to which was the 'means that will let you in, to act those things as a parliament which are for the good of the people', and that would 'give a happy progress and issue to this Parliament'.[20]

The 'somewhat to be offered to you' was the following Recognition to which all members were required to subscribe before they were permitted to re-enter the House: 'I do hereby freely promise and engage to be true and faithful to the Lord Protector and the Commonwealth of England, Scotland, and Ireland, and shall not, according to the tenor of the indentures whereby I am returned to serve in this present Parliament, propose or give my consent

[17] Burton, I, xxi–xxxii; *CJ*, VII, 365–7.   [18] Lomas–Carlyle, II, 366.
[19] Lomas–Carlyle, II, 381–5.   [20] Lomas–Carlyle, II, 389–90.

to alter the Government, as it is settled in one person and a Parliament.'[21] It is very difficult to estimate precisely how many members signed this Recognition. The original document, described by Goddard as a 'long piece of parchment',[22] has apparently not survived and probably perished in the disastrous fire of October 1834 that destroyed most of the old Palace of Westminster and much of the House of Commons archive with it. As a result, there is no record of signatories, and contemporary estimates of the number who signed vary considerably. Goddard thought that about a hundred members signed on 12 September, whereas Whitelocke estimated that 'about 130' did so, Richard Hatter 'about 140', and George Downing 140. Ludlow put the figure 'within a day or two' at 130, *Mercurius Politicus* at 140, and the Dutch ambassadors at 145.[23] Those ambassadors were normally well informed, and they believed that another 50 members signed on 13 September, and that by 27 October around 350 had done so.[24] An account printed in the *Old Parliamentary History* suggests that as many as 193 signed on 14 September.[25] If this figure is at all reliable, the willingness of members to sign was probably enhanced by the House's resolution that same day that the Recognition 'doth not comprehend, nor shall be construed to comprehend therein, the whole [Instrument of] Government, consisting of Forty-two Articles; but that the same doth only include what concerns the Government of the Commonwealth, by a Single Person and successive Parliaments'.[26] According to *Mercurius Politicus*, about 240 members had signed the Recognition by 20 September, and nearly 300 by 5 October.[27] Whitelocke thought the number was 300 by 6 October.[28] Thurloe's claim on 24 October that 'there is not above thirty persons in the whole four hundred and sixty that have refused to sign the Recognition'[29] may, however, have been an exaggeration. Peter Gaunt has shown that we can identify around 310 members who were active in the House after 12 September, and who must therefore have signed the Recognition. The estimate of 350 from the Dutch ambassadors also carries weight. Gaunt points out that the full

[21] *CJ*, VII, 368. [22] Burton, I, xxxv.
[23] Burton, I, xxxv; Whitelocke, *Memorials*, IV, 149; Ludlow, I, 392; *Clarke Papers*, V, 208–9; *Mercurius Politicus*, no. 222 (7–14 September 1654), pp. 3761–4; TSP, II, 606. Cf. TSP, II, 715, for the figure of 'at least 150'.
[24] TSP, II, 606; BL, Add. MS 17677 U, fo. 437, quoted in Gardiner, *Commonwealth and Protectorate*, III, 203, n. 3.
[25] OPH, XX, 371. [26] *CJ*, VII, 368; Burton, I, xxxvii; Whitelocke, *Memorials*, IV, 149.
[27] *Mercurius Politicus*, no. 223 (14–21 September 1654), p. 3780; *Mercurius Politicus*, no. 225 (28 September–5 October 1654), p. 3816. Gilbert Mabbott claimed that 'about 230' members had signed the Recognition by 21 September (*Clarke Papers*, V, 213), while *Severall Proceedings of State Affairs*, no. 261 (21–28 September 1654), p. 4144, puts the figure at 245 by 27 September.
[28] Whitelocke, *Memorials*, IV, 152. [29] Vaughan, I, 71.

strength of the House never reached 460: only 22 Scottish members were returned, and of these probably only 12 or 13 are known to have taken their seats, although it is possible that the actual number may have been higher than this.[30] Some of the double or treble returns were never resolved and at least three members died during the Parliament.[31] A significant number of absences therefore cannot be explained by a conscientious refusal to sign the Recognition. Gaunt has suggested that the number of those who actually refused was probably 'around 80', or at any rate 'somewhere between 50 and 80'.[32]

Those who did withdraw on principle included some of the most committed commonwealthsmen, such as Sir Arthur Hesilrige, John Bradshaw, Thomas Scott, and John Weaver. According to Ludlow's *Memoirs*:

So soon as this visible hand of violence appeared to be upon them, most of the eminent assertors of the liberty of their country withdrew themselves, being persuaded they should better discharge their duty to the nation by this way of expressing their abhorrence of [Cromwell's] tyrannical proceedings, than by surrendering their liberties under their own hands, and then treating with him who was possessed of the sword, to recover some part of them again.[33]

But otherwise there was apparently no overt protest, perhaps because the terms of the Recognition, and the House's subsequent resolution clarifying that members were required to assent only to the principle of government by a single person and a Parliament, in fact asked for no more than the undertaking given on the indenture for the return of each member.[34]

That most members found no great difficulty in making such a pledge is evident in the draft constitutional bill, which maintained the requirement that the election returns should indicate that 'the persons so elected shall not have power to alter the government from one single person and a Parliament'.[35] By contrast, the bill significantly reduced the council's powers to exclude members. It stated that the council would be:

[30] See chapter 3.
[31] These were Humphrey Mackworth, Sir Thomas Pelham, and Henry Shelley: Peter Gaunt, 'Oliver Cromwell and his Protectorate Parliaments: Co-operation, Conflict and Control', in Ivan Roots, ed., *'Into another Mould': Aspects of the Interregnum* (2nd edn, Exeter, 1998), p. 100, n. 32.
[32] Peter Gaunt, *Oliver Cromwell* (Oxford, 1996), p. 180; Gaunt, 'Cromwell and his Protectorate Parliaments', p. 88.
[33] Ludlow, I, 392.
[34] Article 12 of the Instrument mandated electors and the sheriffs, or other returning officers, to seal indentures providing that 'the persons elected shall not have power to alter the government as it is hereby settled in one single person and a Parliament': Gardiner, *Constitutional Documents*, p. 410. Cromwell reminded members of this: Lomas–Carlyle, II, 379, 389. It was certainly one of the considerations that inclined Guybon Goddard and several other Norfolk members to sign the Recognition: Burton, I, xxxvi.
[35] This was in chapter 33 of the draft bill: Gardiner, *Constitutional Documents*, p. 440.

empowered to examine upon oath as touching any articles of popery or delinquency mentioned in chapter 29 against any person or persons returned for members of Parliament, and, if they shall find such charge to be true, and shall certify the same to the Parliament, the first day of the sitting of the Parliament, that then such members shall not sit until the House have adjudged the same.[36]

Tellingly, the council's powers did not extend to policing whether members met the other moral and religious qualifications set out in chapter 31 of the bill.[37] It is also striking that the bill placed ultimate authority to adjudicate such cases in Parliament rather than in the council. This may indicate that most members were more concerned about the issue of pre-sessional exclusions than about the imposition of the Recognition. The events of 1656 would suggest that their concerns were well founded.

EXCLUSIONS BEFORE THE SECOND PROTECTORATE PARLIAMENT

We saw in the previous chapter that the regime monitored the elections to the second Protectorate Parliament very closely. Thurloe received detailed reports from the major-generals, and the depth of anti-military feeling among electors profoundly alarmed the council. It seems that the council was initially planning to enforce the Recognition before the Parliament assembled, in order to avoid any repetition of the events of 1654. Thurloe wrote to Henry Cromwell on 1 July that 'the election is to be, as it was the last Parliament; only all possible care is to be used, that the qualifications in the government be observed, and the Recognition is to be first taken, before they sit in the House'.[38] However, the council was caught off-guard by the unexpectedly large number of candidates unsympathetic to the regime who were returned, and by the beginning of September it had apparently decided that nothing short of a large-scale exclusion would prevent such individuals from taking their seats.

In determining which members should be excluded, the council appears to have relied heavily on the reports sent in by the major-generals during the course of the elections. It therefore comes as no surprise to find that those counties where the major-general or his deputy reported the most active opposition, and experienced the greatest difficulty in securing the return of 'honest men', were often also those that subsequently had the largest number of their members excluded. To illustrate this general point, we can follow through the case studies of individual counties presented in the previous chapter. The greatest number excluded for any county was eight (Kent and Lincolnshire). However, because the number of seats varied considerably

---

[36] This was in chapter 34 of the draft bill: Gardiner, *Constitutional Documents*, p. 441.
[37] Gardiner, *Constitutional Documents*, p. 436.   [38] *TSP*, V, 176.

from county to county, it is also illuminating to measure the proportion of members who were excluded. Chris Durston has found that 'the exclusion rate for the whole Parliament was roughly twenty-six per cent'.[39] There was, however, considerable variation between the different counties, and in some of those areas where most problems had been reported during the elections the rate of exclusion was as high as 50 per cent.

To begin, as before, with Hezekiah Haynes, we find that the proportion of members excluded in Suffolk and Norfolk was almost twice as high as the national average of 26 per cent. In Suffolk, the seven members for the county who had attracted most votes were all excluded, out of sixteen elected: William Bloys, William Gibbs, Edmund Harvey, Edward Le Neve, Henry North, John Sicklemore, and Daniel Wall. In Norfolk, six members were excluded, out of thirteen elected: John Buxton, Sir William D'Oiley, Sir Ralph Hare, Thomas Sotherton, and Philip Woodhouse (all for the county of Norfolk), together with John Hobart (Norwich). As we saw in the previous chapter, Haynes had especially abhorred the election of the last named.

A similarly high rate of exclusion (around 50 per cent) is also evident in the three other counties that emerged in chapter 3 as especially problematic. In Sussex, seven members were excluded out of thirteen returned: George Courthop, Sir John Fagge, Samuel Gott, Herbert Morley, and Sir Thomas Rivers (all for the county of Sussex), together with Henry Peckham (Chichester) and John Goodwin (East Grinstead). In Kent, eight members were excluded out of sixteen: Richard Beale, John Boys, Lambert Godfrey, William James, John Selliard, Daniel Shetterden, and Sir Thomas Styles (all for the county of Kent), along with Thomas St Nicholas (Canterbury). In Lincolnshire, likewise, eight members were excluded out of sixteen: Charles Hall, Charles Hussey, Thomas Lister, William Savile, William Welby, and William Woolley (all for the county of Lincolnshire), together with Sir Anthony Irby (Boston) and John Weaver (Stamford).

By contrast, those areas that appeared in the previous chapter to have been less troublesome to the government generally saw a much lower rate of exclusion. In Disbrowe's association, there were no exclusions at all in Dorset and Gloucestershire. In Cornwall, only three members were excluded out of twelve elected (Walter Moyle for the county, Thomas Gewen for Launceston, and Walter Vincent for Truro), and in Somerset only four out of sixteen (John Buckland, Sir Alexander Popham, and Robert Long for the county, and John Doddridge for Bristol). The only counties within Disbrowe's association that saw a slightly higher rate of exclusion were Wiltshire, where five were excluded out of the fourteen elected (Sir

---

[39] Christopher Durston, *Cromwell's Major-Generals: Godly Government during the English Revolution* (Manchester, 2001), p. 200.

Anthony Ashley Cooper, Sir Alexander Popham (also returned for Somerset), John Bulkeley (also returned for Hampshire), and Henry Hungerford for the county, along with Edward Tooker for Salisbury); and Devon, where the figure was six out of twenty (Sir John Doddridge (also returned for Bristol), John Hale, William Morrice, Sir John Northcote, and Sir John Young for the county, and John Maynard for Plymouth). The overall rate of exclusion within Disbrowe's association was thus 22 per cent (eighteen out of eighty-three seats).

In Bridge's association, the rate was just below this level: 21 per cent, or four members excluded out of nineteen returned. These four were two of the eight members for Lancashire (Thomas Birch for Liverpool and Richard Radcliffe for Manchester), and two of the six members for Staffordshire (Thomas Minors for Lichfield and John Bowyer for Newcastle-under-Lyme). None of the five members for Cheshire was excluded. Finally, in Berry's association, the rate was lower still: 15 per cent (seven members excluded out of forty-six returned). Four out of eight members were excluded in Shropshire (Andrew Lloyd and Samuel Moore for the county, Samuel Jones for Shrewsbury, and John Aston for Ludlow), but only two out of six in Herefordshire (Edward Harley for the county, John Birch for Leominster), none of the seven from Worcestershire, and only one of the twenty-five from Wales (Charles Lloyd for Montgomeryshire).

It seems that no members were excluded for Scotland. There was, however, an attempt to exclude several of the Irish members. We saw in the previous chapter that Henry Cromwell's decision to retain in Ireland some of the officers who had been elected cut the army interest among the Irish members to just one (John Brett). Henry's enemies on the council retaliated by trying to reduce the civilian interest, and sought to exclude three of his closest allies: Tristram Beresford, John Bisse, and Richard Tighe. However, Henry was able to overturn these decisions and all three took their seats by the end of October.[40] Henry agreed to Thurloe's request that John Davies be excluded on the grounds that he was 'as great an intelligencer to the royal party as any man', 'by no means fit to serve in Parliament', and 'a most pestilent fellow'.[41] There was only one case, that of Sir Paul Davies, in which Henry was unable to secure admission for an excluded Irish member whom he actively supported, and it seems that Sir Paul Davies never attended this sitting of Parliament.[42]

The total number of members who were excluded before the Parliament opened cannot be calculated exactly. No official government list of names

[40] *TSP*, V, 477; *CJ*, VII, 427, 439, 456.   [41] *TSP*, V, 398.
[42] This paragraph is based on Patrick Little, 'Irish Representation in the Protectorate Parliaments', *Parl. Hist.*, 23 (2004), 336–56.

appears to exist, while the various contemporary lists that do survive are not consistent. The likeliest figure is probably just over 100, with 105 as perhaps the most probable total.[43] These individuals can be divided into a number of categories. There were, first of all, commonwealthsmen opposed to the Protectorate, most notably Thomas Birch, Henry Darley, Richard Darley, Sir Arthur Hesilrige, Thomas Lister, Henry Mildmay, Thomas Scott, Thomas St Nicholas, and John Weaver.[44] Then there were prominent Presbyterians who had obstructed the extension of liberty of conscience in 1654–5: these included John Birch and John Bulkeley. However, much the largest category appears to have been moderate Presbyterian gentry who were known to be profoundly unsympathetic to the Protectorate and especially to the major-generals. Many of these gentry came from traditional county families and had been conservative Parliamentarians during the 1640s: a few typical examples from the many were Herbert Morley and Sir John Fagge in Sussex, Sir Alexander Popham in Somerset, Sir Ralph Hare in Norfolk, William Bloys in Suffolk, Sir Thomas Bowes and Sir Harbottle Grimston in Essex, Sir Anthony Irby in Lincolnshire, Sir John Northcote and Sir John Young in Devon, and Sir Thomas Styles in Kent. It is worth noting that only a small minority of the individuals thus denied their seats were actually excludable under Articles 14 or 15 of the Instrument of Government. Very few – Thomas Adams, Sir John Gore, and Peniston Whalley among them – had been active royalists in the first Civil War and could thus be excluded under Article 14.[45] In many other cases, the reasons for a member's exclusion remain relatively obscure, and may well have depended on the perceptions and activities of the local major-general or his deputy, and the information that they sent to the council.

---

[43] These lists are: TNA, SP 18/130/29; Bodl., MS Rawlinson A 73, fo. 317r; Bodl., MS Tanner 52, fo. 156r; *CJ*, VII, 425; and BL, Stowe MS 361, fo. 103 (this last list is printed in Whitelocke, *Memorials*, IV, 280, but see below for a discussion of the uncertainty surrounding its authenticity). The numbers of names on these lists are 96, 95, 98, 79, and 95 respectively. Thurloe put the figure at 'near 100' on 16 September, and roughly two weeks later at 'about 100': *TSP*, V, 424, 453. Another contemporary wrote of 'at least a 100 excluded members': *TSP*, V, 456. Carol Egloff estimates that it may have been as high as 107: Carol S. Egloff, 'The Search for a Cromwellian Settlement: Exclusions from the Second Protectorate Parliament', *Parl. Hist.*, 17 (1998), 310. Chris Durston put the figure at 'just over 100': Durston, *Cromwell's Major-Generals*, p. 199. A comparison of the surviving lists establishes 101 names pretty reliably, and a further five slightly less reliably. In addition, there may have been as many as ten more excluded, but it is unlikely that the final total was as high as 115, and a figure in the region of 105 is more probable. For a detailed analysis of the surviving lists, see appendix 1.

[44] Carol Egloff has calculated that no fewer than twenty-five known commonwealthsmen were elected in 1656, but only eleven of these were excluded: Egloff, 'Exclusions', 311 and n. 49.

[45] Egloff, 'Exclusions', 312–13.

An analysis of the surviving lists points to a number of conclusions. First, over seventy of the excluded members represented counties and only about thirty sat for boroughs. This suggests that the regime found its strongest support in urban areas. In the shires, on the other hand, it was running up against growing opposition from traditional, moderate county gentry. A second feature is that sixty or more of those excluded appear to have sat in the first Protectorate Parliament, while at least thirty-eight had no previous parliamentary experience. There thus seems to be no very close correlation between the length of a member's earlier career and whether or not he was excluded. Perhaps the most marked pattern was a geographical one. The previous chapter argued that the regime had encountered the greatest problems in those regions that had been most staunchly Parliamentarian during the 1640s. This is also evident in the geographical profile of those excluded. Areas that were consistently under Parliamentarian control from the spring of 1643 onwards account for approximately seventy (or roughly two-thirds) of the exclusions.[46] This pattern is broadly compatible with the conclusions that emerged from the analysis of election returns in chapter 3: it suggests that the Protectoral regime was often encountering most overt opposition in precisely those areas where Parliamentarian allegiance was sufficiently long established for leading county figures to feel able to express openly their reservations about the Protectorate and its policies.

PROTESTS AND READMISSIONS, 1656–7

The difficulty of calculating the number of those excluded is compounded by the fact that up to sixty more members withdrew in protest. Sir Charles Firth estimated this group at 'fifty or sixty', while Carol Egloff puts it at 'approximately sixty'.[47] The addition of this further group of withdrawals, on top of those already excluded, probably accounts for why figures of 120, 140, or even 160 appear in some contemporary sources.[48] Furthermore, as in 1654,

---

[46] This figure has been calculated by adding up the number of excluded members for the following counties, in addition to London (4): Devon (6), Essex (6), Hampshire (2), Kent (8), Lincolnshire (8), Middlesex (1), Norfolk (6), Nottinghamshire (1), Rutland (1), Somerset (4), Staffordshire (2), Suffolk (7), Sussex (7), Warwickshire (1), Wiltshire (5).

[47] Firth, *Last Years*, I, 16; Egloff, 'Exclusions', 304.

[48] For 120, see BL, Lansdowne MS 821, fo. 314v, printed in Abbott, IV, 418; *Clarke Papers*, III, 73; Bodl., MS Clarendon 52, fo. 287v; *CSPV*, 1655–6, 266. For 140, see TNA, SP 18/130/31. For 160, see TNA, SP 18/130/29; *TSP*, V, 427. Hesilrige's later claim (7 February 1659) that 'two hundred were kept out' was almost certainly exaggerated: Burton, III, 101. Cf. William Packer's statement (9 February 1659) that 'one hundred were kept out', and Richard Knightley's (11 February 1659) that 'one hundred and fifty members were kept out': Burton, III, 160, 215.

it is virtually impossible to distinguish between absence for a whole range of reasons, not least illness, and voluntary secession based on a principled objection to the exclusion.

Two protests were printed shortly after the exclusion. One was entitled *An Appeale from the Court to the Country, made by a Member of Parliament lawfully chosen, but secluded illegally by my L[ord] Protector* (1656). This pamphlet denounced 'so manifest a breach of our laws, so uncolourable a violation of our privileges, so heinous an invasion of our common right, and freedom, and so public a defiance given to the whole nation'. The author went on to 'compare this infringement of our privileges with that of the late King's in demanding the five members', and stressed 'how infinitely this transcends it in all its measures, considering the number of the persons secluded, the insufficiency of this general charge, and how far this does reflect upon the honour of the respective counties, whose delegates they are, to have their messengers reproachfully dismissed'. The author was appalled that 'this qualification of the Instrument admits so great a latitude of interpretation that the most zealous patriots and incorrupt assertors of the people's rights may stand secluded by it', and concluded with a personal denunciation of Cromwell, lamenting that 'this rigid maintainer of the rights and privileges of Parliament, laying aside his now useless religical vizard, [should] subvert the very foundation of that venerable assembly'.[49]

The other pamphlet was a Remonstrance ostensibly signed by ninety-eight of the excluded members.[50] Ralph C. H. Catterall showed that this is almost certainly apocryphal, and that at least two of its purported signatories, Herbert Morley and Sir John Fagge, denied all knowledge of it.[51] On 12 October, Morley wrote from Glynde Place, his home in Sussex, to Sir John Trevor that

I am amazed to hear of it, and do fear it may be done purposely to blemish the integrity of the excluded members. However if my hand be to it, I disavow that ever I knew of it, or gave any direction to affix it to the same, it being my desire, that since I am debarred from exercise of the trust reposed in me by my country to serve them in Parliament, I am well contented I shall ever live quietly at my own house, where if any

---

[49] *An Appeale from the Court to the Country, made by a Member of Parliament lawfully chosen, but secluded illegally by my L[ord] Protector* (1656), pp. 1, 3, 4–5.
[50] *To all the worthy gentlemen who are duely chosen for the Parliament, which intended to meet at Westminster the 17 of September 1656. And to all the good people of the Common-wealth of England. The humble remonstrance, protection, and appeale of severall knights and gentlemen duly chosen to serve their countrey in Parliament; who attended at Westminster for that purpose, but were violently kept out of the Parliament-house by armed men hired by the Lord Protector* ([7 October] 1656). This is printed in *OPH*, XXI, 28–37.
[51] Ralph C. H. Catterall, 'A Suspicious Document in Whitelock's "Memorials"', *EHR*, 16 (1901), 737–9. The text is printed in Whitelocke, *Memorials*, IV, 274–80.

desire to speak with me, they shall assuredly find me; and I know my brother [Sir John] Fagge's practice and opinion to be the same.[52]

The Remonstrance was probably the work of a commonwealthsman – a theory that does not rule out the possibility that one or more of the excluded members may have had some hand in it – and it gives an insight into criticism of Cromwell from that quarter in the autumn of 1656. The pamphlet insisted that elected members had 'an undoubted right to meet, sit and vote in Parliament', and complained that the 'Lord Protector has, by force of arms, invaded this fundamental right and liberty, and violently prevented the meeting of the people's chosen deputies in Parliament'. Once again, the comparison with Charles I's attempted arrest of the five members cast this latest exclusion in a very poor light: 'none of the most wicked kings, in their highest hope to erect a tyranny, ever dared, since members were sent to Parliaments by elections, to throw aside, by force, as many of the chosen members as they thought would not serve their ends'. Cromwell had 'assumed an absolute arbitrary sovereignty', and had in effect asserted 'that the people's choice cannot give any man a right to sit in Parliament, but the right must be derived from his gracious will and pleasure with that of his counsellors'. Not only had the exclusion changed 'the state of the people from freedom into a mere slavery'; it had also ensured that 'the present assembly at Westminster is not the representative body of England', and any laws that it passed were therefore 'null and void in themselves, and of no legal effect or power'.[53]

Perhaps the most striking characteristic of these printed protests is their forthright personal criticism of Cromwell. The Protector, however, remained at pains to distance himself from the exclusions. When George Courthop appealed against his exclusion directly to Cromwell, the latter replied 'that it was an act of the councils, and that he did not concern himself in it'.[54] According to one report of his speech to the army officers on 27 February 1657, Cromwell told them reproachfully that when the members were chosen 'you garbled them, kept out and put in whom you pleased by the Instrument'.[55] Certainly, Cromwell attended only four of the nineteen recorded council meetings during September, and none on the two days (15 and 16 September) when many of the key decisions were apparently taken.[56] He never publicly attempted to defend the exclusions, and when the House came to consider the excluded members it scrupulously recognised that this was a council matter.

[52] *TSP*, V, 490.   [53] *OPH*, XXI, 29–30, 32–5.
[54] S. C. Lomas, ed., 'The Memoirs of Sir George Courthop, 1616–1685', *Camden Miscellany XI* (Camden Society, 3rd series, 13, 1907), pp. 93–157, especially pp. 141–5.
[55] BL, Lansdowne MS 821, fo. 314v, printed in Abbott, IV, 418.
[56] Egloff, 'Exclusions', 191–2.

This debate began on 18 September, the day after the Parliament opened, when Sir George Booth tabled a short letter from the excluded members describing how they had been denied entry to the House.[57] The next day, the Clerk of the Commonwealth in Chancery was summoned, and informed the House that 'he received an order, from his highness's council, that he should deliver tickets to all such persons, and such only, as, being returned to serve in Parliament, should be certified unto him, from the council, as persons by them approved'. He produced the order to this effect, signed by the clerk of the council, William Jessop.[58] On 20 September, the House resolved to ask the council to give 'their reasons why those members who are returned from the several counties and boroughs for members, are not approved, and why they are not admitted to come into the House'.[59] Two days later, the Lord Commissioner Nathaniel Fiennes informed the House on the council's behalf that the latter had 'not refused to approve any who have appeared to them to be persons of integrity *to the government*, fearing God and of good conversation'.[60] The insertion of the words 'to the government' – which did not appear in Article 17 of the Instrument – was surely highly significant, for it defined 'integrity' much more specifically in terms of loyalty to the regime. A motion to adjourn was defeated by 115 votes to 80, with Disbrowe and Fiennes acting as tellers for the Noes. The House then immediately resolved by 125 votes to 29 that those who had not been approved should now 'be referred to make their application to the council for an approbation'.[61] The sudden drop in the total number of those who voted suggests that at least forty-one of the fifty to sixty or so members who withdrew in protest did so in between these two votes on 22 September.

It seems that, from then until January 1657, approximately twenty-seven excluded members were readmitted to the House, although the exact process by which this happened is difficult to reconstruct.[62] Many made no effort to seek readmission, and an army newsletter of 25 September reported that 'some of them are gone into the country discontented and will not apply themselves to the council, and some are guilty and dare not'.[63] Concerned about low attendance, the House resolved on 29 September that 'all the

---

[57] *CJ*, VII, 424.

[58] *CJ*, VII, 425. For the original order, dated 13 September 1656, see Bodl., MS Nalson 16, fo. 346r. For an example of a ticket of admission, see Whitelocke, *Memorials*, IV, 274.

[59] *CJ*, VII, 426.   [60] *CJ*, VII, 426 (emphasis added). Cf. Egloff, 'Exclusions', 181–2.

[61] *CJ*, VII, 426; *Clarke Papers*, III, 74; *TSP*, V, 453; Whitelocke, *Memorials*, IV, 274.

[62] Egloff, 'Exclusions', 305–6. Egloff lists twenty such members at 305, n. 26. However, it can be established from Burton's diary and the *Commons' Journal* that at least seven more members were readmitted: Tristram Beresford, John Bisse, Charles Hall, John Hobart, John Maynard, Richard Tighe, and Walter Vincent. This brings the total of those readmitted to at least 27 out of roughly 100–107 originally excluded.

[63] *Clarke Papers*, III, 74–5.

persons who have been returned to serve in this present Parliament, and have been, and shall be, approved, and either have sat, or may sit, in the House, and are now absent, do give their attendance on the service of this House, in the House, before Monday next [6 October]'.[64] Such concerns appear to have receded by mid-October,[65] and the issue dropped out of sight thereafter, re-emerging only briefly in late December.

On 20 December, as members were beginning to go home for Christmas, Denis Bond moved that the House be called. Lambert agreed, but urged the need to 'distinguish between such as are approved and such as are not'. This gave the prominent Presbyterian Thomas Bampfield an opportunity to reopen the issue of the excluded members and to demand the abandonment of any such distinction: 'I hope the council are by now satisfied of those that are left out, that they are now persons capable to sit.' Peter Brooke seconded him. This proposal 'bred some heat in the House', but the dispute subsided when the Speaker 'very discreetly' moved on to another question in order 'to prevent further debate'.[66] The House simply resolved that it should be called on 31 December.[67] Burton felt that 'none of the excluded persons will be received', and 'few of those that are gone home will return this session'.[68] When the appointed day arrived, the Speaker asked members 'by what book would you call them, by the book that had all the returns, or by the book of those that were approved'.[69] In the end, approved members only were called, and this prompted the Presbyterian Lambert Godfrey to move 'that liberty be given to every creature. I humbly move that you take an account of your own members, and know how, and why, they are detained. It is the common interest of the nation, and the honour of your House.' Other Presbyterians such as Bampfield and Alexander Thistlethwaite supported him, and Richard Meredith was about to do likewise, 'but the Speaker, being sick of the motion, left the chair'.[70] This brought that particular discussion to a close.

The issue of exclusion did not go away, however. The Humble Petition and Advice provided for '41 commissioners . . . appointed by Act of Parliament, who, or any fifteen or more of them, shall be authorised to examine and try whether the members to be elected for the House of Commons in future Parliaments be capable to sit, according to the qualifications mentioned in this Petition and Advice'. Those deemed 'not qualified accordingly' were to be suspended from 'sitting until the House of Commons shall, upon hearing of their particular cases, admit them to sit'. These commissioners were required to 'certify in writing to the House of Commons' the 'causes and

[64] *CJ*, VII, 430.   [65] TNA, PRO 31/3/100, fo. 388.
[66] Burton, I, 190–5; Bodl., MS Carte 228, fo. 81r. See also *Clarke Papers*, III, 85.
[67] *CJ*, VII, 471.   [68] Bodl., MS Carte 228, fo. 81r.   [69] Burton, I, 283.   [70] Burton, I, 290–1.

grounds of their suspensions of any persons so to be elected as aforesaid'.[71] On 21 April, however, Cromwell suggested that these arrangements be modified. He warned that 'truly those commissioners are uncertain persons; and it is hard to say what may happen. I hope they will be always good men; but if they should be bad, then perhaps they will keep out good men.' He wished 'to help – as to the freedom of Parliament', and felt that 'if there be no commissioners it would be never a whit the worse'. In the end, it was up to Parliament to adjudicate its own membership: 'if you make qualifications for membership, and if any man will presume to sit without those qualifications, you may deal with them'. He added: 'If any man sit there that has not right to sit there, if any stranger come in upon a pretended title of election, then perhaps it is a different case, but if any sit there upon pretence of a qualification upon him, you may send him to prison without any more ado. Whether you think fit to do so or no, it is a parliamentary business: I do but hint it to you.'[72] Parliament took the hint: in the light of Cromwell's suggestions, the Additional Petition and Advice revoked the clause providing for forty-one commissioners and declared instead that 'there shall be the penalty and fine of £1000 laid and inflicted upon every such unqualified member (being so adjudged) by the said House of Commons, and imprisonment of his person until payment thereof'.[73] This affirmed more clearly than ever the House's control over its membership and was surely intended to prevent the possibility of any future conciliar exclusions like those of 1654 and 1656. Cromwell had encouraged these changes and accepted them without demur. However, by removing the power of conciliar exclusion, the Humble Petition and Advice, as amended by the Additional Petition and Advice, weakened the government's hand while strengthening that of Parliament, with consequences that will be examined in the next section.

THE RETURN OF THE EXCLUDED, 1658–9

To follow the story of exclusions through to the second sitting of the second Protectorate Parliament and, beyond that, to the third Protectorate Parliament is like considering the dog that did not bark in the night. We are looking at the consequences of something that did not happen. Yet the implications were no less real for that, and they affected the proceedings of

---

[71] Gardiner, *Constitutional Documents*, p. 451; *CJ*, VII, 509–10; Burton, I, 390–1.
[72] Lomas–Carlyle, III, 107–8.
[73] Gardiner, *Constitutional Documents*, p. 460. This amendment appears to have been made by the committee that drafted the Additional Petition and Advice, responding to Cromwell's suggestion, and to have been accepted by the House without debate. There is no evidence that it caused discussion at any of the three readings of the Additional Petition: *CJ*, VII, 545, 557, 571–3; Burton, II, 171–5, 248–54, 283–305.

these remaining sittings in very direct ways. In particular, the return of a sizeable number of committed and vociferous opponents of the Protectoral regime produced a bitter wrangle over the Humble Petition and Advice, and especially over the newly created Other House.

Burton's diary indicates that at least twenty of the excluded members re-entered the House in January 1658.[74] There was no impediment to their return, provided that they were willing to take the oath prescribed for members of Parliament in the Humble Petition and Advice.[75] More than half of these twenty returnees spoke regularly, and some of them, most notably the commonwealthsmen led by Hesilrige and Scott, made repeated interventions in debates. To illustrate the importance of the role that these newly returned members played, it is worth examining the debates over the Other House that took place on 28–30 January and 1–4 February 1658, and that contributed directly to Cromwell's decision to dissolve the Parliament.

On 28 January, Scott, Ashley Cooper, and Weaver were instrumental in securing a debate the following day on the title of the Other House.[76] The next day, Hesilrige and Scott led the attack on the new chamber: the former made a series of fairly short contributions, whereas the latter gave a single, lengthy speech that was a denunciation as much of the old House of Lords as of the new Other House.[77] St Nicholas, Gewen, and Weaver all spoke in support of Hesilrige's motion to debate the matter in Grand Committee, although this was defeated.[78] On 30 January, there were further speeches by Hesilrige, Scott, and Weaver, together with interventions from Thorpe, Ashley Cooper, and Gibbs.[79] Burton's record of proceedings on 1 February was very brief, 'for I went out at twelve ... for I was engaged upon other business', but his diary nevertheless reveals contributions from Scott, Gewen, and St Nicholas.[80] The next day, Boteler, Briscoe, Haynes, and Beake attempted to regain the initiative with lengthy defences of the Other House and the need for the Commons to correspond with it.[81] Formerly excluded members, especially Doddridge, Ashley Cooper, Chute, Weaver, and Hesilrige, were again prominent among those who replied.[82] Many of the familiar names recurred the next day, 3 February: Hesilrige, Gewen,

[74] Anthony Ashley Cooper, Thomas Birch, Chaloner Chute, Henry Darley, John Doddridge, Sir John Fagge, Thomas Gewen, William Gibbs, Sir Arthur Hesilrige, Henry Hungerford, Thomas Lister, Henry Mildmay, Herbert Morley, Thomas Scott, John Sicklemore, Thomas St Nicholas, Sir Thomas Styles, Francis Thorpe, Edward Turner, and John Weaver.
[75] Gardiner, *Constitutional Documents*, p. 463. Cromwell had originally nominated Hesilrige to be a member of the Other House, but he refused to sit there and preferred to take up his seat in the Commons as a member for Leicester: Ludlow, II, 32–3.
[76] Burton, II, 377–9; Bodl., MS Carte 80, fo. 753v.
[77] Burton, II, 380, 392, 393, 394 (for Hesilrige); 382–92 (for Scott).
[78] Burton, II, 392–4; *CJ*, VII, 589–90.   [79] Burton, II, 394–404.   [80] Burton, II, 404–6.
[81] Burton, II, 407–17.   [82] Burton, II, 418–24.

Gibbs, Scott, Weaver, Ashley Cooper, Turner, Fagge, Doddridge, and Hungerford.[83] Finally, on 4 February, Thorpe, Morley, Doddridge, Hesilrige, and Scott all made speeches reaffirming their hostility towards the existence of the Other House, until proceedings were cut short by Cromwell's call to meet him in the House of Lords and his announcement that the Parliament was dissolved.[84] The presence of these newly returned members thus made a very considerable difference to the composition of the House, as did the removal to the Other House of some of Cromwell's most effective supporters.[85] All this evidence surely bears out Ludlow's comment that 'most of the members who had been formerly excluded, took the oath also, and were admitted to sit in the House, where the addition of these last, together with the removal of those of the Other House, who were for the most part taken out of this, made a considerable alteration in that body'.[86]

Many of these individuals played a similarly important – and, from the government's perspective, often destructive – role in the third Protectorate Parliament. This will be examined more closely in chapters 7 and 8; here we should simply note that the removal of the council's powers of exclusion allowed the return of a significant number of members who resented the Protectorate and sought the return of the Commonwealth (or, in some cases, the monarchy). Of the twenty excluded members who re-entered the House in January 1658, at least thirteen were also re-elected to the third Protectorate Parliament a year later.[87] In addition, six of those who had been excluded and subsequently readmitted to the first sitting of the second Protectorate Parliament were returned to the third Protectorate Parliament.[88] There was also a further group of at least twelve members who had been excluded in the autumn of 1656, and who entered Parliament in January 1659 for the first time.[89] In all, at least thirty-one of those originally excluded in the autumn of 1656 thus sat in the third Protectorate

---

[83] Burton, II, 424–41.   [84] Burton, II, 442–64; *CJ*, VII, 592.

[85] Those removed to the Other House included Lord Broghill, John Disbrowe, Nathaniel Fiennes, Charles Fleetwood, George Fleetwood, Henry Lawrence, John Lisle, Sir Richard Onslow, Phillip Skippon, Walter Strickland, Sir William Strickland, William Sydenham, Edward Whalley, and Bulstrode Whitelocke: HMC, *The Manuscripts of the House of Lords, 1699–1702* (1908), pp. 506–7.

[86] Ludlow, II, 32.

[87] Anthony Ashley Cooper, Chaloner Chute, Sir John Fagge, Thomas Gewen, Sir Arthur Hesilrige, Henry Hungerford, Henry Mildmay, Herbert Morley, Thomas Savile, Thomas Scott, Thomas St Nicholas, Edward Turner, and John Weaver.

[88] Lambert Godfrey, John Goodwin, John Hobart, Charles Lloyd, Joachim Matthews, and John Maynard.

[89] Theophilus Biddulph, John Birch, Richard Brown, John Bulkeley, Sir William D'Oiley, Samuel Gott, Sir Anthony Irby, John Jones, Samuel Moore, William Morrice, Walter Moyle, and Sir John Northcote.

Parliament.[90] It is worth briefly assessing the role that these members played in destabilising this Parliament.

First of all, it needs stressing that these members did not form any kind of organised political group, and it is important not to impose upon them a greater coherence than they possessed. By no means all of them were irreconcilably hostile towards the Protectorate, or the Humble Petition and Advice. Some were quite capable of defending the latter as a viable basis for a lasting settlement.[91] Other members disliked the vagueness of the Humble Petition and wished to address its inadequacies, but as a way of preserving the Protectorate rather than of overthrowing it.[92] By contrast, there were others who disliked the Humble Petition because they resented the Protectorate in general, and wanted to see a return to the Commonwealth. Such commonwealthsmen, of whom Hesilrige and Scott were the most vociferous, admired the Rump, in which they had both sat: Hesilrige took great exception when one member referred to it as 'the fag-end of the Long Parliament'.[93] He lamented its dissolution and the creation of the Protectorate, and allegedly claimed that the Instrument of Government was 'made by the sword, and by the sword it must be maintained and not otherwise. That, therefore, perished because it had no right foundation.' He insisted that 'the Petition and Advice may be altered by you if you find inconveniences in it', and he therefore urged members that 'this may be the subject of our debate, and let us be convinced of it by law, right reason and divinity if there be any'.[94] Scott likewise looked back fondly to the Commonwealth, years when 'we never bid fairer for being masters of the whole world'. For him, as for Hesilrige, the expulsion of the Rump and the establishment of the Protectorate were savage blows to the 'good old cause'. Scott claimed that he had 'never met a zealous assertor of that cause, but lamented' the dissolution of the Rump, 'to see faith broken, and somewhat else … It was as much bewailed, at the Instrument of Government.'[95]

---

[90] These thirty-one individuals can be established from Burton's diary as having attended the Parliament. It is, however, possible that up to twelve more of the members excluded in 1656 might have sat in 1659 as well. Their names appear in the returns for the Parliament, but it remains uncertain whether or not they ever actually attended: John Buckland, George Courthop, John Gell, Richard Grenville, Sir Richard Lucy, Thomas Minors, Sir Alexander Popham, Thomas Saunders, John Sicklemore, James Thurbane, Edward Tooker, and Walter Vincent.

[91] For example, Samuel Gott on 7 March 1659: Burton, IV, 56–7. Cf. Schilling, p. 180.

[92] For example, Thomas St Nicholas on 8 February 1659: Burton, III, 118–19; BL, Add. MS 5138 (diary of Guybon Goddard), pp. 134–5. Cf. Schilling, pp. 34–5.

[93] This was on 21 March 1659. The same member, who 'was of no great quality', also accused Hesilrige of seeking to make himself and Sir Henry Vane 'the great Hogn Mogens, to rule the Commonwealth': Burton, IV, 221–3.

[94] Burton, III, 567–9; BL, Add. MS 5138, pp. 265–6. Cf. Schilling, p. 144.

[95] Burton, III, 112. Cf. BL, Add. MS 5138, p. 134.

His attack on the Humble Petition thus reflected a more deep-rooted resentment of the Protectorate. At the other end of the political spectrum, there were crypto-royalists among those previously excluded members who wished to see an end not only to the Protectorate but to the republic as well, and who sought instead the restoration of the monarchy and the House of Lords. One royalist observer noted the presence in the Commons of some 'members that are well affected to His Majesty'.[96] Such members abominated less the events of 1653 than those of 1649. It was, for example, from this royalist perspective that John Hobart opposed the Humble Petition and Advice: 'For this Petition and Advice, if Pope Alexander 6, Caesar Borgia, and Machiavel, should all consent together, they could not lay a foundation for a more absolute tyranny.'[97]

From the viewpoint of Richard Cromwell and his council, the lack of any conciliar power of exclusion allowed exponents of all these various persuasions to return in some numbers, and to make common cause during the prolonged debates over the recognition of Richard Cromwell as Protector (7–18 February),[98] the acceptance of the Other House (19 February–1 March; 26 March–8 April),[99] and the acknowledgement that the elected Irish and Scottish members had a legitimate right to sit in the Commons (8–23 March).[100] The Humble Petition and Advice thus helped to create a problem – in that it antagonised a range of members of very different viewpoints – while simultaneously failing to provide the Lord Protector and the council with a ready means to resolve it. Although members remained conscious of their privileges as a House, they sometimes felt the lack of a clear mechanism for ensuring that those returned fulfilled the necessary qualifications.[101] They were conscious that this work now fell entirely on Parliament and took up a considerable amount of time. The vetting of members, especially in so large an assembly with so many new to Parliament, left a great deal to be desired, and on 5 February it was found that 'a madman' dressed 'in grey clothes' had been sitting in the House for three days without being detected.[102]

[96] Bodl., MS Clarendon 60, fo. 61r.
[97] Burton, III, 542–3; BL, Add. MS 5138, pp. 257–8. Cf. Schilling, p. 137; and BL, Lansdowne MS 823, fo. 235r.
[98] Burton, III, 87–151, 155–94, 204–32, 256–87, 289–95, 316–24, 326–45; BL, Add. MS 5138, pp. 123–95; Schilling, pp. 25–90; *CJ*, VII, 601–5.
[99] Burton, III, 349–69, 403–24, 509–48, 550–94; IV, 7–87, 277–93, 351–9, 370–9; BL, Add. MS 5138, pp. 195–268; Schilling, pp. 91–147; *CJ*, VII, 605–12, 621–32.
[100] Burton, IV, 87–119, 122–39, 143–7, 163–91, 193–202, 204–23, 225–34, 237–43; Schilling, pp. 182–260; Derbyshire Record Office, MS D258/10/9/2 (diary of Sir John Gell), fos. 3r–6r; *CJ*, VII, 613–16, 618–19.
[101] Burton, III, 69–82.
[102] He was named William King, and had been a vintner: see Burton, III, 76–82; *CJ*, VII, 600–1.

CONCLUSION

In conclusion, it seems that the size of the Commons in 1659, and the lack of any conciliar power of exclusion, enabled a broader cross-section of opinion within the political and social elite to find voice in Parliament than had been the case earlier in the Protectorate. This confirmed and strengthened a pattern – already evident in the second sitting of the second Protectorate Parliament – that stemmed from the abolition by the Humble Petition and Advice of the council's power of exclusion. After 1657, unable to debar those whose political and religious views they distrusted, the Protector and the council had to face the return of members who spanned the entire spectrum from crypto-royalists to commonwealthsmen. The consequence was that the Parliaments that sat in 1658–9 presented a marked contrast to those of 1654–7, where the council had possessed the power to exclude members. Although the council used that power on a large scale only in 1656, Cromwell had in addition been willing, in 1654, to impose a Recognition of the Protectorate and the Instrument of Government as a condition for members being allowed to enter the House. Thus deprived of a significant proportion of their duly elected members – in 1654 by forced subscription to the Recognition, and two years later by pre-sessional exclusions – the first Protectorate Parliament, and the first sitting of the second, never embraced the range of opinion that was found within the second sitting of the second Protectorate Parliament, and even more so within the third Protectorate Parliament. The exceptional size of the latter Parliament served only to heighten this contrast. As a result, the third Protectorate Parliament in particular presented the council with considerable difficulties of management and leadership. This problem in turn leads neatly into a closer examination of the relations between the council and Parliament, and the dynamics of the political factions within both institutions. These issues will be addressed further in the next chapter.

5

Factional politics and parliamentary management

Over fifty years have passed since Hugh Trevor-Roper wrote his controversial assessment of the politics of the Protectorate Parliaments. His primary concern was to explain how Oliver Cromwell failed to get what he wanted from the Parliaments that sat in 1654 and 1656; but he was also interested in the nature of parliamentary management. His conclusions on Cromwell are well known, and provocative:

The one English sovereign who had actually been a member of Parliament proved himself as a Parliamentarian the most incompetent of them all. He did so because he had not studied the necessary rules of the game. Hoping to imitate Queen Elizabeth, who by understanding these rules had been able to play upon her 'faithful Commons' as upon a well-tuned instrument, he failed even more dismally than the Stuarts.[1]

According to Trevor-Roper, the corollary of this 'vacuum of leadership' at the centre was that the Protectorate Parliaments were beset by factionalism, with the 'country' party (led by 'Presbyterian' veterans from the 1640s) opposing the 'courtiers' in 1654–5, and the 'kingship' party in 1656–7 trying to foist a new monarchical constitution on Cromwell. The rejection of the crown gave power instead into the hands of the army, and this, together with the return of a republican caucus to Parliament in 1658 and 1659, brought chaos, and the ineffectual Richard Cromwell was forced to dissolve Parliament and resign as Protector.[2]

Historians have praised the 'elegance' of Trevor-Roper's argument, but have expressed concern at its central thrust, which has been described as 'something of a conjuring trick'.[3] Roger Howell 'revisited' the Trevor-Roper thesis in 1988, and modified it, especially as it related to Oliver Cromwell.

[1] Quoted in Roger Howell, 'Cromwell and his Parliaments', in R. C. Richardson, ed., *Images of Oliver Cromwell: Essays for and by Roger Howell, Jr* (Manchester, 1993), p. 125.
[2] Hugh Trevor-Roper, 'Oliver Cromwell and his Parliaments', in his *Religion, the Reformation and Social Change* (3rd edn, 1984), pp. 355, 376–86, 388.
[3] Howell, 'Cromwell and his Parliaments', p. 125; Ivan Roots, 'Introduction to the Revised Edition', in Ivan Roots, ed., *'Into another Mould': Aspects of the Interregnum* (2nd edn, Exeter, 1998), p. xvi.

For Howell, Trevor-Roper's contrast between Cromwell's failings as a manager and the success of Elizabeth I is fundamentally flawed, as it fails to take into account the differences between the sixteenth and the middle of the seventeenth centuries, which meant that 'Elizabethan-style Parliamentary management by itself was not the answer to the political problems of the 1650s.'[4] It might also be added that recent work on the Elizabethan Parliaments – notably that by Sir Geoffrey Elton and Michael Graves – has changed our view of management and factional politics in the earlier period, and has thus rendered Trevor-Roper's comparative approach inadequate, if not entirely obsolete.[5] A new way of approaching factionalism during the Protectorate is badly needed.

Other historians have tried to tackle this problem head-on. Peter Gaunt, in his study of Oliver Cromwell's Parliaments, agrees with Trevor-Roper that 'there is no sign of consistent or coherent Parliamentary management' from above, but argues that this was intentional, as Cromwell 'seems to have believed quite genuinely that his Parliaments ... would work diligently and meet the needs of state and government for which they had been summoned'. This also explains why the councillors were apparently so inactive in the Commons.[6] But Gaunt goes one stage further. Not only were the Protector and his council inactive; there was no government 'party' at all. Instead, the Protector's interests were supported 'by a group of agents and supporters in the House, a loose amalgam of councillor members of Parliament, civilian office holders and army officers ... [and] this was far from being a unified, long-term party'. Furthermore, 'If Cromwell had no permanent party within the House, nor did any other individual or interest group. Opposition was frequently apparent and vociferous, but it was manifested as an *ad hoc* resistance to particular issues, not as an opposition, still less the opposition ... the Protectoral Parliaments were very fluid assemblies, composed of temporary and usually shortlived alliances briefly surfacing amid the ebb and flow of shifting interests and issues.'[7]

Gaunt's work on the first two Protectorate Parliaments fits neatly with Derek Hirst's view of the third. Hirst's ingenious argument sets up for attack the 'conspiracy theories' of Godfrey Davies and other historians of the

[4] Howell, 'Cromwell and his Parliaments', p. 134.
[5] For a convenient summary of the debate on the Elizabethan Parliaments, see David L. Smith, *The Stuart Parliaments, 1603–1689* (1999), pp. 7–8.
[6] Gaunt, 'Oliver Cromwell and his Protectorate Parliaments: Co-operation, Conflict and Control', in Roots, *'Into another Mould'*, pp. 88, 90.
[7] Gaunt, 'Oliver Cromwell and his Protectorate Parliaments', pp. 88–9; see also Carol Egloff's emphasis on 'the fluidity, indeed the confusion, of party groupings during the Protectorate', in her 'John Hobart of Norwich and the Politics of the Cromwellian Protectorate', *Norfolk Archaeology*, 42 (1994), 38.

Restoration, who saw Richard Cromwell's Parliament as being deliberately destroyed by an alliance of republican 'commonwealthsmen' and 'crypto-cavaliers', intent on obstructing business and antagonising the army. Hirst presents instead a Parliament 'unusually sophisticated and purposive by seventeenth-century standards'. Weak leadership from the Protector and (especially) from successive speakers brought debate to a standstill on occasion, but there remained gentlemanly 'constraints upon parliamentary politics', which resulted in a 'positive' attitude among members, not factional animosity. Indeed, in the 'confusing landscape of 1659', no long-term factional objectives were sustainable. Groupings within the Parliament were loose, and the whole tone of the session was one of consensus, with opposing members seeking to persuade rather than coerce their opponents.[8]

This denial of factionalism within the Protectorate Parliaments is startling. Unlike Howell, who argues that the Cromwellian Parliaments were something different, almost intrinsically unmanageable, and open to fighting among factions, Gaunt and Hirst are keen to emphasise that these Parliaments fit into the consensual model modish among historians of the late sixteenth and early seventeenth centuries. As Hirst says, 1659 'was in many respects just one more seventeenth-century Parliament'.[9] These were still traditional Parliaments, governed by a desire for 'consensus not conflict'. Disputes arose almost by accident, rather than by factional design, and members insisted that 'dissidents must be comprehended rather than over-ridden, for the purpose of debate was to persuade and to preserve unity'.[10] Yet in playing down both management and factionalism, Gaunt and Hirst leave important events drifting dangerously far from their evidential moorings. In this chaotic 'ebb and flow' of events, how did such partisan measures as the new Parliamentary Constitution of 1654–5, the militia bill introduced to underpin the government of the major-generals in December 1656, or the proposed monarchical constitution which triggered the kingship debates in February 1657 reach the floor of the House at all? Why was the Parliament in gridlock over the recognition of the government or the status of the Other House in 1659 if the members were so 'positive', and why did stalemate lead to dissolution in this, as in two of the previous three, sitting of Parliament? The question of Oliver and Richard Cromwell's relationships with their Parliaments will be explored in later chapters. Rather, the aim here is to look again at the role of 'party politics' during the Protectorate Parliaments, to identify the composition of the individual factions, to examine the interactions between them, and to consider the ways in which

---

[8] Derek Hirst, 'Concord and Discord in Richard Cromwell's House of Commons', *EHR*, 103 (1988), *passim*, esp. 341, 344, 348–9.
[9] Hirst, 'Concord and Discord', 345.   [10] Hirst, 'Concord and Discord', 349–50.

they supported, obstructed, or even, at times, replaced the Protector and his council in the managing of parliamentary business. The chapter falls into three basic sections, which focus on the main factional groupings: the divided 'court' party, the Presbyterian (or 'country') interest, and the republicans or 'commonwealthsmen'.

THE COURT PARTY

Contemporaries were very certain that they could identify a 'court party' in all three Protectorate Parliaments, but they did not always agree as to what it signified. In the 1654–5 Parliament, the term was used broadly;[11] it included the senior officers, the councillors, and a number of informal advisers, all of whom owed a basic loyalty to Oliver Cromwell. Important parliamentary divisions reveal who the leading 'courtiers' were at this stage. On votes on the constitution, Sir Charles Wolseley acted as teller in divisions with his fellow councillors Walter Strickland and John Lambert;[12] the councillor Philip Jones worked not only with Lambert and John Disbrowe, but also with the non-councillor, Sir William Strickland,[13] while Lord Broghill, who as yet held no formal office but was a loyal Cromwellian, partnered non-councillors with close ties to the Protector, such as the Protector's son, Henry Cromwell, and son-in-law, John Claypole, as well as councillors Sir Charles Wolseley, John Disbrowe, and Edward Montagu.[14] The mixture of councillors and non-councillors, of civilian courtiers and military men, suggests that the court party was united on most issues concerning the constitution, and, although the details are obscure, it seems that some form of management was being deployed by the council. When it came to religion, the court was not so united, as individuals took different lines, and some leading courtiers sided with those who wanted restrictions on liberty of conscience, despite Cromwell's strong views on the matter.[15] Overall, however, in divisions the united court party could usually muster between eighty and one hundred votes.[16] This was a useful bloc, but in most divisions it was just short of a majority.

The unity of the 'court' was not something that could be taken for granted. Even during the 1654–5 Parliament, it was becoming clear that the supporters of the Protectorate could be divided into two categories, 'the soldiery and

[11] Burton, I, xxvii, lxvi, lxxiv, lxxxii; Ludlow, I, 338.
[12] *CJ*, VII, 367, 385.   [13] *CJ*, VII, 406, 414, 418.
[14] Burton, I, lxvi, lxxiv, cvii, cxxxi, cxxxiii; *CJ*, VII, 382, 384, 385, 394, 403, 418, 419, 420, 421.
[15] Patrick Little, *Lord Broghill and the Cromwellian Union with Ireland and Scotland* (Woodbridge, 2004), pp. 79–81.
[16] *CJ*, VII, 367–421.

courtiers'.[17] The diarist Guybon Goddard spoke of the Protector's 'party' as consisting of 'courtiers and officers of the army'.[18] This distinction was not yet politically important, as throughout the 1654 Parliament the civilian and military supporters of the Protectorate worked together to resist the threat to the regime posed by the Presbyterian and 'country' MPs, who were intent on rewriting its founding constitution, the Instrument of Government. But events between the dissolution of the first Protectorate Parliament in January 1655 and the sitting of the second in September 1656 changed the political landscape. During this period the 'army interest' strengthened its already dominant position within the Protector's council at Whitehall,[19] with the most conspicuous example of their influence being the establishment of the major-generals scheme throughout England and Wales, as a reaction to the royalist rising of the spring of 1655. This increase in military influence not only caused tensions with the country gentry, it also encouraged alternative schemes in Scotland and Ireland, where the respective governors, Lord Broghill and Henry Cromwell, were intent on reducing the power of the army and establishing civilian government reliant on the traditional landowners. Their reforms met with a frosty reception in the English council, which oversaw Scottish and Irish policy, and even before the Parliament sat in September 1656 there were signs that the 'civilian' and 'military' approaches to government were incompatible. As the second Protectorate Parliament continued, it became increasingly apparent that the old 'court party' had split into two rival camps, which might be termed the 'civilian' and 'army' interests.[20]

THE CIVILIAN INTEREST

For a brief period at the beginning of the second Protectorate Parliament it looked as if the court party might still hold together.[21] In September 1656, both the civilians and the army officers supported the controversial exclusion from the Commons of suspected royalists and perceived enemies of the regime, and they were also united on the need to continue the war with Spain.[22] But there were soon indications that a coherent civilian interest group was beginning to break away. They were led by a small group of

---

[17] Burton, I, xxvi.   [18] Burton, I, xxxv.

[19] Carol Egloff, 'The Search for a Cromwellian Settlement: Exclusions from the Second Protectorate Parliament', *Parl. Hist.*, 17 (1998), 193, 195.

[20] Carol Egloff, 'Settlement and Kingship: The Army, the Gentry, and the Offer of the Crown to Oliver Cromwell' (Ph.D thesis, Yale University, 1990), pp. 236, 298–9. There were signs of this split long before the winter of 1656–7: see Little, *Broghill*, chapter 4.

[21] See Egloff, 'Exclusions', 303.

[22] Egloff, 'Exclusions', 190, 303; *Clarke Papers*, III, 75; see chapter 11.

perhaps a dozen men, whose names are repeatedly mentioned during the winter and spring of 1656–7. In November 1656, 'five great persons' – probably Sir Charles Wolseley, Edward Montagu, Philip Jones, Oliver St John, and Lord Broghill – openly promoted a hereditary succession and opposed the 'exorbitances' of the army.[23] In January 1657, the attack on the militia bill, which sought to perpetuate the rule of the major-generals in the localities, was mounted by civilian courtiers such as Broghill and his ally, the Irish member, William Jephson, Secretary Thurloe, John Claypole, and Bulstrode Whitelocke, working with disgruntled Presbyterians.[24] A similar group promoted the offer of the crown to Cromwell, under the Remonstrance, in February. Some contemporaries identified the leading lights as Broghill and John Glynne, possibly joined by Whitelocke,[25] while the Coventry member, Robert Beake, was certain that the kingship originated with a 'cabal' made up of four civilian councillors and three non-councillors: Nathanial Fiennes, Wolseley, Montagu, and Jones, and Broghill, Thurloe, and the lord chief justice, John Glynne.[26] When it was debated in the House, early champions of the new constitution included councillors such as Jones, Montagu, Wolseley, and Fiennes,[27] but the passage of the new constitution was managed by non-councillors, notably Lord Broghill. Broghill's 'prudent and dextrous deportments in the House'[28] were crucial in arranging compromises – especially over the religious articles – which ensured the support of the Presbyterian majority in the Commons. He also played an important role in marshalling the votes of the Irish and Scottish members, and the final massive majority in favour of the kingly constitution (renamed the Humble Petition and Advice) on 25 March was a testament to the effectiveness of the coalition built up over the previous few weeks. When Cromwell declined to accept the Humble Petition in its monarchical form on 31 March, the 'royal party' (as it had become known) was 'highly discontented';[29] those who absented themselves from the Commons in protest included such prominent civilians as 'Lord Broghill, Sir Charles Wolseley [and] Lord Chief Justice [Glynne]'.[30] In Broghill's absence, the management of debates was taken on

---

[23] BL, Lansdowne MS 821, fo. 250r; Egloff, 'Settlement and Kingship', p. 296.
[24] For these speeches, see *TSP*, V, 786–8 (but cf. Egloff, 'Settlement and Kingship', p. 225); Bodl., MS Tanner 52, fo. 186r–v; Surrey History Centre, Loseley MS LM/1331/56; Burton, I, 230–43, 310–19; see also Bodl., MS Carte 228, fo. 83r–v; Christopher Durston, *Cromwell's Major-Generals: Godly Government during the English Revolution* (Manchester, 2001), chapter 10.
[25] Ludlow, II, 20–1; Egloff, 'Settlement and Kingship', pp. 314–16.
[26] Coventry City Archives, BA/H/Q/A79/302 (Robert Beake to Leonard Piddock, 28 March 1657). This document is published in Carol Egloff, 'Robert Beake and a Letter Concerning the Humble Petition and Advice, 28 March 1657', *HR*, 68 (1995), 233–9.
[27] BL, Lansdowne MS 821, fo. 294v.   [28] BL, Lansdowne MS 821, fo. 326r–v.
[29] Bodl., MS Carte 228, fo. 84r.   [30] BL, Lansdowne MS 822, fo. 29r.

by John Thurloe, who used his position as secretary of state and spymaster to good effect.[31] But even his labours were to be in vain; and Oliver's rejection of the crown on 8 May caused Thurloe and many other civilians to 'hang down their heads'.[32] In the last weeks of the Parliament, Thurloe was again prominent, urging on the financial bills and the Additional Petition and Advice which had to be passed before the sitting was adjourned on 26 June.[33]

The ability of the civilian interest to manage the 1658 sitting was hampered by the absence through illness of Thurloe, whose 'presence in time had prevented much of what happened amiss', and by the promotion of Broghill to the Other House, where he found his ability to manage the Commons severely restricted.[34] Broghill's predicament was shared by the eight other leading civilian courtiers, who had been appointed to an upper chamber which had yet to be recognised by the Commons.[35] Faced with a hostile Lower House, Cromwell was forced to bring the Parliament to a premature end on 4 February 1658. The problem of the secondment of leading courtiers to the Other House continued in the 1659 Parliament, and many of the most prominent courtiers again had little influence at Westminster, even though Richard Cromwell still relied on their advice in private.[36] Although contemporaries routinely referred to 'the court party' in the Commons in 1659,[37] once again the meaning of the term had shifted. Of the old civilian courtiers, only Thurloe was still in the Commons; although he was ably assisted by members such as the Scottish councillor, Samuel Disbrowe, the solicitor-general, William Ellis, and the Presbyterian (and now the Protector's sergeant-at-law), John Maynard, none of these had the standing of English councillors, and there seems to have been little of the teamwork that had characterised the court's involvement in Parliament in 1654–5 or 1656–7.[38] Thurloe was undoubtedly an important spokesman for the Protector in the 1659 Parliament,[39] introducing the bill of recognition of the government,[40] taking part in the management of financial matters and foreign policy,[41] and acting as

[31] *CJ*, VII, 521–2, 524; Burton, II, 2–4, 22, 32, 36, 42–3, 44, 88, 91.

[32] BL, Lansdowne MS 822, fo. 75r.   [33] Burton, II, 259, 289, 296, 306.

[34] *TSP*, VI, 762, 768, 775.

[35] Broghill, Claypole, Fiennes, Glynne, Jones, Montagu, Pierrepont, St John, Whitelocke, Wolseley.

[36] See Ivan Roots, 'The Debate on "the Other House" in Richard Cromwell's Parliament', in Richard Ollard and Pamela Tudor-Craig, eds., *For Veronica Wedgwood these Studies in Seventeenth-Century History* (1986), pp. 190–1.

[37] Bodl., MS Clarendon 60, fo. 61r; Guizot, *Richard Cromwell*, I, 307, 316.

[38] For the 'court' party, see Austin Woolrych, 'Historical Introduction', in R. W. Ayers, ed., *The Complete Prose Works of John Milton*, vol. VII (New Haven and London, 1980), p. 16.

[39] BL, Lansdowne MS 823, fo. 279r; see also Ludlow, II, 54–5.   [40] *TSP*, VII, 605.

[41] [Slingsby Bethel,] *A True and Impartial Narrative* (1659), p. 7; Burton, IV, 365–7, 383; see chapter 11.

teller on crucial divisions over the future of the Scottish and Irish MPs and the Other House.[42] But Thurloe's role could often be secondary, even in crucial matters such as foreign affairs, which he had controlled in 1656–7. In 1659 he introduced foreign business into the Commons, but then played no part in the debate until the very end, leaving the argument to be won by others.[43] Thurloe's weakened position made him vulnerable to increasingly vicious personal attacks from the commonwealthsmen.[44] Furthermore, as the session continued, effective control of policy began to fall into others' hands.

THE ARMY INTEREST

In December 1656 one commentator wrote of 'the council and army men' as if they formed one integrated interest group,[45] and it is true that the 'army interest' was led by powerful soldier-councillors – John Lambert, Charles Fleetwood, John Disbrowe, and William Sydenham – supported by non-military allies, Sir Gilbert Pickering and Walter Strickland. Despite its strength in the council at this time, the army's influence over the government as a whole was about to be challenged. The great test case was the militia bill, introduced by John Disbrowe on 25 December, which would decide the future of the major-generals. Unsurprisingly, the bill was debated with much heat by 'the major-generals' party', led by John Lambert.[46] The stakes were high. As one contemporary put it, 'the soldiers and their friends are for it and if I may speak plain I guess it is to keep up the reputations of the major-generals, and so a revolution feared'.[47] When it came to the vote whether or not to proceed with the militia bill, senior officers acted as tellers,[48] and when the bill was 'cast out … many of the major-generals etc. complained to his highness how much the House … discouraged the godly'.[49] The Protector's cool reaction to such pleas suggested that the influence of the civilian courtiers in Cromwell's counsels was growing stronger. The defeat of the militia bill in January 1657 not only destroyed the rule of the major-generals in the localities, it also forced the army interest at Westminster on to the back foot.

Proposed changes to the Protectoral Constitution also worried the army interest. Major-General Berry and John Disbrowe, supported by Pickering, were among those who argued against hereditary succession when it was first raised by the civilian courtiers in November 1656.[50] When the civilian

---

[42] *CJ*, VII, 616, 619, 621.
[43] The key figures were John Maynard, John Swinfen, and Sir Richard Onslow: see Burton, III, 376–84, 461–5, 471–2, 477–80, 481–93.
[44] Bodl., MS Clarendon 60, fos. 135r, 152r–v.   [45] Bodl., MS Carte 228, fo. 81r.
[46] *TSP*, VI, 20–1.   [47] Bodl., MS Carte 74, fo. 22r.
[48] *CJ*, VII, 483.   [49] *TSP*, VI, 37.
[50] BL, Lansdowne MS 821, fo. 250r–v; Bodl., MS Carte 74, fo. 47r.

courtiers introduced the Remonstrance in February 1657, the tellers against discussing it were Sydenham, Strickland, and Lambert, and Lambert's ally, Luke Robinson.[51] In the initial debates on the Remonstrance, it was noted that Lambert, Disbrowe, Sydenham, Fleetwood, Walter and Sir William Strickland, Pickering, and another Lambert associate, Adam Baynes, were all opposed to it, along with Colonels Thomas Cooper, John Hewson, and Jerome Sankey and the Yorkshire members who followed Lambert.[52] This was a well-defined, and widely feared, political grouping. Critics persisted in calling it 'the major-generals and their party' long after January 1657,[53] while its supporters spoke of it as representing the 'interest of the saints' or 'interest of the people of God'.[54] Neither the army nor the saints had ever been a popular group, either in the country or in Parliament, and in 1657 the army interest could not command enough votes to prevent the introduction of the new monarchical constitution, or its progress from Remonstrance to Humble Petition. As Thurloe reported in March 1657, 'Lambert and his party opposeth very much, but without any effect in the House.'[55] In an admission of this, after their initial protest in February, the leaders of the army interest withdrew from the Commons,[56] and looked to use their influence elsewhere.

The power of the army interest was dependent on two factors: their intimate relationship with Oliver Cromwell and their authority, as senior officers, over the army itself. The latter worried its opponents, who were mindful of the military violence used against the Parliament in 1647, 1648, and 1653. Meetings of officers caused nervousness among the civilian courtiers and their allies. 'A meeting of 30 officers' at Wallingford House, the seat of Charles Fleetwood, in November 1656 had 'resolved vigorously to oppose a settlement', leaving the civilian leaders much alarmed.[57] The defeat of the militia bill in January 1657 brought threats from the army leaders, who warned Cromwell that they would not co-operate with other legislation; and it was noted that, in the debates on raising money for the Spanish war, 'those that were for the decimation bill ... were exceeding cold'.[58] Immediately after the Remonstrance was introduced into the Commons on 23 February, there were reports that 'the soldiery are against it in the House [and] without doors';[59] Thurloe feared that 'Lambert will, if it can be done, put the army into a distemper';[60] and another commentator noted, with concern, that 'Lambert and all the major-generals violently oppose it.'[61]

[51] *CJ*, VII, 496.   [52] BL, Lansdowne MS 821, fo. 294r–v; see also *TSP*, VI, 74, 93.
[53] BL, Lansdowne MS 821, fo. 364r; see also *ibid.*, MS 822, fos. 3r, 11v, 29r; *Clarke Papers*, III, 91.
[54] BL, Lansdowne MS 822, fos. 15r, 41r.   [55] *TSP*, VI, 93.   [56] Bodl., MS Carte 228, fo. 84v.
[57] BL, Lansdowne MS 821, fo. 250r.   [58] *TSP*, VI, 37.
[59] *Clarke Papers*, III, 91.   [60] *TSP*, VI, 74; BL, Egerton MS 2618, fo. 51r (24 February 1657).
[61] Bodl., MS Tanner 52, fo. 197v.

The 'officers of the army' were prominent agitators against the new constitution, and the group that confronted Oliver Cromwell in the famous interview on kingship on 27 February included both members and non-members.[62] Senior officers lobbied Cromwell assiduously during April and early May.[63] The threat of mutiny within the army, as well as noises by Lambert, Fleetwood, Disbrowe, and 'other officers of quality' that they would resign their commands if kingship were accepted, may have played its part in influencing the Protector in his rejection of the offer of the crown in May 1657.[64]

Despite their public expressions of satisfaction at Cromwell's decision, the army interest was still not comfortable with the amended Humble Petition, and criticised the Protectoral version as being too close to a monarchical structure.[65] Their disappointment with the Humble Petition was the first step in gradual distancing of the army interest from the Protectorate. The signs were already there in April 1657, when the moderate army officer, Edward Whalley, told Henry Cromwell that unless a compromise could be found over the constitution, they would have 'only this bad expedient left us, to dissolve into a commonwealth, which many aim at, but I hope their expectation will be frustrated'.[66] Cromwell's sacking of Lambert from his civil and military offices in July 1657 did not cause an immediate mutiny in the army; its effects were longer term, and more subtle. Lambert's fate came as a reminder to other members of the army interest, especially Fleetwood and Disbrowe, that their own positions were also insecure.[67] For the time being, however, the army interest still publicly supported the Protectorate, and in 1657–8 the ailing Oliver Cromwell allowed the senior officers to retain a degree of power over the central government. Fleetwood, Disbrowe, Sydenham, and their allies remained in the council, whereas civilians such as Broghill and Whitelocke were frozen out. The Other House, chosen by Oliver in December 1657, included many senior officers,[68] and when it reconvened in Richard's Parliament in 1659 there were complaints that it was a military chamber, not a proper House of Lords. Those kicked upstairs included Fleetwood, Pickering, Disbrowe, Sydenham, the two Stricklands, Berry, and Hewson. The army also returned a number of important officers to the Commons in 1659, including Lambert and his sidekick, Adam Baynes, who were veterans of the faction-fighting of 1657, and remained implacable enemies of the Protectorate and the Humble Petition.[69] There were fears that

---

[62] *TSP*, VI, 93; BL, Lansdowne MS 821, fo. 312r; see also *Clarke Papers*, III, 92.
[63] *TSP*, VI, 281.   [64] *TSP*, VI, 219, 261, 281.
[65] See especially Thurloe's comment: *TSP*, VI, 310–11.
[66] BL, Lansdowne MS 822, fo. 49r (14 April 1657).
[67] Pickering was another rumoured to be prepared to refuse his oath as a councillor: see TNA, SP 78/113, fo. 261r.
[68] *TSP*, VI, 745, 753.   [69] See, for example, Burton, IV, 124, 175.

Fleetwood, Disbrowe, and 'that gang' would again cause trouble, both inside and outside Parliament,[70] and, sure enough, the army interest began to 'renew their old practice of remonstrating' soon after the opening of the 1659 Parliament.[71] The resulting situation was extremely volatile, as 'these divisions [in the Commons] were not confined within the walls of that House, but broke out in the army itself, the officers everywhere discovering their jealousies, one of another'.[72]

There was a new twist, however. In 1657 the army interest was opposing changes to the Protectorate from within; by 1659 it was increasingly willing to work with the enemies of the Protectorate, the republican commonwealthsmen, in both Houses. The first signs of this development could be seen as early as January 1658, when it was reported that 'Lambert and Hesilrige ... have made they say a strong party',[73] but it was only in Richard's Parliament that this new political configuration began to have a political impact. As the royalist agent John Barwick noted on 16 February 1659, 'the republicans reckon on 12 colonels (now in command) that will be for them, and 6 of them at least are of that [the Other] House'. He also reported that leading figures, including the Protector's powerful brother-in-law, Charles Fleetwood, had 'fallen off to the republicans'.[74] During this Parliament, Richard Cromwell had to intervene repeatedly to keep the army councils in order,[75] and in March it was reported that a new 'congregation' had been set up in London, led by the disaffected Independent divine, Dr John Owen, and including among its members Lambert, Fleetwood, Disbrowe, and other senior officers.[76] By mid-April, there were warnings that members would soon have a stark choice: 'you will either have a commonwealth, or Disbrowe instead of Cromwell'.[77] When the Commons, dominated by Presbyterian critics of the army, voted to dissolve the general council of the army and to cashier officers who opposed Parliament, the gauntlet was down. It was only a matter of time before the army once again intervened in parliamentary politics.

THE END OF THE CROMWELLIAN CONSENSUS

The rift between the civilian and military courtiers after 1656 had a dramatic effect on the balance of power within the Protectorate. The Protector's

---

[70] *TSP*, VII, 605, 612; see Woolrych, 'Historical Introduction', pp. 10–12.
[71] *TSP*, VII, 612; see also BL, Lansdowne MS 823, fos. 216r, 223r, 251r.   [72] Ludlow, II, 61.
[73] Bodl., MS Tanner 52, fo. 218r.   [74] Bodl., MS Clarendon 60, fos. 129v–130r.
[75] *Clarke Papers*, III, 182–3, 187; Guizot, *Richard Cromwell*, I, 306.
[76] Stephen, II, 158; BL, Lansdowne MS 823, fos. 251–2.
[77] Bodl., MS Clarendon 60, fo. 322v; see also *Clarke Papers*, V, 284.

council, which was expected to assist in the government of the country as well as to arrange the management of Parliament, was now split in two. This became apparent when the Remonstrance was debated in February 1657, as the council fell into distinct halves, with six members in favour and six against,[78] and it soon affected matters of less consequence as well.[79] Such a division made the co-ordination of parliamentary policy through the council almost impossible during the spring and summer of 1657. The declining political importance of the council was not only a reflection of this split, it was also a by-product of Oliver Cromwell's increasing willingness to seek advice from outside his council chamber. Even before the Remonstrance was unveiled, it was reported that two non-councillors, William Pierrepont and Oliver St John, 'have been often, but secretly, at Whitehall' to advise Cromwell.[80] The 'cabal' behind the Remonstrance was made up of non-councillors as well as councillors. An account of a private meeting in May 1657 to discuss 'great businesses' named five politicians as being closeted with Cromwell, only one of whom was a councillor.[81] The effect was to sideline the council when it came to parliamentary management, which was increasingly left to others, notably John Thurloe and (in 1657) Lord Broghill. The important players were those who commanded the loyalty of interest groups within the Commons. Broghill could call upon a solid phalanx of Irish and Scottish members (thanks to his Irish estates and his office as president of the Scottish council). Others with regional interests included Philip Jones and John Glynne, in south and north Wales respectively, and a professional interest group – the lawyers – which had by 1659 come under the leadership of a small clique loyal to the regime, including Attorney-General Prideaux, Solicitor-General Ellis, and the Presbyterian-turned-courtier, John Maynard, who was 'well assisted [in the House] by other gentlemen of the long robe'.[82] To lump these groups together as the 'kingship party' or 'court party' is to miss the distinctive influence of politics by coalition, which was both the cause and the effect of the polarisation of politics in the later 1650s. From 1657, the army interest, unable to win votes on its own, also began to look for support to a coalition of enemies of the Protectorate; in the same period, the civilian courtiers came increasingly to depend on the largest faction in the Commons, the Presbyterians.

---

[78] BL, Lansdowne MS 821, fo. 294v.
[79] In March 1657, when debating the Scottish Kirk, Fleetwood, Lambert, Pickering, and Strickland squared up to Fiennes, Jones, and Wolseley: see Stephen, II, 20; Little, *Broghill*, pp. 133–4.
[80] *TSP*, VI, 37.
[81] Whitelocke, *Diary*, p. 464 (Broghill, Pierrepont, Thurloe, Whitelocke, and Wolseley).
[82] Bodl., MS Clarendon 60, fos. 224r, 248r.

THE PRESBYTERIANS

Like the lawyers, the Presbyterians formed a large and amorphous group, which included moderate 'country' gentry and a wide range of trimmers and 'neuters'. Historians have been wary of this political group. Peter Gaunt emphasises that the blanket term 'Presbyterian' can be a misleading one, and he avoids its use.[83] Carol Egloff also counsels caution, saying that 'political Presbyterianism in the 1650s comprehended a wide range of opinion and behaviour, ranging from whole-hearted co-operation with the Protectoral system on the one hand to active opposition on the other', although she does not dismiss the term altogether.[84] J. T. Cliffe embraces the term with fewer qualms, partly because he chooses to define it broadly, as including those former Parliamentarians who were opposed to army rule and 'deeply concerned about the state of religion and more particularly the widespread anarchy which prevailed', although few were keen to introduce a truly Presbyterian church on the Scottish model.[85] With these considerations in mind, there are two good reasons for retaining the use of the word Presbyterian as an umbrella term for this, the largest group of members in the Protectorate Parliaments: it was a term widely used by contemporaries – who, for a change, seem to have used it fairly consistently – and it also reflects the fact that many of the leaders were old 'political Presbyterians', who had been staunchly loyal to Parliament during the first Civil War, but were then secluded from the Commons at Pride's Purge in December 1648. These men formed a tight circle, cemented by kinship, friendship, and religious ties, as well as by a shared ambivalence towards the Protectorate, and a bitter hatred of its predecessor, the Commonwealth.

In 1654–5, there is no doubt that the Presbyterians were the main opposition party, and they made it their business to dissect the Instrument of Government, seeking at each stage to reduce the power of the Protector and his council, and to promote Parliament as a bastion against oligarchy. The tellers in the important constitutional divisions were mostly drawn from a small group of men, including Sir Richard Onslow, John Birch, John Bulkeley, Sir John Hobart, and Sir Ralph Hare.[86] The leaders of this core group seem to have worked in teams, with Onslow and Birch acting together as tellers on important motions no fewer than six times.[87] The most active tellers, Birch, Bulkeley, and Onslow, were experienced members from the

---

[83] Gaunt, 'Oliver Cromwell and his Protectorate Parliaments', p. 89.
[84] Egloff, 'Exclusions', 313.
[85] J. T. Cliffe, *The Puritan Gentry Besieged* (1993), pp. 5–8.
[86] *CJ*, VII, 384, 385, 394, 403, 409, 413, 418, 419, 420, 421.
[87] *CJ*, VII, 384, 413, 414, 417, 421.

1640s who had been imprisoned after Pride's Purge,[88] and they were now joined by a number of new members who shared their distrust of the Protectorate, and also agreed that the religious toleration granted by the Instrument went too far. The result was a formidable and apparently well-organised party in the House, which was usually able to muster around 100 votes in the Commons, and therefore could challenge, and often defeat, the court interest. Oliver Cromwell's decision to dissolve the Parliament reflects the strength of this opposition to the government, and his angry speech was mostly aimed at the supposedly conservative Presbyterians: 'dissettlement and division, discontent and dissatisfaction, together with real dangers to the whole, has been more multiplied within these five months of your sitting, than in some years before'.[89]

The lingering resentment between the government and the Presbyterians was all too evident at the opening of the second Protectorate Parliament. As we saw in chapters 3 and 4, the biggest challenge to the major-generals in the parliamentary elections of 1656 came from the old Parliamentarian heart-lands, and it is significant that leading Presbyterians were excluded, including Birch, Bulkeley, and Hare. Yet there were some who were willing and able to take their places from the very beginning, and others who 'had formerly withdrawn themselves out of some discontent' would return to the Commons by the end of 1656.[90] Their identity can be seen in the debates during the winter of 1656–7. When the return of the excluded members was discussed in December, there was 'some heat in the House' between two leading Presbyterians, Thomas Bampfield and Lambert Godfrey, and the councillors Sir Gilbert Pickering and Walter Strickland. Bampfield and Godfrey were joined by Alexander Thistlethwaite in debate on 31 December, and all three questioned the legality of the exclusion.[91] The militia bill, introduced a few days before, was strongly opposed by the Presbyterians. Richard Hampden and Sir John Hobart opposed its introduction,[92] and dur-ing the debate that followed Bampfield, assisted by Francis Drake and John Trevor, led the attack on the bill, working closely with the civilians.[93] The militia bill marked an important factional shift, as the old tensions between the Presbyterians and the civilian courtiers were glossed over in their common opposition to military government as exemplified by the army-dominated council and the major-generals. The greatest passion in debate came from the Presbyterians, not the civilians, and personal 'exceptions' occurred

---

[88] David Underdown, *Pride's Purge: Politics in the Puritan Revolution* (Oxford, 1971), pp. 368–9, 381.
[89] Lomas–Carlyle, II, 409.   [90] Vaughan, II, 77.
[91] Burton, I, 290–1; Egloff, 'Exclusions', 308.   [92] *CJ*, VII, 475.
[93] Burton, I, 230–43, 310–19.

between James Ashe and John Disbrowe, and between Henry Cromwell (the Protector's cousin) and Major-General Boteler.[94] When motions were passed preventing a second reading of the bill and then rejecting it outright, the tellers were not civilian courtiers but leading Presbyterians, John Trevor, Henry Cromwell II, Francis Drake, and Griffith Bodurda.[95]

Carol Egloff is right to draw attention to the strong connection between 'anti-militarism' and the drive towards a 'pro-monarchical' settlement.[96] The Presbyterians were naturally inclined to support a return to the 'ancient constitution' of king, Lords, and Commons; and the initial divisions that ensured the Remonstrance was read in detail saw an alliance between civilians and Presbyterians, with Sir Charles Wolseley and John Fitzjames working together on 23 February, and Sir Richard Onslow and Philip Jones a day later. The majorities in favour were substantial.[97] The modified version of the Remonstrance, eventually presented as the Humble Petition and Advice at the end of March, was widely accepted and, through the efforts of Broghill and others, the Presbyterian majority remained committed to it, even though the religious and financial articles were still somewhat unpalatable. Bampfield and Thomas Grove were tellers against allowing a 'constant revenue' for the new monarch, and this vote was only narrowly carried by the civilian courtiers. The religious measures also needed careful management, and for men such as Onslow and Joachim Matthews this was the main obstacle.[98] Others hoped for further reforms in the future, and the loopholes and loose ends which made the Humble Petition so unsatisfactory as a constitution may have been crucial politically, in ensuring Presbyterian support in the Commons. As Robert Beake told his Coventry constituents at the end of March, the Humble Petition was to be welcomed despite its flaws: 'I can assure you there is much of English freedom in this constitution, and I would not have too much prejudice conceived against it upon account of religion, for though it be not provided for as it ought, yet the provision is better than what we have had.'[99]

Despite their doubts, the Presbyterians were among the strongest advocates of the new constitution. Eight of those readmitted after being excluded went on to vote for kingship on 25 March,[100] and Sir Richard Onslow,

---

[94] Bodl., MS Carte 228, fo. 88r.   [95] *CJ*, VII, 483.

[96] Egloff, 'Settlement and Kingship', pp. 7, 16, and *ibid.*, chapters 1 and 3 *passim*.

[97] *CJ*, VII, 496.

[98] See *CJ*, VII, 502, 504, where Grove and Bampfield act as tellers against religious settlement; and *ibid.*, 508–9, where Fitzjames and Markham oppose Wolseley and Thurloe; see also Little, *Broghill*, chapter 5; see chapter 2 in the present book for more about Onslow and Matthews.

[99] Coventry City Archives, BA/H/Q/A79/302: Beake to Leonard Piddock, 28 March 1657.

[100] Egloff, 'Settlement and Kingship', p. 93.

Richard Hampden, Francis Drake, Henry Cromwell II, Sir John Trevor, his son John, Francis and Nathanial Bacon, Robert Beake, John Fitzjames, and Griffith Bodurda were also among the kinglings.[101] Others needed to be convinced. During the debates that followed Cromwell's equivocal reaction to the original Humble Petition, in April and early May, some Presbyterians, led by Bampfield and Trevor, pushed for further safeguards on the monarch, with Parliament having a greater say over the nomination of officers and control of the revenue; they were joined by Thistlethwaite, Godfrey, Hobart, and Bodurda in pushing for changes in the religious articles.[102] Such measures were not a rejection of the new constitution, rather a call for further modification. Indeed, the Presbyterians in general were firmly in favour of a monarchical settlement. When Cromwell rejected the crown on 8 May, prominent Presbyterians such as Bodurda and John Goodwin led the protests in the Commons;[103] Richard Hampden, Sir John Hobart, and John Trevor were reported to be 'very angry';[104] and Thurloe feared 'the country gentlemen … being under great discouragement and discontent, it is very probable many of them will be gone', jeopardising the pro-civilian majority in the Commons.[105] Thurloe's pessimism was not proved correct, however. In later debates, the Presbyterian interest proved robust in its defence of the Humble Petition, even while attempting to modify parts of it (especially the religious clauses) to their taste. Indeed, in June 1657 it was a section of the Presbyterian party (now characterised as 'Bampfield, Godfrey, Grove and their gang') which was seen as the most bitter enemy of the army interest in the Commons.[106]

After the 1654–5 session, the Presbyterians had been abused and excluded; after the 1656–7 sitting, they were honoured. Bitter critics from 1654–5, such as Onslow and Hobart, were now appointed to the Other House that they had helped to create, and many of those excluded in 1656 (including Thomas Gewen, John Birch, John Maynard, and John Bulkeley) were active supporters of the regime nine months later.[107] By 1659, even those, such as John Swinfen, who had refused to take office in the early years of the Protectorate, were now willing to sit as members of Parliament, and to defend the government against the republicans and their military allies.[108] Whether through the promise of preferment (as some contemporaries suggested)[109] or the recognition that the regime was softening its line towards

---

[101] *A Narrative of the Late Parliament* (1657), pp. 22–3; see also Egloff, 'Exclusions', 317.
[102] Burton, II, 22, 28, 33–4, 51, 54.   [103] BL, Lansdowne MS 822, fo. 71r.
[104] BL, Lansdowne MS 822, fo. 75r.   [105] *TSP*, VI, 281.
[106] BL, Lansdowne MS 822, fo. 84r.
[107] Egloff, 'Exclusions', 317; Cliffe, *Puritan Gentry Besieged*, p. 21.
[108] For Swinfen, see *ODNB*; see also Roots, 'The Debate on "the Other House"', p. 197, and Stephen, II, 156.
[109] Guizot, *Richard Cromwell*, I, 319.

them and their concerns, under Richard Cromwell the Presbyterians were no longer merely 'prepared to support whatever in the present government stood for social order and political moderation'[110] – they had become active supporters of the Protectorate. They still had problems with the Humble Petition, but these were minor compared with the threat posed by the commonwealthsmen in the Parliament and the army without, and Richard, who lacked his father's close association with the army and the sectaries, was worth supporting.[111] On 29 January 1659, John Fitzjames summed up the Presbyterian attitude: 'our eyes are all upon the Parliament now, and from there, we expect ease, and peace and plenty and all sorts of blessings, and what not'.[112]

In the Commons, the Presbyterians led the defence of the Protectorate against the republican commonwealthsmen. As one commentator put it, 'most Presbyterians, amongst whom Swinfen, Birch, Knightley, Godfrey, Bampfield, [and] Grove are chief ... to avoid the hazard of casting matters into the hands of the republican party, or of being brought under the cavalier power, do sway to the Protector's party'.[113] An analysis of tellers for important votes confirms the importance of the Presbyterians to the court interest, with old stagers such as Bodurda, Bulkeley, Hampden, Birch, Grove, Trevor, Swinfen, and Nathaniel Bacon all turning out to support the government line.[114] In the crucial division on 18 April, banning any meetings of army officers without express permission, the tellers were Hugh Boscawen and Edward Rossiter – both of whom had been Presbyterians in the 1640s – and it was passed by 163 votes to 87.[115] In the early weeks of this Parliament, Sergeant John Maynard – a political Presbyterian from the 1640s who had been imprisoned for opposing the government (and questioning its legitimacy) during Cony's case in 1655, and was subsequently excluded in 1656 – was probably the government's most active parliamentary manager in the Commons, eclipsing even Secretary Thurloe.[116]

Contemporary reports underline the importance of the Presbyterians in debate. Thomas Burton identifies John Trevor, George Starkey, Francis Drake, and others as defenders of the Humble Petition, with Starkey even describing the new constitution as 'the ark that has preserved us in the deluge

---

[110] Woolrych, 'Historical Introduction', p. 17.
[111] See, for example, Guizot, *Richard Cromwell*, I, 285.
[112] Alnwick, Northumberland MS 552, fo. 71v.   [113] Stephen, II, 156.
[114] *CJ*, VII, 603–41. There were some exceptions, notably Thomas Gewen, who remained a critic of the regime: see Burton, III, 181; *ibid.*, IV, 23.
[115] *CJ*, VII, 641.
[116] [Bethel,] *Narrative*, p. 8; Vaughan, I, 176; Whitelocke, *Diary*, p. 489; *Clarke Papers*, III, 40. According to Sir John Gell, Maynard even claimed (on 28 February 1659) that 'the Protector is king as to all intents and purposes' (Schilling, p. 135).

of anarchy and confusion'.[117] Other sources agree. On 8 February it was reported that, when the recognition of Richard Cromwell had been debated, the commonwealthsmen had been 'briefly and fully answered by Mr Bulkeley, Major Beake and Serjeant Maynard',[118] and the motion was 'urged by Mr Trevor, Birch, Swinfen, with many lawyers and a great many ayes', with Godfrey, Bulkeley, and Grove joining in the debate.[119] On 15 February Robert Beake himself reported to Henry Cromwell the success of the vote on the Recognition, carried by a majority of 110, which had been opposed by the commonwealthsmen, with 'the Presbyterians with vigour driving the other way'. When it came to the status of the Other House, the Presbyterians were also prepared to support the government with 'the addition of some Lords'.[120] The question of the old peers being admitted to the Other House was divisive, as it was a conscious step to return Parliament to its pre-1649 form, but the vote was carried by a cadre of Presbyterians, led by Maynard and Birch, as well as 'Mr Bulkeley, Mr Grove, Mr Swinfen, Mr Bampfield, [and] Mr Godfrey', who 'fell in with the court party', and influenced the outcome.[121]

By this stage, an important development was apparent. As the court party in the Commons contracted, the Presbyterians seem to have become important not just in winning votes, but in formulating policy and managing it in the House. This can be seen in the gradual sidelining of the leading court spokesman, Secretary Thurloe. In the foreign policy debates of February 1659, Thurloe's role as manager was apparently taken over by Maynard, Onslow, and Swinfen, among others.[122] In the same month, Thurloe apparently lost the confidence of the House when he was the only member to oppose moves to 'bound the powers of the chief magistrate' in the recognition bill.[123] In the debates on the Other House in March, the Presbyterians forced the acceptance of the old peers, leaving Thurloe to opine that he 'liked not the addition, but could not tell how to help it, unless to bring in confusion by the loss of the question'.[124] Increasingly, the Presbyterians, not Thurloe and the civilian courtiers, were calling the shots. This takeover was disconcerting, but it did not lead to an attack on the Protectorate – quite the

---

[117] Burton, III, 72, 349, 510; not all Presbyterians were so positive: see Bulkeley's comments *ibid.*, IV, 55–6, 61–2; see also Jason Peacey, 'The Protector Humbled: Richard Cromwell and the Constitution', in Patrick Little, ed., *The Cromwellian Protectorate* (Woodbridge, 2007), pp. 32–52.

[118] BL, Lansdowne MS 823, fo. 212r.

[119] BL, Lansdowne MS 823, fo. 231v; according to Sankey (*ibid.*, fo. 232r), Godfrey and Bampfield had refused to take the oath on taking their seats.

[120] BL, Lansdowne MS 823, fo. 221r.

[121] BL, Lansdowne MS 823, fo. 247v; Bodl., MS Clarendon 60, fo. 209r–v.

[122] See Burton, III, 461–5, 471–2, 477–80.   [123] *CJ*, VII, 603; [Bethel,] *Narrative*, sig. A3–4.

[124] BL, Lansdowne MS 823, fo. 247v.

opposite. At the end of March, votes on the continued sitting of Irish and Scottish MPs and on the viability of the Other House were passed by large majorities thanks to Presbyterian support, and when, on 29 March, Sir Henry Vane questioned whether the present assembly was indeed a Parliament, he was 'called to the bar' not by a courtier but by a leading Presbyterian, Thomas Grove, seconded by John Bulkeley.[125] Money matters had always been a cause of concern for the Presbyterians, but in this Parliament the excise bill was introduced by Bulkeley, and championed in debate not only by Thurloe but also by Birch, Swinfen, and other Presbyterians.[126] By doing this, the Presbyterians were once again pushing issues further than the courtiers were comfortable with. Birch's aggressive stance when dealing with army pay arrears (which the excise was designed to tackle) certainly contrasted with attempts at conciliation made by Thurloe, and by Richard Cromwell himself;[127] and when the Commons moved against the army council on 18 April, the harshest criticism of the military came from Swinfen, Maynard, and Birch.[128] This deliberate, and dangerous, provocation of the army was not something that Thurloe and the other courtiers could countenance, and it serves to reinforce the impression that by April 1659 the Presbyterians in the Commons were not merely in the Protector's party – they had effectively hijacked it.[129]

THE COMMONWEALTHSMEN

Unlike the Presbyterians, the commonwealthsmen could not be lured from their opposition to the Protectorate government. Largely made up of old Rumpers and other republicans, their opposition to the Protectorate was principled and consistent from 1653 until 1659. The leaders were excluded in 1654 and 1656, but under the Humble Petition the government no longer had that luxury, and the commonwealthsmen returned in force in the brief, chaotic sitting of January–February 1658, their activities being responsible for its premature demise. In 1659 the commonwealthsmen were better organised and more effective in their relentless criticism of the regime.[130] Thurloe noted that Sir Henry Vane, Sir Arthur Hesilrige, Edmund Ludlow, Henry Neville, and Thomas Scott were the leaders of the commonwealth party.[131] Other commentators added to this list John Bradshaw and the former Cromwellian councillor, Sir Anthony Ashley Cooper, as well as a

---

[125] BL, Lansdowne MS 823, fo. 274r; Burton, IV, 294–5; Guizot, *Richard Cromwell*, I, 335.
[126] Burton, IV, 296–8, 312–15, 320–3, 383–6, 417, 419, 438; see chapter 10.
[127] Burton, IV, 383–4.
[128] Burton, IV, 450–1, 452, 455–6, 458, 460, 463; Schilling, pp. 160–1, 172, 176–7.
[129] *TSP*, VII, 647.   [130] Woolrych, 'Historical Introduction', pp. 16–17.
[131] *TSP*, VII, 588, 605.

small number of less prominent members.[132] Hesilrige, Vane, and their friends were men of great parliamentary experience and of political and rhetorical skill, bitterly opposed to the Protectorate and the Humble Petition and Advice, which they counted 'destructive to the liberties of the people'.[133] The weight of their experience made up for the 'republic party' being the 'weaker' in voting strength, and, as one contemporary reported, by the end of January it was clear that 'there will be two for one for confirming of the present settlement'.[134] This was no exaggeration. In mid-March it was calculated that there were only forty-seven 'true patriots of liberty' in the Commons,[135] and throughout this Parliament the commonwealthsmen did not win a single division.[136] Quality could help to counterbalance this lack of quantity, but only to an extent. As one contemporary put it, 'the republicans are the lesser party, but are all speakers, zealous, diligent, and have the better cause ... and yet the other can outvote them when they please'.[137] The need to reduce the voting strength of their enemies encouraged the commonwealthsmen to attack the Protector for cancelling the assizes (which would have taken the lawyer-members out of London), and to call for the sixty Scottish and Irish members to be removed from the Commons.[138] Both attempts failed, and on 25 March there were reports that 'the commonwealthsmen are silenced in the House' and 'hang down their heads'.[139]

Faced with the uncomfortable fact of their own impotence, the commonwealthsmen tried to discredit the Protector's advisers and thus disrupt attempts to manage the Commons. Vane and Hesilrige attacked Thurloe, casting aspersions on his character, and drawing parallels between him and Charles I's secretary of state, Sir Francis Windebanke.[140] Another effective tactic was filibustering. This is obvious from the pages of Burton's diary, which includes lengthy speeches by Hesilrige and Vane in particular, and from angry comments by their enemies.[141] Contemporaries saw delay and obfuscation as only two of many advantages enjoyed by the

---

[132] Bodl., MS Clarendon 60, fos. 98r, 248r; BL, Lansdowne MS 823, fo. 212r; Vane and Ludlow had refused to take the oath on sitting: see Lansdowne MS 823, fos. 221r, 247r.
[133] [Bethel,] *Narrative*, p. 5.
[134] *Clarke Papers*, III, 176; see also Bodl., MS Clarendon 60, fos. 61r, 119r; and Guizot, *Richard Cromwell*, I, 287, 300.
[135] Bodl., MS Clarendon 60, fo. 224r.　　[136] *CJ*, VII, 603–41.
[137] Bodl., MS Clarendon 60, fo. 129r; see also BL, Lansdowne MS 823, fo. 239r.
[138] The success of the latter would have allowed the commonwealthsmen 'to turn the scales and carry all clear before them' (Bodl., MS Clarendon 60, fo. 213v); see also BL, Lansdowne MS 823, fo. 261r; [Bethel,] *Narrative*, pp. 7, 9, 10.
[139] Bodl., MS Clarendon 60, fos. 254r, 256r. See also *ibid.*, fos. 275r, 279r, 292r, for similar comments.
[140] Bodl., MS Clarendon 60, fo. 152v. This is dated 15 February: see BL, Lansdowne MS 823, fo. 223r; see also Burton, III, 308–9; BL, Lansdowne MS 823, fo. 345r.
[141] BL, Lansdowne MS 823, fo. 212r.

commonwealthsmen.[142] On 12 February 1659, one royalist agent commented that 'Cromwell's friends' would have forced through the bill of recognition, 'but the republic men have given some stop to them, as by setting on foot petitions both here in the city and in the army'.[143] The connection between the commonwealthsmen and the army is an interesting one, as it relates not only to unrest among the radical junior officers at this time (who were rumoured to be in talks with the commonwealthsmen from mid-February)[144] but also to the alienation of the senior officers of the 'army interest' from the Protectorate. On certain issues the commonwealthsmen were openly supported in the Commons by John Lambert and Adam Baynes;[145] by mid-February not just Lambert but Fleetwood and Disbrowe were linked to the republican party;[146] and in early March it was reported that 'the commonwealth party are ... labouring to bring in the officer party to espouse their interest'.[147] Some believed the army's Remonstrance in April 'smells much of a commonwealth', and by the end of the month there was little doubt that the army officers favoured the 'commonwealth's men' above the 'Whitehall party'.[148] 'Reason or choler'[149] in the chamber could get the commonwealthsmen nowhere as long as the Protector's friends could muster a majority in the Commons; but the newly forged links with the army interest outside the House would prove far more damaging to the survival of the Protectorate, when push came to shove.

THE CRYPTO-ROYALISTS

As well as the army interest, in 1659 the commonwealthsmen were joined by another, more unlikely, ally: the crypto-royalist caucus in the Commons. This group, characterised as 'the sons and allies of old cavaliers with their proselytes',[150] was apparently awaiting an opportunity to emerge as champions of the Stuart cause when the time was right. Yet the identification of this group is difficult, and even royalist commentators seemed uncertain how to describe them and their political objectives. Although clearly considered to be 'the king's party',[151] in the early weeks of the Parliament they tended to side with the republicans in the House, 'thereby to endeavour the subversion

[142] Guizot, *Richard Cromwell*, I, 303.   [143] Bodl., MS Clarendon 60, fo. 116r.
[144] Bodl., MS Clarendon 60, fos. 135r, 209v.
[145] TSP, VII, 605; BL, Lansdowne MS 823, fo. 247r.
[146] TSP, VII, 612; see also Bodl., MS Clarendon 60, fos. 130r, 224v, 225r, 322v, 347v.
[147] Stephen, II, 157.   [148] Bodl., MS Clarendon 60, fo. 354r; TSP, VII, 662.
[149] Bodl., MS Clarendon 60, fo. 197r.
[150] Bodl., MS Clarendon 60, fo. 224r; for similar comments, see Ludlow, II, 60, and Schilling, p. 24.
[151] Bodl., MS Clarendon 60, fo. 119r.

of the present government, which cannot settle elsewhere without giving his majesty fair opportunity';[152] and some thought their support for the return of the 'old peers' to the Other House was a 'cloak' to 'carry Charles Stuart'.[153] As a result, they became known as 'hypocrite patriots' or 'counterfeit commonwealthsmen', as well as 'the cavaliers',[154] and there was probably a considerable overlap between them and the 'neuters' among the country gentry on the fringes of the Presbyterian interest. In addition, royalist agents were naturally reluctant to specify who these fifth columnists were. At the beginning of the 1659 Parliament there were only 'five or six that make scruple to sit unless they may have particular warrants from his majesty', although there were many others who did not require such safeguards.[155] Others calculated that they 'and such neuters as usually concur' ranged in strength from 100 to 140 members,[156] and Sergeant Maynard 'protested in the lobby with just indignation that he thought Charles Stuart had more friends in the House than the Protector'.[157] Among these wildly differing estimates, it is possible to identify at least the nucleus of a pro-Stuart group. Two unusually frank reports by a 'Mr Hancock', on 25 March and 10 April, named names. In the first, he mentioned a few 'of these men', led by Lord Falkland ('by many degrees the most eminent in zeal and forwardness'), and including John Howe, Sir Horatio Townshend, Edward Hungerford, and 'others of great estates'.[158] Later he again described Falkland as 'the most active young man in the House', while Howe, Townshend, Ralph Delaval, and 'young Morgan' were 'as forward but not so active', and Hungerford and Richard Howe were 'as honest, but not so forward'.[159] To these can be added a few others, such as Sir George Booth, John Hobart, and the renegade Irish member, Arthur Annesley.[160] As Hancock's reports suggest, the number of true royalists in the Commons was probably small; and, except as a satellite to the commonwealthsmen, their factional influence was correspondingly limited. Moreover, as the Parliament continued, there was no disguising the fact that the aims of the crypto-royalists and the commonwealthsmen were

---

[152] Bodl., MS Clarendon 60, fo. 61r–v; see also the comments in Roots, 'The Debate on "the Other House"', p. 194.
[153] BL, Lansdowne MS 823, fos. 245–6.   [154] Bodl., MS Clarendon 60, fos. 209r, 224r, 248r.
[155] Bodl., MS Clarendon 60, fo. 18r; see also fo. 22r for a Gloucestershire MP requiring warrant.
[156] Bodl., MS Clarendon 60, fo. 224r.   [157] Bodl., MS Clarendon 60, fo. 248r.
[158] Bodl., MS Clarendon 60, fo. 248r.
[159] Bodl., MS Clarendon 60, fo. 336v; Mabbott, for one, thought Falkland's arrival in the Commons as newsworthy as that of Sir Henry Vane: BL, Lansdowne MS 823, fo. 212v.
[160] Morgan told Henry Cromwell on 8 March 1659 that Annesley 'divides with the commonwealth' and was opposed to the Humble Petition: see BL, Lansdowne MS 823, fo. 346r. For Hobart, see Egloff, 'John Hobart'; John Hobart is not to be confused with his kinsman, the Presbyterian turned Cromwellian, Sir John Hobart (*ibid.*, 39).

fundamentally incompatible. In the middle of April 1659, as tensions over the army increased, Falkland, Hungerford, Annesley, and others could be seen joining the courtiers and Presbyterians against their former allies.[161] When it came to it, the crypto-royalists were not prepared to plunge the country into anarchy in the short term in the hope that the long-term result might be the return of the Stuarts. The emergence of a coherent royalist party at Westminster would have to wait until the more settled conditions of the spring of 1660.

CONCLUSION

Historians, often focusing on individual Parliaments during the Protectorate, or on those of one Protector and not the other, have tended to oversimplify or overcomplicate the factional history of the period. This present survey, which has taken the three Parliaments as a continuous political dialogue, suggests a pattern which is at once clear and complex. There were three basic factional groupings. First was the 'court' interest, made up of the supporters of Oliver Cromwell. In 1654–5 there seems to have been a united 'court', centred on the Protector's council, but during the 1656–7 sitting it split into antagonistic groups, which can be characterised (with some reservations) as the 'army' and 'civilian' interests. The rivalry between these two interests continued through to the 1659 Parliament, when the army came out in opposition to the Protectorate of Richard Cromwell. The civilian group was the larger and more diverse of the two, but it was more of a coalition than a party; and in divisions the 'courtier' leadership relied on bloc votes from Irish, Scottish, and Welsh members, the lawyers, and (increasingly) the Presbyterians. The Presbyterians formed the largest interest in the Commons. Its centre was made up of a close-knit group of veterans from the 1640s, who could usually count on support from a larger peripheral group which easily dominated the division lobbies in the Commons. Their power can be seen in all three Parliaments, whether in opposition to the Instrument of Government in 1654–5, in support of the Humble Petition in 1657, or in defence of the Protectorate in 1659. In the last, their most dangerous opponents were the commonwealthsmen – a small number of republicans ardently opposed to the Protectorate – but, like the civilian court interest, they could only come close to winning votes through an uneasy coalition with other groups: the crypto-royalists (who also stood to benefit from the collapse of the Protectorate) and, more importantly, the disgruntled army interest.

[161] Burton, IV, 448, 453, 456–7, 460–1.

Despite this pattern of central cores and peripheral groups, of coalitions and alliances, the various interests and factions were fairly consistent in their beliefs and desires. The army interest remained wedded to the 'good old cause', with military might guaranteeing civil and religious liberty. Whether such a scheme included government by a Protector and council was another matter. It was this question that divided them from the commonwealthsmen until 1658–9. The civilians and the Presbyterians both detested army involvement in politics, and (on the whole) were wary of religious radicalism. Their agreement from 1657 onwards was an acknowledgement of their similar views. The different groups were remarkably consistent in personnel and policies throughout the Protectorate, even though their factional alignments were constantly changing. And it was from the heart of these factions that the parliamentary managers emerged. Management was assumed by the council only in 1654–5 and the autumn of 1656; thereafter business was influenced by men associated with particular interest groups, such as Broghill, Thurloe, and Maynard, and it could be argued that they were (with varying degrees of subtlety and success) pushing for their own policies, rather than merely taking orders from the two Protectors. The nature of factionalism and political management in this period seems to be far more complex than Trevor-Roper or Godfrey Davies have suggested, but far clearer than the chaotic alternative provided by more recent historians.

The basic factional dynamic during the Protectorate Parliaments – the gradual alienation of the army, and the growing alliance between the Presbyterians and the civilian court – reflected changes in the Protectorate as a whole. The regime established in December 1653 was hardly a popular one, and measures such as the major-generals (introduced in 1655) were deeply resented throughout England, as the election results in 1656 show. From the summer of 1657, and the passing of the Humble Petition and Advice, the regime attained a degree of stability, even popularity, as civilian rule replaced the rule of the army in central and local government. This move towards stability did not come to an end with the death of Oliver Cromwell in September 1658. In fact, the succession of Richard was welcomed across the country, and by the Presbyterians in particular, as it broke the personal ties which had until recently bound the Protector and the army so closely together. In the words of Austin Woolrych,

Moderate men everywhere took hope that the new government would stand as a bulwark against all that they had most disliked in recent years – the power of the sword, the excesses of the saints, the meddling with private morality in the name of 'reformation of manners', the whole receding threat of social revolution.[162]

---

[162] Woolrych, 'Historical Introduction', p. 7.

The later 1650s did not witness a retreat to a conservatism that presaged a return of the Stuarts: it marked instead the growing confidence of a Protectoral government shorn of its unacceptable military connotations. Richard Cromwell's brother-in-law, Lord Fauconberg, was upbeat at the end of March, saying that in the Parliament and in the country as a whole, 'things seem to have a fairer temper than formerly, so that all sober, honest men begin now to renew their hopes of a settlement'.[163] The French ambassador had also registered this change of mood by the middle of April 1659: 'the court party are full of hope of a happy issue of all their designs'.[164] Contemporaries seem to have recognised that the Presbyterian dominance in Parliament in 1659 was only a symptom of a wider change throughout Protectoral Britain and Ireland, encouraged by Richard Cromwell and his civilian advisers. In the face of this, the republicans and royalists in Parliament could only disrupt and delay proceedings at Westminster; and the senior officers, led by Fleetwood, could only fall back on the threat of military force. The military coup of April 1659 was not proof of endemic weakness in the regime; it was an admission by the army grandees that there was no place for them in a new Presbyterian-influenced Protectorate.[165]

---

[163] BL, Lansdowne MS 823, fos. 272–3.   [164] Guizot, *Richard Cromwell*, I, 360.

[165] For a preliminary attempt to work these ideas through, albeit from a rather different angle, see Patrick Little, 'Year of Crisis or Turning Point? 1655 in its British Context', *Cromwelliana*, new series, 3 (2006), 28–43.

6

Oliver Cromwell and Parliaments

Oliver Cromwell's inability to achieve an effective working relationship with successive Parliaments during the 1650s remains one of the greatest ironies of the English Revolution. It was also a crucial reason why the English Republic failed to generate lasting political stability. This chapter will reconsider this problem and suggest that the principal difficulty lay in Cromwell's desire to use Parliament to reconcile the interests of the English nation as a whole with those of a godly minority (including himself) who embraced a radical religious agenda. He hoped that through Parliaments the nation and the godly people could become coterminous. His refusal to acknowledge the essential incompatibility of these two interests lay at the heart of his failure to find any Parliament that fulfilled his high hopes. This chapter will argue that the main reason for that failure ultimately lay in the incompatibility between the sort of reforms that Cromwell wanted Parliament to pursue – the vision of a godly commonwealth that he wished it to promote – and the attitudes and priorities of the majority of members of Parliament. Although, as Ivan Roots and Peter Gaunt have argued, and as is demonstrated elsewhere in this book, it is important not to overlook the legislative achievement of the Protectorate Parliaments, equally, their performance fell far short of what Cromwell desired.[1] Always he searched for a Parliament that would promote his vision of a godly commonwealth, and always it eluded him.

An earlier version of this chapter, 'Oliver Cromwell and the Protectorate Parliaments', appeared in Patrick Little, ed., *The Cromwellian Protectorate* (Woodbridge, 2007), pp. 14–31.

[1] Ivan Roots, 'Lawmaking in the Second Protectorate Parliament', in H. Hearder and H. R. Loyn, eds., *British Government and Administration: Essays Presented to S. B. Chrimes* (Cardiff, 1974), pp. 132–43; Peter Gaunt, 'Oliver Cromwell and his Protectorate Parliaments: Co-operation, Conflict and Control', in Ivan Roots, ed., *'Into another Mould': Aspects of the Interregnum* (2nd edn, Exeter, 1998), pp. 70–100; Peter Gaunt, 'Law-making in the First Protectorate Parliament', in Colin Jones, Malyn Newitt, and Stephen Roberts, eds., *Politics and People in Revolutionary England: Essays in Honour of Ivan Roots* (Oxford, 1986), pp. 163–86.

THE LONG PARLIAMENT

This failed quest reached its climax in the first and second Protectorate Parliaments of 1654–5 and 1656–8. But, to set that failure in context, we need first to examine briefly why Cromwell had earlier fallen out with the Long Parliament, in whose armies he had played such a critical role during the Civil Wars. He clearly believed in the justice of Parliament's cause against Charles I in that conflict. As he wrote to Colonel Valentine Walton in September 1644: 'We study the glory of God, and the honour and liberty of the Parliament, for which we unanimously fight, without seeking our own interests ... I profess I could never satisfy myself of the justness of this war, but from the authority of the Parliament to maintain itself in its rights; and in this cause I hope to approve myself an honest man and single-hearted.'[2] However, it is important to notice that even here Cromwell's loyalty to Parliament was not unconditional. He believed that it had a trust imposed upon it and that it should be held accountable, above all to God's cause and to the godly people. Parliament's responsibility to protect both liberty of conscience for the godly and the liberty of the whole nation became more explicit in a letter that Cromwell wrote to William Lenthall, Speaker of the House of Commons, on the evening of 14 June 1645, the day of the great Parliamentarian victory at Naseby. After insisting that 'this is none other but the hand of God, and to Him alone belongs the glory, wherein none are to share with Him', Cromwell told Lenthall: 'Honest men served you faithfully in this action. Sir, they are trusty; I beseech you in the name of God, not to discourage them. I wish this action may beget thankfulness and humility in all that are concerned in it. He that ventures his life for the liberty of his country, I wish he trust God for the liberty of his conscience, and you for the liberty he fights for.'[3] Parliament thus had an obligation not to betray the 'honest' people, a word that recurs in Cromwell's letters and speeches as a synonym for 'godly'.[4]

Cromwell's belief in the importance of that parliamentary obligation grew ever more apparent during 1647–8, as Parliament struggled to reach a settlement with the King. Convinced that the worst possible outcome would be for Parliament to betray those who had fought for it by selling out to the King, Cromwell argued that it would be better if necessary to break

---

[2] Lomas–Carlyle, I, 181.
[3] Lomas–Carlyle, I, 204–5. The Commons ordered this passage to be omitted when the letter was printed, but Cromwell's allies in the Lords subsequently reinstated it in the version that they had privately printed. See Abbott, I, 360; *LJ*, VII, 433–4; and J. S. A. Adamson, 'Oliver Cromwell and the Long Parliament', in John Morrill, ed., *Oliver Cromwell and the Long Parliament* (Harlow, 1990), pp. 49–92, especially pp. 66–8.
[4] See, for example, Lomas–Carlyle, I, 146.

off negotiations with Charles by passing a Vote of No Addresses. On 3 January 1648 he made an impassioned speech in support of this vote, urging members of the Commons to 'look on the people you represent, and break not your trust, and expose not the honest party of the kingdom, who have bled for you, and suffer not misery to fall upon them for want of courage and resolution in you, else the honest people may take such courses as nature dictates to them'.[5] That strangely menacing final line raised the possibility of some very radical courses of action, although these were as yet left vague.

In Cromwell's eyes, the army's decisive victory in the second Civil War, culminating in its defeat of Scottish royalists at the battle of Preston in August 1648, gave Parliament both a divine mandate and a responsibility to bring the King to justice. Writing to the Speaker Lenthall the day after Preston, Cromwell described this latest victory as 'nothing but the hand of God ... for whom even Kings shall be reproved', and urged him to 'take courage to do the work of the Lord, in fulfilling the end of your magistracy, in seeking the peace and welfare of the people of this land, that all that will live quietly and peaceably may have countenance from you, and they that are implacable and will not leave troubling the land may speedily be destroyed out of the land'.[6] Cromwell and other army leaders were deeply disappointed when the Parliament instead resumed talks with the King on terms that were essentially unaltered since 1642. This frustration eventually prompted Colonel Pride's decisive intervention on 6 December 1648 when he excluded the more conservative members of the Commons and thus opened the way for setting up a special high court to try the King.

Historians have found Cromwell's behaviour in the closing weeks of 1648 and the beginning of 1649 deeply enigmatic. He carefully distanced himself from Pride's Purge, not arriving in London until after it was over, probably because he did not wish to be personally associated with such a breach of constitutional propriety. It is likely, as John Morrill and Philip Baker have recently argued, that he wanted Charles to be tried and to cease to be king, either by deposition or abdication, but that he hoped that an alternative short of executing him could be found.[7] Cromwell wanted the King brought to account, yet he was a reluctant regicide and he had no wish to see monarchy abolished. Once the King was dead, however, he did not resist the abolition of the monarchy as 'unnecessary, burdensome and dangerous to the liberty,

---

[5] David Underdown, ed., 'The Parliamentary Diary of John Boys', *Bulletin of the Institute of Historical Research*, 39 (1966), 156.
[6] Lomas–Carlyle, I, 343–4.
[7] John Morrill and Philip Baker, 'Oliver Cromwell, the Regicide and the Sons of Zeruiah', in Jason Peacey, ed., *The Regicides and the Execution of Charles I* (Basingstoke, 2001), pp. 14–35; reprinted in David L. Smith, ed., *Cromwell and the Interregnum* (Oxford, 2003), pp. 17–36.

safety, and public interest of the people', and of the House of Lords as 'useless and dangerous to the people of England'.[8] The ancient parliamentary trinity of Crown, Lords, and Commons was thus reduced to the purged remnant of the Commons, the Rump Parliament. This was the body, comprising barely seventy active members, which Cromwell hoped would now embrace the cause of godly reform.

THE RUMP AND BAREBONE'S

Once again, he was to be profoundly disappointed. He regarded his conquests of Ireland and Scotland during 1649–51 as further mandates from God. Yet, in his eyes, the Rump wholly failed to live up to its trust and to fulfil God's purpose. Cromwell's disillusionment deepened until in April 1653, convinced that the Rump was no longer 'a Parliament for God's people' and fearing that it intended to hold fresh elections without adequate safeguards to exclude the ungodly, he stormed down to Westminster and expelled it, protesting to members that 'you have sat too long here for any good you have been doing lately'.[9] Two days later he issued a declaration justifying his action and complaining that the Rump 'would never answer those ends which God, His people, and the whole nation expected from them'. Instead, 'this cause, which the Lord has so greatly blessed and borne witness to, must needs languish ... and, by degrees, be wholly lost; and the lives, liberties and comforts of His people delivered into their enemies' hands'.[10] Those words reveal much about his vision of Parliament and its role: in Cromwell's view, a Parliament that had committed 'an high breach of trust' against God and godly people could not be permitted to continue.[11] Furthermore, a 'more effectual means' had to be found to 'secure the cause which the good people of this Commonwealth had been so long engaged in, and to establish righteousness and peace in these nations'.[12] This last statement rested on an assumption that the advancement of the godly cause and the peaceful settlement of the whole nation were compatible, an assumption that ultimately turned out to be mistaken.

At that moment, immediately after his expulsion of the Rump Parliament, Cromwell probably wielded greater power than at any other stage of his career. Interestingly, he did not try to assume dictatorial powers but instead attempted to find another way towards a parliamentary settlement. Believing that the Rump had betrayed the godly, he now adopted Major-General Thomas Harrison's scheme of an assembly consisting exclusively of the

---

[8] Gardiner, *Constitutional Documents*, pp. 384–8 (quotations at pp. 385, 387).
[9] Lomas–Carlyle, II, 264–5.   [10] Gardiner, *Constitutional Documents*, p. 401.
[11] Lomas–Carlyle, II, 284.   [12] Gardiner, *Constitutional Documents*, p. 402.

godly. Modelled on the ancient Jewish Sanhedrin of saints, this body comprised 140 carefully selected godly souls, nominated by the radical religious congregations of London, and added to by the army council. This was a very different kind of assembly, unique in English constitutional history. Its members were nominated rather than elected (hence one name given to it, the Nominated Assembly); it consisted of a single chamber of 140 members, rather than the customary House of Commons which by 1640 contained 507 seats (hence another name, the Little Parliament); and it contained staunch Puritans, of whom one typical and prominent example was Praise-God Barebone (hence a third name, Barebone's Parliament).[13] The members were to be 'persons fearing God, and of approved fidelity and honesty'; people, as Cromwell would have put it, with 'the root of the matter' in them.[14]

Once again, his underlying hope was that the interests of the godly and of the whole nation could be reconciled. In his summons to members of Barebone's, Cromwell spoke in the same breath of their 'love to, and courage for, God and the interest of His cause, and of the good people of this Commonwealth'.[15] His opening speech to members on 4 July 1653 contained the following visionary call to them to embrace the trust that God had placed in them: 'Truly God has called you to this work by, I think, as wonderful providences as ever passed upon the sons of men in so short a time ... It's come, therefore, to you by the way of necessity; by the wise Providence of God ... God has owned you in the eyes of the world; and thus, by coming hither, you own Him ... Therefore, own your call!'[16] Interestingly, in this speech and elsewhere Cromwell never referred to Barebone's as a Parliament but rather as an 'assembly': he was surprised and disappointed when on its first full day of business it declared itself a Parliament, elected a Speaker, and restored the Rump's Clerk of the Parliament and Sergeant-at-Arms to their offices. Cromwell anticipated that Barebone's would sit no longer than 3 November 1654, and he apparently hoped that before the end of 1655 the people would be sufficiently settled to resume their right to elect regular Parliaments. He probably envisaged it less as a Parliament in itself than as an interim expedient to provide for a parliamentary settlement.[17] However, after less than six months, beset

---

[13] By far the most detailed study of Barebone's and its members is Austin Woolrych, *Commonwealth to Protectorate* (Oxford, 1982).

[14] Gardiner, *Constitutional Documents*, p. 405; Lomas–Carlyle, III, 121.

[15] Gardiner, *Constitutional Documents*, p. 405.   [16] Lomas–Carlyle, II, 290, 296.

[17] Austin Woolrych, *Britain in Revolution, 1625–1660* (Oxford, 2002), chapter 17; Woolrych, *Commonwealth to Protectorate*, pp. 144–53; Gardiner, *Commonwealth and Protectorate*, II, 283–9; David Farr, *John Lambert, Parliamentary Soldier and Cromwellian Major-General, 1619–1684* (Woodbridge, 2003), pp. 123–4.

by internal divisions, Barebone's dissolved itself and surrendered power back to Cromwell, who later referred to the episode as 'a tale of my own weakness and folly'.[18]

It was indicative of the constitutional ferment of these years that one of Cromwell's army colleagues, John Lambert, had already drafted an alternative constitution, the Instrument of Government, which was adopted on 16 December 1653.[19] Under its terms, Cromwell was appointed Lord Protector, an office he held until his death in September 1658. The central principle of this paper constitution was that 'the supreme legislative authority' should 'reside in one person, and the people assembled in Parliament'.[20] This constitutional arrangement, revealingly reminiscent of that which had existed under the monarchy, made the relationship between the Protector and Parliaments crucially important. Cromwell certainly wanted to rule with *a* Parliament. Throughout the Protectorate, he greeted each new Parliament with an optimistic welcome, such as his claim that the first Protectorate Parliament was 'a door of hope opened by God to us'.[21] He emphasised the solemn trust that God had placed in Parliament, and the awesome responsibility to God's cause and the godly people that this imposed on members: 'you have upon your shoulders the interests of three great nations with the territories belonging to them; and truly, I believe I may say it without any hyperbole, you have upon your shoulders the interest of all the Christian people in the world'.[22] Parliament had an absolutely crucial role to play, and Cromwell declared that 'it's one of the great ends of calling this Parliament that this ship of the Commonwealth may be brought into a safe harbour; which, I assure you, it will not well be, without your counsel and advice'.[23] But Cromwell was to be bitterly disappointed: his optimism turned to frustration when the Parliament, rather than embarking on the moral reforms for which he yearned, instead started tinkering with the Instrument of Government. The crux of the problem was that he wanted *a* Parliament but it had to be a Parliament *on God's terms.*

This in turn helps to explain why, although he was committed to Parliaments in principle, Cromwell did not feel committed to any individual Parliament. In his view, 'that Parliaments should not make themselves

[18] Lomas–Carlyle, III, 98.

[19] The full text of the Instrument of Government is printed in Gardiner, *Constitutional Documents*, pp. 405–17. For Lambert's role in drafting the Instrument, see Farr, *John Lambert*, pp. 124–45.

[20] Gardiner, *Constitutional Documents*, p. 405.   [21] Lomas–Carlyle, II, 340.

[22] Lomas–Carlyle, II, 339.   [23] Lomas–Carlyle, II, 358.

perpetual is a fundamental', and he asked: 'Of what assurance is a law to prevent so great an evil, if it lie in one or the same legislature to unlaw it again? Is this like to be lasting? It will be like a rope of sand; it will give no security, for the same men may unbuild what they have built.'[24] It was his principal grievance against the members of the Rump Parliament that they wished (or so he believed) 'to perpetuate themselves'.[25] Cromwell felt that 'a continual sitting of Parliaments' raised the hazard of 'a Parliament … executing arbitrary government without intermission, saving of one company, one Parliament, leaping into the seat of another just left warm for them; the same day that one left, the other was to leap in'. Cromwell thought that this was 'a pitiful remedy … and it will always be so when and whilst the legislative is perpetually exercised'.[26] To institute perpetual Parliaments was to run the risk of a Parliament assuming 'an absolute power without any control, to determine the interests of men in property and liberty'.[27]

Instead of a perpetual Parliament, Cromwell's criterion for a successful Parliament was whether it encouraged godliness in ways that would enable the godly people gradually to become coterminous with the nation as a whole. This meant pursuing both 'liberty of conscience and liberty of the subjects', and Cromwell called these 'two as glorious things to be contended for as any God has given us'.[28] He welcomed the Instrument of Government as a means of promoting *both* 'a just liberty to the people of God, *and* the just rights of the people in these nations'; and he insisted that he had no desire to retain the office of Lord Protector 'an hour longer than I may preserve England in its just rights, and may protect the people of God in … a just liberty of their consciences'.[29] The yoking together of these broad aims in the same breath affords an important insight into Cromwell's vision of Parliament's role. He wanted it to set a lead not only by promoting godly behaviour but also by extending 'liberty of conscience' broadly among Protestant groups. He regarded 'liberty of conscience' as 'a fundamental', and argued that: 'Liberty of conscience is a natural right; and he that would have it ought to give it … Liberty of conscience – truly that's a thing ought to be very reciprocal.'[30] This idea of reciprocal liberty of conscience recurs in Cromwell's speeches, and was very dear both to his heart and to those of many army officers.

---

[24] Lomas–Carlyle, II, 382.
[25] Lomas–Carlyle, II, 284. That Cromwell's belief was almost certainly mistaken is brilliantly unravelled in Blair Worden, *The Rump Parliament, 1648–1653* (Cambridge, 1974), chapters 15–17. For subtly different accounts, see Woolrych, *Commonwealth to Protectorate*, chapters 2–3; and Adamson, 'Oliver Cromwell and the Long Parliament', pp. 81–92.
[26] Lomas–Carlyle, III, 93–5.   [27] Lomas–Carlyle, III, 98.   [28] Lomas–Carlyle, II, 345.
[29] Lomas–Carlyle, II, 419 (emphasis added).   [30] Lomas–Carlyle, II, 382–3.

However, only a minority of members of the first and second Protectorate Parliaments were sympathetic to such a radical agenda, and most consistently regarded liberty of conscience as a much lower priority than the prevention of errors, heresies, and blasphemies, and the maintenance of public order. On 15 December 1654, for example, the first Protectorate Parliament resolved that any bills that it passed against 'atheism, blasphemy, damnable heresies, ... popery, prelacy, licentiousness, or profaneness' were to 'become laws, within twenty days after their presentation to the Lord Protector', even if he did not give his consent to them.[31] This remarkable clause formed part of the Parliament's attempts to define and curtail a number of Protectoral powers established in the Instrument of Government, and it directly obstructed Cromwell's promotion of liberty of conscience. The prevailing mood within Parliament was utterly at odds with the attitudes not only of Cromwell but also of many of his army colleagues who, in late 1654, presented a petition to him requesting that 'liberty of conscience be allowed', and that 'a law be made for the righting [of] persons wronged for liberty of conscience'.[32] Again and again, that conflict of outlooks caused Cromwell's high hopes of Parliament to be dashed. He and the Protectorate Parliaments needed each other, yet found it impossible to work together, and this aroused – on both sides – a mixture of mistrust, frustration, and bafflement. Cromwell's reactions and dilemmas were similar to those of someone in a relationship that they can neither break off nor make to work. Each time he met a new Parliament, he welcomed it in the hope that it might succeed where its predecessors had failed; but each time the mismatch between his priorities and those of the majority of members ensured that he was disappointed.

Cromwell's frustration and disappointment were most starkly evident in his periodic decisions to dissolve Parliament. In the case of the first Protectorate Parliament, he took this step at the earliest possible constitutional opportunity, after five *lunar* months rather than five *calendar* months, on 22 January 1655. The dissolution took members by surprise: Cromwell had allowed them to believe that the Parliament would last a minimum of five *calendar* months, until 3 February, and they were on course to present

---

[31] *CJ*, VII, 401. For a fuller discussion, see chapter 9 in the present book, and David L. Smith, 'Oliver Cromwell, the First Protectorate Parliament, and Religious Reform', *Parl. Hist.*, 19 (2000), 38–48. This article was reprinted in R. Malcolm Smuts and Arthur F. Kinney, eds., *Responses to Regicide* (Amherst, 2001), pp. 49–70; and also in Smith, *Cromwell and the Interregnum*, pp. 167–81.
[32] *To His Highness the Lord Protector, etc. and our General: The Humble Petition of Several Colonels of the army* (1654); *Clarke Papers*, III, 13; Vaughan, I, 80; Barbara Taft, 'The Humble Petition of Several Colonels of the army: Causes, Character, and Results of Military Opposition to Cromwell's Protectorate', *Huntington Library Quarterly*, 42 (1978–9), 15–41.

him with their bills on that day.[33] Instead, on 22 January he summoned members to the Painted Chamber and denounced them for getting side-tracked on constitutional issues and missing the chance to extend toleration of the godly. That would have involved challenging the natural instinct of many people to demand greater toleration for themselves than they were willing to extend to others, as well as imposing penalties upon the overtly ungodly. Yet the Parliament had, Cromwell claimed, 'done just nothing'.[34] In his peroration, Cromwell lamented that 'the Lord has done such things amongst us as have not been known in the world these thousand years, and yet notwithstanding is not owned by us', and he then concluded, devastatingly: 'I think it my duty to tell you that it is not for the profit of these nations, nor fit for the common and public good, for you to continue here any longer. And therefore I do declare unto you, that I do dissolve this Parliament.'[35] Such rhetoric makes it possible to imagine why so many members of Parliament, and of the wider political elite, questioned Cromwell's motives and perceived him as a self-seeking hypocrite who invoked God's will as a cloak for his own ambitions.[36]

Those accusations are difficult either to prove or to disprove. What we can be sure of is that Cromwell's personality was full of paradoxes, one of the most striking of which was that a man so committed to 'government by a single person and a Parliament' as 'a fundamental'[37] also possessed a deeply authoritarian streak. Cromwell was willing to rule, as he put it in July 1647, 'for [the people's] good not what pleases them'.[38] His readiness to impose godly rule and a 'reformation of manners' regardless of public opinion came through most strongly during the period of the major-generals, which lasted from the late summer of 1655 until the beginning of 1657.[39] Cromwell argued that the 'sole end of this way of procedure was the security of the peace of the nation, the suppressing of vice and encouragement of virtue, the very end of magistracy';[40] and he later praised the major-generals as 'more effectual towards the discountenancing of vice and settling religion, than

---

[33] The earliest hints that the Parliament might be dissolved before 3 February appeared only during the first week of January 1655: Gardiner, *Commonwealth and Protectorate*, III, 240; Lomas–Carlyle, II, 402–4.
[34] Lomas–Carlyle, II, 417–18.　[35] Lomas–Carlyle, II, 429, 430.
[36] See, for example, Ludlow, I, 398–401; and Lucy Hutchinson, *Memoirs of the Life of Colonel Hutchinson*, ed. Julius Hutchinson (1968), pp. 293–4, 298–9.
[37] Lomas–Carlyle, II, 381.　[38] Lomas–Carlyle, III, 345.
[39] The fullest study of the major-generals is Christopher Durston, *Cromwell's Major-Generals: Godly Government during the English Revolution* (Manchester, 2001). For Cromwell's use of the phrase 'reformation of manners', see for example Lomas–Carlyle, II, 538, 540; III, 113–14.
[40] Ivan Roots, ed., *Speeches of Oliver Cromwell* (1989), p. 78. This text is derived from Charles L. Stainer, ed., *Speeches of Oliver Cromwell, 1644–1658* (1901), p. 209.

anything done these fifty years'.[41] However, Christopher Durston's recent study of the major-generals has concluded that, although they had some success in improving the regime's security, their campaign for moral reform was 'a clear failure'.[42] Their remit was too ambitious, and they were given too little time and insufficient support for them to achieve more than fairly minimal progress towards godly reformation. Where they had the assistance of sympathetic local commissioners, as in Staffordshire,[43] a degree of success was possible, but in general there was a striking lack of popular enthusiasm for Cromwell's vision. What the experiment did succeed in generating was considerable resentment of rule by 'swordsmen' and a conviction among many of those elected to the second Protectorate Parliament that the Instrument of Government left the Protector's powers dangerously vague and open-ended. In early 1657, a group of members led by Lord Broghill therefore developed a plan to make Cromwell king, an ancient office whose powers had been defined in relation to centuries of English laws far more explicitly than those of the new office of Lord Protector. It was perhaps the supreme irony of Cromwell's career that this man, who had led the Long Parliament's struggle against Charles I, should himself be offered the Crown by the second Protectorate Parliament.

OLIVER CROMWELL AND THE PARLIAMENTS, 1657–8

That offer presented Cromwell with the most agonising dilemma of his career, and it took him three months (from February to May 1657) to make up his mind.[44] As early as December 1651 he had reflected that 'a settlement of somewhat with monarchical power in it would be very effectual'.[45] Nearly a year later, in November 1652, in a private conversation with Bulstrode Whitelocke in St James's Park, Cromwell lamented the 'pride and corruption' of many members of the Rump Parliament and then asked Whitelocke: 'What if a man should take upon him to be king?' Whitelocke replied that he thought

---

[41] Lomas–Carlyle, II, 543.   [42] Durston, *Cromwell's Major-Generals*, p. 179.
[43] John Sutton, 'Cromwell's Commissioners for Preserving the Peace of the Commonwealth: A Staffordshire Case Study', in Ian Gentles, John Morrill, and Blair Worden, eds., *Soldiers, Writers and Statesmen of the English Revolution* (Cambridge, 1998), pp. 151–82.
[44] The fullest accounts of this episode remain C. H. Firth, 'Cromwell and the Crown', *EHR*, 17 (1902), 429–42, and 18 (1903), 52–80; Firth, *Last Years*, I, 128–200. Also helpful is Clive Holmes, *Why Was Charles I Executed?* (2006), chapter 7. For Lord Broghill's role in the offer of the kingship to Cromwell, see Patrick Little, *Lord Broghill and the Cromwellian Union with Ireland and Scotland* (Woodbridge, 2004), pp. 145–60.
[45] Whitelocke, *Memorials*, III, 374 (10 December 1651). The previous September, following the battle of Worcester, one highly placed observer, John Dury, described Cromwell as 'in effect King': Leo Miller, ed., *John Milton and the Oldenburg Safeguard* (New York, 1985), p. 49. Cf. Ludlow, II, 9.

such a move would be even more difficult to achieve than a Stuart restoration.[46] When Cromwell was formally offered the kingship in 1657, he indicated that part of the reason why he took it so seriously was precisely because it came from Parliament itself. He informed representatives of the Parliament on 8 April that 'no man can put a greater value than I hope I do, and shall do, upon the desires and advices of the Parliament'.[47] Five days later, he declared: 'I had rather have any name from this Parliament, than any other name without it; so much do I think of the authority of the Parliament.'[48] If a majority of members of Parliament felt that it was desirable for Cromwell to become king, then that carried considerable weight with him: 'If the wisdom of this Parliament should have found a way to settle the interests of this nation, upon the foundations of justice and truth and liberty to the people of God, and concernments of men as Englishmen, I would have lain at their feet, or at anybody else's feet, that this might have run at such a current.'[49] However, in the end he remained unconvinced by the Parliament's case, finding in it only arguments from 'expediency' rather than 'necessity'.[50] When he eventually decided to decline the Crown, his rhetoric characteristically stressed the importance of providence:

Truly the Providence of God has laid aside this title of King providentially de facto . . . God has seemed providentially, seemed to appear as a Providence, not only to strike at the family but at the name . . . God has seemed so to deal with the persons and with the family that He blasted the very title . . . I will not seek to set up that, that Providence has destroyed, and laid in the dust; and I would not build Jericho again.[51]

Equally, it is possible that Cromwell realised that he was perhaps more powerful as Lord Protector than he would have been as king. Arguably the most crucial considerations in his own mind were a desire not to antagonise the army (whose opposition he interpreted as a sign of God's disapproval), and a fear that to accept the Crown might indicate sinful ambition and greed.[52] As a result, when a new constitution, the Humble Petition and Advice, was adopted in June 1657, Cromwell remained as Protector.

---

[46] Whitelocke, *Diary*, pp. 281–2. These same words are attributed to Cromwell in the other account that Whitelocke left of this conversation: Whitelocke, *Memorials*, III, 471. On the differences between these two accounts, see Blair Worden, 'The "Diary" of Bulstrode Whitelocke', *EHR*, 108 (1993), 122–34, especially 129.
[47] Lomas–Carlyle, III, 34–5.   [48] Lomas–Carlyle, III, 57.
[49] Lomas–Carlyle, III, 79–80. Cf. *TSP*, VI, 219–20.
[50] This was a particular theme of his speech to the representatives of the second Protectorate Parliament on 13 April 1657: Lomas–Carlyle, III, 53–73.
[51] Lomas–Carlyle, III, 70–1.
[52] On this, see especially Blair Worden, 'Oliver Cromwell and the Sin of Achan', in Derek Beales and Geoffrey Best, eds., *History, Society and the Churches: Essays in Honour of Owen Chadwick* (Cambridge, 1985), pp. 125–45; reprinted in Smith, *Cromwell and the Interregnum*, pp. 39–59. It is, however, possible that Cromwell did not regard this as the

That constitution reflected a further dimension of Cromwell's view of Parliament, which was his growing anxiety about the extent of parliamentary powers. This was closely related to his frustration at the Parliament's reluctance to extend liberty of conscience as widely as he hoped. He particularly regretted its harsh punishment of the Quaker James Nayler for blasphemy, which seemed to him indicative of members' religious intolerance. On 25 December 1656, he wrote to the Speaker, Sir Thomas Widdrington, asking 'that the House will let us know the grounds and reasons whereupon they have proceeded' in the Nayler case.[53] That case strongly reinforced Cromwell's growing belief in the need for a second chamber to act as 'a check or balancing power' on the Commons. According to a contemporary report, Cromwell allegedly told the army officers on 27 February 1657:

> It is time to come to a settlement and lay aside arbitrary proceedings, so unacceptable to the nation. And by the proceedings of this Parliament, you see they stand in need of a check or balancing power (meaning the House of Lords or a House so constituted) for the case of James Nayler might happen to be your own case. By their judicial power, they fell upon life and member, and doth the Instrument in being enable me to control it?[54]

Cromwell therefore welcomed the Humble Petition and Advice's provision for an Other House comprising at least forty and not more than seventy members. These were to be nominated by the Lord Protector and approved by the Commons, and they were subject to stringent religious and moral checks.[55] But the Other House turned out to be another big disappointment, for only forty-two of the sixty-three people whom Cromwell nominated actually accepted. Those nominees included seven English peers, but only two relatively obscure ones (Lord Fauconberg and Lord Eure) agreed to serve; one of the five who declined was Lord Saye and Sele, a former patron of Cromwell's, who now bitterly resented his willingness to countenance the abolition of the Lords.[56] To Saye, the Other House was merely a surrogate to appease peers and make the abolition of the Lords seem slightly more palatable. Saye wrote

---

end of the matter. According to one royalist agent, he 'privately assured his monarchical friends that as soon as he can weed out those that opposed him he will then revive the business': Bodl., MS Clarendon 55, fo. 6r.

[53] Lomas–Carlyle, III, 20. On the Nayler case, see especially Firth, *Last Years*, I, 98–106; Theodore A. Wilson and Frank J. Merli, 'Nayler's Case and the Dilemma of the Protectorate', *University of Birmingham Historical Journal*, 10 (1965–6), 44–59; Leo Damrosch, *The Sorrows of the Quaker Jesus: James Nayler and the Puritan Crackdown on the Free Spirit* (Cambridge, Mass., 1996), chapter 4; and Kate Peters, *Print Culture and the Early Quakers* (Cambridge, 2005), chapter 8.

[54] Lomas–Carlyle, III, 488.

[55] The text of the Humble Petition and Advice is printed in Gardiner, *Constitutional Documents*, pp. 447–59.

[56] Firth, *Last Years*, II, 7–16. Lord Fauconberg married Cromwell's daughter Mary in November 1657. Lord Eure sat for Yorkshire in Barebone's Parliament, and for the North Riding in the first and second Protectorate Parliaments.

to another nominated peer, Lord Wharton, on 29 December 1657 urging him not to attend, arguing that the Other House was evidence that there was a 'design of overthrowing the House of Peers, and in place thereof to bring in and set up a House chosen at the pleasure of him [i.e., Cromwell] that has taken power into his hands to do what he will'.[57]

Yet there were others, especially the commonwealthsmen such as Sir Arthur Hesilrige and Thomas Scott, for whom the Other House was far *too* reminiscent of the Lords. They also lamented the fact that, even though Cromwell had declined the title of king, he was by this stage king in all but name. When Cromwell opened the second sitting of the second Protectorate Parliament on 20 January 1658, his habitual optimism was still not quite extinguished. He hoped that the Parliament would promote the 'cause', which he defined as 'the maintaining of the liberty of these nations; our civil liberties, as men; our spiritual liberties, as Christians'.[58] In a further speech five days later, he vigorously urged members to ensure that 'liberty of conscience may be secured for honest people, that they may serve God without fear, that every just interest may be preserved; that a godly ministry may be upheld and not affronted by seducing and seduced spirits; that all men may be preserved in their just rights, whether civil or spiritual'.[59] However, from 28 January onwards, the House became embroiled in a heated debate over the Other House and what it should be called.[60] Deeply annoyed, Cromwell dissolved the Parliament after only two weeks.[61] His bitterness came through in his final speech (the last speech he made to any Parliament) on 4 February 1658, when he declared: 'I think it high time that an end be put to your sitting. And I do dissolve this Parliament! And let God be judge between you and me!'[62] Later that day, Cromwell complained to Colonel Alban Cox that the Parliament had 'done nothing in fourteen days but debated whether they should own the government of these nations, as it is contained in the Petition and Advice, which the Parliament at their former sitting had invited us to accept of, and had sworn us unto'. Cromwell, 'judging these things to have in them very dangerous consequences to the peace of this nation, and to the loosening [of] all the bonds of government; and being hopeless of obtaining supplies of money, for answering the exigencies of the nation, from such men as are not satisfied with the foundations we stand upon', had therefore 'thought it an absolute necessity to dissolve this present Parliament'.[63] On that bitter note, Cromwell's troubled

[57] C. H. Firth, ed., 'A Letter from Lord Saye and Sele to Lord Wharton, 29 December 1657', *EHR*, 10 (1895), 107.
[58] Lomas–Carlyle, III, 151.   [59] Lomas–Carlyle, III, 184.   [60] See chapter 8.
[61] Firth, *Last Years*, II, 16–41.   [62] Lomas–Carlyle, III, 192. Cf. *TSP*, VI, 778–9, 781–2.
[63] Lomas–Carlyle, III, 308–9.

relationship with Parliaments came to a close, and he died seven months later, weary and disillusioned, on 3 September 1658.

Over fifty years ago, Hugh Trevor-Roper suggested that the problems in that relationship lay primarily in a failure of management. He argued that Cromwell was a 'natural back-bencher' who lacked the ability and the willingness to manage Parliaments really effectively.[64] But this was perhaps less crucial than the complex nature of Cromwell's vision of Parliament itself. The underlying problem was that Cromwell wanted Parliament to pursue a cause that most members did not accept. He hoped that Parliament would encourage godliness and extend liberty of conscience until the godly ultimately became coterminous with the nation as a whole. This proved incompatible with his other 'great end' of reuniting the nation after the Civil Wars through 'healing and settling'.[65] Yet always he hoped that these goals might be reconciled, as for example in his speech on 21 April 1657 to representatives of the second Protectorate Parliament that had framed the Humble Petition and Advice: 'I think you have provided for the liberty of the people of God, and for the liberty of the nation. And I say he sings sweetly that sings a song of reconciliation betwixt these two interests! And it is a pitiful fancy, and wild and ignorant to think they are inconsistent. Certainly they may consist!'[66] Just how central this was to Cromwell's vision of a godly nation, and to what he believed he had been fighting for all along, was clear from another speech to representatives of this Parliament a few weeks earlier, on 3 April 1657:

If anyone whatsoever think the interest of Christians and the interest of the nation inconsistent, or two different things, I wish my soul may never enter into their secrets . . . And upon these two interests, if God shall account me worthy, I shall live and die. And . . . if I were to give an account before a greater tribunal than any earthly one; and if I were asked why I have engaged all along in the late war, I could give no answer but it would be a wicked one if it did not comprehend these two ends.[67]

However, in a nation where by the time of Cromwell's death many parishes were still using all or part of the old Prayer Book, those two interests surely *were* inconsistent.[68]

---

[64] Hugh Trevor-Roper, 'Oliver Cromwell and his Parliaments', in his *Religion, the Reformation and Social Change* (3rd edn, 1984), pp. 345–91. This article first appeared in Richard Pares and Alan J. P. Taylor, eds., *Essays Presented to Sir Lewis Namier* (1956), pp. 1–48.
[65] Lomas–Carlyle, II, 341.   [66] Lomas–Carlyle, III, 101.   [67] Lomas–Carlyle, III, 31.
[68] See, for example, Derek Hirst, 'The Failure of Godly Rule in the English Republic', *Past and Present*, 132 (1991), 33–66; Ann Hughes, 'The Frustrations of the Godly', in John Morrill, ed., *Revolution and Restoration: England in the 1650s* (1992), pp. 70–90.

The two 'fundamentals' of 'liberty of conscience' and 'government by a single person and a Parliament' that Cromwell outlined on 12 September 1654 thus cut against each other. In the end, Cromwell and a majority of members of the Protectorate Parliaments were at cross-purposes. He was expecting fruits that were not realistic when he told the second Protectorate Parliament on 17 September 1656: 'I think for the keeping of the Church and people of God, and professors, in their several forms in this liberty, I think, as it ... has been a thing that is the root of visible profession, the upholding this I think you will find a blessing in it, if God keep your hearts to keep things in this posture and balance, which is so honest and so necessary.'[69] These were the priorities on which he believed a Parliament should most appropriately concentrate. As he told members of that same Parliament on 8 May 1657, in the Humble Petition and Advice 'it is also exceeding well provided there for the safety and security of honest men, in that great, natural, and religious liberty, which is liberty of conscience. These are the great fundamentals ... the intentions of the things are very honourable and honest, and the product worthy of a Parliament.'[70] Yet it was a product that most members of the Protectorate Parliaments consistently shied away from, thereby undermining their relationship with the Protector.

These tensions within Cromwell's vision of Parliament can be located within a wider intellectual framework, for they stemmed in part from the specific form that Calvinist thought had assumed in England during the later sixteenth and early seventeenth centuries. From the reign of Elizabeth I onwards, one characteristic feature of English national identity was the application of the Calvinist doctrine of the Elect to the whole nation, producing the idea of an elect nation that had withstood the threat from international Catholicism led by Spain.[71] A somewhat similar pattern was evident in the Dutch Republic, the only other major West European state in which Calvinists constituted more than a minority of the population.[72] This in turn generated a problem: were the Elect those who felt a sense of assurance that they were among God's saints; or were they all members of the elect nation? This was an issue that Cromwell never succeeded in resolving. His speeches to Parliaments constantly assumed that the two were compatible and would

[69] Lomas–Carlyle, II, 538.   [70] Lomas–Carlyle, III, 126–7.

[71] See, for example, R. T. Kendall, *Calvin and English Calvinism to 1649* (Oxford, 1979); Patrick Collinson, 'England and International Calvinism, 1558–1640', in Menna Prestwich, ed., *International Calvinism, 1541–1715* (Oxford, 1985), pp. 197–223; and the essays in the *Douglas Southall Freeman Historical Review* (Richmond, Va.; spring 1999).

[72] On this theme, see in particular G. Groenhuis, 'Calvinism and the National Consciousness: The Dutch Republic as the New Israel', in A. Duke and C. Tamse, eds., *Church and State since the Reformation* (The Hague, 1981), pp. 118–33; Alastair Duke, 'The Ambivalent Face of Calvinism in the Netherlands, 1561–1618', in Prestwich, *International Calvinism*, pp. 109–34.

ultimately be reconciled. He recognised that this would inevitably be a lengthy and painful process. As he told the first Protectorate Parliament:

These are but entrances and doors of hope, wherein through the blessing of God you may enter into rest and peace. But you are not yet entered. You were told today [in Thomas Goodwin's sermon that preceded the opening of the Parliament] of a people brought out of Egypt towards the land of Canaan, but, through unbelief, murmuring, repining and other temptations and sins, wherewith God was provoked, they were fain to come back again, and linger many years in the wilderness, before they came to the place of rest.[73]

This was where Parliament's role became so crucial, for 'if the Lord's blessing and His presence go along with the management of affairs at this meeting, you will be enabled to put the topstone to this work, and make the nation happy'. But he added that 'this must be by knowing the true state of affairs; that you are yet, like the people under circumcision, but raw. Your peaces are but newly made.'[74] In other words, England bore the marks of being a chosen people; now, Cromwell believed, they had to embrace that responsibility by liberating the godly, encouraging the ungodly towards the ways of godliness, and thereby furthering God's purpose for England.

That God had such a purpose Cromwell did not doubt. Five months later, when he dissolved the first Protectorate Parliament, he declared:

I look at the people of these nations as the blessing of the Lord; and they are a people blessed by God. They have been so, and they will be so, by reason of that immortal seed, which has been and is among them. Those regenerated ones in the land, of several judgements, who are all the flock of Christ, and lambs of Christ, though perhaps under many unruly passions and troubles of spirit, whereby they give disquiet to themselves and others, yet they are not so to God, as to us. He is a God of other patience, and he will own the least of truth in the hearts of his people.[75]

In Calvinist terms, this meant affirming – and ensuring peaceful coexistence between – those who already believed themselves to be among the Elect, and encouraging their numbers to expand until they synchronised with the nation as a whole, thus turning the ideal of an elect nation, so dear to English Calvinists of the period, into a reality. As Cromwell later told the second sitting of the second Protectorate Parliament, membership of the Elect could apply to nations as well as individuals: 'As God pardons the man whom He justifies . . . sometimes God pardons nations also.' He believed that the course

[73] Lomas–Carlyle, II, 358.
[74] Lomas–Carlyle, II, 358. Roots, *Speeches of Oliver Cromwell*, p. 40, follows Stainer, *Speeches of Oliver Cromwell*, p. 145, in giving this phrase as 'you are *not* yet like the people under circumcision, but raw'. Although this apparently reverses the sense, Cromwell's underlying meaning in the passage as a whole – that England needed to face up to the challenges and responsibilities of being a chosen people – remains clear enough.
[75] Lomas–Carlyle, II, 425.

of England's history from the Reformation onwards pointed to its special destiny as an elect nation:

Truly I hope this is His land: and in some sense it may be given out that it is God's land. And He that has the weakest knowledge and the worst memory can easily tell that we are a redeemed people. We were a redeemed people, when first God was pleased to look favourably upon us, and to bring us out of the hands of Popery in that never-to-be-forgotten reformation, that most significant and greatest the nation has felt or tasted.

England's redemption was 'comprehensive of all the interest of every member, of every individual of these nations'.[76]

Cromwell was flexible about the institutional means that might most appropriately further this process of redemption. At the Putney Debates in the autumn of 1647, he had insisted that he was not 'wedded and glued to forms of government' for these were 'but dross and dung in comparison of Christ'.[77] Nevertheless, his natural constitutional reflex was to believe that Parliaments should play a central role in any settled form of government. He felt that 'whatsoever is done without authority of Parliament in order to settlement, will neither be very honest, nor to me very comprehensible'.[78] Even during the 1650s, however, Parliament was still sufficiently the 'representative of the realm' to provide an authentic reflection of the wider lack of enthusiasm for the godly reforms that Cromwell sought. The first and second Protectorate Parliaments were both elected on a revised franchise, set out in the Instrument of Government, which implemented a major redistribution of seats towards the counties and a £200 property qualification for the county franchise. The outcome was a membership that constituted at most a shift *within* the existing social and political elite rather than a shift *away from* it.[79] As a result, civilian unease about attempts to widen liberty of conscience and liberate the religious sects was directly expressed in Parliament. Here, perhaps, there was an ironic echo of the problems that the early Stuarts had faced with their Parliaments. Just as Conrad Russell has written that these were 'not difficulties with their Parliaments; they were difficulties which were reflected in their Parliaments',[80] so much the same was true of Cromwell and his Parliaments. By a profound irony, Cromwell recognised that Parliament was 'the truest way to know what the mind of the nation is';[81] but he failed to grasp fully the devastating implications

---

[76] Lomas–Carlyle, III, 153–4.   [77] Lomas–Carlyle, III, 362, 373.   [78] Lomas–Carlyle, III, 81.
[79] The revised distribution of seats in the Instrument of Government, and its implications, are discussed more fully in chapter 3.
[80] Conrad Russell, *Parliaments and English Politics, 1621–1629* (Oxford, 1979), p. 417.
[81] Lomas–Carlyle, III, 58.

that this fact had for his hopes that Parliaments would implement radical religious reforms.

Those implications in turn take us deep into the problems and paradoxes of the English Revolution more generally. Indeed, they can be related to the issues of the nature and responsibilities of political and religious freedom that were profoundly explored in England during this period. This chapter began with Cromwell's declared commitment in September 1644 to defend the honour, liberty, and rights of Parliament. He never ceased to espouse this ideal, and throughout the 1650s he regularly asserted that Parliaments should be free. He welcomed the first Protectorate Parliament as 'a free Parliament, and that it may continue so, I hope, is in the heart and spirit of every good man in England ... It is that which, as I have desired above my life, so I shall desire to keep it so above my life.'[82] He felt that it was his duty to give the Parliament 'all possible security'; to care for its 'quiet sitting; caring for [its] privileges ... that they might not be interrupted'; he wished to keep the Parliament 'from any unparliamentary interruption' and to give it 'no interruption' himself.[83] Yet it is one of the greatest paradoxes of Cromwell's relations with Parliaments that, while defending their freedom against others, he was willing to intervene and even exclude members if he disapproved of some of the uses that they made of that freedom. In a sense, he became during the 1650s a victim of the very parliamentary freedom that he had himself taken up arms to defend in the 1640s. To be sure, we have already seen that he carefully distanced himself from the council's pre-sessional 'purges' of somewhere between seven and eleven members from the first Protectorate Parliament, and just over a hundred from the second.[84] Equally, he believed that Parliament's freedom was conditional on the acceptance of certain fundamentals of government. He told members of the first Protectorate Parliament: 'You were a free Parliament, and truly so you are, whilst you own the government and authority that called you hither.'[85] That qualification was crucial, for Cromwell went on to assert that government rested on four fundamentals: that Parliaments should not be perpetual; 'government by one single person and a Parliament'; 'liberty of conscience' in religion; and shared control of the militia between Parliament and the Lord

[82] Lomas–Carlyle, II, 354.   [83] Lomas–Carlyle, II, 408.
[84] Peter Gaunt, 'Cromwell's Purge? Exclusions and the First Protectorate Parliament', *Parl. Hist.*, 6 (1987), 1–22; Carol S. Egloff, 'The Search for a Cromwellian Settlement: Exclusions from the Second Protectorate Parliament', *Parl. Hist.*, 17 (1998), 178–97, 301–21. See also chapters 3 and 4.
[85] Lomas–Carlyle, II, 366.

Protector.[86] Only those members who subscribed to a Recognition promising not to try to 'alter the government, as it is settled in a single person and a Parliament' were to be permitted to enter the House. Cromwell insisted that he had the right to do this: 'Though I told you in my last speech that you were a free Parliament, yet I thought it was understood withal that I was the Protector, and the authority that called you, and that I was in possession of the government by a good right from God and men.'[87] We saw earlier that somewhere between fifty and eighty members subsequently withdrew in protest rather than sign this Recognition.[88] Cromwell clearly regarded such an authoritarian intervention as permissible, and he told members: 'The making of your minds known in that by giving your assent and subscription to it, is that means, that will let you in to act those things as a Parliament which are for the good of the people.'[89] To paraphrase Cromwell's own words of July 1647, he wanted members of Parliament to act for the good of the people, even if the methods he adopted to ensure this were not what pleased them.

Such actions were of a piece with Cromwell's willingness in certain circumstances to bypass Parliament and if necessary even to breach the rule of law. For example, he argued that in a national emergency it was sometimes essential to raise funds without parliamentary authority. As he put it to the first Protectorate Parliament on 22 January 1655: 'Though some may think it is an hard thing without parliamentary authority to raise money upon this nation, yet I have another argument to the good people of this nation, if they would be safe, and have no better principle: whether they prefer the having of their will though it be their destruction, rather than comply with things of necessity? That will excuse me.'[90] Such an argument was disconcertingly similar in substance (though not in rhetorical expression) to that used by Charles I to justify the raising of the Forced Loan (1627) and Ship Money (1634–9). Even more disturbing to many of Cromwell's contemporaries was his willingness to contemplate breaches of the very liberties and privileges for which he had fought in the Civil Wars. Later in that same speech, he declared: 'A temporary suspension of caring for the greatest liberties and privileges (if it were so, which is denied) would not have been of that damage that the not providing against free quarter has run the nation upon. And if it be my liberty to walk abroad in the fields, or to take a journey, yet it is not my wisdom to do so when my house is on fire.'[91] The logical extension of this

---

[86] Cromwell discussed these four 'fundamentals' in turn: Lomas–Carlyle, II, 381–5.
[87] Lomas–Carlyle, II, 379–80.
[88] CJ, VII, 367–8; Gaunt, 'Cromwell and his Protectorate Parliaments', pp. 87–8. This episode is discussed more fully in chapter 4.
[89] Lomas–Carlyle, II, 390.   [90] Lomas–Carlyle, II, 424–5.   [91] Lomas–Carlyle, II, 430.

argument was that the abrogation of liberties was justifiable in a national emergency. Moreover, since those liberties rested on the laws, then the rule of law itself was not sacrosanct. Cromwell confronted this problem explicitly in his opening speech to the second Protectorate Parliament when he asserted that:

If nothing should ever be done but what is according to law, the throat of the nation may be cut while we send for some to make a law. Therefore certainly it is a pitiful beastly notion to think that though it be for ordinary government to live by law and rule, yet ... if a government in extraordinary circumstances go beyond the law even for self-preservation, it is yet to be clamoured at and blottered at.[92]

Such attitudes mark Cromwell as very much a man of his times. He held the view, highly characteristic of early seventeenth-century England, that a mild tyranny was preferable to anarchy.[93] That view, which had helped to hold parliamentary opposition to Charles I in check until a later stage in England than in Charles's other two kingdoms, remained almost instinctive within the political elite during and after the Civil Wars. Cromwell addressed this issue head-on in one of his last speeches, on 25 January 1658, when he stated that: 'It were a happy thing if the nation would be content with rule. Content with rule, if it were but in civil things, and with those that would rule worst; because misrule is better than no rule, and an ill government, a bad one, is better than none.'[94] In this quotation, we see the logical working out of a doctrine that one of Cromwell's earlier patrons, Lord Wharton, had expressed in Parliament in 1643, that they were 'not tied to a law for these were times of necessity and imminent danger'.[95] That belief was so central to the Parliamentarian war effort that it could not be shed even after (perhaps *especially* after) the King had been executed, the monarchy abolished, and the republic established.

Those dilemmas were intrinsic not only to the Parliamentarian 'cause' but also to the Revolution itself, and Cromwell himself embodied them. This lay behind many of the contemporary criticisms of him. The commonwealthsman Edmund Ludlow, for example, in a conversation with Cromwell on 14 August 1656, told him bluntly that he 'was heartily sorry to see one who

[92] Lomas–Carlyle, II, 543–4. Roots, *Speeches of Oliver Cromwell*, p. 100, follows Stainer, *Speeches of Oliver Cromwell*, p. 246, in omitting the phrase 'if a government in extraordinary circumstances go beyond the law even for self-preservation'. There is a blank in the manuscript account at this point (Burton, I, clxxii), but the extrapolation of the meaning in Lomas–Carlyle is entirely plausible.

[93] Cf. John Morrill, *The Nature of the English Revolution* (Harlow, 1993), especially chapters 1, 15, and 18.

[94] Lomas–Carlyle, III, 175.

[95] John Morrill, *Revolt in the Provinces: The People of England and the Tragedies of War, 1630–1648* (2nd edn, Harlow, 1999), p. 75.

had been so forward in the cause of the public, not to discern any difference between a sword in the hands of a Parliament to restore the people to their ancient rights, and a sword in the hands of a tyrant to rob and despoil them thereof'.[96] In that sense, Cromwell was not just an important individual; he was an emblematic figure who epitomised many of the central issues and tensions of his time. In the Civil Wars of the 1640s, he had thought it possible to fight for God and for Parliament without any sense of contradiction; but from 1648 onwards these priorities became ever more incompatible.[97] Desperately, and most vividly in his dealings with the first and second Protectorate Parliaments, he tried to reconcile his relationship with God and his relationship with Parliaments. He yearned to find a rapport with Parliaments, as for example in his words to the second Protectorate Parliament on 17 September 1656:

It is an union, really it is an union, this between you and me, and both of us united in faith and love to Jesus Christ, and to his peculiar interest in the world, that must ground this work. And in that, if I have any peculiar interest that is personal to myself, that is not subservient to the public end, it were no extravagant thing for me to curse myself, because I know God will curse me, if I have ... I say, if there be love between us, that the nations may say, these are knit together in one bond to promote the glory of God against the common enemy, to suppress everything that is evil, and encourage whatsoever is of godliness, – yea, the nation will bless you![98]

Yet the very language that he used to extol this union was liable to alienate many of the members he so wished to win over. The final, crowning irony was not only that Cromwell failed to achieve the 'union' with Parliaments that he desired, but also that he was himself the biggest single reason for that failure.

---

[96] Ludlow, II, 13–14.
[97] On this, see especially Adamson, 'Oliver Cromwell and the Long Parliament'.
[98] Lomas–Carlyle, II, 549.

7

Richard Cromwell and Parliaments

Richard Cromwell's relationship with Parliaments inevitably stands in marked contrast to his father's relationship with them. Lord Protector for less than nine months compared to nearly five years, Richard's only Parliament consisted of a single session lasting less than three months. Furthermore, although Richard had been a member of both the first and second Protectorate Parliaments, he lacked the extended parliamentary experience that helps to set his father's handling of his Parliaments within a much longer context. Nevertheless, Richard's relations with Parliament deserve to be examined in their own right as an integral part of the parliamentary and political history of the Protectorate, and not merely to be seen as a codicil to the story told in chapter 6. This chapter will consider Richard's early career and parliamentary experience, and explore the development of his political and religious attitudes as reflected principally in his surviving speeches and correspondence. We will then turn to examine his relationship with the third Protectorate Parliament in 1659, and the reasons why that Parliament ultimately collapsed.

RICHARD CROMWELL'S EARLY CAREER

Richard was one month short of his 32nd birthday when he was proclaimed Lord Protector. Born on 4 October 1626, he was the third son of Oliver Cromwell and Elizabeth Bourchier. He was educated at Felsted School, probably served briefly in the Parliamentarian armies during 1647, and was admitted a member of Lincoln's Inn on 27 May 1647.[1] After lengthy negotiations, on 1 May 1649 he married Dorothy, daughter of Richard

---

[1] Probably the best life of Richard to date is that by Peter Gaunt in the *ODNB*. In addition, the following are all quite useful: R. W. Ramsey, *Richard Cromwell* (1935); Earl Malcolm Hause, *Tumble-Down Dick: The Fall of the House of Cromwell* (New York, 1972); John A. Butler, *A Biography of Richard Cromwell, 1626–1712, the Second Protector* (Lampeter, 1994); and Jane Ross Hammer, *Protector: A Life History of Richard Cromwell, Protector of the United Kingdom 1658–1659/60* (New York, 1997). We are also most grateful to Jason Peacey for

Maijor, a prosperous landowner from Hursley in Hampshire, where the couple went to live.[2] Richard Cromwell's early life revealed little in the way of outstanding ability or determination: there is some evidence that his father thought him idle but was determined to prepare him for a life of public service. Oliver wrote to Richard Maijor on 13 August 1649: 'I have committed my son to you; pray give him advice ... I would have him mind and understand business, read a little history, study the mathematics and cosmography: these are good, with subordination to the things of God. Better than idleness, or mere outward worldly contents. These fit for public services, for which a man is born.'[3] That same day, Oliver told his daughter-in-law Dorothy: 'I desire you both to make it above all things your business to seek the Lord: to be frequently calling upon Him, that He would manifest Himself to you in His son, and be listening what returns He makes to you, for He will be speaking in your ear and in your heart, if you attend thereunto.' He desired her 'to provoke your husband likewise thereunto', and went on: 'as for the pleasures of this life, and outward business, let that be upon the bye. Be above all these things, by faith in Christ, and then you shall have the true use and comfort of them, and not otherwise.'[4]

A subsequent letter from Oliver directly to his son on 2 April 1650 helps to illuminate their relationship and the grooming that Richard received from his father. Oliver began by urging Richard to 'seek the Lord and His face continually: let this be the business of your life and strength, and let all things be subservient and in order to this'. In a passage that reveals something of his personal faith, Oliver argued that 'the true knowledge is not literal or speculative, but inward, transforming the mind to it. It's uniting to, and participating of, the divine nature (2 *Peter*, I. 4): it's such a knowledge as Paul speaks of (*Philippians* the 3rd, 8, 9, 10). How little of this knowledge of Christ is there among us.' He enjoined Richard to 'take heed of an unactive vain spirit. Recreate yourself with Sir Walter Raleigh's *History*: it's a body of History, and will add much more to your understanding than fragments of story. Intend [= endeavour] to understand the estate I have settled: it's your concernment to know it all, and how it stands.' Oliver concluded with some advice on marriage: 'though marriage be no instituted sacrament, yet where the undefiled bed is, and love, this union aptly resembles Christ and His

---

allowing us to see prior to publication his article on 'The Protector Humbled: Richard Cromwell and the Constitution', in Patrick Little, ed., *The Cromwellian Protectorate* (Woodbridge, 2007), pp. 32–52.

[2] Lomas–Carlyle, I, 299–302, 411–12, 432–4.   [3] Lomas–Carlyle, I, 451.

[4] Lomas–Carlyle, I, 452–3. A parallel can perhaps be drawn with a similar letter that Oliver Cromwell sent to Richard's younger brother Henry in October 1657, in which he wrote: 'though all things answer not, be you humble, and patient, place value where it truly lies, viz., in the favour of God, in knowing Him, or rather in being known of Him. If your heart be truly here, you cannot miscarry' (Lomas–Carlyle, III, 498).

Church. If you can truly love your wife, what love does Christ bear to His Church and every poor soul therein, who gave Himself for it and to it.'[5]

It seems, however, that Richard did not live up to his father's hopes, for on 28 June 1651 Oliver told Richard Maijor very candidly of his concerns about his son. Having heard that Richard had 'exceeded his allowance, and is in debt', he did not 'grudge him ... laudable recreations, nor an honorable carriage of himself in them'. 'But if', he continued, 'pleasure and self-satisfaction be made the business of a man's life, so much cost laid out upon it, so much time spent in it, as rather answers appetite than the will of God, or is comely before His saints, I scruple to feed this humour.' Oliver was determined that Richard's 'being my son should [not] be his allowance to live not pleasingly to our heavenly Father, who has raised me out of the dust to what I am!' He asked Maijor to advise Richard 'to approve himself to the Lord in his course of life; and to search His statutes for a rule to conscience, and to seek grace from Christ to enable him to walk therein'. He felt that 'it lies upon me to give him (in love) the best counsel I may; and know not how better to convey it to him than by so good a hand as yours. Sir, I pray you acquaint him with these thoughts of mine.'[6] It is possible that this provides an early indication of a difference of attitude towards religion between Richard and his father.

Oliver's anxieties about his son did not prevent the council from entrusting Richard with certain responsibilities in local government. In April 1651 he was asked to enquire into 'the wastes of timber' in the New Forest; he was among those commissioned in October 1653 to find 'godly and able ministers' for vacant livings in Southampton; and the following December he was appointed to a committee to reconcile the mayor and aldermen of Winchester.[7] In April 1654, he was made Keeper and Warden of the New Forest.[8] He emerged for the first time on to the national stage later that year when he was returned to the first Protectorate Parliament for both Monmouthshire and Hampshire, and chose to sit for the latter.[9] He was appointed to about a dozen committees on a wide range of subjects, including those for privileges, for enquiring into the proceedings of the judges at Salters' Hall, for considering naval and land forces, for Irish affairs, for Scottish affairs, for considering the Chancery ordinance, for the corn trade, for the draining of the Lincolnshire fens, for public accounts, for taking away purveyance, and for reviewing the profession of civil law.[10] He acted as a

---

[5] Lomas–Carlyle, II, 53–4.   [6] Lomas–Carlyle, II, 209–10.
[7] TNA, SP 25/96, p. 125; SP 25/71, pp. 166–7; SP 25/72, pp. 171–2.
[8] Bodl., MS Rawlinson A 328, fos. 33–4, quoted in Abbott, III, 270–1.
[9] *Return of Members of Parliaments of England, 1213–1702* (2 vols., 1878), I, 501.
[10] *CJ*, VII, 366, 368, 370–1, 373–4, 380, 387, 407, 415.

teller twice, on both occasions in defence of the Instrument of Government or of the Protector's powers. On 27 November, he was teller against restoring the county franchise to the forty-shilling freeholders, but was defeated by 53 votes to 96. On 15 January 1655, he was teller in favour of making an annual grant of £700,000 to the Protector for the army until 25 December 1659 (rather than only until 25 December 1656), and, although he was defeated on that occasion, the vote was overturned the following day.[11] There appears to be no evidence that he made any speeches during this Parliament.

Richard's earliest surviving letter, to his brother Henry, was dated 27 November 1655 and offers a valuable insight into his religious attitudes. It is unclear how far he shared his father's profound belief in a providentialist God. Richard wrote: 'I can boast of the love of God who affords me restraining grace, keeping me within the compass of my place ... what God will do more for me I know not, I am certain his divine goodness has exceeded my desert.'[12] It seems, however, that Richard lacked his father's strong commitment to Independency and to religious liberty of conscience. There is a hint, in another letter to Henry dated 1 January 1656, that Richard sought to extend toleration broadly: 'I desire God to continue such a spirit to you, as may be public, it being comprehensive, you are certain by its large circumference, to take in all sorts of people, and so consequently the people of God, you making no difference but when the seal is upon a Saint, and the mark of the Beast upon an enemy to Jesus Christ.'[13] However, other surviving evidence shows that Richard's own sympathies lay more with the Presbyterians than the Independents. The letter-book of the leading Presbyterian John Fitzjames reveals that he was on friendly terms with Richard from the summer of 1655 onwards,[14] while according to the French ambassador Bordeaux, early in 1657 Richard, 'in order to make himself agreeable to the Presbyterians', was 'frequenting their churches'.[15] Furthermore, in March 1659, the Scottish minister James Sharp reported that the Independents were 'very observant and grieved when this Protector does take special notice of those of the Presbyterial way'.[16] This evidence suggests that Richard inclined more towards the Presbyterians than did his father.

In June 1655 Oliver expressed the hope that his two surviving sons would live 'private lives in the country'.[17] He nevertheless appointed Richard to the committee for trade and navigation the following November.[18] In 1656,

---

[11] *CJ*, VII, 391, 417–18.   [12] BL, Lansdowne MS 821, fo. 38r.

[13] BL, Lansdowne MS 821, fo. 64r.

[14] Alnwick Castle, Northumberland MS 551 (letter-book of John Fitzjames, V), fos. 21v, 27v; Northumberland MS 552 (letter-book of John Fitzjames, VI), fo. 14r.

[15] TNA, PRO 31/3/101, fo. 44r.   [16] Stephen, II, 153.   [17] Lomas–Carlyle, II, 451.

[18] TNA, SP 25/76, pp. 358–9.

Richard was returned to the second Protectorate Parliament to sit for both Hampshire and the University of Cambridge, and chose to serve for the latter.[19] Once again, he was appointed to a wide variety of committees.[20] He acted as a teller only once, on 9 October 1656, for those in favour of a small quorum of three judges for ensuring the security of the Protector's person, but was defeated by 59 votes to 117.[21] There is evidence that he spoke briefly on two occasions: on 9 December, he suggested that the bill for Wigston's Hospital be referred to an existing committee on the University of Cambridge in order 'to save your time', and the next day he nominated Richard Hampden and Griffith Bodurda to be added to the committee for debts upon the public faith.[22] Richard's choice of two leading Presbyterians for this purpose again suggests that his own sympathies lay in that direction. So, too, may Thomas Burton's report that on 12 December, at a private dinner, Richard expressed the view that 'Nayler deserve[d] to be hanged' and 'for his part was clear in that Nayler ought to die'.[23] Richard seems, however, to have played little further part in the Parliament. According to Bordeaux, Richard had seen the Remonstrance inviting Oliver to become king prior to its introduction by Sir Christopher Packe on 23 February 1657,[24] but once the debates on the Remonstrance began in earnest he retreated to Hursley. He congratulated his brother Henry on being well 'out of the spattering dirt which is thrown about here', and warned that 'things that might be whispered ought not to be committed to paper'.[25]

Thereafter, he played an increasingly prominent role in public life and, following the adoption of the Humble Petition and Advice, came to be widely perceived as his father's likely successor. He was appointed chancellor of the University of Oxford in succession to Oliver in July 1657, and the following December he became a member of the council.[26] Richard was among those nominated to the Other House, and he was present at all fourteen of its meetings between 20 January and 4 February 1658. He was appointed to the committees for privileges and for petitions, but there is no evidence that he made any speeches.[27] In *A Second Narrative of the late Parliament*, the commonwealthsman Sir George Wharton mocked the members of the

---

[19] *Return of Members*, I, 505; *CJ*, VII, 432.
[20] *CJ*, VII, 424, 427–9, 435, 438, 444, 453, 456–7, 466, 473, 493.   [21] *CJ*, VII, 437.
[22] Burton, I, 84, 95. In the event, however, a new committee (including Richard) was established for settling Wigston's Hospital, and Bodurda and Hampden were not added to the committee for debts upon the public faith: *CJ*, VII, 466.
[23] Burton, I, 126.   [24] Firth, *Last Years*, I, 129.   [25] BL, Lansdowne MS 821, fo. 324r.
[26] *Mercurius Politicus*, no. 372 (16–23 July 1657), pp. 7948, 7957; TNA, SP 25/78, pp. 331, 379. For Richard as chancellor of Oxford, see Butler, *Biography of Richard Cromwell*, chapter 4.
[27] HMC, *The Manuscripts of the House of Lords, 1699–1702* (1908), pp. 505–25; Whitelocke, *Memorials*, IV, 329–30.

Other House, and offered a finely ironic portrait of Richard as 'a person of great worth and merit, and well skilled in hawking, hunting, horse-racing, with other sports and pastimes; one whose undertakings, hazards and services for the cause, cannot well be numbered or set forth, unless the drinking of King Charles's, or (as is so commonly spoken) his father's landlord's health'. Wharton noted that Richard was 'very likely to be his father's successor',[28] and by 1658 this perception was increasingly widespread.[29] It was even rumoured in mid-January 1658 that Richard might become king in his father's lifetime. Samuel Hartlib informed John Pell that 'the city-statesmen here begin to talk as if my Lord Richard, the eldest son to his highness, is to be made k[ing], and that very shortly, his father remaining still Lord Protector till the government be more and more settled'.[30] When Oliver died on 3 September, Richard was proclaimed Protector the next day.[31]

THE CALLING OF THE THIRD PROTECTORATE PARLIAMENT

Despite the mystery that remains over precisely when, and indeed whether, Oliver formally designated Richard as his heir, the latter's succession was outwardly smooth and peaceful.[32] He was proclaimed throughout the three kingdoms, and a pamphlet was published containing the loyal addresses presented to him.[33] Thurloe informed Henry Cromwell on 7 September that 'it has pleased God hitherto to give his highness your brother a very easy and peaceable entrance upon his government. There is not a dog that wags his tongue, so great a calm are we in.' 'But I must needs acquaint your

---

[28] [Sir George Wharton], *A Second Narrative of the late Parliament (so called)* (1658), p. 11.
[29] See, for example, *CSPD, 1657–8*, 266–7.   [30] Vaughan, II, 436.
[31] For the text of the proclamation, see *OPH*, XXI, 228–9.
[32] The controversy over Richard's nomination arose because eyewitnesses reported that Cromwell did not name a successor on his deathbed. He had previously stated that he had left a written nomination, but Thurloe claimed that this could not be found. It is, however, possible that Thurloe and the council suppressed it because it nominated Charles Fleetwood and they preferred Richard as more malleable and a civilian. The lack of a written nomination of Richard made the issue of his recognition as Protector more sensitive and problematic than it might otherwise have been. The mystery remains insoluble because it is impossible to prove either that Cromwell *did* nominate Richard (see Hause, *Tumble-Down Dick*, pp. 36–74) or that he did *not* (see Austin Woolrych, 'Milton and Cromwell', in Michael Lieb and John T. Shawcross, eds., *Achievements of the Left Hand: Essays on the Prose of John Milton* (Amherst, 1974), pp. 185–218). For judicious reviews of the surviving evidence relating to this subject, see G. B. Nourse, 'The Nomination of Richard Cromwell', *Cromwelliana* (1979), 25–31; and Peter Gaunt's life of Richard in the *ODNB*.
[33] *A true catalogue, or, An account of the several places and most eminent persons in the three nations, and elsewhere, where, and by whom Richard Cromwell was proclaimed Lord Protector of the Commonwealth of England, Scotland, and Ireland. As also a collection of the most material passages in the several blasphemous, lying, flattering addresses, … which were sent to the aforesaid* (1659).

excellency', he continued ominously, 'that there are some secret murmurings in the army, as if his highness were not general of the army, as his father was; and would look upon him and the army as divided.'[34] A week later, Lord Fauconberg wrote that 'certainly somewhat is brewing underhand. A cabal there is of persons, and great ones, held very closely, resolved, it's feared, to rule themselves, or set all on fire.'[35] Richard's close connections with the Presbyterians and the civilian courtiers made him a figure of suspicion in the eyes of the army.

The army soon proved to be a serious problem, and early in October a group of officers petitioned Richard for the appointment of a commander-in-chief (Charles Fleetwood) who was a soldier and who would have power to commission all officers below field rank. One royalist observer wrote that 'there are many of the officers that will not call him Protector, but the young gentleman; they say that it is not fit that the Protector should have both the places being one that never drew a sword in the behalf of the Commonwealth'.[36] On 18 October, Richard responded to the petition with a speech, drafted by Thurloe, to the officers who were then in London. He admitted, candidly: 'it is my disadvantage, that I have been so little amongst you, and am no better known to you. I hope a little time will remove that disadvantage, which indeed is upon us both, not doubting, but as I come to know you better, and you to know more of me, our mutual confidence in each other will increase.' However, he resisted the officers' request and insisted that to entrust the filling of vacant commissions to anyone other than the Protector would be contrary to the Humble Petition and Advice: he should 'therein break [his] trust, and do otherwise than the Parliament intended'. He concluded by admitting that 'there is one thing I am troubled at very much, which is, that the army is so much in arrear of their pay ... I can assure you, both myself and the council do consider nothing so much, as to pay the arrears, and to settle your pay better for the future.'[37] This answer apparently pacified the army officers for the time being, and 'they parted with kindness'.[38]

A few weeks later, however, further disputes at the officers' prayer meetings prompted Richard to request another 'meeting with them to uphold the good correspondency that ought to be betwixt him and the army' on 19 November. He 'hoped they would assist him in the government, for he stood in much need of their advice, being young and not fitted for so great a work, and had a disadvantage, that he succeeded one who was so extraordinarily able to undergo such a burden, which would sink him, if he had not the advice and also the prayers of good men'. This speech again met with a

---

[34] *TSP*, VII, 374.   [35] *TSP*, VII, 386.   [36] Bodl., MS Clarendon 59, fo. 116v.
[37] *TSP*, VII, 447–9.   [38] *Clarke Papers*, III, 165.

favourable reception: it was reported that 'the officers seemed to be much affected with what [Richard] said, except some few of the inferior sort who muttered a little after they were gone, but they were persons inconsiderable, so that in all probability things will tend to unity in the army'.[39] Bordeaux, however, thought that the speech 'somewhat irritated them',[40] and the officers' underlying mistrust of Richard would surface again dramatically the following year.

Although there was some discontent within the army, many contemporaries were impressed by Richard's bearing, poise, and evident sincerity. On 18 October, he gave an audience to the French ambassador and, according to Whitelocke, 'did carry himself discreetly, and better than was expected'.[41] Four days earlier, a group of ministers presented to Richard 'a declaration of faith and order owned and practised in the congregational churches in England'. His response was characteristically self-deprecating. He told the ministers: 'I must say I am not moulded to make speeches, I have infirmity, I want experience, and I want understanding; but I desire that I may learn to do my duty, as to the nation in general, and as to the good people of the nation in particular.' Once again, he stressed the power and providentialism of God:

We are all in the keeping of a better hand. And what soever shall become of us, truth will live, and the interest of God will remain; as we are under his hand, and in his hand, we have cause to hope and not to fear, and in that respect I have very great hopes, that God will appear more and more in the behalf of his people, and will bring forth purity in his worship, and will bring forth unity and agreement of brethren.

He emphasised the importance of unity again in his conclusion, 'desiring of God that we may study peace and unity one to another, and that we may incorporate the interest of the people of God, as much as we can ... let us endeavour for a right understanding of one another'.[42]

Richard's desire to promote 'peace and unity' can only have been reinforced by the existing divisions within the council. Here again, considerable tension between the military and civilian members soon became apparent. At the beginning of November, Thurloe was so stung by the slurs spread by some councillors and army officers that he 'was a very evil counsellor' that he offered to resign, but Richard declined this offer.[43] According to one royalist agent, Fauconberg allegedly claimed that 'Thurloe governs Cromwell, and St John and Pierrepont govern Cromwell.'[44] Thomas Clarges felt that Richard 'showed a great prudence and moderation' in his handling of these

---

[39] *Clarke Papers*, III, 168–9. [40] Guizot, *Richard Cromwell*, I, 264.
[41] Whitelocke, *Memorials*, IV, 337.
[42] C. H. Firth, 'A Speech by Richard Cromwell, 14 October 1658', *EHR*, 23 (1908), 736.
[43] *TSP*, VII, 490. [44] *Clarendon SP*, III, 425.

'little umbrages', and thought that, given 'how little his highness was here-
tofore exercised in public affairs, and the great grief that almost overwhelmed him for the loss he had of so dear a father', it was 'miraculous
how he waded through his difficulties at this time'.[45] Richard's strongest
supporters on the council, besides Thurloe, were reported to be mainly its
civilian members, notably the Lord President, Henry Lawrence; the Lord
Keeper, Nathaniel Fiennes; and Sir Charles Wolseley. Of the military officers, only Admiral Lord Edward Montagu and the Comptroller of the
Household, Colonel Philip Jones, were firmly loyal to Richard and can be
counted among the civilian interest.[46] By early November, Bordeaux thought
that Richard was allowing 'the council to act with entire liberty and authority', and that 'most resolutions [were] adopted in accordance with the wishes
of the officers of the army'.[47] About a week later, Thurloe wrote that 'it goes
for current, that some of the ill counsellors must be removed, before any
thing can well go on'; and by the end of December he felt that 'things seem
sometimes to be skinned over, but break out again'.[48] Richard's attempt to
strengthen his support base by adding Lords Broghill and Fauconberg to the
council aroused fierce opposition from the army interest, led by Disbrowe,
and two officers, Major-General James Berry and Colonel Thomas Cooper,
were appointed instead.[49]

One of the issues over which the council was most deeply divided was
whether or not – and on what franchise – a Parliament should be called.
According to Bordeaux, in mid-September there was 'talk of a Parliament
being called', although it was 'a very general opinion that the Parliament will
not be assembled just yet, for fear lest, under the shadow of that body,
factions might be formed which would not venture to show themselves at
any other time'.[50] By early October, 'more positive statements' were 'afloat'
'in reference to the assembling of a Parliament', but 'the principal matter in
debate' was 'how to regulate the form of the elections'. Fleetwood likewise
told Henry Cromwell on 19 October that 'we are still upon our old debate,
but can come to no resolve; the difficulties we meet with about the manner of
calling Parliament being great'.[51] Bordeaux wrote presciently at the beginning of November that if Richard were 'necessitated to call a Parliament, it
may with some reason be apprehended that that body, feeling itself supported by a part of the army, will weaken his authority, although the

[45] *TSP*, VII, 491–2.   [46] *TSP*, VII, 495.   [47] Guizot, *Richard Cromwell*, I, 254.
[48] *TSP*, VII, 510, 581.
[49] Guizot, *Richard Cromwell*, I, 271; Richard Baker, *A Chronicle of the Kings of England*
(1670), p. 657; Patrick Little, *Lord Broghill and the Cromwellian Union with Ireland and
Scotland* (Woodbridge, 2004), p. 167.
[50] Guizot, *Richard Cromwell*, I, 234, 238.
[51] Guizot, *Richard Cromwell*, I, 243, 244; *TSP*, VII, 451.

Presbyterians and all the nobility are favourable to him'.[52] By mid-November, Richard was reported to be 'think[ing] of assembling the Parliament, as the payment of arrears due to the army can no longer be delayed without very great inconvenience',[53] and he and the council eventually decided informally on 29 November to summon a Parliament for January 1659.[54] Thurloe told Henry Cromwell the following day that a Parliament was 'always usual at the beginning of every prince's reign', and that the main reasons for the decision were 'the great necessities we have for money, which cannot be supplied but by Parliament'; 'the good opinion the people in general now have of his highness'; and 'other reasons, which are more fit to be told your excellency by word of mouth, than by this way'.[55]

The elections to this Parliament have already been examined (in chapter 3), as has the return in significant numbers of members who had been excluded from the second Protectorate Parliament in 1656 (in chapter 4). When the results came in, Thurloe wrote that 'there is so great a mixture in the House of Commons, that no man knows which way the major part will incline'.[56] A royalist agent predicted that 'there never met any Parliament in England so full of animosities as this will do', while the Venetian Resident, Giavarina, thought that 'it would not be remarkable if such a heterogeneous mixture had a bitter taste'.[57] Some other observers, however, thought that the position looked rather more encouraging for the government than had initially been anticipated. One writer believed that members would probably divide 'two to one for confirming of the present settlement by a Protector and two Houses against a standing Commonwealth council'.[58] Bordeaux similarly reported that 'there appears to be a great number of members of Parliament inclined to peace, and that the party of those who are discontented with the government will probably be numerically the weakest'.[59] Indeed, a few days before the Parliament duly assembled on 27 January 1659, Ralph Josselin observed that 'a spirit of slumber and remissness is wonderfully upon the nation'.[60]

---

[52] Guizot, *Richard Cromwell*, I, 252.

[53] Guizot, *Richard Cromwell*, I, 260. Sir Archibald Johnston of Wariston recorded a similar rumour a few days earlier: James D. Ogilvie, ed., *The Diary of Sir Archibald Johnston of Wariston*, vol. III, *1655–1660* (Scottish History Society, 3rd series, 34, Edinburgh, 1940), 104.

[54] *TSP*, VII, 541. It appears, however, that the *formal* council decision to summon Parliament for 27 January 1659 was taken only on 3 December 1658: TNA, PRO 31/17/33, p. 243. See also Bodl., MS Clarendon 59, fos. 273r, 278v–279r; Guizot, *Richard Cromwell*, I, 270–1; Whitelocke, *Memorials*, IV, 338.

[55] *TSP*, VII, 541. Cf. *CSPV*, 1657–9, 261.   [56] *TSP*, VII, 594.

[57] Bodl., MS Clarendon 59, fo. 409r; *CSPV*, 1657–9, 288.   [58] *Clarke Papers*, III, 176.

[59] Guizot, *Richard Cromwell*, I, 287. One of Ormond's informants likewise wrote that 'the republican party ... are as yet judged much the weaker': Bodl., MS Clarendon 60, fo. 61r.

[60] Alan MacFarlane, ed., *The Diary of Ralph Josselin, 1616–1683* (British Academy, Records of Social and Economic History, new series, 3, Oxford, 1976), p. 438.

THE THIRD PROTECTORATE PARLIAMENT

Richard Cromwell's opening speech to the two Houses of Parliament on 27 January 1659 lasted about fifteen minutes, and a number of contemporaries were impressed by his delivery. One wrote that Cromwell 'spoke to both Houses with such a grace and presence, and with such oratory and steadiness, without the least interruption and so pertinently to the present occasion, as it was beyond all expectation', while another reported that 'it was very taking, and much approved of by most of the members, which they signified by their general hummings of him whilst he was speaking'.[61] Others recorded that the speech was 'much applauded' and 'much commended, it being good language and pithy'.[62] Richard's words offer some insight into his view of Parliament and what he hoped it might achieve. He had, he declared, 'thought it for the public good to call a Parliament of the three nations'. He believed it to be 'agreeable not only to my trust, but to my principles, to govern these nations by the advice of my two Houses of Parliament'. He quoted approvingly from the Humble Petition and Advice that 'Parliaments are the great council of the Chief Magistrate, in whose advice both he and these nations may be most safe and happy.'[63] He assured members that he had 'that esteem of them' and that, just as he had 'made it the first act of [his] government to call [them] together', so he would let them 'see the value' he placed upon them by the answers he would 'return to the advice' they gave him 'for the good of these nations'. He insisted that he had 'nothing in my design, but the maintenance of the peace, laws, liberties, both civil and Christian, of these nations; which I shall always make the measure and rule of my government, and be ready to spend my life for'. After briefly addressing issues of foreign policy, religion, and legal reform,[64] he closed with a characteristic plea to members to 'maintain and conserve love and unity among yourselves, that therein you may be the pattern of the nation ... and to this let us all add our utmost endeavours for the making this an happy Parliament'.[65] Like Richard's other recorded speeches, the tone was very temperate and irenic, a far cry from his father's impassioned and uncompromising calls for radical action.

[61] *Clarke Papers*, III, 176.   [62] Bodl., MS Clarendon 60, fos. 40br, 41r.
[63] This was derived from article 2 of the Humble Petition, which stated that Parliament is 'your great council, in whose affection and advice yourself and this people will be most safe and happy': Gardiner, *Constitutional Documents*, p. 449.
[64] These sections of Richard's speech are analysed more fully in chapters 8, 9, and 11.
[65] [Richard Cromwell,] *The Speech of His Highness the Lord Protector, made to both Houses of Parliament at their first meeting on Thursday the 27th of January 1658[/9]* (1658[/9]), . pp. 4–5, 9.

Bills for the recognition of Richard as Protector were initiated shortly afterwards in both Houses, but neither came to fruition. In the Other House, a bill 'for recognizing his highness the Lord Protector and disclaiming the title of Charles Stuart' received its first reading on 31 January and its second the following day.[66] It was then committed, and the committees recommended that the recognition of Richard Cromwell and the disclaiming of Charles Stuart's title should be enacted by two separate bills.[67] The amended bill for Richard's recognition then passed its third reading on 5 February, but nothing further was heard of it.[68] In the Commons, meanwhile, Thurloe introduced a bill for 'an Act of Recognition of his highness' right and title to be Protector and Chief Magistrate of the Commonwealth of England, Scotland, and Ireland, and the dominions thereunto belonging': this received its first reading on 1 February and its second on 7 February.[69] It was then debated on 8–12 and 14–18 February.[70] On 14 February, the House voted by 191 to 168 to retain the word 'recognise', with the commonwealthsmen Hesilrige and Neville as tellers for the minority who sought its deletion, but it was agreed to drop the word 'undoubted' from the bill. The Commons also resolved that 'before this bill be committed, this House do declare such additional clauses to be part of the bill, as may bound the power of the chief magistrate; and fully secure the rights and privileges of Parliament, and the liberties and rights of the people'.[71] The House considered the additional clauses on 17 and 18 February, but on the second day voted by 217 to 86 not to 'proceed to determine the power of the negative voice in the chief magistrate, in the passing of laws, before the constitution of the Parliament, as to two Houses, be first resolved on'.[72] As a result, the House then turned its attention to the knotty problem of the nature and title of the Other House, and the bill for the recognition of Richard's title as Lord Protector disappeared from view for the rest of the Parliament.

Although there is apparently no surviving evidence of the debates in the Other House, extensive records exist of proceedings in the Commons that

---

[66] HMC, *MSS of the House of Lords*, pp. 529–30; *Clarke Papers*, III, 176.
[67] HMC, *MSS of the House of Lords*, p. 531.
[68] HMC, *MSS of the House of Lords*, p. 533.
[69] *CJ*, VII, 596, 601; *Clarke Papers*, III, 176; Burton, III, 25–6; BL, Add. MS 5138 (diary of Guybon Goddard), pp. 114–15, 122–3; Bodl., MS Clarendon 60, fo. 83r; Schilling, p. 25; Ludlow, II, 54. For the draft act, see TNA, SP 18/201/1; and *TSP*, VII, 603–4.
[70] *CJ*, VII, 601–5; Burton, III, 118–94, 204–32, 256–87, 289–95, 316–45; BL, Add. MS 5138, pp. 123–95; Schilling, pp. 25–90; *Clarke Papers*, III, 181; Whitelocke, *Memorials*, IV, 339–40.
[71] *CJ*, VII, 603; Burton, III, 284–7; BL, Add. MS 5138, p. 176; Schilling, p. 80; BL, Lansdowne MS 823, fos. 219r, 223r–v; *Clarke Papers*, III, 181; *TSP*, VII, 617; Guizot, *Richard Cromwell*, I, 303–4; *CSPV*, 1657–9, 293.
[72] *CJ*, VII, 605; Burton, III, 345; *TSP*, VII, 619; BL, Lansdowne MS 823, fo. 229r.

enable us to reconstruct something of how members perceived Richard and his title as Lord Protector. The initial reaction to the bill for recognition at its first reading on 1 February did not seem particularly hostile. Later that day, Thomas Clarges told Henry Cromwell: 'I hope it will be the happiest Parliament that ever sat in England ... Some few made sharp reflections on the bill, but the spirit of the House was so much for it, that by this day's action, I perceive, things will go fairly on.' However, he added more cautiously: 'on Monday next there will be a tough debate upon the second reading of the recognition; but there is no danger'.[73] Exactly a week later, as the debate got underway, he wrote: 'I perceive a great (I think I may say, the greatest) sense of the House is with [the recognition]; but those that oppose, are able speakers, which makes the considerations long before they come to a question.' Clarges did 'not observe any, that can object any thing against his highness's person; those that have been sharp, and have seemed to doubt of his due nomination to the succession, but yet concluded to approve it'. 'Others', he noted, 'have glanced at the establishing a commonwealth to consist of a single person, a senate, and the people; but nothing of this kind has been gratefully received.'[74]

Certainly members were generous in their personal tributes to Richard, and stressed his goodness, honesty, and integrity. Such positive views coexisted with a wide variety of different political and constitutional positions. Many members emphasised their deep personal loyalty, including swordsmen such as Lambert, who reportedly stated that 'we are all for this honourable person that is now in the power'. Lambert's ally William Packer was typical in also urging the need for firmer constitutional foundations: 'I concur that the gentleman deserves the government as well as any man in the world, but I would have him settled upon a better foundation; against which there is no just exception.' The attorney-general, Sir Edmund Prideaux, echoed him: 'No man is so unwise, but he will circumscribe the Chief Magistrate. I hope we shall have a concurrence. I have served here many years. I find no man give just exception against the man. Without guile or gall, was a good expression. I hear of none to remove him, nor in competition with him. Why should not we willingly own him, and cheerfully, against whom there are no exceptions?'[75] Many Presbyterian members spoke in a similar vein, although they too sometimes suggested the need for tighter definition of Protectoral powers. John Bulkeley, for example, 'would trust him more than any man ... I would have those gentlemen that think of

---

[73] *TSP*, VII, 605. Bordeaux also noted the lack of opposition at the bill's first reading although, like Clarges, he went on to observe that it would 'shortly call forth all forms of discontent': Guizot, *Richard Cromwell*, I, 299–300.

[74] *TSP*, VII, 609.   [75] Burton, III, 132, 161, 232; BL, Add. MS 5138, p. 150.

another government, lay it aside, and only look to the fitting the government to this single person, making it neither too wide nor too narrow . . . I take him not to be a person ambitious of power, but to rule with the love of his people, not to grasp at greatness.'[76] Richard Knightley apparently echoed him: 'It is some happiness that the single person is of good disposition, free from guile; but he is but a man. I have heard the judges say, that the Chief Magistrate, man or woman, must be bound; law must not cease.'[77] These warnings indicated the persistence of the anxieties about sweeping Protectoral powers that some Presbyterians had expressed in the first two Protectorate Parliaments.

It is important to notice that encomia of the new Protector were in no way the exclusive preserve of courtiers or Presbyterians. Commonwealthsmen were anxious to stress their lack of personal animus towards him. Hesilrige, for instance, reportedly declared: 'I never knew any guile or gall in him. I honour the person.' Or, on another occasion: 'I confess, I do love the person of the Lord Protector. I never saw nor heard either fraud or guile in him. I wish only continuance of wealth, health, and safety to his family. I wish the greatest of honour and wealth of any man in this nation to him and his posterity.'[78] Henry Neville likewise moved 'to declare the Protector to be Chief Magistrate' on the grounds that 'he is the fittest person of any man in England'.[79] Other commonwealthsmen, while echoing such plaudits, regretted the vagueness of the Humble Petition and Advice and urged the need to define the Protector's powers more clearly. Thus Thomas Scott: 'I would not hazard a hair of his present highness's head. Yet I would trust no man with more power than what is good for him and for the people . . . If you think of a single person, I would have him sooner than any man alive.'[80] Lambert's close ally Adam Baynes took a similar line and reminded members of the possibility that a future chief magistrate might be less attractive than Richard: 'I do honour him; but he cannot always live. It is an unhappiness oftentimes for the people to have a good Chief Magistrate . . . Let us set the Government so, that the worst of men cannot hurt us.'[81] Such concerns notwithstanding, the chorus of praise for Richard was remarkable, and even a political maverick of possible royalist sympathies like Robert Reynolds joined in: 'I heard not one man against the single person: against *the* single person there is not one exception. Not any other man in this nation

[76] Burton, III, 146. Cf. Schilling, p. 43.
[77] Burton, III, 262. Cf. BL, Add. MS 5138, p. 176; and Schilling, p. 71.
[78] Burton, III, 27, 104. Cf. BL, Add. MS 5138, p. 113; and Schilling, p. 31.
[79] Burton, III, 134. Cf. Schilling, pp. 39–40.   [80] Burton, III, 112.
[81] Burton, III, 216–17; BL, Add. MS 5138, p. 168. Cf. Schilling, p. 58.

would pass so clearly. I have particular and personal reasons. I would venture my life rather than he should be in danger.'[82]

Whatever the sincerity of these claims, this apparent goodwill towards Richard suggests that the third Protectorate Parliament was not doomed to failure from the outset. Indeed, by late February the situation looked more promising for Richard and his allies than it had done a few weeks earlier. Bordeaux reported that 'before the meeting of Parliament', everyone, 'even the most enlightened ministers of state', suspected that 'the Protector was threatened with an alliance between the disaffected officers of the army and the republican members, and that these two parties, acting together, would be capable of effecting a change in the government'. Since then, however, 'the Protector's party gained strength in Parliament'. The main danger, Bordeaux observed shrewdly, was that 'the public belief that the Protector has failed in regaining the adherence of the leaders of the army, without putting himself entirely in their hands, [might] yet alienate from him the support of many'.[83] Nevertheless, by the end of March, after the Parliament had sat for a couple of months, Richard had gained significant measures from it, although not as many as he would ideally have liked. He had secured a resolution recognising his title as Lord Protector (although the bill to that effect languished), the recognition of the Other House, and an acknowledgement of the legitimacy of the Scottish and Irish members of the Commons. Sir Richard Browne thought that the 'admission of the Scotch and Irish to sit and have voice in Parliament seems to manifest the prevalence of the Court party (as they call it) over the republican, and by the accession of those voices not a little to fortify Cromwell in all future deliberations and debates'.[84] The disposal of the fleet was also left in the Protector's hands rather than in those of a committee.[85] However, a bill to settle certain taxes on the Protector for life was defeated by a resolution on 1 April that 'from and after the end, or other determination of this present Parliament, no excise, customs, or other imposts be demanded, levied, received, or paid, by any of the people of this Commonwealth, by virtue of any Act, ordinance, order, or declaration whatsoever now in being ... other than what shall be agreed upon and consented to by this House'.[86] This resolution was another manifestation not so much of hostility towards Richard or the Protectorate as of a reluctance to give him too much financial independence, at any rate until his powers were defined more specifically.

---

[82] Burton, III, 211. Cf. Schilling, pp. 54–7.   [83] Guizot, *Richard Cromwell*, I, 314–17.
[84] *Nicholas Papers*, IV, 87.
[85] Burton, III, 493; BL, Add. MS 5138, p. 245; Schilling, p. 122; *CJ*, VII, 607; *TSP*, VII, 626.
[86] Burton, IV, 327. Cf. Derbyshire Record Office, MS D258/10/9/2 (diary of Sir John Gell), fo. 13v.

Despite these disputes and tensions, the Parliament did not seem to be on the verge of collapse at the end of March, and events appeared to be moving in Richard's favour. James Sharp noted on 24 March that 'there is a great change in the House of Commons by the passing of two votes this week for the sitting of the Scottish and Irish members during this present Parliament, which, being critical votes, give occasion to a general apprehension that the Republican party are upon the declining hand, and so the P[resbyterian] party shall gain many proselytes'.[87] Similarly, Giavarina wrote the following day that 'there is good reason to look for a happy issue in conformity with the wishes of the Protector because it is noteworthy that notwithstanding the disputes and delays his party prevails at every decision', and as late as 8 April he reported that 'in spite of the numerous difficulties raised by opponents everything has proceeded in accordance with the Protector's desires'.[88] That same day, a royalist agent observed that 'it is now very apparently manifest, which before was suspected, that Cromwell's party is abundantly the more powerful, and that what they want in reason they supply in number, and will by that advantage in a short time (without the ... interposition of some accident) work all things to their own will'.[89] The Parliament's subsequent disintegration – culminating in its dissolution on 22 April – was remarkably rapid and was due primarily to the intervention of the army. As so often during Oliver's Protectorate, tensions between army officers and civilian politicians helped to destabilise Parliament. Richard was treading the same uneasy path between the army and Parliament as his father had done, and when the two ultimately fell out the consequences were disastrous for both the Parliament and the Protectorate. Although this process owed much to deep-rooted and longer-term incompatibilities of outlook between the civilian interest and the army leaders that can be traced back to the inception of the Protectorate and beyond, the final unfolding was quite short-term. To his credit, Richard perceived the potential hazard that the army presented, and lost 'no opportunity of caressing the soldiers': he was, for example, 'present when they received their pay' on 25 February and 'addressed them with much confidence and friendship'.[90] Indeed, the army's apparent loyalty came as a pleasant surprise to Thurloe, who wrote on 22 March: 'it is a miracle of mercy that we are yet in peace, considering what the debates are, and what underhand working there is to disaffect the officers of the army: but for ought I can perceive, they remain pretty staunch, though they are in great want of pay, for which no provision is at all made, nor do I see that we are likely to have any yet'.[91]

[87] Stephen, II, 160.   [88] *CSPV*, 1659–61, 1, 6.   [89] Bodl., MS Clarendon 60, fo. 307r.
[90] Guizot, *Richard Cromwell*, I, 321.   [91] *TSP*, VII, 636.

Nevertheless, mistrust of Richard was steadily growing among the senior army officers, and especially among those whom Ludlow referred to as the 'Wallingford House, or army-party', notably Fleetwood, Disbrowe, Sydenham, Kelsey, and Berry.[92] Their view of Richard was not improved when, probably in March, a cornet in Richard Ingoldsby's regiment was summoned before Richard for insubordination, and denounced his major as ungodly. Richard allegedly responded: 'Go thy way, Dick Ingoldsby, thou canst neither preach nor pray, but I will believe thee before I believe twenty of them.' This incident appears to have reinforced the fears of leading army officers that Richard's religious sympathies were less in tune with theirs than his father's had been. According to Ludlow, 'from this time all men among them who made but the least pretences to religion and sobriety began to think themselves unsafe whilst he governed'.[93] Around the end of March, Richard, possibly in an attempt to mollify the army leaders, apparently consented to a request from Fleetwood and Disbrowe that a general council of officers be convened, although the details of this agreement are difficult to reconstruct.[94] It was a fateful step, for when the army council met at Wallingford House on 2 April, it authorised the drafting of a 'humble representation and petition' to the Protector. Whitelocke later wrote in his *Diary*: 'On the 6 of this month a representation was signed by all the officers of the army, and afterwards presented to his highness setting forth their want of pay, the insolences of the enemies, and their designs together with some in power to ruin the army and the good old cause.' The officers urged Richard 'to advise with the Parliament, and to provide effectual remedy'. Whitelocke commented that 'this was the beginning of Richard's fall': he observed that it was 'set on foot by' Fleetwood and Disbrowe, and that 'the Parliament disputed about the Other House but took no course to provide money, but exasperated the army, and all those named of the Other House'.[95] Indeed, the army council's representation contained a barely concealed threat towards the Houses when it spoke of 'plucking the wicked out of their places, wheresoever they may be discovered'.[96]

Although, according to *Mercurius Politicus*, Richard publicly received the representation 'with a very great affection and respect to the whole body of officers which presented it, using many expressions of tenderness and endearment to them, as the old friends of his renowned father', in private he allegedly ordered Fleetwood to suppress it.[97] He yielded under pressure,

[92] Ludlow, II, 61–2.   [93] Ludlow, II, 62–3.   [94] Ludlow, II, 65–6.
[95] Whitelocke, *Diary*, p. 511. The same passage also appears in Whitelocke, *Memorials*, IV, 341–2. The full text of 'the humble representation and petition of the General council of the officers of the armies of England, Scotland and Ireland' is printed in *OPH*, XXI, 340–5.
[96] *OPH*, XXI, 344. See also *Nicholas Papers*, IV, 101–2; *CSPV*, 1659–61, 6–7.
[97] *Mercurius Politicus*, no. 561 (31 March–7 April 1659), p. 352; *Clarendon SP*, III, 451–2.

however, and forwarded the representation to both Houses of Parliament on 8 April.[98] If the representation showed the army leaders' growing antagonism towards Richard and the Parliament on various issues ranging from the payment of arrears to the promotion of the 'good old cause', the Commons' response revealed both a lack of empathy with the officers and a reluctance to treat their grievances with any degree of urgency. For a full ten days, they continued to discuss a range of matters including the public revenue (especially the excise), certain disputed elections, two Quaker papers, and complaints against Major-General Boteler. Only on 18 April did they belatedly turn to consider the army's representation.[99]

Ironically, the debate in the Commons that day helped to bring the two Houses closer together, for most of those who spoke advocated conferring with the Other House about how best to proceed. Among those most deeply hostile to the army's meetings were members as diverse as the crypto-royalist Viscount Falkland ('I am against their meetings, and would have them suppressed'), the Presbyterian John Swinfen ('I am against these general meetings ... They are both unnecessary and dangerous'), the Presbyterian-courtier John Maynard ('I would have plain English spoken ... Lord have mercy upon us, if we cannot speak to our army, to go to their stations and charges, but we must discontent and disoblige them'), and the solicitor-general, William Ellis ('If we cannot be obeyed in this, we sit to very little purpose ... Surely such an extraordinary meeting must have an extraordinary end').[100] The commonwealthsmen tended to take a more sympathetic line: Hesilrige, for example, 'would have you also to court them, by providing them pay ... Go upon that which will draw the affections of the army after you.'[101] Yet such sympathy was predicated on an insistence that any concessions to the army should not be detrimental to Parliament's authority. It is worth remembering, as Derek Hirst has argued, that Hesilrige was 'a Parliament-man as well as a republican'.[102] Likewise, it is telling that according to Burton, Scott not only said that 'there is a "good old cause". If their meetings be to manage that, I shall not be against them', but also added the crucial qualification: 'while their counsels are in subordination to you'.[103] After lengthy debate, the Commons passed two resolutions that Whitelocke thought 'distasteful to the army':[104] first, 'that, during the sitting of the Parliament, there shall be no General council or meeting of the officers of

[98] Burton, IV, 379; *CJ*, VII, 632.
[99] Burton, IV, 380–448; *CJ*, VII, 632–41; Guizot, *Richard Cromwell*, I, 362; BL, Lansdowne MS 823, fo. 293r.
[100] Burton, IV, 449, 451, 452, 459.   [101] Burton, IV, 450.
[102] Derek Hirst, 'Concord and Discord in Richard Cromwell's House of Commons', *EHR*, 103 (1988), 356.
[103] Burton, IV, 454.   [104] Whitelocke, *Diary*, p. 512; Whitelocke, *Memorials*, IV, 342.

the army without the direction, leave, and authority of his highness the Lord Protector, and both Houses of Parliament'; and, secondly, 'that no person shall have or continue any command or trust in any of the armies or navies of England, Scotland or Ireland ... who shall refuse to subscribe, that he will not disturb or interrupt the free meetings in Parliament of any the members of either House of Parliament, or their freedom in their debates and counsels'. The Commons then resolved to seek 'the concurrence of the Other House ... to these votes'. Only after passing these resolutions did the House then agree to consider, the following day, 'how the arrears of the armies and navies may be speedily satisfied'.[105]

The army's representation had also been forwarded on 8 April to the Other House which, possibly swayed by the presence of such senior officers as Sydenham, Whalley, Fleetwood, Berry, and Goffe, acted with greater despatch than the Commons and resolved to consider the matter on Monday, 11 April.[106] That day, they referred the matter to a committee (which included all these grandees as well as Disbrowe), and ordered them to report the following day. The committee found it impossible to report within the time available, and the item was postponed and then disappeared from view until the Commons' two resolutions of 18 April were brought to the Other House the next day.[107] According to Thomas Clarges, 'the Other House was in a great consternation upon receipt of' the Commons' resolutions, 'and were so high, as many moved to lay them aside, and it was carried but by one voice in the contrary, which I somewhat admire; for without doubt, if they disagree with us in these, a further transaction may be doubtful'.[108] The House voted, by a majority, to set aside all other business and to consider the Commons' resolutions the next day. This they did throughout 20 April, without reaching a conclusion; further discussion was then deferred until 22 April to allow for consideration of amendments to a bill for 'securing the nation against the common enemy', but the debate was never resumed, and the Parliament was dissolved that day.[109]

It was ironic, given the government's protracted efforts to secure the recognition of the Other House, that Richard did not wait for that House to come to a view: indeed, John Barwick thought that the second chamber was 'another clog upon him' and had 'encouraged the army to their late interposition into the affairs of state'.[110] Instead, on 18 April, Richard immediately informed the officers of the Commons' resolutions, forbade them from holding further meetings, and ordered them to return to their respective posts. Disbrowe 'attempted to justify what had passed at their meetings', but Richard insisted

[105] *CJ*, VII, 641. See also BL, Lansdowne MS 823, fo. 297r; *TSP*, VII, 657–8, 662.
[106] HMC, *MSS of the House of Lords*, pp. 557–8.
[107] HMC, *MSS of the House of Lords*, pp. 558–63.   [108] *TSP*, VII, 658.
[109] HMC, *MSS of the House of Lords*, pp. 564–7.   [110] *TSP*, VII, 662.

that they repair to their commands, whereupon they 'withdrew without replying'.[111] Although the army council meeting scheduled for 20 April appears not to have taken place, the officers failed to disperse. Richard summoned Fleetwood to Whitehall, 'but the messenger returned without an answer'; instead, Fleetwood ordered a rendezvous of the army at St James's for 21 April, whereupon Richard ordered a counter-rendezvous for the same time at Whitehall.[112] Meanwhile, on the morning of 21 April, the Commons began to debate the settling of the armed forces as a militia, possibly under Parliament's control, which was precisely what the army most feared.[113] According to Ludlow, at about noon that day Disbrowe came to Richard at Whitehall and told him that 'if he would dissolve his Parliament, the officers would take care of him; but that, if he refused so to do, they would do it without him, and leave him to shift for himself'.[114]

It soon became clear on 21 April that virtually all the regiments in London were attending Fleetwood's rendezvous rather than Richard's, and the latter was left 'a general without an army'.[115] That evening Disbrowe led a deputation of about a dozen officers to Richard to repeat the demand for Parliament's dissolution.[116] Bordeaux had written the previous day, with characteristic insight, that Richard 'will yield to the wishes of the [army] leaders, and will prefer this to placing himself in the hands of the Parliament, which is composed of men of no solidity, who would desert him at a pinch, and some of whom are on his side only so long as they believe it to be consistent with the design of restoring the king'.[117] Bordeaux was proved correct. Whitelocke recorded that, faced with the army's demand, Richard conferred with Broghill, Fiennes, Thurloe, Wolseley, and himself. 'Most of them were for it', Whitelocke wrote, although he claimed that he himself was not, 'and wished a little longer permission of their sitting, especially now they had begun to consider of raising money, whereby they would engage the soldiery.' 'Most were for the dissolving of the Parliament', and 'it [was] said that the Lord Broghill persuaded his highness to sign the commission for dissolution of the Parliament'.[118] This was delivered to the Houses the following morning.[119] The Other House promptly obeyed, but the Commons initially tried to resist and locked their doors. Faced with

[111] Guizot, *Richard Cromwell*, I, 364. See also *TSP*, VII, 658; BL, Lansdowne MS 823, fos. 299r–v, 301r–302r.
[112] Ludlow, II, 68–9. See also *CSPV*, 1659–61, 10–12.   [113] Burton, IV, 472–81.
[114] Ludlow, II, 69. See also Guizot, *Richard Cromwell*, I, 366; *Nicholas Papers*, IV, 124–5.
[115] Ludlow, II, 69. See also *Clarke Papers*, III, 193–4.   [116] Guizot, *Richard Cromwell*, I, 370.
[117] Guizot, *Richard Cromwell*, I, 367.
[118] Whitelocke, *Diary*, p. 512; Whitelocke, *Memorials*, IV, 343; *Clarke Papers*, V, 285.
[119] Whitelocke, *Diary*, p. 512; Whitelocke, *Memorials*, IV, 343. See also Guizot, *Richard Cromwell*, I, 371; Burton, IV, 482–3; Ludlow, II, 70–1; *CSPV*, 1659–61, 13–14; BL, Lansdowne MS 823, fo. 304r; Little, *Broghill*, p. 168.

the threat of military force, however, they adjourned: the army then barred entry to the House and the members dispersed.[120] So ended the third and last of the Protectorate Parliaments.

RICHARD CROMWELL AND PARLIAMENTS: A REASSESSMENT

The dissolution of the third Protectorate Parliament is perhaps best understood as one in a long line of army interventions that sought either to dissolve a Parliament or to manipulate its membership, following those of August 1647, December 1648, April 1653, and September 1654. It was strangely fitting that the Protectorate, which had been conceived after the expulsion of the Rump and the self-destruction of Barebone's, itself survived the end of the last Protectorate Parliament by barely a month. The fundamental problem remained the lack of understanding between the army leadership and many ordinary members of Parliament. This manifested itself in contrasting political and religious priorities, and different conceptions of the 'good old cause'. Whereas under Oliver Cromwell a military Lord Protector excited the suspicion of many within Parliament, under his son a civilian, pro-Presbyterian Lord Protector excited the suspicion of many within the army. Both Cromwells tried in different ways to straddle two essentially incompatible worlds, yet their attempts to do so often tended to destabilise parliamentary proceedings between 1653 and 1659. This did not mean that the Parliaments were unable to function effectively or productively, but it did represent an inherent source of weakness that had potentially disastrous consequences if the 'single person and Parliament' failed to govern harmoniously together.

It was indicative of the deep dilemma facing Richard Cromwell that on 21 April 1659 he conferred with his closest advisers, all of whom were civilians, and then capitulated to the army's demand that the Parliament be dissolved. He thus ended up gaining the worst of both worlds. Many courtiers lamented the passing of the Parliament and felt that he had sold out to the army, yet in spite of that the army leaders still did not see him as one of their own. John Maidstone, steward and cofferer of the Protectoral household, wrote that the army always 'reflected on [Richard] as a person true to the civil interest, and not fixed to them'.[121] Although technically Richard remained Protector for about another four weeks, his powers in effect came to an end with the dissolution of the third Protectorate Parliament.

---

[120] HMC, *MSS of the House of Lords*, pp. 566–7; Burton, IV, 482–3; *CJ*, VII, 644; Ludlow, II, 70–1; *Clarke Papers*, IV, 20–1; *Nicholas Papers*, IV, 116–18; Bodl., MS Clarendon 60, fo. 432r–v.
[121] *TSP*, I, 767.

Thereafter, he was 'little better than a prisoner' at Whitehall, left in a 'state of abandonment' and 'a melancholy posture'.[122] By the beginning of May, 'the whole army, officers and soldiers, [spoke] with such contempt of the person of this Protector and abomination of his father's memory as amazes all the hearers'.[123] On 7 May the army secured the return of the Rump Parliament and with it the Commonwealth; then, on 19 May, the Rump elected a new council, and a few days later demanded Richard's resignation.[124] As one royalist writer put it, 'his late highness Richard is now a very Dick with them'.[125] On 14 May the Rump passed an act to destroy the Great Seal of the Protectorate and revert to that of the Commonwealth.[126] It was, perhaps, the betrayal of his brother-in-law Fleetwood and his uncle Disbrowe that hurt Richard most deeply. Of them he wrote: 'they tripped up my heels before I knew them, for though they were relations, yet they forsook me ... They are pitiful creatures. God will avenge innocence.'[127]

Despite his youth and his relative lack of political experience, Richard displayed considerable skill in handling the difficult and complex circumstances that he inherited from Oliver. At first sight, perhaps his greatest weakness was that he succeeded his father. Most obviously, he lacked his father's exceptional military record, and his own sympathies inclined more towards Presbyterians than Independents. Richard nevertheless attempted to make the best of the situation and to turn these traits to his own advantage. The proceedings of the third Protectorate Parliament suggest that the failure of his efforts to build political support was far from inevitable. Despite the evident difficulties of the session, by March 1659, events were steadily moving in Richard's direction until the decisive army intervention in April–May proved fatal first to the Parliament and then to the Protectorate itself. That intervention reflected long-term anxieties among the army officers that can only have been exacerbated by Richard's civilian background and Presbyterian leanings. Yet the actual coup, led by Fleetwood and Disbrowe, took place suddenly and for essentially short-term reasons. It reflected army fears that Richard was gaining too firm a hold on the Parliament, and that he was guiding it in directions that would ultimately prove prejudicial to the army's aims and interests. Richard's misfortune was thus that he fell foul of the army before he had had sufficient time to construct a secure parliamentary base. His own benign character and

[122] Bodl., MS Clarendon 60, fo. 456r; Guizot, *Richard Cromwell*, I, 385; *Nicholas Papers*, IV, 122. See also *CSPV*, 1659–61, 16–18.
[123] Bodl., MS Clarendon 60, fo. 465r.
[124] Ludlow, II, 77–85; Whitelocke, *Diary*, pp. 513–16; Whitelocke, *Memorials*, IV, 343–50; *A & O*, II, 1272–6.
[125] *Nicholas Papers*, IV, 135.   [126] *A & O*, II, 1271; *CJ*, VII, 654.
[127] BL, Lansdowne MS 823, fo. 370r. See also *CSPD*, 1658–9, 336.

attitudes could well have enabled him to become an effective leader of a broad and moderate coalition, within which a large number of Presbyterian members were playing a more supportive and co-operative role than they had in the first two Protectorate Parliaments.

During much of his brief career as Protector, and in his dealings with the third Protectorate Parliament, Richard had grappled with what was perhaps the central constitutional problem of the Protectorate: whether, and how far, its institutions should resemble older forms of government. This applied in particular to the franchise, the powers of the head of state, the privileges of Parliament, and the existence of an Other House. Some members thought the Instrument of Government too radical while others thought it too conservative, and the Humble Petition and Advice was if anything less satisfactory than the Instrument because in seeking to construct a basis for settlement its terms were vaguer, less clearly defined. Much of the third Protectorate Parliament's time was spent trying to achieve greater definition of Protectoral powers and parliamentary structures, and these attempts produced rambling and inconclusive debates that soon ran up against the problems of Parliament's legal role and judicature. This was in turn closely connected to a cluster of longstanding issues that dogged Parliament throughout the Protectorate, namely the relationship between Parliament and the legal system, the role that Parliament might play in promoting legal reform, and the nature and scope of parliamentary judicature. All three Protectorate Parliaments tried to address these closely related questions, and the story of their attempts will form the subject of the next chapter.

8

Law reform, judicature, and the
Other House

During the medieval and Tudor periods, the English Parliament had developed in close conjunction with the legal and judicial systems. Parliament was the monarch's 'high court' and exercised justice in the monarch's name.[1] In addition to joint proceedings of the two Houses, for example, in cases of impeachment, the House of Lords possessed an appellate judicature and from 1621 re-established itself as a formidably effective and popular court of appeal.[2] The abolition of the monarchy and the House of Lords in 1649 therefore raised major questions about Parliament's judicial and legal role. How far had the Lords' judicial powers been transferred to the unicameral Parliaments of the Interregnum? This issue emerged most starkly during the trial of James Nayler in 1656, and prompted calls for another House that would fulfil some of the functions of the old House of Lords and constrain the Commons' actions. Yet the creation of the Other House by the Humble Petition and Advice proved highly controversial, and sparked major debates over its status and powers during 1658–9. Furthermore, the Protectorate Parliaments regularly addressed issues relating to law reform, although the reality of what was achieved in this area fell far short of what Cromwell desired. Parliament's relationship with the law and the legal system remained highly contested throughout the Protectorate and was a further source of division both among members and between Cromwell and Parliament.

LAW REFORM IN THE FIRST AND SECOND
PROTECTORATE PARLIAMENTS

The reform of the law was discussed repeatedly during the English Revolution from about 1646 onwards, and especially during the

---

[1] For an overview of this aspect of Parliament, see David L. Smith, *The Stuart Parliaments, 1603–1689* (1999), pp. 32–8.
[2] James S. Hart, *Justice upon Petition: The House of Lords and the Reformation of Justice, 1621–1675* (1991).

171

Interregnum.[3] The Rump debated these matters extensively during 1649–50, and in January 1652 it appointed a commission chaired by the lawyer Matthew Hale to draw up proposals for law reforms.[4] The Hale Commission, as it is generally known, drafted sixteen bills, by far the longest of which was the last, which proposed a major decentralisation of legal proceedings, for example, through the creation of county registries to record land transactions and titles, and also to grant probate and administration of wills. This draft bill also provided for the establishment of county courts to hear ordinary cases with a procedure for appeal to the Upper Bench and Common Pleas; fundamental reform of the court of Chancery; and significant changes to the law of debt. These reforms represented a skilful compromise between more far-reaching (especially Leveller) demands for radical restructuring of the legal system, and more conservative influences, especially within the legal profession.[5] However, when they were presented to the Rump in January 1653, not one of them was adopted, probably due to the caution of some of the lawyers in the Parliament, and also to a desire among many members not to antagonise moderates and Presbyterians. The sum total of the Rump's legal reforms consisted of acts for probate of wills, the reform of debt law, and the conversion of legal proceedings into the English language. Some of the Hale Commission's proposals were taken up by Barebone's Parliament, which passed acts for civil marriages and for the relief of creditors and poor prisoners. Barebone's also voted to abolish Chancery, but did not take this further.[6] There things stood when the Parliament dissolved itself on 12 December 1653 and the Protectorate was established a few days later.

The importance that Cromwell attached to legal reform was evident in the various Protectoral ordinances on this subject that he issued between late December 1653 and 2 September 1654. Among the most notable were ordinances continuing the Rump's act for probate of wills and granting administration (24 December 1653 and 3 April 1654), an ordinance for

---

[3] For a helpful survey, see James S. Hart, *The Rule of Law, 1603–1660: Crown, Courts and Judges* (Harlow, 2003), especially chapters 7 and 8. Also useful are Stuart E. Prall, *The Agitation for Law Reform during the Puritan Revolution, 1640–1660* (The Hague, 1966), and Donald Veall, *The Popular Movement for Law Reform, 1640–1660* (Oxford, 1970).

[4] Blair Worden, *The Rump Parliament, 1648–1653* (Cambridge, 1974), pp. 105–18; G. B. Nourse, 'Law Reform under the Commonwealth and Protectorate', *Law Quarterly Review*, 75 (1959), 512–29, especially 515–18.

[5] Mary Cotterell, 'Interregnum Law Reform: The Hale Commission of 1652', *EHR*, 83 (1968), 689–704; Alan Cromartie, *Sir Matthew Hale, 1609–1676: Law, Religion, and Natural Philosophy* (Cambridge, 1995), pp. 70–3; Nourse, 'Law Reform', 518–22; Veall, *Popular Movement*, pp. 79–84, 153–60, 180–90.

[6] Austin Woolrych, *Commonwealth to Protectorate* (Oxford, 1982), pp. 262–73; Prall, *Agitation for Law Reform*, pp. 79–98; Nourse, 'Law Reform', 522–6.

the relief of creditors and poor prisoners (9 June 1654), one for establishing a High Court of Justice (13 June 1654), and another 'for the better regulating and limiting the jurisdiction of the High Court of Chancery' (21 August 1654).[7] William Sheppard, a Gloucestershire lawyer and religious Independent whom Cromwell had invited to London in March 1654 to serve as his legal adviser, almost certainly drafted the last of these ordinances, and it reflected Cromwell's wish to make Chancery more efficient and less expensive for litigants.[8] In particular, the Chancery ordinance sought to reduce the delays for which the court was notorious, and the lengthy ordinance (comprising sixty-seven clauses) introduced major reforms: for example, justices of the peace were authorised to take depositions from litigants in the localities, without waiting for them to travel to London; the court was to sit in the afternoons as well as mornings in order to expedite business; a court of appeal was established that included two judges from each of the four common-law courts in addition to Chancery commissioners; and the scope of the court's jurisdiction was reduced.[9] Stephen Black has described this wide-ranging measure as 'the only piece of comprehensive legislation in the field of law reform enacted during the Interregnum'.[10]

When the first Protectorate Parliament assembled on 4 September 1654, Cromwell warmly praised this ordinance, and stressed the need to pursue further legal reforms. He informed members that the government 'desired to reform the laws. I say to reform them: and for that end it has called together persons ... of as great ability and as great integrity as are in these nations, to consider how the laws might be made plain and short, and less chargeable to the people; how to lessen expense, for the good of the nation'. He went on to observe that 'those things are in preparation; which in due time, I make no question, will be tendered to you', and that 'in the mean while there has been care taken to put the administration of the laws into the hands of just men; men of the most known integrity and ability'. He took particular pleasure in the fact that 'the Chancery has been reformed; and I hope, to the just satisfaction of all good men: and as to the things and causes, depending there, which made the burden and work of the honourable persons entrusted in those services too heavy for their ability, it has referred many of them to places where Englishmen love to have their rights tried, the Courts of Law at Westminster'.[11]

---

[7] *A & O*, II, 824, 869, 911–15, 917–18, 949–67.
[8] On William Sheppard's role and significance, see Nancy L. Matthews, *William Sheppard, Cromwell's Law Reformer* (Cambridge, 1984).
[9] *A & O*, II, 949–67; Prall, *Agitation for Law Reform*, pp. 105–11.
[10] Stephen F. Black, '*Coram Protectore*: The Judges of Westminster Hall under the Protectorate of Oliver Cromwell', *American Journal of Legal History*, 20 (1976), 52.
[11] Lomas–Carlyle, II, 353.

However, in this, as in other respects, the Parliament proved a great disappointment to Cromwell. Of the more than forty bills that this Parliament considered, several addressed issues of legal reform, including 'an Act for creditors and prisoners', 'an Act for taking away the Court of Wards', 'an Act for taking away purveyance', 'an Act for probate of wills', and 'an Act for settling a Court of Justice at York'.[12] Yet in the event very little progress was made on any of these measures, and instead the House concentrated on reviewing the Protectoral ordinances issued earlier that year. For example, on 5 October the Chancery ordinance was referred to a committee, and eight days later the House accepted their recommendation that the ordinance be suspended until 28 November.[13] On 25 November, this suspension was further extended until 25 December, and this was later renewed to 1 March 1655.[14] In the meantime, an act 'for the better regulating and limiting the jurisdiction of' Chancery passed its first reading on 4 December, but got no further before the Parliament's dissolution.[15] Similarly, on 25 October the judges' proceedings under the ordinance for the relief of creditors and poor prisoners were suspended and a committee was appointed to consider this ordinance.[16] However, the committee did not report back during the Parliament's lifetime. On 31 October, a committee was appointed to bring in a bill 'for taking away the Court of Wards'.[17] This passed its first reading on 15 December and its second a week later, but no more was heard of it.[18] A bill for taking away the Court of Wards in Ireland likewise passed its first reading on 22 December but then disappeared.[19] On 21 November, the committee for the Court of Wards bill was also instructed to 'bring in a bill for the taking away of purveyance': this passed its first two readings and was committed, but was then lost.[20] On 14 December, a committee was appointed to consider 'how the probate of wills, and granting administration, and recovery of legacies, may be settled throughout all England and Wales, for the greatest ease and advantage of the people; and to prepare one or more bills to that purpose, if they think fit', but this again left no

[12] See the draft list of bills intended for the first Protectorate Parliament in BL, Stowe MS 322 (Revenue Papers), fo. 74r–v.

[13] *CJ*, VII, 373–4, 376; Burton, I, xlviii; *Mercurius Politicus*, no. 226 (5–12 October 1654), pp. 3830–1; *Mercurius Politicus*, no. 227 (12–19 October 1654), p. 3847.

[14] *CJ*, VII, 390, 414; Burton, I, xcvi; *Mercurius Politicus*, no. 233 (23–30 November 1654), p. 4054; Whitelocke, *Memorials*, IV, 158.

[15] *CJ*, VII, 394.

[16] *CJ*, VII, 378; *Severall proceedings in Parliament*, no. 265 (19–26 October 1654), p. 4208; Whitelocke, *Memorials*, IV, 154.

[17] *CJ*, VII, 380.

[18] *CJ*, VII, 402, 407; *Mercurius Politicus*, no. 237 (21–28 December 1654), p. 5017.

[19] *CJ*, VII, 407.

[20] *CJ*, VII, 387, 402, 407; *Mercurius Politicus*, no. 237 (21–28 December 1654), p. 5017.

further trace in the parliamentary record.[21] That same committee was also entrusted to prepare a similar bill regarding probate of wills in Ireland but it never reported back, while a bill for 'the uniting of Ireland unto the Commonwealth of England', which would have involved 're-establishing the courts of judicature there', passed its first reading on 15 January and was due for its second reading the day the Parliament was dissolved.[22] This lack of any solid legislative achievement helps to explain Cromwell's lament, in his speech of dissolution on 22 January 1655, that the Parliament had failed where it 'might have proceeded to have made those good and whole-some laws which the people expected from you, and might have answered the grievances, and settled those things proper to you as a Parliament'.[23]

In the interval between the first and second Protectorate Parliaments, Cromwell continued to support the cause of law reform. At the same time, however, his relations with the legal profession in general, and with the judiciary in particular, steadily deteriorated. Some professional lawyers felt uneasy about Cromwellian attempts at legal reform, possibly in part because of innate conservatism and caution, and in part because they perceived them as a threat to their own vested interests. Perhaps more significantly, the fact that the first Protectorate Parliament never confirmed the Instrument of Government led some of them to question the legal validity of the Protector's powers. This issue came to a head during 1655–6 over two matters above all: the implementation of the Chancery ordinance and the case of George Cony.

Parliament's suspension of the Chancery ordinance lapsed on 1 March 1655, and Cromwell assumed that the ordinance therefore resumed effect from that date. On 23 April, the three commissioners of the Great Seal, Bulstrode Whitelocke, Sir Thomas Widdrington, and John Lisle, together with the Master of the Rolls, William Lenthall, were summoned before a committee of the council and instructed to enforce the ordinance as soon as possible. Lenthall, Whitelocke, and Widdrington refused on the grounds that the ordinance had never received parliamentary ratification, and on 1 May they wrote to the Lord President of the council informing him that they could not give themselves 'satisfaction so as to be free to proceed upon' the ordinance touching Chancery, notwithstanding 'the great trouble of our own thoughts in our unhappiness in this dissatisfaction'.[24] Whitelocke later recounted that 'for me to execute this ordinance as law, when I knew that those who made it had no legal power to make a law, could not be justified

---

[21] *CJ*, VII, 400–1; Whitelocke, *Memorials*, IV, 161.   [22] *CJ*, VII, 401, 415–16.
[23] Lomas–Carlyle, II, 407.
[24] TNA, SP 25/76, p. 57. For the appointments of Widdrington, Whitelocke, and Lisle, see *CJ*, VII, 378.

in conscience, and would be a betraying of the rights of the people of England, and too much countenancing of an illegal authority'.[25] Cromwell remained equally determined that the ordinance should be enforced, and on 6 June he summoned the commissioners and the Master of the Rolls to appear before him and the council. Whitelocke insisted that 'our scruple was not upon the authority of his highness and the council, as to the command of all matters concerning the government of the commonwealth, but only as to the effect of this ordinance, to be executed as a law, the which we apprehended . . . would be of great prejudice to the public, and would be contrary to what we had formerly by our oath promised'.[26] Lisle capitulated, but Whitelocke and Widdrington stood firm: as a result, they were removed from the bench and replaced as commissioners of the Great Seal by Nathaniel Fiennes. However, this proved to be a pyrrhic victory for Cromwell because it soon became clear that Fiennes lacked the stature to ensure the ordinance's implementation.[27]

The case of George Cony similarly hinged on the legality of Protectoral ordinances that Parliament had not confirmed. In November 1654, Cony, a London merchant, refused to pay customs duties on imported silk and was imprisoned. His lawyers asserted that the customs duties were 'due by no law since' an ordinance of December 1647 that had expired in 1653 with the dissolution of the Rump.[28] This case was deeply problematic for Cromwell because the Instrument of Government had authorised the Protector and his council to raise customs; Cony's refusal thus posed a direct challenge to the Instrument's legitimacy.[29] The case was heard before Chief Justice Henry Rolle in the Upper Bench on 12 May, and six days later he and Cony's lawyers were ordered to appear before the council. There Cromwell berated them and according to one (possibly biased) royalist account declared that, 'if they would have Magna Carta (which they had talked so much of in Westminster Hall), they must put on each a helmet and troop for it'.[30] Clarendon's even more colourful account alleged that 'when they with all humility mentioned the law and *Magna Charta*, Cromwell told them, that their *magna farta* should not control his actions, which he knew were for the safety of the commonwealth'.[31] Rolle was so offended that according to Ludlow 'he desired by a letter to Cromwell to have his quietus': his resignation was duly accepted on 7 June and about a week later John Glynne, a loyal Cromwellian, was appointed to succeed him. Cony recognised that Glynne's

[25] Whitelocke, *Memorials*, IV, 204.   [26] Whitelocke, *Memorials*, IV, 205.
[27] Black, 'Coram Protectore', 53–5.   [28] TNA, SP 18/97/48; Vaughan, I, 175–6.
[29] Gardiner, *Constitutional Documents*, p. 414 (article 27 of the Instrument).
[30] *Nicholas Papers*, II, 346. For Rolle's appointment, see *CJ*, VII, 378.
[31] Clarendon, *History*, VI, 93 (Book XV, § 150).

appointment rendered his case hopeless: shortly afterwards he paid both the customs duties and a fine, and was then released.[32] These altercations with the judiciary served both to expose the Instrument's uncertain legal status and to increase Cromwell's determination to pursue legal reform. They thus help to explain why, in the second Protectorate Parliament, Cromwell tried to advance the cause of reform while a significant number of members remained at best indifferent and preferred instead to devise a new written constitution in the form of the Remonstrance and later the Humble Petition and Advice.

During 1655 and 1656, Cromwell's legal adviser William Sheppard worked on a comprehensive and eloquent blueprint for the reform of English law entitled *Englands Balme*. In this book, Sheppard developed the earlier proposals of the Hale Commission, while also drawing upon other influences such as *The Lawes and Liberties of Massachusetts* (1648).[33] Published in October 1656, *Englands Balme* was dedicated to Sheppard's patrons with the words: 'there is none that may more justly challenge a share in the dedication of it, than your highness and your council, by whose care it has been brought forth ... At your and the Parliament's feet therefore I do lay it down: and (knowing well your resolutions to the work), I shall not need to use any quickenings, to move you forward therein.'[34] In a prefatory letter 'to the right honourable the Lords and Gentlemen assembled in Parliament', Sheppard offered the book to 'this Parliament now convened and sitting'. The main text, comprising 215 pages and 13 chapters, presented a systematic body of proposals designed to ensure:

that offensive, oppressive, and superfluous laws be removed, defective laws supplied, doubtful laws cleared, and all the good laws abridged and well executed: that quick and speedy justice be done for the recovery of right, relief against wrong, and for this, that all the Courts of Justice be regulated: that men's properties and liberties be well settled and secured: that men may make the uttermost improvement of their estates, without prejudice to the public; that evil men and masters be discouraged, and the good encouraged: and such-like things as these.[35]

In particular, Sheppard called for a much more elaborate system of county and borough courts; the creation of a superior court of appeal containing all the judges of the four courts at Westminster; enhanced responsibilities for justices of the peace, who would be increased in number and carefully chosen for their honesty and ability; standardised fees and new rules for reducing delays in all courts; the registration of wills and the bringing of grants of

---

[32] Ludlow, I, 413; Black, '*Coram Protectore*', 58.
[33] Matthews, *William Sheppard*, pp. 144–86.
[34] William Sheppard, *Englands Balme* (1656), sigs. A3v–A4r.
[35] Sheppard, *Englands Balme*, sig. [a3r–v].

probate and letters of administration (historically the preserve of the ecclesiastical courts) within the remit of the common-law courts; the registration of land; and new procedures for enabling creditors to regain money due to them.[36] Sheppard concluded the preface to his book, signed at Whitehall on 1 October 1656, with the hope 'that this Parliament may do it'.[37]

Two weeks earlier, on 17 September, Cromwell developed very similar themes in more general terms during his opening speech to the second Protectorate Parliament. There was, he argued, 'one general grievance in the nation. It is the law. Not that the laws are a grievance; but there are laws that are a grievance; and the great grievance lies in the execution and administration.' He told members that:

there are wicked and abominable laws, that it will be in your power to alter. To hang a man for six pence, thirteen pence, I know not what; to hang for a trifle, and pardon murder, is in the ministration of the law, through the ill-framing of it. I have known in my experience abominable murders acquitted. And to come and see men lose their lives for petty matters: this is a thing that God will reckon for.

He hoped that it would 'not lie upon this nation a day longer than you have an opportunity to give a remedy; and I hope I shall cheerfully join with you in it. This has been a great grief to many honest hearts and conscientious people; and I hope it is in all your hearts to rectify it.'[38] Over the weeks that followed, several bills were introduced, consistent with the hopes of Cromwell and Sheppard, and these found some support among council members such as John Disbrowe, Sir Charles Wolseley, Walter Strickland, Sir Gilbert Pickering, Philip Jones, and John Lambert. By contrast, resistance to the reforming bills was sometimes led by prominent legal officers, including Chief Justice John Glynne, Solicitor-General William Ellis, Attorney-General Sir Edmond Prideaux, Attorney for the Duchy of Lancaster Nicholas Lechmere, and Master of the Rolls William Lenthall.[39] The result was that this Parliament's legislative achievement in the field of law reform, although not negligible, nevertheless fell well below what Cromwell had hoped for.

The Parliament produced two acts that introduced specific reforms. First, on 23 September, a committee was established to prepare a bill 'for taking away the Court of Wards and Liveries', and also for taking away wardships in Ireland and Scotland. This bill passed its third reading on 22 November

---

[36] Sheppard, *Englands Balme*, *passim*; see also the excellent analysis in Matthews, *William Sheppard*, pp. 144–86.

[37] Sheppard, *Englands Balme*, sig. [a4r–v].

[38] Lomas–Carlyle, II, 541. There are close resemblances between this section of Cromwell's speech and parts of Sheppard, *Englands Balme*: see, for example, Sheppard's discussion of 'hard laws' at pp. 191–207.

[39] Matthews, *William Sheppard*, p. 187.

and received Protectoral assent five days later. The act confirmed the abolition of the Court of Wards on 24 February 1646, and also stated that from
that date all tenures *in capite* or by socage in chief were converted into free
and common socage (freehold). The act nevertheless safeguarded certain
rents and heriots due to lords or other private individuals through ward-
ship.[40] The second measure that successfully completed its passage through
the House was an act abolishing purveyance: this passed its third reading on
12 December and received Protectoral assent on 9 June 1657. It described
purveyance as a 'great and insupportable grievance', and stipulated that 'all
statutes, laws, customs or usages touching purveyance or pre-emption, or
compositions for purveyance of pre-emption, are hereby repealed and
declared to be utterly void to all intents and purposes'.[41]

These were the only two acts implementing legal reforms that the
second Protectorate Parliament passed. In both cases the changes endured:
although – like all ordinances passed since 1642 – they were declared null and
void at the Restoration, the abolition of the Court of Wards and of purveyance was enshrined in statute in 1660–1.[42] Otherwise, however, the
Parliament's handling of legal reform presents a story of initiatives begun
but then abandoned or swamped by other business, such as the Nayler case,
or the Remonstrance and later the Humble Petition and Advice. The initial
impetus described by Thurloe on 4 November, when he informed Henry
Cromwell that 'the Parliament is going on upon several bills for reforming
the law', soon petered out.[43] Several bills introduced during the Parliament's
opening weeks addressed a number of the reforms earlier proposed by
William Sheppard, some of which had also been considered in previous
Parliaments and by the Hale Commission. For example, on 23 September,
the House ordered that 'a bill be brought in for the probate of wills in the
North, and in other parts of England'.[44] This bill passed its first reading on
24 October and its second three days later, whereupon it was committed.[45]
The bill was amended on 1 and 2 December.[46] Further amendments were
reported on 24 December, but the solicitor-general, the attorney-general,
and the chief justice all spoke 'against the registering of such wills'; the bill

---

[40] *CJ*, VII, 427, 439, 447, 450, 453, 456, 457, 460; *A & O*, II, 1043; Whitelocke, *Memorials*,
IV, 282.
[41] *CJ*, VII, 447, 449, 465, 467, 552; *A & O*, II, 1057; *The Publick Intelligencer*, no. 61 (8–15
December 1656), p. 1052; Whitelocke, *Memorials*, IV, 282, 302. See also G. E. Aylmer, 'The
Last Years of Purveyance, 1610–1660', *Economic History Review*, new series, 10 (1957),
81–93, especially 90.
[42] The relevant statutes were 12 Car. II, c. 4 (Court of Wards), and 12 Car. II, c. 24
(purveyance).
[43] *TSP*, VII, 557. Thurloe similarly told John Pell on 16 November that 'the Parliament do
mostly intend the reformation of the law': Vaughan, II, 56.
[44] *CJ*, VII, 427.   [45] *CJ*, VII, 445, 446.   [46] *CJ*, VII, 462–3.

was then, at Disbrowe's suggestion, recommitted.[47] On 24 March, the House ordered amendments to be reported six days later, but this never happened.[48] On 28 April, the reporting of these amendments was again postponed until 5 May, and then until 11 May, when minor changes were incorporated.[49] On 15 June, the bill's third reading was scheduled for three days later but, after further postponements and despite the efforts of Walter Strickland in particular, it did not in fact take place before the Parliament was adjourned on 26 June.[50] During this Parliament's second sitting in 1658, the House agreed on 22 January that the bill should be read on 1 February, but this did not occur.[51]

On 25 September 1656, a committee was established to tackle another longstanding legal issue by preparing 'a bill for settlement of marriages; and to prevent the taking away of heirs and infants, and registering of births, burials and marriages'.[52] This was tendered on 20 October, but 'exceptions were taken thereunto, for that the same was in divers places razed, interlined, and half of one of the sheets cut off', and it was therefore returned to the committee.[53] The bill then received its first reading on 15 November.[54] When it was debated on 29 April, Disbrowe, Strickland, Jones, and Lambert all expressed support for the bill, but resistance was led by Glynne, Prideaux, Lechmere, and Lenthall, all of whom argued that it should apply for six months only.[55] The bill's second reading was postponed until 23 May, but in fact occurred only during the Parliament's second sitting, on 22 January 1658.[56] The committee for the bill was afforced on 3 February, but the Parliament was dissolved the following day.[57]

A number of other bills initiated during the Parliament's opening days also soon languished. A bill 'for settling registers [of land] in every county' passed its first reading on 23 September and its second on 10 October, when it 'received a very large debate because of the opposition it received from the long robe'. In the end, the House resolved that this bill would not apply retrospectively and referred the matter to a committee, but nothing further was heard of it.[58] On 25 September, a committee was appointed 'to prepare a bill to compel those who are of ability and lie in prison, to pay their debts'. This produced a bill 'for relief of creditors and poor prisoners' that passed its first reading on 3 December.[59] On 27 April 1657, the House ordered that it be read on 6 May, but this was postponed for two weeks, and then again

---

[47] *CJ*, VII, 474; Burton, I, 226–7; Whitelocke, *Memorials*, IV, 283.
[48] *CJ*, VII, 510, 514–15.   [49] *CJ*, VII, 524, 531, 532; *Clarke Papers*, III, 108.
[50] *CJ*, VII, 558, 570, 573; Burton, II, 253–4, 283, 303.   [51] *CJ*, VII, 581; Burton, II, 338.
[52] *CJ*, VII, 428.   [53] *CJ*, VII, 441.   [54] *CJ*, VII, 454.
[55] *CJ*, VII, 526–7; Burton, II, 68–77.   [56] *CJ*, VII, 537, 581; Burton, II, 337–8.
[57] *CJ*, VII, 591–2.   [58] *CJ*, VII, 427, 437, 439, 441; Matthews, *William Sheppard*, pp. 191–2.
[59] *CJ*, VII, 428, 463.

repeatedly thereafter – despite the efforts of Disbrowe and Wolseley – until the Parliament's adjournment on 26 June.[60] On 25 September 1656, a committee was established 'to consider of the abuses in granting writs of *certiorari*', but never reported back to the House.[61] A bill 'for ascertaining of arbitrary fines, upon descent or alienation of copyholds of inheritance' passed its first reading on 29 September and its second four days later, but proceeded no further.[62]

During the first two weeks of October 1656, a number of committees were appointed to address various other aspects of legal reform, notably those 'to revise the Acts and laws touching bastardy, adultery and fornication; and to reduce them into one law'; 'to consider of the statutes and laws touching the wages of artificers, labourers and servants, and to present a bill for further redress herein'; to review 'the number and quality of attornies' and 'the number of solicitors'; and 'to revise the statutes touching wandering, idle, loose, and dissolute persons, beggars, rogues, and vagabonds, and to reduce them into one law, with such alterations and additions as shall be necessary'. However, it seems that none of these committees ever reported back to the House.[63]

Certain other measures attempted to deal with longstanding legal issues, but did not make much headway. For example, a bill 'for recovery of small debts, and relieving persons in cases of small trespasses', sought the relief of creditors: it passed its first reading on 16 October and its second two weeks later, whereupon it was committed. It then disappeared from view until 18 June 1657, when the House ordered that amendments to the bill should be reported on 'the second Thursday after the next meeting of the Parliament', but in fact no more was ever heard of it.[64] On 3 November, Lambert introduced a bill 'for the erecting a court of law and a court of equity at the City of York'. This allegedly 'startle[d] the lawyers to see the administration of law like to be carried into [the] provinces'. The bill passed its first reading on 3 November and its second on 20 November, whereupon it was committed. On 3 March 1657, the House ordered that amendments be reported a week later, but this never happened.[65] A bill 'for laying and trials of actions in their proper counties, and restraining the travelling of jurors out

---

[60] *CJ*, VII, 524, 531, 546, 549; Burton, II, 100, 245.

[61] *CJ*, VII, 428. *Certiorari* was a writ that removed a case from a lower court to either Chancery or the Upper Bench, and thus had the effect of delaying prosecution of a suit. Although this bill was apparently never drafted, the act 'for the better observation of the Lord's Day' forbade the use of writs of *certiorari*: Matthews, *William Sheppard*, p. 204; *A & O*, II, 1169–70.

[62] *CJ*, VII, 429–30, 433.   [63] *CJ*, VII, 433, 435, 438, 439.   [64] *CJ*, VII, 439, 449, 561.

[65] *CJ*, VII, 449, 456, 498, 501; *Clarke Papers*, III, 80; Matthews, *William Sheppard*, p. 199.

of their proper counties for trial of actions' passed its first reading on 11 November, but proceeded no further.[66]

Another perennial issue was the court of Chancery. On 19 February 1657, the House voted not to receive a 'report touching the Chancery, and the new rules there'. This report was hostile towards the Cromwellian Chancery ordinance, and it is consistent with their usual alignments that Disbrowe was one of the tellers for the majority who voted against receiving it, whereas Lechmere was a teller for the minority who wished to do so.[67] On 29 April, the House resolved 'that the ordinance for the better regulating and limiting of the jurisdiction of the Court of Chancery, be continued in force, until the end of this Parliament, and no longer, without further ado in Parliament'. The following day, on Disbrowe's motion, a committee was established 'to take into consideration the regulation of the Court of Chancery, and to bring in a bill in that behalf, if they see cause', but nothing further happened.[68] On 2 April, the House ordered the bill 'touching tithes' to receive its first reading on 6 April, but this did not take place.[69] On 24 April, the first reading was ordered for three days later but was repeatedly postponed until 29 May.[70] This bill finally received its first reading – on Sir William Strickland's motion – on 1 June, when it was strongly supported by Disbrowe, but opposed by Whitelocke and Lenthall; it proceeded no further thereafter.[71]

This rather desultory record was, not surprisingly, a great disappointment to Cromwell. By 21 April 1657, speaking to members of Parliament, he was beginning to wonder if 'the legislature would be almost as well in the four courts of Westminster Hall. And if they could make laws and judge too, you would have excellent laws; and the lawyers would be able to give you excellent counsel.' He went on: 'I hope you will think sincerely, as before God, that the laws must be regulated . . . surely the laws need to be regulated.' While admitting that he was no legal expert, he insisted that the problem was urgent: 'the delays in suits, and the excessiveness of fees, and the costliness of suits, and those various things that I do not know what names they bear – I have heard talk of demurrers and such-like things, which I scarce know – but I say certainly that the people are greatly suffering in this respect; they are so'. He was 'persuaded that this will be one thing that will be upon your hearts, to do something that is honourable and effectual in it'.[72] However, as we saw above, all efforts to push further bills through the House failed. Instead, from December 1656 onwards, it was with other slightly different legal issues, especially those regarding parliamentary

---

[66] *CJ*, VII, 452.   [67] *CJ*, VII, 494.   [68] *CJ*, VII, 527, 528; Burton, II, 80.
[69] *CJ*, VII, 519, 520.   [70] *CJ*, VII, 523, 524, 528–9, 531, 535, 538, 540.
[71] *CJ*, VII, 543; Burton, II, 165–6.   [72] Lomas–Carlyle, III, 95, 113.

judicature, that the second Protectorate Parliament became deeply concerned. These problems arose over two connected matters – the case of James Nayler and the establishment of the Other House – and it is to these that we now turn.

THE SECOND PROTECTORATE PARLIAMENT: JUDICATURE AND THE OTHER HOUSE

In December 1656, the case of James Nayler raised the question of how, and by what authority, the Parliament could try and sentence him. Some members argued that the original judicature of the old House of Lords had been transferred automatically to the unicameral Parliaments of the Interregnum, and that the House could therefore proceed against Nayler judicially. Others denied this, and instead urged the House to proceed by passing legislation in the form of an act of attainder. These debates deserve close examination because they addressed fundamental matters of parliamentary judicature more directly than any other case during the Protectorate.

The issues began to come into focus on 5 December, when the Presbyterian Thomas Bampfield reported back to the House from the committee appointed to make a preliminary report about Nayler's case. Chief Justice Glynne advised that 'whatsoever authority was in the Houses of Lords and Commons, the same is united in this Parliament'. The Presbyterian Sir Richard Onslow suggested that, 'in Strafford's case, you proceeded upon the legislative power. I would have you, this afternoon, debate it, whether you will proceed upon the legislative way or the judicatory way.' Whitelocke similarly urged 'the committee to resolve you how you will proceed, whether upon your judicatory or legislative power'.[73] The discussion continued the next day, when Nayler appeared at the bar of the House. Charles Lloyd called on members to 'make a court for the trial of Nayler, that you may keep your legislative power, and proceed judicially . . . I would have a particular court erected to hear and determine.' Walter Strickland added: 'it is a hard case that we should have no law in force to try this gentleman, but you must have recourse to your legislative power'.[74] Other members took different views. The Presbyterian John Ashe suggested adopting a blend of the judicial and legislative processes – 'you ought first to declare him guilty of such a crime: then draw up the bill of attainder against him, and then call him to the bar' – while Lambert's close ally Adam Baynes, mindful of setting a precedent, declared: 'I would have him so tried as to bring in a bill of attainder against him, or leave him to the law. It is below you to honour him with a

---

[73] Burton, I, 30–2.   [74] Burton, I, 38.

trial here; but if it must be otherwise, let him be called to the bar, and proceed judicially against him, lest the precedent be of dangerous and ill consequence to other persons, whose lot it may be, in other cases.'[75] On 8 December, Whitelocke stated that he had 'not found that the Parliament has given judgement in any matter where there was not a law before. They have not proceeded in that case, but by Act of Parliament.' His 'humble opinion' was 'to go by way of bill' of attainder.[76]

As the debate continued over the days that followed, it became ever clearer that the members of council who sat in the House were deeply divided over how to proceed against Nayler, and proved quite unable to set any firm or consistent lead. Some council members advocated proceeding by act of attainder. Walter Strickland, for example, was reported as telling the House: 'nor can you properly pass any sentence upon him but you must do it by bill. I am not satisfied in your judicial way of proceeding.' Skippon likewise 'would have a bill of attainder, with a blank, brought in', while Thurloe insisted: 'You must now proceed upon *lex terrae*, the legislative power.'[77] Equally, those who took this line also included noted opponents of the Protectoral regime such as the Presbyterian Sir Richard Onslow, who 'would have a blank brought in for the punishment, in the bill of attainder. Make the punishment what you will, you must have recourse to the legislative power.'[78] Some leading members of the army interest echoed him, for example, Major-General Boteler who desired that 'a bill of attainder may be brought in to that purpose' of imposing a death sentence.[79]

By contrast, certain other prominent councillors opposed an act of attainder. Sydenham professed himself 'against the bill of attainder', while Wolseley felt that 'it is most orderly, first to agree of the punishment, and then to bring in a bill, if a bill be proper; which I question. The legislative power of Parliament is great, but not so great as to be taken up upon this occasion. I am afraid of an ill precedent.'[80] Thomas Burton reported that many of the 'grandees' were 'against the legislative way, for fear of an ill precedent, and they mainly incline to the moderate kind of punishment'.[81] Again, support for this view can be discerned across the whole political spectrum. The former Rumper Luke Robinson 'would not have you trouble yourselves with a bill of attainder, which will take up two or three days of your time, but pass some such moderate punishments as offered to you, by a vote'. Colonel Thomas Cooper was of a similar mind: 'This House may proceed to fine, imprisonment, and corporal punishment, and this in a judicial way, without preparing a bill. In my opinion there needs no bill.' So too was the Presbyterian Lambert Godfrey, who had been among the members excluded

[75] Burton, I, 43–4.   [76] Burton, I, 58.   [77] Burton, I, 88, 101, 111.   [78] Burton, I, 90.
[79] Burton, I, 115.   [80] Burton, I, 86, 89.   [81] Bodl., MS Carte 228, fo. 79v.

at the beginning of the session, and who now advised the House 'to proceed in your judicial way, as has been instanced to you in several cases'. One of the most vocal of the Scottish members, Dr Thomas Clarges, was likewise 'against the troubling ourselves with a bill in this case. I think it is altogether needless. Your judicial power will extend further than to such a vote as this, without the help of your legislative.'[82]

During the Nayler debates, council members were thus hopelessly divided over whether to proceed judicially or by an act of attainder: this left them unable to offer a lead in a House where members of many different persuasions lined up for and against each course of action. Small wonder, then, that some members remained genuinely uncertain: the Presbyterian Griffith Bodurda, for example, allegedly suggested that the House 'proceed either by your judicial or legislative way. I doubt whether you have all the power of the House of Lords transferred to you, or especially in this thing. You did take off the grand and high delinquent, the late king, by your legislative law, but this was just.'[83] In the end, on 16 December, the House voted by 96 to 82 not to prepare a bill imposing the death penalty on Nayler. Instead, it sentenced him to a series of savage penalties: he was to be placed in the pillory at Westminster for two hours, and then whipped through the streets from there to the Old Exchange, where he would again be placed in a pillory for another two hours. Then his tongue would be bored through with a hot iron, he would have the letter B (for blasphemer) branded upon his forehead, and he would finally be sent to Bridewell where he would be kept to hard labour.[84] In imposing this sentence on Nayler, the House thus eschewed an act of attainder but asserted instead that it exercised a judicature that might extend to the most savage of corporal punishments.

In making this assertion, the House inadvertently encouraged calls for the creation of a second chamber, a highly contentious issue that was to dog the rest of the Protectorate. On 25 December, Cromwell wrote to the Speaker, Sir Thomas Widdrington, asking 'that the House will let us know the grounds and reasons whereupon they have proceeded' in the Nayler case.[85] The House then spent three days (26, 27, and 30 December) discussing how to reply.[86] In these rather rambling debates, a marked contrast became apparent between those speakers who were members of the council and those who were not. Most of the latter robustly defended the House's judicature and argued that it did not need to be debated at length. Luke Robinson warned against getting involved in any discussion over 'the jurisdiction of this House', and felt that 'this demurrer to your jurisdiction puts

[82] Burton, I, 92, 97, 142, 157.   [83] Burton, I, 120.
[84] *CJ*, VII, 468–9; Burton, I, 158; *TSP*, VII, 708–9; Whitelocke, *Memorials*, IV, 283.
[85] Lomas–Carlyle, III, 20.   [86] *CJ*, VII, 475–7.

all your business to a stop'. He would 'be pulled out of this House' before he would 'condescend to speak to this jurisdiction. If you preserve not that, which is *salus populi*, the privilege of Parliament, you overthrow all the people's liberties.' Convinced that 'it is neither for [the Protector's] service nor ours to decline our jurisdiction', he argued that 'if you be not a judicatory, you are nothing'.[87] The Presbyterian John Goodwin insisted that 'if you be a Parliament you have a judicatory power to pass this sentence', and he knew 'no reason why you should appoint a committee to examine your jurisdiction ... If you arraign your own judgment, what shall we be called ... I wonder what his highness will think of us, if we should not assert our jurisdiction.'[88] Sir William Strickland declared: 'If you arraign the jurisdiction of your Parliament, I shall desire to go home ... I hope we shall be able to dispute and assert our jurisdiction. This is the essence and being of a Parliament.' He did not doubt that the House could 'make it out that we had a jurisdiction to do what we did. If there be not a judicial power in Parliament, I know not what principles are. I hope we have lost none of our privileges ... I take it we have all the power that was in the House of Lords, now in this Parliament.'[89] Those who took this line included some of the major-generals who were not councillors, for example, Boteler, who was 'satisfied that this House had a judicatory power to pass this judgment'.[90] Such members typically advocated replying with a brief assertion of their judicature, and the avoidance of a more protracted debate. Thus George Downing: 'I would have us return this short answer to the letter, that we take ourselves to be a Parliament, with all appurtenances; and, therefore, we did it by our judicatory power, being the supreme judicatory of this nation.'[91]

The councillors, by contrast, tended to take a more moderate line: they were more cautious in their defence of Parliament's judicature, and more emphatic in urging the need to examine that jurisdiction carefully and to satisfy Cromwell about their grounds for proceeding in the Nayler case. Chief Justice Glynne urged that 'a way may be found out to preserve a right understanding between his highness and us, without the need of a *tertius arbiter*'. He warned that 'the judicial power is not boundless, for this is against the natural power of a court of justice, this is a court of will and power. There must be rules to all judicial power.'[92] The Lord President of the council, Henry Lawrence, asserted that 'you must give a liberty to speak to the jurisdiction. Otherwise you will neither satisfy the ends of his highness, nor of the people, to ascertain what may be done for the future in these cases.'[93] Lambert was likewise reported as insisting that: 'It is not without good reason that his highness should be satisfied in the grounds. He knows

[87] Burton, I, 251–2, 261, 272.   [88] Burton, I, 252.   [89] Burton, I, 253, 275–6.
[90] Burton, I, 258.   [91] Burton, I, 262.   [92] Burton, I, 251, 278.   [93] Burton, I, 254.

not by what way you have proceeded, whether upon the judicatory or legislative ... Not that I would recede from any thing we have done, nor that his highness should retract any thing that he has offered; but that we might candidly understand one another after the business is fully debated.' He stressed that 'a right understanding between his highness and the Parliament is certainly the *salus populi*. I hope it will also be thought *suprema lex*.'[94] Sir Gilbert Pickering took a similar line: 'It is very fit this jurisdiction should be debated. It seems, though the judicatory power of Parliament cannot extend to life, yet, by this means, by a vote of today, you may pull out a man's eyes tomorrow; slit his nose, or cut off his hands, ears, or tongue. This is very hard, and ought to be considered.' He urged the House 'fully to debate the business, that you may give his highness a clear account, who, being under the obligation of an oath, ought certainly to have satisfaction in this matter'.[95] William Sydenham expressed the same view: he would 'have it freely considered here, what may be the rights of Englishmen, what due bounded liberty we shall have ... If you intend such an answer, as in plain terms to assert your jurisdiction, and say you have done it because you have done it, this will neither stand with the honour nor wisdom of a Parliament.' Sydenham granted that 'this House has a judicial power, as to judge of your own members, or to judge of appeals from inferior courts, for you are the supreme jurisdiction. But to send for men up out of the country, and to judge them without a law, what encroachment is this upon the liberties of the people! ... We have not a power here to do what we please.'[96] Another major-general, Disbrowe, urged that 'if there have been any error in our proceedings, we ought to rectify it ... It is fit we should satisfy his highness, and one another, in this thing.'[97] On the question of how to respond to Cromwell's letter, the majority of councillors thus appear to have taken a consistent line, albeit one at odds with a significant number of other members of the House.

On 30 December, the debate was adjourned until 2 January, but in the event it was never resumed.[98] It had raised some knotty issues and, although the debate blew over without reaching a conclusion, Thurloe was somewhat overoptimistic when he wrote to Pell on 1 January that: 'There has lately fallen out some question between his highness and the Parliament, as to the jurisdiction of the Parliament as to their judicature without the Protector's consent; but that business is like to end in love.'[99] Not least among the questions that emerged during these debates was whether there should be a *tertius arbiter* between the House and the Protector, possibly in the form of a second chamber. The Presbyterian Lambert Godfrey put the dilemma very

---

[94] Burton, I, 256, 281.   [95] Burton, I, 256.   [96] Burton, I, 257–8, 275.
[97] Burton, I, 271.   [98] *CJ*, VII, 477–8.   [99] Vaughan, II, 77.

neatly: 'Here is your power asserted on one hand; the supreme magistrate, on the other hand, desiring an account of your judgment. Where shall there be *tertius arbiter?*[100] Cromwell was also much exercised by this question: he told the army officers on 27 February 1657 that 'the proceedings of this Parliament' demonstrated the 'need of a check or balancing power (meaning the House of Lords or a House so constituted)', and he was disturbed that 'by their judicial power' the House 'fell upon life and member'.[101] It was against this background that the authors of the Remonstrance, led by Broghill, developed the idea of a second chamber or Other House, comprising between forty and seventy members.[102]

The brevity and vagueness of the Remonstrance's proposal for the Other House have been discussed already.[103] In particular, it did not address the question of the judicature of the Other House.[104] However, on 17 March the House passed a series of resolutions – subsequently incorporated into the fifth article of the Humble Petition and Advice – that defined the Other House's jurisdiction in ways that rendered it significantly more limited than that of the old House of Lords. Specifically, the Other House could 'not proceed in any civil causes, except in writs of error, in cases adjourned from inferior courts into the Parliament for difficulty, in cases of petitions against proceedings in Courts of Equity, and in cases of privileges of their own House'. Furthermore, the Other House could 'not proceed in any criminal causes whatsoever against any person criminally, but upon an impeachment of the Commons assembled in Parliament, and by their consent', and it could only 'proceed in any cause, either civil or criminal, ... according to the known laws of the land, and the due course and custom of Parliament'. Lastly, such judicature was vested in the Other House as a whole, not in individual members: 'no final determinations or judgments be by any members of that House, in any cause there depending, either civil, criminal or mixed, as Commissioners or Delegates, to be nominated by that House; but all such final determinations and judgments to be by the House itself, any law or usage to the contrary notwithstanding'.[105]

The creation of a second chamber possessing an appellate judicature coincided with a number of calls for a revival of the Lords that were voiced during the later years of the Protectorate. One of the most forceful came from

[100] Burton, I, 249.
[101] Lomas–Carlyle, III, 488. This episode is discussed more fully in chapter 6 of the present book.
[102] Patrick Little, *Lord Broghill and the Cromwellian Union with Ireland and Scotland* (Woodbridge, 2004), pp. 145–60.
[103] See chapter 2, above, and appendix 2.   [104] See appendix 2.
[105] Gardiner, *Constitutional Documents*, p. 452; *CJ*, VII, 506; Burton, I, 387–8. Cf. *TSP*, VI, 107; TNA, PRO 31/3/101, fo. 111r.

that inveterate defender of parliamentary privileges, the lawyer William Prynne, who, in December 1657, wrote a preface to a new edition of his *A Plea for the Lords*, originally published in 1647. In this preface, he asserted that 'the judicial power, judicature, and judgements in Parliament, belong wholly and solely to the King and House of Lords, not to the Commons House'.[106] Similarly, when the second Protectorate Parliament reconvened on 20 January 1658, the Lord Keeper, Nathaniel Fiennes, urged members not to forget 'that each House' should take 'a more especial care of what is most proper for it, and it most proper for'. Whereas the Commons 'provides and strengthens the sinews of war to preserve the commonwealth from destruction in gross, by public force and violence', the Other House 'will preserve it from destruction by retail, through the due administration of justice, suppressing particular wrongs and oppressions, which would soon break out into open flames and public rapines, if they were not prevented by the courts of judicature, whereof the highest and last resort is there'.[107] However, such an emphasis on the Other House's judicature served only to highlight its resemblance to the old Lords, and this proved so controversial that it led to a vigorous debate between 28 January and the Parliament's dissolution on 4 February.[108] The leading protagonists in this debate have already been identified and analysed;[109] here we shall briefly consider what was said in relation to parliamentary judicature.

The crux of the issue was that if the second chamber were regarded as the Other House then it presumably possessed only those functions granted to it in the Humble Petition and Advice and the Additional Petition and Advice. If, however, it were called the House of Lords, then it would logically have all the powers and privileges of the old Lords. Some members were convinced that the second chamber was *a* House of Lords, although not *the* House of Lords. With typical bluntness, Major-General Boteler declared: 'A House of Lords they are, and they will be so.'[110] The Presbyterian Robert Shapcote reportedly expressed the same view at greater length:

It is clear, nothing clearer, that they are a House of Parliament; and if so, it was never known that two Houses of Commons were in England ... If we dispute grounds and foundations, we shall soon dispute ourselves out of doors. If they be not a House of Parliament, it may be the same of us ... You cannot own them to be a House of Parliament unless you call them a House of Lords.[111]

---

[106] William Prynne, *A Plea for the Lords, and House of Peers* (1658), sig. a†2[r]. Prynne's preface was dated 6 December 1657.
[107] *CJ*, VII, 586.
[108] *CJ*, VII, 589–92; Burton, II, 374–462; *Clarke Papers*, III, 134–5; Whitelocke, *Memorials*, IV, 329–30.
[109] See chapter 4.   [110] Burton, II, 409.   [111] Burton, II, 402.

But to make the leap from the name of the House of Lords to the full powers and privileges of the old Lords was highly problematic. Colonel Joachim Matthews acknowledged that the House of Lords had formerly possessed 'a judicial power' and handled 'complaints from courts of justice and equity, which would take up much of your time'. He was 'not against the name of the Lords by way of appellation, as an honour to them; but to give it with all the powers and privileges, I cannot consent'.[112] Leading commonwealthsmen took a similar view. Thomas Scott observed that 'you have settled them only as a High Court of Justice; but if you make them a co-ordinate power with you, you give them the power of your purses, of peace and war, of making laws; and magistrates to execute them'.[113] Hesilrige concurred: 'They are another House, and that is enough ... Grant once Lords, then you will find tenderness, of course, to maintain the privileges of that House as Lords.' He demanded: 'shall we now rake them up, after they have so long laid in the grave? Will it not be infamous all the nation over? Shall we be a grand jury again?'[114] By contrast, some lawyers suggested a pragmatic solution: that, for the newly constituted bicameral Parliament to function at all, the House at least needed to communicate with the second chamber, regardless of what it was called. As Solicitor-General William Ellis put it: 'If they be a legislature, how can you pass laws without a correspondence? We can do nothing. We may as well go home again ... For my part, I know not the difference of the name. We must, for our safety and peace, correspond with the Other House.'[115]

The debate gradually became less and less focused, however, and it had still not reached a conclusion when Cromwell dissolved the Parliament on 4 February. In his closing speech, he defended the Other House and those whom he had nominated to it: 'I named it of men that can meet you wheresoever you go and shake hands with you and tell you that it is not titles, it is not lordship, it is not this nor that, that they value, but a Christian and an English interest.' They were men, he went on, whom he 'hope[d] would not only be a balance to a Commons House of Parliament but to themselves, having honest hearts, loving the same things that you love, whilst you love England and whilst you love religion'. He told members that he 'thought it would have satisfied you. But if everything must be either too high or too low, you are not satisfiable.' He insisted that he had chosen 'such a House as I thought I might answer for, upon my life, that they would be true to those ends that were the ground and state of our war with the Cavalier party all along.' 'And', he asked, 'what will satisfy if this will not?'[116] Cromwell's words reflected deep frustration with the hostility that had been voiced

---

[112] Burton, II, 451.   [113] Burton, II, 391.   [114] Burton, II, 403, 407.
[115] Burton, II, 419.   [116] Lomas–Carlyle, III, 505–6.

towards the Other House by some members of the Commons. Whitelocke also suspected that 'the protector looked upon himself as aimed at by them, though with a side wind, and testimonies of their envy towards him'.[117] This widespread opposition to the second chamber persisted, and it resurfaced dramatically the following year in Richard Cromwell's Parliament. As Thurloe observed on the eve of that Parliament: 'the Other House will be the great question, and that most certainly sticks in the throats of many of our friends'.[118]

THE THIRD PROTECTORATE PARLIAMENT

The third Protectorate Parliament saw the effective abandonment of attempts at legal reform: not one of the bills that had languished in the previous Parliament was revived in either House in 1659.[119] Sheppard had retired to his Gloucestershire home in the late summer of 1657, and only from May 1659 onwards, after the dissolution of the Parliament, was there a resurgence of pamphlet calls for legal reform.[120] Richard Cromwell's opening speech to the Parliament on 27 January urged that 'the good and necessary work of reformation, both in manners and in administration of justice', be continued, that profaneness may be discountenanced and suppressed, and that righteousness and justice may be executed in the land'.[121] In his lengthy speech immediately afterwards, Lord Commissioner of the Great Seal Nathaniel Fiennes said of Oliver Cromwell that 'as to the outward Court of God's House, the administration of judgement, and justice amongst men, what were his desires and endeavours, and what his care from time to time to fill the benches with able and learned judges, we all know'. Fiennes went on to advocate 'that law and justice may be executed with equity and mercy; that neither craft nor cruelty may take advantage of the rigour of the law, or of the hands of God, to turn judgement into wormwood, and justice into gall: that judgement and justice may run down with a clear and swift stream'.[122] In the event, however, such calls appear to have been ignored, and no further progress was made with legal reform. Instead, the Parliament became heavily preoccupied with constitutional issues. Once again, prominent among these

---

[117] Whitelocke, *Memorials*, IV, 330.   [118] *TSP*, VII, 589.

[119] *CJ*, VII, 593–644; HMC, *The Manuscripts of the House of Lords, 1699–1702* (1908), pp. 525–67.

[120] Matthews, *William Sheppard*, p. 223; Veall, *Popular Movement*, pp. 95–6.

[121] [Richard Cromwell,] *The Speech of His Highness the Lord Protector, made to both Houses of Parliament at their first meeting on Thursday the 27th of January 1658[/9]* (1658[/9]), pp. 8–9.

[122] [Nathaniel Fiennes,] *The speech of the right honourable Nathaniel Lord Fiennes, one of the Lord Keepers of the Great Seale of England, made before his Highnesse, and both Houses of Parliament on Thursday the 27th of January, 1658[/9]* (1658[/9]), pp. 11, 15.

was the controversy surrounding the nature and status of the Other House, and Bordeaux predicted in early January that 'the new House of Lords' was likely to prove 'the first stumbling block'.[123]

This debate lasted from 19 February until 1 March and then again from 26 March until 8 April. It hinged upon a series of closely related questions: whether the Commons should correspond and transact business with the newly created second chamber; whether that chamber should be recognised as the House of Lords or simply as an Other House; whether its powers should be 'bounded' and, if so, in what ways; how far the attributes of the old House of Lords had been automatically transferred to it; and what functions – particularly legislative and judicial – it should perform. The debate was rambling, prolonged, and somewhat confused. One of Henry Cromwell's informants reported on 1 March that, 'in this grand affair, the House is much divided, some being for the old peers only, some for the new lords only, and others for both together, while the commonwealth party sit still, resolving to give their vote to the greatest disadvantage of his highness'.[124] Some commonwealthsmen, notably Hesilrige and Scott, opposed the Other House as yet another quasi-monarchical feature of the Protectorate. Others were less vehemently hostile, and simply sought clarification of the rather vague and ambiguous arrangements contained in the Humble Petition and Advice. As Derek Hirst has argued, 'those who challenged the "Other House" were not necessarily seeking to destroy the Protectorate but rather to remedy what many genuinely saw as objectionable anomalies'.[125] In the end, the House proceeded to a sequence of resolutions: that Parliament consisted of two Houses (19 February); that the Commons would 'transact with the persons now sitting in the Other House, as an House of Parliament, during this present Parliament', and that it was 'not hereby intended to exclude such peers, as have been faithful to the Parliament, from their privilege of being duly summoned to be members of that House' (28 March); and that messages from one House to the other should be carried only by members of the House that sent the message (8 April).[126]

Among the issues explored during the course of this debate were the judicial and legislative functions of the new House. Some members argued

123 Guizot, *Richard Cromwell*, I, 285.
124 *TSP*, VII, 626. For a similar assessment, see *ibid.*, 627.
125 Derek Hirst, 'Concord and Discord in Richard Cromwell's House of Commons', *EHR*, 103 (1988), 351.
126 *CJ*, VII, 605, 621, 632; Burton, III, 366; IV, 293, 374–5, 378; BL, Add. MS 5138 (diary of Guybon Goddard), pp. 194–5; BL, Lansdowne MS 823, fos. 229r, 272r, 276r–v, 278r; Bodl., MS Carte 73, fo. 250r; Whitelocke, *Memorials*, IV, 340–1; *TSP*, VII, 640; *Nicholas Papers*, IV, 84.

that legal and constitutional balance demanded the existence of a second chamber, and the range and diversity of those who took this line were striking. One of the many members who sat for the first time, John Stephens, spoke in favour of 'the ancient constitution by two Houses. Justice is always pictured with a pair of scales. The two Houses were so. Sometimes the Lords were too heavy, and sometimes the Commons were too heavy.' He therefore urged members 'to restore the ancient House of Lords ... We must restore the House of Lords, as a point of policy and prudence. They may be a good screen on both sides; between the magistrate and the people.'[127] A much more experienced member, the Presbyterian Robert Beake, similarly took 'the single person and the Commons as two scales, the House of Lords as the beam. Both scales are subject to factions and tyranny and extravagances. The beam is prudential.' He saw the Lords as intimately bound up with the laws: 'By no law of England can the Judges sit in the House of Commons. They must sit in the Lords' House, else we want their grave and sage advice. We have sworn by the covenant to maintain the two Houses; and the Parliament might as well take away *meum* and *tuum*, as a House of Lords.'[128] This led some members to defend the Lords as guardians of England's liberties. As Edmund Fowell put it: 'The Barons anciently were the great bulwarks and defence of the liberties of the nation. How oft did they fight for *Magna Charta*. They did great service in old times, and so did those in the quarrel. There is a necessity for a House of Lords.'[129] Such claims for the necessity of the Lords or an Other House drew further strength from the traditional legislative supremacy of the parliamentary trinity, in which the consent of all three elements was needed for a bill to become law. Several members cited Sir Edward Coke in support of this principle. The Presbyterian-courtier John Maynard reminded members that 'Lord Coke, no flatterer of prerogative, tells you plainly, it is no law that is not made by the three estates', while one of the Irish members, the former Presbyterian and crypto-royalist Arthur Annesley, observed that 'Lord Coke is clear that no law is of force but what is made by the three estates'.[130] The most that a commonwealthsman such as Hesilrige could advance by way of a counterargument was that 'they were intended, doubtless, only to survey laws'.[131]

The judicial functions proved rather more difficult to define, not least because they were so closely related to the issue of how similar the new chamber was to the old House of Lords. On 22 February, the Presbyterian

---

[127] Burton, III, 358. Cf. BL, Add. MS 5138, pp. 191–2; and Schilling, p. 94.
[128] Burton, III, 363. Cf. BL, Add. MS 5138, p. 193.
[129] Burton, III, 354; BL, Add. MS 5138, p. 191.
[130] Burton, III, 574, 592. Cf. Schilling, p. 156.   [131] Burton, IV, 14. Cf. Schilling, pp. 161–2.

John Trevor urged the House to focus on the judicature of the Other House. He argued that there was 'a necessity of bounding those powers which have been formerly exercised, which did consist of two parts, the judicial and legislative, that our late revolutions have awakened us to care for'. He asked members 'to consider, first, how far it is bounded, and then it is fit to consider what boundaries, in reference to the people's safety, should be given to them; and first begin with the judicial part'.[132] Other Presbyterians, such as Richard Knightley and Robert Jenkinson, concurred: both supported this 'motion to begin with the power of judicature in that House'.[133] The issue then focused on how far the ancient judicial powers of the Lords had been transferred to the new second chamber, or to the Commons. Here the debate became steadily more diffuse, and the House never proceeded to a specific resolution on this point. Some members argued that the Commons had simply absorbed most of the powers formerly exercised by the Lords. According to Jenkinson, 'the Commons began to grow upon the Lords, and all their glass is now run out. Almost all that power is in this House, the Commons having now whatever possessions and tenures made them considerable. The Lords have no interest now, and signify no more than you.'[134] Others believed that the old Lords' powers were now vested in the Other House: 'Whatever the old Lords claimed', opined Edward Turner, 'these may claim it.'[135]

This in turn raised two further questions regarding the judicature of the Other House. The first was whether it was right for any chamber with an element of hereditary membership to exercise judicial powers. As another of the new members, John Hewley, put it: 'The debate leads to examine the persons. Let us examine the rights. The old Lords first, as to their rights as barons, then as to their judicial powers. They have claimed an hereditary right. We must examine the reason. I think *ab initio non fuit sic.*' He insisted that a 'judicial office cannot in reason be granted to a man and his heirs. It requires skill and science. A man cannot be steward of a Court-Baron, to him and his heirs. If this be so, how can such a power be inherent that is the highest judicature? ... Virtue is not derivative ... Further is not safe. *Salus populi suprema lex.*'[136] The commonwealthsman Thomas Chaloner reportedly made the same point even more starkly: 'I would have no one sort of men to be hereditary judges of the nation, to them and their heirs for ever.'[137] By contrast, the crypto-royalist Arthur Annesley offered a very different view:

---

[132] Burton, III, 410; BL, Add. MS 5138, pp. 217–18. Cf. Schilling, p. 102.
[133] Burton, III, 410–11; BL, Add. MS 5138, p. 218.
[134] Burton, III, 365. Cf. Schilling, p. 96.
[135] Burton, IV, 68.   [136] Burton, III, 558–9. Cf. Schilling, pp. 140–1.
[137] Burton, III, 540. Cf. BL, Add. MS 5138, pp. 255–6; and Schilling, p. 136.

noting that 'it is objected against them … that it is contrary to reason, that there should be an hereditary judicial power in them', he wished that 'such new reason may not proceed from our new lights. Practice and experience many hundred years, show the reasonableness of them.'[138] John Maynard insisted that the new chamber's powers were already sufficiently limited: 'These new Lords are bounded already; what more bounds would you put upon them? For their judicial power, they cannot meddle with *meum* and *tuum*, nor appeals and errors. This was a great privilege never denied to the House of Lords. Now they cannot meddle with any thing but what comes from this House. They cannot vote by proxies.'[139] For Maynard, the bounds already placed on the Other House by the Humble Petition and Advice were strong enough to prevent their judicial powers from being abused or from becoming too sweeping.

The second question was whether the judicial powers of the Other House in effect made them the House of Lords. The Presbyterian Sir John Northcote had been 'against transacting; but now you have voted them a court, you must pursue the ceremony fit for a court'. However, 'as to that of calling them Lords, you have not yet agreed'.[140] He wished to keep the title of the Other House separate from its judicial powers. As Adam Baynes put it, the Humble Petition and Advice 'had not made them a House of Lords, unless going into that House made them Lords. It was not intended for them to be Lords. You denied that, the last Parliament. It was in consideration, whether they should have a negative or co-ordinate power with you; some negative as to the judicial power, but nought as to the legislative.'[141] Similarly, Scott hoped that the House 'would not restore those that are but two years old to have all the privileges of the old Lords'.[142] Once again, however, the discussion of this point did not produce any kind of resolution.

CONCLUSION

From all these tangled debates, there thus emerged a widespread sense of the need for some kind of second chamber, even though its precise form and functions – and even its name – remained highly controversial. It was therefore unsurprising, perhaps, that barely a year later the old House of Lords was restored, complete with the judicial and legislative powers that it had exercised prior to the Civil Wars. This reversion to the *status quo ante* also

---

[138] Burton, III, 592; BL, Add. MS 5138, p. 273. Cf. Schilling, pp. 155–7.
[139] Burton, IV, 52.   [140] Burton, IV, 354.
[141] Burton, IV, 32. Cf. BL, Add. MS 5138, p. 282; and Schilling, p. 170.
[142] Burton, IV, 352.

had the effect of resolving at a stroke, albeit in a conservative manner, the controversy that surrounded the powers and judicature of the Commons during the Protectorate, and that erupted so dramatically in the House's deep uncertainty over how to proceed in the case of James Nayler.

Just as the abolition of the Lords in 1649 gave way to the creation of an Other House in 1657, and three years later to the return of the House of Lords, so the calls for legal reform from the later 1640s onwards produced at best very partial and incomplete measures in the Protectorate Parliaments. Very few of the initiatives examined in this chapter were actually enshrined in legislation, and even fewer survived the Restoration. Although the achievement of the second Protectorate Parliament in this respect was not negligible, in general many more bills for legal reform were initiated than actually ever became acts. The parliamentary record suggests that the underlying reason for this was a lack of agreement, both between Cromwell and Parliament, and among the members themselves, as to what reforms were needed and how they should be implemented. Again and again, members became deeply divided and got bogged down in unfocused debates over how best to proceed. Those who were also members of the council proved unable to set any kind of lead or to advance a consistent and coherent line of their own. At the same time, many of the professional lawyers in Parliament generally opposed any significant legal reforms that they perceived as at all prejudicial to their own vested interests. Against these various obstacles, Cromwell's apparently genuine desire to promote cheaper, more accessible, and speedier justice – most notably by means of the Chancery ordinance – ran aground and ultimately broke apart.

If the Protectorate saw little in the way of lasting changes to the legal system, or Parliament's relationship with it, this surely stemmed primarily from insufficient agreement within Parliament, and between Parliament and the Protector, over precisely what reforms were desirable, and what balance should be struck between change and continuity following the abolition of the monarchy and the House of Lords in 1649. While, like Cromwell, many members might have agreed on what they did not want, they found it impossible to agree on what they did want, and to devise ways of filling the vacuum that commanded general support. A broadly similar pattern of disagreement and uncertainty is evident – only even more emotively and with even more disruptive implications for the relationship between the 'single person and Parliament' – when we turn to the issue of religious reform during the Protectorate, and this will form the subject of the next chapter.

9

Religious reform

The Protectorate saw various attempts, especially by Oliver Cromwell and his army allies, to use Parliament as a means to introduce radical religious reforms. These included efforts to improve the quality of the ministry and to extend liberty of conscience more widely. However, all three Protectorate Parliaments contained numerous members who sought a much more structured national church with penalties for those who refused to conform to it, and who therefore wished to frustrate the more libertarian aspects of the army's religious agenda. In the bitter debates that ensued about liberty of conscience, and particularly over the cases of John Biddle and James Nayler, the collision between Cromwell's religious vision and the attitudes and preferences of many within the Protectorate Parliaments became starkly apparent. This chapter will examine the causes and consequences of that collision, and the ways in which it destabilised the Protectorate Parliaments and forced changes within the Protectorate.

THE FIRST PROTECTORATE PARLIAMENT

The heart of the problem lay in Cromwell's desire to use a body designed as 'the representative of the whole realm' to advance what remained a minority agenda, 'liberty of conscience'. In the end his wish to liberate the godly proved incompatible with the determination of many members to prevent the spread of heresies and blasphemies. The principal source of disagreement between Cromwell and a majority of members seems not to have been over whether religious reform was necessary, but over what sort of religious reform was desirable. Thus, in the first Protectorate Parliament more than forty bills were considered,[1] several of which addressed issues of religious

---

[1] Peter Gaunt, 'Law-making in the First Protectorate Parliament', in Colin Jones, Malyn Newitt, and Stephen Roberts, eds., *Politics and People in Revolutionary England: Essays in Honour of Ivan Roots* (Oxford, 1986), p. 174; Sarah E. Jones, 'The Composition and Activity of the Protectorate Parliaments' (Ph.D thesis, University of Exeter, 1988), p. 128.

reform, including a bill 'for settling tenths [= tithes], and all impropriations, belonging to the State, for the maintenance of ministers', a bill 'against the Quakers, heresies, and blasphemies', and another 'for the restoring [of] cathedrals'.[2] Religion was undoubtedly a priority, and the French ambassador Bordeaux recorded that, during Cromwell's opening speech on 4 September 1654, 'as often as he spoke ... of liberty and religion ... the members did seem to rejoice with acclamations of joy'.[3] But the more specific the debates became, the more divergences opened up over what kind of religious settlement Parliament should promote and construct.

It is virtually impossible to reconstruct the religious attitudes of most members of the Protectorate Parliaments. Sarah Jones has argued that only a minority were 'active' or 'expressed opinions' that reveal their religious sympathies, and that the religious affiliations of nearly 70 per cent of members of the first Protectorate Parliament may remain unknown. Jones tentatively suggests that, of the remainder, Presbyterians constituted 18 per cent, Independents 4 per cent, 'radicals' (such as Quakers or Baptists) 3 per cent, and Anglicans 2 per cent.[4] However, these figures are necessarily approximate and provisional, and it is often difficult to make distinctions with any degree of precision: in particular, identifying those who were religious Presbyterians and Independents is even more problematic by 1654 than in the later 1640s. It is nevertheless worth noting that various contemporary observers reported the prominence of what they termed Presbyterians: Sir Edward Nicholas wrote that 'there are many that now persuade the King to some extraordinary compliance with the Presbyterian party, for that so many of that faction are chosen to sit in the approaching mock Parliament',[5] while the Venetian secretary in England, Lorenzo Paulucci, observed that 'the members returned for the new Parliament are not quite to the Protector's satisfaction. He wanted a majority of his own creatures, whereas a great part of those already chosen prove to be Presbyterians, the enemies of the dominant military party on which the government depends.'[6]

---

[2] See the draft list of bills intended for the first Protectorate Parliament in BL, Stowe MS 322 (Revenue Papers), fo. 74r–v.
[3] *TSP*, II, 588.   [4] Jones, 'Composition and Activity of the Protectorate Parliaments', p. 74.
[5] TNA, SP 18/74/115.
[6] *CSPV*, 1653–4, 235–6. This situation was not significantly altered by the fact that before the Parliament assembled the council 'purged' somewhere between seven and eleven members, only two of whom apparently had Presbyterian sympathies. Nor was it decisively changed when around fifty to eighty members withdrew on 12 September rather than sign a Recognition promising to accept 'the [Instrument of] Government, as it is settled in a single person and a Parliament': see Peter Gaunt, 'Cromwell's Purge? Exclusions and the First Protectorate Parliament', *Parl. Hist.*, 6 (1987), 1–22; Gardiner, *Commonwealth and Protectorate*, III, 173–8, 193–7; and chapter 3, in the present book.

The influence of such people among the Parliament's most active members can be discerned in the religious reforms that were adopted for inclusion in the draft 'constitutional bill' to which this Parliament devoted so much of its time.[7] Initially, the Parliament had envisaged creating an assembly of divines that would advise members on religious reform.[8] However, on 5 October, a grand committee for religion was appointed to meet on two afternoons a week, to discuss 'matters of religion' with the advice of between twelve and twenty ministers.[9] The religious measures that the House subsequently adopted fell into two main categories: the provision and maintenance of the ministry, and the suppression of what were deemed religious errors, heresies, and blasphemies. On both issues, the principal concern was to create structures that would regulate the nation's religious life. As Bordeaux observed in late October: 'the Parliament is still taken up about religion: I am afraid they are not good enough to be fathers of the Church, to form a true canonical one. In all likelihood, they will set the Presbytery uppermost, and give toleration to the others.'[10]

Within a month of its assembling, the Parliament turned to the question of the ministry. Before it met, Cromwell had issued two Protectoral ordinances specifically designed to improve the quality of the ministry: that of March 1654 established a national body of 'triers' to vet all new clergy, while the following August county commissioners known as 'ejectors' were set up to expel 'scandalous, ignorant and insufficient ministers and schoolmasters'.[11] The Parliament referred both of these ordinances to a large committee of ninety-four members.[12] This committee initially suggested suspending the ordinance for the 'ejectors' while they drafted a new bill, but that proposal was narrowly defeated.[13] There are apparently no hints in the surviving sources as to the contents of this new bill. It is clear, however, that it was read twice during the course of November and after the second reading was referred back to the committee, 'upon some exceptions', never to resurface during the Parliament's lifetime.[14] Pending further progress on that bill, the Parliament resolved on 7 December that, 'until some better provision be

---

[7] The text of this 'constitutional bill' is printed in Gardiner, *Constitutional Documents*, pp. 427–47.

[8] *CJ*, VII, 367. See also Burton, I, xxvii.   [9] *CJ*, VII, 373; Burton, I, xlvi.   [10] *TSP*, II, 697.

[11] *A & O*, II, 855–8, 968–90. On the establishment and activities of the 'triers' and 'ejectors', see Jeffrey R. Collins, 'The Church Settlement of Oliver Cromwell', *History*, 87 (2002), 18–40; and Christopher Durston, 'Policing the Cromwellian Church: The Activities of the County Ejection Committees, 1654–1659', in Patrick Little, ed., *The Cromwellian Protectorate* (Woodbridge, 2007), pp. 189–205.

[12] *CJ*, VII, 370, 371. See also Burton, I, xli.   [13] *CJ*, VII, 377, 381, 382. See also Burton, I, lxii.

[14] *CJ*, VII, 377, 381, 382, 384, 385–7. See also Burton, I, lxii, lxxv, lxxix, lxxxix; *Mercurius Politicus*, no. 232 (16–23 November 1654), p. 4038; *Mercurius Politicus*, no. 233 (23–30 November 1654), p. 4053; Whitelocke, *Memorials*, IV, 156.

made by the Parliament, for the encouragement and maintenance of able, godly, and painful ministers, and public preachers of the Gospel, for instructing the people, and for discovery and confutation of errors, heresy and whatsoever is contrary to sound doctrine, the present public maintenance shall not be taken away, nor impeached'.[15] This was accompanied by a resolution that 'the true reformed Protestant Christian religion as it is contained in the Holy Scriptures of the Old and New Testament, and no other, shall be asserted and maintained as the public profession of these nations'.[16] The next day (8 December), after 'a long debate',[17] the Parliament resolved that any subsequent bills that required:

> from such ministers and preachers of the Gospel as shall receive public maintenance for instructing the people, a submission and conformity to the public profession aforesaid, or enjoining attendance unto the preaching of the word and other religious duties on the Lord's day ... shall pass into and become laws within twenty days after the presentation to the Lord Protector, although he shall not give his consent thereunto.[18]

This was a clear indication of the importance that the majority of members attached to public conformity by a national ministry.

These steps to maintain the ministry and the 'public profession' of religion were complemented by measures to stamp out 'damnable heresies' and blasphemies. Throughout the deliberations on this subject, liberty of conscience remained a much lower priority, to be denied whenever it conflicted with the prevention of errors, heresies, and blasphemies, or the maintenance of public order. Thus, on 15 December, after two days of 'long debates',[19] the House resolved that 'without the consent of the Lord Protector and Parliament, no law or statute be made for the restraining of such tender consciences as shall differ in doctrine, worship or discipline, from the public profession aforesaid and shall not abuse this liberty to the civil injury of others, or the disturbance of the public peace'. To this, however, was added the crucial proviso that:

> such bills as shall be agreed upon by the Parliament, for the restraining of atheism, blasphemy, damnable heresies, to be particularly enumerated by this Parliament, popery, prelacy, licentiousness, or profaneness; or such as shall preach, print, or

---

[15] *CJ*, VII, 397. See also Burton, I, cxii. This clause was adopted as chapter 44 of the draft 'constitutional bill': Gardiner, *Constitutional Documents*, p. 443.

[16] *CJ*, VII, 397. See also Burton, I, cxii. This clause was adopted as chapter 41 of the 'constitutional bill': Gardiner, *Constitutional Documents*, p. 442.

[17] Whitelocke, *Memorials*, IV, 159.

[18] *CJ*, VII, 398. See also Burton, I, cxii–cxiii; *Mercurius Politicus*, no. 235 (7–14 December 1654), pp. 4085–6. This clause was adopted as chapter 42 of the 'constitutional bill': Gardiner, *Constitutional Documents*, pp. 442–3.

[19] Whitelocke, *Memorials*, IV, 161; Burton, I, cxviii–cxix.

avowedly maintain any thing contrary to the fundamental principles of doctrine held forth in the public profession ... shall pass into, and become laws, within twenty days after their presentation to the Lord Protector, although he shall not give his consent thereunto.[20]

This final clause constituted a further attempt by the Parliament to obstruct Cromwell's promotion of liberty of conscience.

The most specific illustration of the difference between Cromwell and the first Protectorate Parliament over liberty of conscience was the case of the Socinian John Biddle. In his two books, *A Two-Fold Catechism* and *The Apostolical and True Opinion, concerning the Holy Trinity, revived and asserted*, Biddle had denied the Trinity and the divinity of Christ, and London Presbyterians were quick to identify him as a target.[21] He was interrogated by a parliamentary committee, and the House subsequently endorsed the committee's verdict that the *Two-Fold Catechism* expressed 'many blasphemous and heretical opinions', and that *The Apostolical and True Opinion* was 'full of horrid, blasphemous, and execrable opinions, denying the Deity of Christ and of the Holy Ghost'.[22] Biddle was imprisoned and his books burnt; and his case soon led to a broader attack on the Quakers, against whom a bill was prepared. The campaign against the Quakers was also prompted by the bizarre protest outside the Palace of Westminster of Theauraujohn Tany: on 30 December, he threw a Bible, a saddle, a sword, and a pistol into a bonfire, alleging that these were the Gods of England, and then laid about him with a drawn sword.[23] Although Cromwell did not prevent Biddle's punishment, it was characteristic that he ensured that Biddle was imprisoned on the Scilly Isles, beyond the

[20] *CJ*, VII, 401. See also Burton, I, cxviii–cxix; *Mercurius Politicus*, no. 236 (14–21 December 1654), p. 5002. This clause was adopted as chapter 43 of the 'constitutional bill': Gardiner, *Constitutional Documents*, p. 443. Earlier, the Parliament had resolved by 85 votes to 84 (11 December) to provide 'a particular enumeration of heresies' after the words 'damnable heresies' (*CJ*, VII, 399), and then (13 December) to include the specific words 'blasphemy', 'popery', 'prelacy', 'licentiousness', and 'profaneness' (*CJ*, VII, 400). These resolutions were subsequently confirmed on 3, 12, and 15 January 1655 (*CJ*, VII, 412, 414, 416).

[21] Blair Worden, 'Toleration and the Cromwellian Protectorate', in W. J. Sheils, ed., *Persecution and Toleration* (Studies in Church History, 21, Oxford, 1984), pp. 199–233, especially pp. 218–21.

[22] Burton, I, cxxix–cxxx. The Parliament's handling of Biddle's case can be reconstructed from Burton, I, cxiv–cxvii, cxxiii, cxxviii–cxxx; *CJ*, VII, 400, 404, 416; *Mercurius Politicus*, no. 235 (7–14 December 1654), p. 4086; *Mercurius Politicus*, no. 236 (14–21 December 1654), p. 5002; *Severall proceedings in Parliament*, no. 277 (11–18 January 1654[/5]), pp. 4393–5; Whitelocke, *Memorials*, IV, 160–1.

[23] *CJ*, VII, 410; Burton, I, cxxvii; *Mercurius Politicus*, no. 238 (28 December 1654–4 January 1654[/5]), pp. 5033–4; *Severall proceedings in Parliament*, no. 275 (28 December 1654–5 January 1654[/5]), pp. 4360, 4365–6; Whitelocke, *Memorials*, IV, 163. For Tany, see especially Ariel Hessayon, '"Gold Tried in the Fire": The Prophet Theauraujohn Tany and the Puritan Revolution' (Ph.D thesis, University of Cambridge, 1996).

Parliament's reach, and also granted him a weekly allowance of ten shillings, apparently out of his own pocket.[24]

To Cromwell, who in his opening speech on 4 September 1654 had called 'liberty of conscience and liberty of the subjects' 'two as glorious things to be contended for, as any God has given us',[25] the attitudes of some of the Parliament's most able and active members were profoundly disappointing. In that speech he went on to lament that there was 'too much of an imposing spirit in matter of conscience; a spirit unchristian enough in any times, most unfit for these; denying liberty of conscience to those who have earned it with their blood; who have gained civil liberty, and religious also, for those who would thus impose upon them'.[26] In his speech of 12 September 1654, Cromwell declared that 'liberty of conscience in religion' was 'a fundamental' and 'a natural right'.[27] But such 'a thing ought to be very reciprocal' and, when he dissolved the Parliament on 22 January 1655, Cromwell denounced its failure to give 'a just liberty to godly men of different judgments', and to settle 'peace and quietness amongst all professing godliness', adding: 'is there not upon the spirits of men a strange itch? Nothing will satisfy them unless they can put their finger upon their brethren's consciences, to pinch them there.'[28] On this point Cromwell was fundamentally at odds with the prevailing mood of the Parliament. Moreover, the specific limitations that the 'constitutional bill' placed on his capacity to promote liberty of conscience must have heightened his resentment of the Parliament's systematic curtailing of other Protectoral powers established in the Instrument of Government.

Cromwell's anger at the Parliament's failure to safeguard liberty of conscience was widely shared among the soldiery. Towards the end of 1654, the army presented a petition to him that included the demands that 'liberty of conscience be allowed, but not to papistry in public worship', and that 'a law be made for the righting [of] persons wronged for liberty of conscience'.[29] The Venetian ambassador noted wryly that when, 'in spite of the article in the paper presented by some of the army against interference in religion', the Parliament 'decided that the religion generally professed here must be the Protestant', this outcome 'possibly dissatisfied the military'.[30] In fact, a number of the most prominent members, including figures such as

---

[24] Worden, 'Toleration', pp. 221–2; J. C. Davis, 'Cromwell's Religion', in John Morrill, ed., *Oliver Cromwell and the English Revolution* (Harlow, 1990), pp. 196–7.
[25] Lomas–Carlyle, II, 345.
[26] Lomas–Carlyle, II, 346. At this point in his edition, Carlyle interpolated: 'stifled murmurs from the Presbyterian sect'.
[27] Lomas–Carlyle, II, 382.   [28] Lomas–Carlyle, II, 416–17.
[29] *Clarke Papers*, III, 13; Vaughan, I, 80. Cf. *A Perfect Account of the Daily Intelligence from the Armies in England, Scotland and Ireland, and the Navy at Sea* (1–8 November 1654), sig. 9Q.
[30] *CSPV, 1655–6*, 1.

John Fitzjames, John Bulkeley, Sir Richard Onslow, John Birch, John Ashe, and Robert Shapcote, had a long history of Presbyterian antipathy towards the Independent cause espoused by the army. With the exception of Fitzjames, who had not sat in the Long Parliament, all these members had been imprisoned or secluded at Pride's Purge.[31] The tensions that erupted during the first Protectorate Parliament between on the one hand Cromwell and the army, and on the other a number of active members of Presbyterian sympathies, thus represented in part the continuation of a long-term fissure within the Parliamentarian cause that can be traced back to the later 1640s.

Furthermore, it is likely that at least some of the newly arrived Irish and Scottish members were of Presbyterian sympathies and that their presence therefore tended to strengthen the Parliament's hostility towards liberty of conscience. The member for County Cork, Lord Broghill, provides a good case study of this. Broghill was well connected in both Ireland and Scotland: the owner of extensive lands in Ireland, he was appointed Lord President of the Scottish council in 1655, and in the second Protectorate Parliament he sat for both County Cork and Edinburgh.[32] In the first Protectorate Parliament he was appointed to the committee to review the ordinance 'for ejecting scandalous, ignorant and insufficient ministers and schoolmasters', and acted as a teller for the Noes who opposed its suspension.[33] On 12 December 1654, he was appointed to a committee 'to consider of the particular enumeration of damnable heresies'.[34] Later, on 3 January 1655, he acted as a teller for the Yeas in favour of retaining the words 'to be particularly enumerated by the Parliament' after 'damnable heresies' in the House's resolution of 15 December.[35] Broghill's friends included the Presbyterian minister Richard Baxter, and Broghill nominated Baxter to

---

[31] For Bulkeley, see David Underdown, *Pride's Purge: Politics in the Puritan Revolution* (Oxford, 1971), p. 369. For Onslow, see Mary Frear Keeler, *The Long Parliament, 1640–1641: A Biographical Study of its Members* (Memoirs of the American Philosophical Society, 36, Philadelphia, 1954), p. 290; Underdown, *Pride's Purge*, p. 381; and the *ODNB* (Sir Richard Onslow). For Birch, see Underdown, *Pride's Purge*, p. 368; and the *ODNB* (John Birch). For Ashe, see Keeler, *Long Parliament*, p. 91; and Underdown, *Pride's Purge*, p. 367. For Shapcote, see Underdown, *Pride's Purge*, p. 385.

[32] For Broghill's career, see especially Patrick Little, *Lord Broghill and the Cromwellian Union with Ireland and Scotland* (Woodbridge, 2004); Patrick Little, 'An Irish Governor of Scotland: Lord Broghill, 1655–1656', in A. MacKillop and Steve Murdoch, eds., *Military Governors and Imperial Frontiers, c. 1600–1800: A Study of Scotland and Empires* (Leiden and Boston, 2003), pp. 79–97; and Frances Dow, *Cromwellian Scotland, 1651–1660* (Edinburgh, 1979), pp. 162–210.

[33] *CJ*, VII, 370, 382. The Noes carried the day by 77 votes to 67.   [34] *CJ*, VII, 399.

[35] *CJ*, VII, 412; *Mercurius Politicus*, no. 238 (28 December 1654–4 January 1654[/5]), p. 5034. The Yeas carried the day by 81 votes to 75. This resolution is quoted p. 134.

the group of divines chosen to confer with Parliament's sub-committee on religion.[36] Baxter subsequently wrote of his hostility to 'a universal toleration for all that shall seek the subversion of the faith of Christ'. Although keen to 'distinguish between tolerable and intolerable errors, and restrain only the latter', he was vehemently opposed to 'licentious toleration of Church destroyers'.[37] Broghill's role on committees and as a teller during the first Protectorate Parliament suggests that his own stance on religious issues was consistent with Baxter's position.

The lack of sympathy within the Parliament towards liberty of conscience was important in explaining why Cromwell did not find the assembly, in Bulstrode Whitelocke's phrase, 'pliable to his purposes'.[38] The chances of achieving such pliability were not enhanced by the fact that those councillors who sat in the Parliament do not appear to have formed a coherent group: there is little sign that they attempted to co-ordinate their activities or to set a lead in the House. The government did not introduce any clear legislative programme, and parliamentary business proceeded on an *ad hoc* basis.[39] In part this reflected Cromwell's conviction that he should not interfere directly in the Parliament's deliberations.[40] However, the problem went much deeper, and it ultimately revealed a basic tension within Cromwell's own concept of the role of Parliament that prevented him from achieving a stable working relationship with any of the Protectorate Parliaments.[41] Cromwell wished to use Parliament to unify the interests of the nation with those of the people of God. He was attracted to the Instrument of Government because he felt that within it 'a just liberty to the people of God, and the just rights of the people in these nations [were] provided for'.[42] He believed that if Parliament, the 'representative of the whole realm', promoted liberty of conscience, then the interests of the nation and of the godly would eventually be reconciled. He hoped that Parliament, by promulgating liberty of conscience and fostering peaceful coexistence among 'God's children', would play a central part in this process: this was what a 'pliable' Parliament would have done.

---

[36] N. H. Keeble and Geoffrey F. Nuttall, eds., *Calendar of the Correspondence of Richard Baxter* (2 vols., Oxford, 1991), I, 160, 162, 189. Broghill's religious sympathies in the first Protectorate Parliament are discussed in Little, *Broghill*, pp. 79–81, 224–7, and 232–3, and his friendship with Baxter at pp. 80–1. See also the section on 1654–5 in N. H. Keeble's life of Baxter in the *ODNB*.

[37] Keeble and Nuttall, *Calendar of Correspondence of Baxter*, I, 222–6 (Baxter to Edward Harley, 15 September 1656); quotations at 223, 226.

[38] Whitelocke, *Diary*, p. 400. The same phrase also appears in Whitelocke, *Memorials*, IV, 182.

[39] Peter Gaunt, 'The Councils of the Protectorate, from December 1653 to September 1658' (Ph.D thesis, University of Exeter, 1983), pp. 129–42.

[40] See, for example, Lomas–Carlyle, II, 359, 407. Cromwell's desire to stand back from parliamentary proceedings as much as possible is discussed more fully in chapter 6.

[41] This issue is explored at length in chapter 6.   [42] Lomas–Carlyle, II, 419.

The first Protectorate Parliament, however, contained a core of members who were vehemently opposed to any measures that might lift the lid off a seething mass of sectarian errors and blasphemies. As Cromwell complained to his confidant Lieutenant-Colonel Wilks in January 1655, 'whosoever labours to walk with an even foot between the several interests of the people of God for healing and accommodating their differences is sure to have reproaches and anger from some of all sorts'.[43] This Parliament, like those before and after, continued to reflect the widespread Presbyterian unease about liberating the sects. We have already seen that it had been elected on a revised franchise, with a major redistribution of seats towards the counties and a £200 property qualification.[44] As a result, it manifested many of the attitudes that were apparently mainstream within the political and social elite, and it was deeply reluctant to espouse what remained a minority agenda. Cromwell's commitment to liberty of conscience thus generated profound tensions between the 'single person and a Parliament' which dogged the entire history of the Protectorate.[45]

1656–7

The religious complexion of the second Protectorate Parliament was probably very similar to that of the first. According to Sarah Jones's (again necessarily very approximate and tentative) figures, the religious affiliations of over 60 per cent of members of the second Protectorate Parliament remain unknown, and she suggests that committed Presbyterians constituted perhaps one-fifth of members.[46] When this Parliament assembled on 17 September 1656, the dean of Christ Church and vice-chancellor of Oxford University, John Owen, who was well known for his Independent sympathies, exhorted members to promote a 'coalescence in love and truth' and a 'mutual forbearance of one another' among 'the people of God'.[47] The

---

[43] Lomas–Carlyle, III, 460.
[44] Vernon F. Snow, 'Parliamentary Reapportionment Proposals in the Puritan Revolution', *EHR*, 74 (1959), 409–42. The revised distribution of seats is set out in the Instrument of Government, printed in Gardiner, *Constitutional Documents*, pp. 407–9. These reforms and the elections of 1654 are discussed more fully in chapter 3.
[45] The above account of the issue of religious reform in the first Protectorate Parliament draws in part on material already published in David L. Smith, 'Oliver Cromwell, the First Protectorate Parliament, and Religious Reform', *Parl. Hist.*, 19 (2000), 38–48. This article was reprinted in R. Malcolm Smuts and Arthur F. Kinney, eds., *Responses to Regicide* (Amherst, 2001), pp. 49–70; and also in David L. Smith, ed., *Cromwell and the Interregnum* (Oxford, 2003), pp. 167–81.
[46] Jones, 'Composition and Activity of the Protectorate Parliaments', p. 74.
[47] John Owen, *God's Word in Founding Zion, and His Peoples Duty thereupon. A Sermon Preached in the Abby Church at Westminster, … Septemb[er] 17th 1656* (Oxford, 1656), p. 42.

most important criterion for adopting any policy, he argued, was how well it 'suite[d] the design of God in establishing Sion', and he urged members to 'secure your spirits, that in sincerity you seek the public good of the nations, and the prosperity of the good people therein, who have adhered to the good cause of liberty, and religion'.[48] Later that day, Cromwell echoed Owen in his opening speech when he called for a 'reformation of manners' and set out both his commitment to liberty of conscience and the limits to it. He insisted that 'whatever pretensions to religion would continue quiet, peaceable, they should enjoy conscience and liberty to themselves'; but he was 'against all liberty of conscience' that tended 'to combination, to interests and factions'. 'Truly', he declared, 'I am against all liberty of conscience repugnant to this.'[49] The crucial requirement was to live quietly and to respect the liberty of others, regardless of outward forms:

Men that believe the remission of sins through the blood of Christ, and free justification by the blood of Christ, and live upon the grace of God: that those men that are certain they are so, they are members of Jesus Christ, and are to Him as the apple of His eye. Whoever has this faith, let his form be what it will; [if] he [be] walking peaceably, without the prejudicing of others under another form: it is a debt due to God and Christ, and He will require it, if he that Christian may not enjoy this liberty.[50]

It was the duty of the civil magistrate to ensure peaceful coexistence between the different 'forms': to 'keep things equal' and to prevent 'any one religion to impose upon another'. Cromwell acknowledged that the provision and maintenance of a godly ministry were crucial in advancing the cause of Reformation. He opposed the abolition of tithes, but hoped that in due course other means could be found to maintain 'this ministry of England'. He praised the triers and ejectors, and told members that 'in these things, in these arrangements made by us, that tend to the profession of the Gospel and public ministry, I think you will be so far from hindering that you will further it. And I shall be willing to join with you.'[51]

The second Protectorate Parliament certainly did not neglect measures that implemented religious reform, but the majority of members felt more enthusiastic about maintaining a godly ministry and improving the religious education of the nation than about extending liberty of conscience more widely. Even the renewal of the ordinances for the triers and ejectors on 28 April 1657 was not straightforward. Leading Presbyterians such as Sir Richard Onslow, Lambert Godfrey, and Thomas Bampfield ensured that

---

[48] Owen, *God's Word in Founding Zion*, pp. 44, 47.
[49] Lomas–Carlyle, II, 535. [50] Lomas–Carlyle, II, 536.
[51] Lomas–Carlyle, II, 537–9. On Cromwell's opposition to the abolition of tithes until other means to support the ministry had been found, see Collins, 'Church Settlement', 31–2.

these renewals were only for three years, and that any triers 'named in the intervals of Parliament, shall be afterwards approved by Parliament'.[52] Less contentious was the passage of no fewer than six private acts for the maintenance of godly ministers in particular towns or cities: these were for Great Yarmouth (1 December 1656), Northampton (12 February 1657), Plymouth (14 March 1657), Exeter (27 March 1657), Newport on the Isle of Wight (30 March 1657), and Bristol (26 June 1657).[53] Cromwell gave his assent to the first five of these acts on 9 June, and to the sixth on 26 June 1657.[54] Insofar as the principal promoters of some of these bills can be identified, they appear to have been as follows: for Northampton, Beake and Claypole; for Exeter, Bampfield; for Newport, Bampfield, Sydenham, and Sir William Strickland; and for Bristol, Prideaux and Whitelocke.[55] This roster of names suggests that members who were, as we shall see, deeply divided over Nayler's fate could co-operate over the maintenance of the ministry.

Two other very similar private bills for the maintenance of the ministry failed to complete their passage through the House: one was for Totnes and the other for Portsmouth.[56] On 18 June 1657, a committee was appointed to prepare a bill 'for the maintenance of some preaching ministers' in York, Durham, Carlisle, Newcastle, and Berwick, but this bill was not ready prior to the adjournment on 26 June.[57] A similar concern for the maintenance of a godly ministry was evident in a bill 'enabling several Trustees to purchase in impropriations, and other revenues, to maintain several ministers and lecturers in several parishes within this nation', which passed its first two readings in March 1657 but proceeded no further; another 'for settling several ministers in their livings in Norfolk and Suffolk' received only a first reading.[58] Cromwell welcomed such measures, and told the Parliament on 21 April: 'truly we have settled very much the business of the ministry ... If I have anything to rejoice in before the Lord in this world ... it has been [this].'[59] Two further pieces of private legislation reflected the fact that during the Interregnum cathedrals had become the property of the state. On 26 June 1657, Cromwell assented to 'an Act for settling the late Cathedral Church of Gloucester upon the Mayor and Burgesses of the City of Gloucester, and their successors, for public, religious, and charitable uses' (passed on 5 December 1656).[60] A bill 'for vesting the Church, commonly called the Cathedral Church of Winchester, in certain Trustees for public and religious uses' passed its first reading on 21 May 1657 but then got no further.[61]

---

[52] *CJ*, VII, 524; Burton, II, 51–6, 58–60. See also chapter 1.
[53] *CJ*, VII, 462, 490, 503, 513, 514, 576.   [54] *CJ*, VII, 552–3, 577.
[55] Burton, I, 81, 223, 224, 244–5, 267–8; Whitelocke, *Memorials*, IV, 287.
[56] *CJ*, VII, 489, 496, 538.   [57] *CJ*, VII, 562.
[58] *CJ*, VII, 502, 514–15; Whitelocke, *Memorials*, IV, 287.   [59] Lomas–Carlyle, III, 118.
[60] *CJ*, VII, 464, 552.   [61] *CJ*, VII, 536.

In addition, the Parliament also produced three public acts that applied to the whole Commonwealth of England, Scotland, and Ireland. The first to complete its passage through the House was an act 'for quiet enjoying of sequestered parsonages and vicarages by the present incumbent'. This stated that all those ministers who, on 1 July 1657, were settled in any parsonage or vicarage that had been sequestered by Parliament would henceforth be regarded as the lawful incumbent, regardless of whether the ejected or sequestered minister was still alive. Any ejected or sequestered minister whose real estate was worth less than £30 a year, or whose personal estate was valued at less than £500, was permitted to receive one-fifth of the income from the parsonage or vicarage. This act was passed on 17 June 1657 and received the Protectoral assent on 26 June.[62]

The second of these public acts was 'for convicting, discovering and repressing of popish recusants': it was passed on 18 June and received the Protectoral assent on 26 June.[63] This act was intended to combat the recent 'great increase of popish recusants within this Commonwealth', and required all those aged sixteen or over who were 'papists or popishly affected' to take an Oath of Abjuration before local justices at the next assizes or quarter sessions. By this oath, they renounced the Pope's supremacy, denied the doctrines of transubstantiation and salvation by works, repudiated the existence of purgatory, and rejected the doctrine that the Pope could excommunicate or deprive 'princes, rulers, or governors'. Those who refused to take this oath were to be committed to custody, 'there to remain without bail or mainprise', until the next quarter sessions. Those convicted of recusancy would forfeit 'two third parts of all lands, tenements, leases, farms, copyhold lands, goods and chattels'. Individuals who were not recusants themselves, but who married 'any woman that he shall know to be a popish recusant convict', were also to 'be taken and adjudged a popish recusant convict'. Finally, it was declared illegal 'for any subject of this Commonwealth ... at any time to be present at Mass, at the house of any ambassador or agent, or any other place whatsoever, upon pain and penalty of one hundred pounds and imprisonment, by the space of six months'.

At this bill's second reading, concerns were voiced about the penalties imposed on those who married recusants (Denis Bond), about the lack of legal safeguards on those justices who convicted people of recusancy

---

[62] *CJ*, VII, 560, 577; Whitelocke, *Memorials*, IV, 305. This act is printed in *A & O*, II, 1266–8. It passed its first and second readings on 1 and 4 October 1656 respectively (*CJ*, VII, 431, 434), and subsequently received minor amendments, mainly to clarify patrons' rights of presentation: *ibid.*, 449, 461, 490, 560–1.

[63] *CJ*, VII, 461, 463, 541, 544, 561–2, 577; Whitelocke, *Memorials*, IV, 305. This act is printed in *A & O*, II, 1170–80, from which the following quotations are taken.

(Whitelocke, Luke Robinson), about the need to secure a positive commitment to Protestantism rather than merely a renunciation of popery (Sir William Strickland), and about whether those who renounced papal supremacy should be punished for other privately held beliefs (Sir Gilbert Pickering).[64] Subsequent amendments did more to tighten the legal processes surrounding conviction for recusancy than to soften the doctrinal demands contained in the Act of Abjuration. On 2 June, the House resolved to retain the requirement that recusants repudiate the doctrines of transubstantiation and salvation by works, despite the committee's recommendations; and at the bill's third reading on 18 June the House rejected a proposed amendment that would have given receivers and collectors power of distraint over recusants' property.[65] Once again, the anxiety of many members that due legal process be observed and that personal liberties not be violated was very evident.

Thirdly, there was an act – passed on 20 June and assented to six days later – 'for the better observation of the Lord's Day'.[66] This set out a large number of activities deemed to constitute profanation of the Sabbath, including 'dancing, or profanely singing or playing upon musical instruments'; 'setting up, burning or branding beet, turf or earth'; brewing or baking; attending 'any fairs, markets, wakes, revels, wrestlings, shootings, leaping, bowling, ringing of bells for pleasure, or upon any other occasion (saving for calling people together for public worship), feasts, church-ale, may-poles, gaming, bear-baiting, bull-baiting, or any other sports and pastimes'; and 'travelling, carrying burdens, or doing any worldly labour or work of their ordinary calling' on Sunday. All those aged fourteen or over who were convicted of any such offence were to be fined ten shillings. Justices, constables, churchwardens and overseers of the poor were authorised 'to demand entrance into any dwelling-house, or other place whatsoever suspected by them to harbour, entertain or suffer to be any person or persons profaning the Lord's Day', and those convicted of denying such entrance were liable to be fined twenty shillings. Those who molested, disturbed, or in any way troubled any minister or public preacher were to be fined five pounds and might, at the justices' discretion, be 'sent to the house of correction or work-house, to be set to hard labour . . . for some time, not exceeding six months'. Perhaps most significantly, this act reintroduced compulsory church attendance on Sundays, which the Rump Parliament's Toleration Act

---

[64] Burton, II, 6–8. All these individuals were among those added to the committee for this bill following the debate: *CJ*, VII, 463.
[65] *CJ*, VII, 544, 561–2.
[66] *CJ*, VII, 480, 493, 567, 577; Whitelocke, *Memorials*, IV, 306. This act is printed in *A & O*, II, 1162–70, from which the following quotations are taken.

of 1650 had abolished: 'all and every person or persons shall ... upon every Lords-Day diligently resort to some church or chapel where the true worship and service of God is exercised, or shall be present at some other meeting-place of Christians, not differing in matters of faith from the public profession of the nation'. Those convicted of failing to do this without 'reasonable excuse for their absence' were to be fined 'two shillings and six pence'.

This wide-ranging act was promoted by major-generals such as Whalley and Kelsey, as well as Presbyterians such as Sir William Strickland and Thomas Bampfield.[67] The act passed its first and second readings straightforwardly,[68] but at its third reading (20 June 1657) some of the lawyers in the House expressed concern over the sweeping powers of entry that the bill gave to justices. Burton recorded that Chief Justice Glynne moved 'against the clause for entering into men's houses' on the grounds that 'it may be a snare to all the nation; and knaves, in the night-time, may enter and rob men's houses under this pretence. When an Act of Parliament gives a liberty of entry, then a man may break open doors.' Whitelocke reportedly supported him, arguing 'against all liberty of this kind, to enter men's houses', and asserting that 'the law has always been tender of men's houses. I would not have the people of England enslaved.' Whitelocke's motion to amend the bill to 'demand entrance' was carried.[69] After further debate, another clause against 'all profane and idle sitting openly at gates or doors, or elsewhere', was dropped.[70] The debate continued into the evening, candles were brought in, but eventually Whalley pushed for the question to be put and the bill was passed.[71]

The successful progress of these three public bills into acts indicates that they were all measures on which the Protectoral regime and the majority of members could agree. Yet Cromwell's own sympathies continued to lean further towards liberty of conscience than did those of most members. It is significant that the only occasion on which Cromwell ever used his veto as Protector was on 9 June when he rejected a public bill 'enjoining ministers, and others, to perform the duty of catechising' with words that echoed the old royal veto: 'I am desirous to advise of this bill.'[72] The bill received minor amendments after its second reading, principally to clarify that it applied to Scotland, Ireland, and Wales as well as England.[73] At its third reading on 20–21 May, after an extended debate, a proviso was inserted in the bill stipulating that it did not extend 'to compel any person or persons, being members of particular congregational churches, or children of such

[67] Burton, II, 260–1, 295.   [68] *CJ*, VII, 462, 482.   [69] Burton, II, 263; *CJ*, VII, 567.
[70] Burton, II, 264–5; *CJ*, VII, 567.   [71] Burton, II, 266–8; *CJ*, VII, 567.
[72] Burton, II, 205; *CJ*, VII, 535.   [73] *CJ*, VII, 482, 493, 512; Burton, I, 376.

members, or persons married, who, upon private examination by the minister of such parish church, shall be found to be competently instructed in the principles of the True Christian Reformed Protestant Religion, to come to be catechised in public at the parish church'.[74] A further proviso stated that the bill likewise did not apply to 'any person or persons who shall produce unto the minister of such parish a certificate under the hand of the pastor of a congregated church, agreeing in matters of faith with the public profession, that such person or persons are members of such congregation, or the children or servants of such members, and are under his or their care, for their instruction'.[75] Yet even the addition of these concessions to the congregational churches did not incline Cromwell to assent to this bill, probably because to him it still smacked too much of obliging members of those churches to conform to the practices of the national church.[76]

Indeed, Cromwell's correspondence shows that he remained preoccupied with the issue of liberty of conscience. He was anxious to reassure the Independent-minded mayor and aldermen of Newcastle, who had feared that he might become too sympathetic towards Presbyterians: 'I, or rather the Lord, require of you, that you walk in all peaceableness and gentleness, inoffensiveness, truth and love towards them, as becomes the servants and churches of Christ; knowing well that Jesus Christ, of whose diocese both they and you are, expects it.'[77] Such issues undoubtedly weighed heavily with Cromwell during December 1656, the month that saw the Parliament examine the Quaker James Nayler for blasphemy. The previous October, Nayler had ridden into Bristol on a horse, with admirers shouting hosannas and strewing garments in his path. This episode prompted allegations that 'he assumed the gesture, words, names, and attributes of our Saviour Christ'.[78] In addition to raising the difficult issues of judicature discussed in the previous chapter, the Nayler case also marked a continuation of the debates over liberty of conscience and religious blasphemies and errors that had arisen in 1654–5 regarding Biddle and Tany.[79]

During the lengthy debates over Nayler's fate between 5 and 16 December 1656, the most lenient speakers were consistently two members of the army

---

[74] *CJ*, VII, 535. [75] *CJ*, VII, 536.

[76] The Venetian Resident, Giavarina, thought that Cromwell vetoed this bill because 'he did not wish to offend the sectaries': *CSPV, 1657–9*, 72.

[77] Lomas–Carlyle, III, 2–3. [78] Burton, I, 24.

[79] For accounts of the Nayler case, see especially Firth, *Last Years*, I, 98–106; Theodore A. Wilson and Frank J. Merli, 'Nayler's Case and the Dilemma of the Protectorate', *University of Birmingham Historical Journal*, 10 (1965–6), 44–59; Leo Damrosch, *The Sorrows of the Quaker Jesus: James Nayler and the Puritan Crackdown on the Free Spirit* (Cambridge, Mass., 1996), chapter 4; and Kate Peters, *Print Culture and the Early Quakers* (Cambridge, 2005), chapter 8.

interest on the council, Lambert and Sydenham, together with Whitelocke.[80] Nayler had been Lambert's quarter-master for two years, and the latter described him as 'a man of very unblameable life and conversation, a member of a very sweet society of an independent church': Lambert could not determine how 'he comes (by pride or otherwise) to be puffed up to this opinion'.[81] What Sydenham most regretted was 'the nearness of [Nayler's] opinion to that which is a most glorious truth, that the spirit is personally in us'. He felt that an act of attainder 'scarcely agrees with the rule of the Gospel', and argued that Nayler's opinions 'do border so near a glorious truth' that he could not regard them as blasphemy.[82] Whitelocke adopted a characteristically legalistic position, and reportedly declared that he could find 'neither law nor precedent' for passing the death sentence on Nayler, and objected most to 'the disturbance of the public peace of the nation'.[83] A number of councillors also spoke in favour of leniency towards Nayler, including the Lord President of the council, Henry Lawrence, the Lord Keeper, Nathaniel Fiennes, Major-General John Disbrowe, Sir Gilbert Pickering, Sir Charles Wolseley, and Walter Strickland.[84] As Thomas Burton put it, the 'grandees ... mainly incline to the moderate kind of punishment'.[85]

By contrast, among the most vehemently hostile speakers were prominent Presbyterians such as Sir William Strickland, Thomas Bampfield, and Robert Beake.[86] Strickland declared: 'I would have us put on courage; and let not the enemies of God have the upper hand, to have liberty to blaspheme his name'; he was convinced that Nayler had committed 'blasphemy, nay horrid blasphemy'.[87] Bampfield believed 'that it was the mind of God to punish this offence with death', and felt that 'if this be not blasphemy, then there is no blasphemy in the world'.[88] Beake concurred, and asked more cautious members: 'you agree lesser sins to be blasphemy, and why do you stick to call it horrid blasphemy?'[89] Of the Presbyterian members who had spoken most robustly against errors and blasphemies in the previous Parliament, John Bulkeley and John Birch were among those excluded before the second

---

[80] See Burton, I, 33, 182 (for Lambert); 34, 41–2, 51, 68–9, 86, 172 (for Sydenham); and 32, 57–8, 125, 128–31, 162, 164, 170 (for Whitelocke).
[81] Burton, I, 33.   [82] Burton, I, 69, 86.   [83] Burton, I, 130, 170.
[84] See Burton, I, 62–3, 90, 154 (for Lawrence); 29, 90 (for Fiennes); 31, 39, 54–5, 71–2, 75, 149, 153 (for Disbrowe); 36, 48, 64–5, 150, 153 (for Pickering); 89–90 (for Wolseley); and 28, 38, 56–7, 87–8 (for Walter Strickland).
[85] Bodl., MS Carte 228, fo. 79v.
[86] See Burton, I, 24, 29–30, 32–3, 40–1, 91–2, 118, 147–8, 156–7, 164–5, 173, 218, 263–4 (for Bampfield, who reported from the committee that investigated the case: CJ, VII, 464); Burton, I, 28, 33, 35–6, 44–5, 51, 53, 75, 79, 131, 147–9, 155, 157, 220, 247–8 (for Sir William Strickland); and 43–4, 58–9, 90 (for Beake).
[87] Burton, I, 51, 75.   [88] Burton, I, 91.   [89] Burton, I, 59.

Protectorate Parliament opened.[90] Fitzjames, Onslow, and Ashe, while clearly hostile towards Nayler, did not play a prominent part in these debates.[91] Robert Shapcote, on the other hand, urged members not to become distracted from the case and he spoke so regularly that on 17 December he was 'cried down'. Five days earlier he had argued that 'by the old law this very blasphemy is punishable by death', and had declared himself 'satisfied for this offence Nayler ought to die'.[92] After lengthy debates, however, the House voted against a death sentence and instead imposed savage corporal punishments on Nayler that included whipping, tongue-boring and branding.[93]

Cromwell intervened only after this sentence had been passed, and then it was to ask the Speaker to explain 'the grounds and reasons whereupon they have proceeded'.[94] It is possible that Cromwell's known commitment to liberty of conscience played a part in inclining a majority of members to commute the death sentence, although the limits of their sympathy towards his position were sometimes barely concealed. For example, on 6 December one councillor, Major-General Philip Skippon, reportedly declared:

These Quakers, Ranters, Levellers, Socinians, and all sorts, bolster themselves under [clauses] thirty-seven and thirty-eight of [the Instrument of] Government ... I heard the supreme magistrate say, 'It was never his intention to indulge such things'; yet we see the issue of this liberty of conscience. It sits hard upon my conscience; and I choose rather to venture my discretion, than betray conscience by my silence. If this be liberty, God deliver me from such liberty. It is to evil, not to good, that this liberty extends.[95]

That a major-general spoke in such terms indicated the extent to which Cromwell risked becoming beleaguered not only from many civilian politicians but also from some of his army colleagues. It seems that Cromwell's sympathies did not exercise as much influence as he might have hoped. In mid-January 1657, Humphrey Robinson wrote: 'Though Parliament has been so moulded, and so many made incapable, yet Whitehall's expectations are not answered ... Nayler at last was sentenced by Parliament ... The

---

[90] *CJ*, VII, 425. For their exclusion, see chapter 4.

[91] Burton, I, 31–2, 36, 42, 50, 69, 77, 90, 150. Fitzjames twice acted as teller in divisions, against adjourning the debate on 13 December and, four days later, against allowing Nayler to say anything before judgement was passed: *CJ*, VII, 468, 469.

[92] Burton, I, 161, 165. This quotation is at 125; for Shapcote's other interventions regarding Nayler, see 36–7, 77, 85–6, 104, 155, 157.

[93] *CJ*, VII, 468–9. The House's sentence on Nayler is described more fully in chapter 8.

[94] Lomas–Carlyle, III, 20. See also pp. 138, 185.

[95] Burton, I, 50–1. For articles 37 and 38 of the Instrument, see Gardiner, *Constitutional Documents*, p. 416. Skippon appears to have been alluding to the passage in Cromwell's speech of 17 September 1656 found in Lomas–Carlyle, II, 536–7.

Protector wrote a letter for some moderation, but the House would not hearken to it.'[96]

The Nayler case should be seen in the context of a wider concern over whether tougher measures were needed to prevent religious liberty from running to licence. In the mid-1650s, Quakerism appeared to present an especially urgent problem, and on 18 December 1656 petitions 'containing complaints against Quakers' were presented to Parliament from Cornwall, Devon, Northumberland, Durham, Newcastle, Cheshire, and Bristol. These petitions sparked off a series of denunciations of Quakerism from members. Sir William Strickland complained that Quakers were 'a growing evil, and the greatest that ever was', while Major-General Skippon was reported as saying that 'we are all full of the sense of the evils spread all the land over, and our indulgence to them may make God to cause them to become disturbers of our peace'. The fears that had arisen over Biddle resurfaced as Skippon continued: 'I am for enumeration of their blasphemies, for I would not have any honest man surprised by a general law. I would have Biddle, and his sect, also considered by the same committee [as examined Nayler's case], which are also dangerous, as well as Quakers.'[97] On the other hand, councillors again tended to take a more moderate line and warned of the dangers of a general law against Quakers: Sydenham 'would not bring in a law against Quakers by a general word', while Walter Strickland insisted, 'You will not find in all your statute-books a definition of Quaker or Blasphemy. Other States never do it, further than as disturbers of the peace.'[98] In the end, the House referred the petitions to the Nayler committee 'to consider of them, and to collect such heads out of them, as may be fittest for the suppression of the mischiefs and inconveniences complained of therein; and report the same to the House'.[99] In the event, however, this committee did not report back before the Parliament was adjourned on 26 June. Pending a bill against Quakers, Bampfield and another Presbyterian and London member Sir Christopher Packe moved the third reading of a bill against vagrants on 5 May, and this received Protectoral assent on 9 June.[100]

The Parliament confronted the issue of liberty of conscience again in March 1657 when it discussed the Remonstrance and agreed on a clause that defined the limits of liberty of conscience more precisely than the Instrument of Government had done. Article 37 of the Instrument had stated that: 'so [long] as they abuse not this liberty to the civil injury of others and to the actual disturbance of the public peace on their parts: provided this liberty

---

[96] TNA, SP 18/153/41.   [97] Burton, I, 169, 170.
[98] Burton, I, 172, 173.   [99] CJ, VII, 470; Vaughan, II, 72–3.
[100] Burton, II, 112–14; CJ, VII, 530, 552. This act is printed in A & O, II, 1098–9; it carefully did not mention Quakers by name.

be not extended to popery or prelacy, nor to such as, under the profession of Christ, hold forth and practise licentiousness'.[101] The equivalent clause (article 10) of the Remonstrance – which was identical to that subsequently incorporated into the Humble Petition and Advice (article 11) – toughened this by explicitly mentioning 'horrible blasphemies' and referring to 'profaneness' as well as 'licentiousness', thus: 'whilst they abuse not this liberty to the civil injury of others, or the disturbance of the public peace; so that this liberty be not extended to popery or prelacy, or to the countenancing such who publish *horrible blasphemies*, or practise or hold forth licentiousness or *profaneness* under the profession of Christ'.[102] This represented a compromise that was acceptable to Cromwell, to his army colleagues, and to the majority of members, and the issue receded for the rest of that sitting.

1658 AND 1659

When Cromwell opened the second sitting of this Parliament on 20 January 1658, he remained very concerned about the preservation of 'our civil liberties as men, our spiritual liberties as Christians'. He told members: 'you have now a godly ministry; you have a knowing ministry; such a one as, without vanity be it spoken, the world has not'.[103] The Lord Keeper, Nathaniel Fiennes, took a similar line, and called for 'the advancement of the kingdom of Christ amongst us, and the glory of God, in the good of all men, but especially of the churches of God amongst men'. Fiennes urged members to steer between 'the rock' – 'a spirit of imposing upon men's consciences, where God leaves them a latitude, and would have them free' – and 'the quicksand' – 'an abominable licentiousness, to profess and practise any sort of detestable opinions and principles'.[104] However, this brief sitting achieved virtually nothing in the way of religious reform. In the Other House, a bill 'for the better levying the penalties for profanation of the Lord's Day' passed its first and second readings but got no further before the Parliament was dissolved on 4 February.[105] The Commons meanwhile was so preoccupied with constitutional issues, especially the status and title of the Other House, that it found little time to devote to religious matters. It revived the committee for the bill 'for enabling trustees to purchase in impropriations' that had

[101] Gardiner, *Constitutional Documents*, p. 416.
[102] Gardiner, *Constitutional Documents*, p. 455 (emphasis added). See also *CJ*, VII, 507; *Clarke Papers*, III, 98. For the text of the Remonstrance, see appendix 2. The only minor variation between the two texts was that the Remonstrance referred to 'civil injuries' (plural). This amendment is not referred to in *CJ*, VII, 507, and may be a typographer's change.
[103] Lomas–Carlyle, III, 151, 156.   [104] *CJ*, VII, 583–4.
[105] HMC, *The Manuscripts of the House of Lords, 1699–1702* (1908), pp. 511, 516.

been initiated in the first sitting.[106] It also resurrected another committee to prepare a bill 'for raising maintenance for ministers' and extended its remit to 'parishes that are in counties at large'.[107] But the only bill to emerge was one 'for the uniting the parishes and parish churches of Huntingdon, and for the better maintenance of preaching ministers there': this passed its first and second readings in January but proceeded no further before the dissolution.[108] For Cromwell this was another source of deep frustration. He lamented that 'each sect' wished to 'be uppermost', to 'be not only making wounds, but widening those already made, as if we should see one making wounds in a man's side, and would desire nothing more than to be groping and grovelling with his fingers in those wounds'.[109] He hoped that 'a godly ministry may be upheld, and not affronted by seducing and seduced spirits';[110] but he feared that during this Parliament's brief second sitting the nation 'was in likelihood of running into more confusion'.[111]

We have already seen in chapters 7 and 8 that the constitutional uncertainty surrounding the status of the Other House continued to dog the third Protectorate Parliament, and that there were also lengthy debates over the recognition of Richard Cromwell as Protector. It is also significant that Richard was, by the time he became Protector, known to be sympathetic to Presbyterianism, and less committed to liberty of conscience than his father. In his opening speech on 27 January 1659, Richard recommended to Parliament's 'care the people of God in these nations, with their concernments', adding that 'the more they are divided among themselves, the greater prudence should be used to cement them'. He also commended 'the good and necessary work of reformation, both in manners and in the administration of justice, that profaneness may be discountenanced and suppressed, and that righteousness and justice may be executed in the land'.[112] Lord Keeper Fiennes echoed him by urging that 'Christian liberty may be preserved without unchristian licentiousness', and that 'godliness may be set on the throne, and profaneness thrown out on the dunghill'.[113] However, the Commons

---

[106] *CJ*, VII, 502, 515, 588.   [107] *CJ*, VII, 580–1.   [108] *CJ*, VII, 580, 588.

[109] Lomas–carlyle, III, 174–5. Ivan Roots, ed., *Speeches of Oliver Cromwell* (1989), p. 180, follows Charles L. Stainer, ed., *Speeches of Oliver Cromwell, 1644–1658* (1901), p. 378, in omitting the words 'widening those already made', but this does not affect the overall sense of this passage.

[110] Lomas–carlyle, III, 184.

[111] Lomas–carlyle, III, 191. Roots, *Speeches of Oliver Cromwell*, p. 191, follows Stainer, *Speeches of Oliver Cromwell*, p. 395, in omitting the word 'more' before 'confusion'.

[112] [Richard Cromwell,] *The Speech of His Highness the Lord Protector, made to both Houses of Parliament at their first meeting on Thursday the 27th of January 1658[/9]* (1658[/9]), pp. 8–9.

[113] [Nathaniel Fiennes,] *The speech of the right honourable Nathaniel Lord Fiennes, one of the Lord Keepers of the Great Seale of England, made before his Highnesse, and both Houses of Parliament on Thursday the 27th of January, 1658[/9]* (1658[/9]), pp. 14–15.

soon became so deeply involved with constitutional issues that very little space was given to religious business. The only attempt to initiate any legislation was on 5 February when, following a motion from Bennet Hoskins, member for Herefordshire, the House appointed two committees: one was to consider how Wales and Monmouthshire 'may be supplied with a learned, pious, sufficient and able ministry', to examine the revenues of the church there, 'and to present such bills as they shall think fit, for redress of all grievances concerning the same'; the other was given the same remit for Yorkshire, Cumberland, Westmorland, Northumberland, and Durham.[114] The Other House established a committee 'to peruse the Acts and laws already made against cursing, swearing, breach of the Sabbath and drunkenness, and to see wherein the same are defective and have need to be supplied'; and another to 'consider of the law for restraining the use of the Book of Common Prayer' and to suggest ways of 'putting the same more effectually into execution'. The latter produced a bill for abolishing the Prayer Book but this passed only its first reading prior to the dissolution.[115]

The religious complexion of members of this Parliament was probably broadly similar to that of the first two Protectorate Parliaments. Sarah Jones's research suggests that once again the religious affiliations of nearly 70 per cent of members of the Commons in 1659 remain unknown, and that committed Presbyterians again constituted about 20 per cent of members.[116] The Presbyterian influence within the Commons was first revealed on 5 April 1659, when the House passed a declaration appointing 18 May 'a day of solemn fasting and humiliation'. This declaration complained that 'these nations are overspread with many blasphemies, and damnable heresies against God himself': it condemned the 'too much remissness and connivance of the civil magistrates ... in permitting the growth of these abominations, by suffering persons under the abuse of liberty of conscience to disturb the public ordinances, and to publish their corrupt principles and practices, to the seducing and infecting of others'.[117] Richard Cromwell was more sympathetic to such a declaration than his father would have been.[118] The Scottish minister James Sharp noted at the beginning of March that Richard took 'special notice of those of the Presbyterial way'.[119] Later, on 5 April, Sharp reported that the declaration for a fast day 'does exceedingly

---

[114] *CJ*, VII, 600; Burton, III, 82–4.   [115] HMC, *MSS of the House of Lords*, pp. 529, 534, 560.
[116] Jones, 'Composition and Activity of the Protectorate Parliaments', p. 74.
[117] *A Declaration of the Lord Protector and both Houses of Parliament* (1659), pp. 4–6. See also *CJ*, VII, 625–6. The Other House discussed this declaration on 14, 15, and 18 April, but had not passed it by the time of the dissolution: HMC, *MSS of the House of Lords*, pp. 560–3.
[118] The evidence for Richard's Presbyterian sympathies is also discussed in chapter 7.
[119] Stephen, II, 153.

storm and irritate all the Republican party',[120] whereas Richard treated Sharp 'very civilly'.[121] Further evidence that Richard's sympathies inclined towards the Presbyterians lies in the fact that according to Sharp, the Commons committee for religion, which had begun going through the Confession of the Westminster Assembly, received

assurances given to them from the Court … [that] none are to be countenanced or enjoy public maintenance who do not own it that Presbyterian government shall be that which shall be owned in the nation; that the Triers of Whitehall, the great state engine for Independency, shall be put down, and 8 or 9 commissioners only of ministers for ordination and approving shall be set up in its place.[122]

The Independents felt that the declaration 'import[ed] a design in the Presbyterians … to bring the magistrate to impose upon others',[123] and in this respect the new Protector appeared more in tune with the majority of members than his predecessor had been. Parliament voted through a return to the 1647 Westminster Confession (albeit shorn of its articles on church discipline) on 11 April, and, as Sharp reported, this was supported by 'both the Protector and the major part of the Parliament'.[124] Nor was this return to the lame Erastian presbytery of the 1640s to be the final word on religion, for 'this they think to be the farthest step they can make for the time towards a further settlement which they say will carry on afterwards'.[125] It seems that there were moves afoot to create a national church that would draw conservative Independents closer to the Presbyterian position established under the amended Westminster Confession. Sharp recounted that he had 'seen lately a piece called *Irenicum*, for an union betwixt Presbyterians and Independents', written 'by one of the Presbyterian judgement' (Matthew Newcomen), in which 'he shows how the way of the Independents now is far different from the way of the old puritans and nonconformists (to whom the Independents pretend to conform in their new way) and from citations out of the chief for the congregational way in New England, he proves an agreement in the most points, with the Presbyterian principles'.[126] It was entirely consistent with such a resurgent Presbyterian outlook that when, on 16 April, Quakers delivered two papers to the House, they were ordered immediately to 'resort to their respective habitations, and there apply themselves to their callings; and submit themselves to the laws of the nation, and the magistracy they live under'.[127] The prevailing mood within the House

---

[120] Stephen, II, 167.   [121] Stephen, II, 172.   [122] Stephen, II, 168.
[123] Stephen, II, 169.   [124] Stephen, II, 171.   [125] Stephen, II, 171–2.
[126] Edinburgh University Library, Special Collections, D.K.3.29 (correspondence relating to James Sharp), fo. 115r–v. Sharp was referring here to [Matthew Newcomen,] *Irenicum; or, An essay towards a brotherly peace & union* (1659). See also Keeble and Nuttall, *Calendar of Correspondence of Baxter*, I, 378–9.
[127] *CJ*, VII, 640. See also Burton, IV, 440–6.

thus remained as fearful as ever that religious liberty might turn to licence. It was therefore not surprising, perhaps, that when the Parliament was dissolved on 22 April one of the army's informants wrote that 'there are very many godly men, both ministers and others, who do account the dissolution of the Parliament a merciful as well as an extraordinary providence of God at the time it was done'.[128]

CONCLUSION

In conclusion, most members of the Protectorate Parliaments would have agreed with Oliver Cromwell and the army leaders that Parliament had a crucial role to play in settling the religious life of the nation. They differed, however, over what sort of settlement was to be constructed, over how rigid the national structures should be, and over what measure of liberty of conscience was acceptable. Perhaps more than on any other single issue, the differences of opinion on religious matters, especially between Oliver Cromwell and a significant core of members, were responsible for destabilising the Parliaments of the Protectorate. On certain priorities, such as the maintenance of a godly, preaching ministry, they could co-operate relatively easily. But on other issues – in particular on how widely liberty of conscience should be extended – they were not instinctively in tune. As we argued in chapter 6, a tension existed within Cromwell's own vision between his commitment to Parliament and his pursuit of liberty of conscience that ultimately doomed both to failure. The consequence was that he and most members of the Protectorate Parliaments actively sought religious reform, but they remained unable to achieve lasting agreement over what reforms were desirable and how best to secure them.

Finally, in 1659, events took a rather different turn. The accession of a new Protector more sympathetic towards the Presbyterian majority in Parliament helped to defuse one source of tension, but at the cost of alienating a diverse coalition of army officers, Independents, and commonwealthsmen. This helped to spark off an army coup that forced Richard Cromwell to dissolve the Parliament, and ultimately to resign as Protector, before he had had time to build a secure Presbyterian base in Parliament. Religion thus remained a deeply divisive issue, and the inability to reconcile the Presbyterian majority in Parliament with the Independent majority among the army officers dogged both Protectors. In the first two Protectorate Parliaments, Oliver Cromwell's commitment to liberty of conscience alienated many Presbyterians within Parliament, whereas in the third his son's Presbyterian

---

[128] *Clarke Papers*, IV, 7.

sympathies offended many Independents within the army. In the end, the army had the power to bring down the Protectorate, and it used this to devastating effect in April–May 1659. Throughout the Protectorate, religious controversy was thus one of the crucial sticking points that stood in the way of a settlement, and a key reason why the regime was unable to generate lasting stability.

10

Representation and taxation in England and Wales

Did the voters take their turn at the hustings and then go home, forgetting and forgotten, or did the member maintain close and constructive links with his constituency? In other words, were the wishes and interests of the people outside Parliament effectively represented?[1]

This was the question posed by Derek Hirst as part of his important study of representation in early Stuart England. His answer, after a detailed investigation of the surviving evidence, was that the relationship between members of Parliament and their constituents was growing ever closer in the early seventeenth century. Indeed, at the beginning of the Long Parliament, 'to many both in Parliament and country ... the people were no longer merely to be governed, but they were to act in partnership with their representatives in the House'.[2] Despite Hirst's optimistic prognosis, this situation was eminently reversible. The experience of the Civil Wars, purges of Parliament, the execution of the King, and the repeated forced dissolutions of Parliament all had the potential to erode that 'partnership'. The Protectorate itself could be seen to mark another stage in that process of erosion. In chapters 3 and 4, we saw the way in which elections were managed, with varying degrees of success, the extent to which changes to the constituencies, the new franchise, and the qualifications demanded of voters influenced the make-up of the Protectorate Parliaments, and how exclusions moulded the Commons in 1654 and 1656, creating what some contemporaries viewed as 'forced' Parliaments. These changes to the rules for sitting in the Commons – as well as the growth of distinct political 'parties', the strength of feeling generated by the great constitutional debates, and the depth of religious and ideological belief that lay behind them – risked creating even more distance between members and their constituents. In this chapter, therefore,

---

[1] Derek Hirst, *The Representative of the People? Voters and Voting in England under the Early Stuarts* (Cambridge, 1975), p. 157.
[2] Hirst, *The Representative of the People?*, p. 187.

it is necessary to ask Hirst's question once again, and to attempt to answer it by looking at the theory and reality of representation during the Protectorate Parliaments, before concentrating on an issue of abiding interest to members and constituents alike: taxation.

THE RHETORIC OF REPRESENTATION

During the 1640s and 1650s, Parliament's position as the collective repre-sentative of the people of England and Wales had become something of a cliché. Theorists in the early 1640s, such as Henry Parker, nurtured the 'concept of the derivation of power from the people . . . directly transmitted to the members of the House of Commons', and by the end of the first Civil War in 1646 'the claim to be representative of the people was central to Parliament's stand in the war'.[3] It was as the people's representative that the Rump Parliament claimed the sovereignty that allowed it to bring the King to trial in 1649 and to rule as a republic thereafter.[4] According to such theories, the Protectorate, founded on a written constitution drawn up by army officers, was of questionable legitimacy. Oliver Cromwell's attempt to ratify the Instrument of Government in the 1654–5 Parliament and his evident pleasure at accepting the Humble Petition and Advice from Parliament's hands in 1657 show that the principle of Parliament as the representative of the people of England was accepted as a necessity by the Protector and most of his advisers.[5] This was still the case even as the second Parliament was dissolved amid acrimony. As Oliver opined on 4 February 1658, 'I would not have accepted of this government unless I knew that there would be a reciprocation between the government and the governed, . . . the general representative or the whole collective body, those that were the representative of the whole body of the nation.'[6]

This view of Parliament, as being of its essence the representative of the people, was shared by members of all political persuasions, and was readily used as a tool of debate. Thus the courtiers tried to justify the Protectorate in September 1654 by citing 'the addresses and approbation of the nation' that had supported the regime, and they also argued 'that the whole nation had concluded themselves and us from altering it, by the sealing of the indenture of the return of the election'.[7] The Presbyterian-led opposition naturally rejected this, and instead emphasised Parliament's role as the people's

---

[3] Hirst, *The Representative of the People?*, p. 157.
[4] See Jason Peacey, ed., *The Regicides and the Execution of Charles I* (Basingstoke, 2001), *passim*, especially chapters 5 and 6.
[5] See chapter 6.
[6] Ivan Roots, ed., *Speeches of Oliver Cromwell* (1989), p. 190; cf. Lomas–Carlyle, III, 189–90.
[7] Burton, I, xxix.

bastion against encroachment by the Protector and his council. On 10 November, for example, when the Protector's right of veto was opposed, the Presbyterian argument turned on fears that 'a free people' would become 'slaves' if the Protector had power to block legislation, 'for the legislature was ever in the people, represented in Parliament'.[8] Such arguments were difficult to answer, as the government had called Parliament precisely because it recognised the need for the representatives of the people to give the regime some legitimacy.

During the 1656–7 sitting of the second Protectorate Parliament, the emphasis was on unity among the membership. Those who called for harsh penalties against the Quaker James Nayler repeatedly reminded members that 'the eyes of the nation are upon you',[9] while those who called for leniency also argued that the Parliament should 'do things so as to justify us before both the face of God and the nation too'.[10] Throughout this period, there were concerns that the Parliament should conduct business, rather than dissolve into conflict, and members intervened to dampen down a bad-tempered exchange over the readmission of excluded members on 20 December 1656, reminding their colleagues 'what will be said abroad, that we were upon a debate and would not end it, but rose in anger and so let the sun go down on our wrath'.[11] News of the failure of Miles Sindercombe's plot against Oliver Cromwell in January 1657 was seized on as a way of emphasising the unity of the Parliament. As Lord Broghill put it, a public thanksgiving day 'will be a means to stop the mouths of your enemies'; and William Lenthall agreed: 'This will be a very good expedient to let the world see that there is a right understanding between his highness and us, and that we are cemented.'[12]

The kingship debates, which dominated proceedings from February 1657, exploded this attempt to demonstrate the Parliament's unity to the wider population, and 'the people' once again became a rhetorical football between the warring factions. The Remonstrance of 23 February and its successor, the Humble Petition and Advice, were framed as pleas to Cromwell from the people – they called upon him to restore the 'ancient constitution' not just as 'the knights, citizens and burgesses now assembled' but also as 'men and Christians' and the spokesmen of 'the good people of these nations'.[13] At the same time, the government was keen not to allow too much information into the public domain. The two government newsbooks were deliberately vague about the nature of the debates in the last days of February, and this suggests

---

[8] Burton, I, lxv.   [9] Burton, I, 28–9, 32, 38, 128, 137.   [10] Burton, I, 31.
[11] Burton, I, 195.   [12] Burton, I, 357–8, 360.
[13] See appendix 2 and Gardiner, *Constitutional Documents*, p. 448.

an attempt to keep the Parliament's initial deliberations quiet.[14] But the cat could not be kept in the bag quite so easily, as Sir John Reynolds admitted to Henry Cromwell on 24 February: 'I suppose your Lordship will receive it from other hands, and indeed I wish it were so carried as that common fame did not carry abroad our debates in Parliament.'[15] The offer of the crown, in particular, caused widespread alarm among the radical congregations, with Baptist ministers in London and 'many thousand' others signing addresses and petitions to the Protector; beyond London petitions arrived from twelve congregations in Warwickshire, Oxfordshire, Worcestershire, and Gloucestershire, and from 'the good people of many parts', opposing the creation of a new monarchy. They were soon joined by army officers from across the country,[16] and, even as the Protector walked to the meeting where he would decline the offer of the crown on 8 May, he was intercepted by a group of Baptist officers clutching yet another petition. The incident made Oliver 'extreme angry' not least because 'it did make people abroad say he is afraid of his army'.[17]

From January 1658 the factional sides were drawn up even more rigidly. The commonwealthsmen, still smarting from the forced closure of the Rump Parliament and the end of commonwealth government in April 1653, were quick to play the representative card in 1658 and 1659. In January and early February 1658, Sir Arthur Hesilrige raised questions as to 'the privileges of this House and liberties of England', and attacked the Protectorate as comprising those who 'invade the liberties of the free-born people of England'.[18] His views, and those of his allies, had not changed by the time the third Protectorate Parliament met in January 1659. Thus, on 2 February, Thomas Scott upheld Parliament's privileges by asking: 'for whom do you sit? Is it not for the people of England?'[19] On the same day, Henry Neville attacked the Humble Petition and Advice as a threat to 'the liberties of the people'.[20] Hesilrige's long speech on 7 February argued that 'the right [of government] is, originally, in the people' and that the dissolution of the Rump had taken that right away from them by force; the Protectorate was illegal even when ratified under the Humble Petition because the 1656 Parliament was 'a forced Parliament', with many members excluded. The new Parliament, however, was made up of the 'freest, and clearest and most undoubted representatives', and had a duty to restore the 'privileges and liberties' of

[14] *Mercurius Politicus*, no. 350 (19–26 February 1656[/7]), p. 7624, refers to 'a public business in reference to the settlement of the nation' but gives no details; this is echoed in *The Publick Intelligencer*, no. 72 (23 February–2 March 1656[/7]), p. 1228.
[15] BL, Lansdowne MS 821, fos. 296–7.
[16] Firth, *Last Years*, I, 154–5, 191–2; *Clarke Papers*, III, 95–6.
[17] BL, Lansdowne MS 822, fos. 71–2.   [18] Burton, II, 380, 439.   [19] Burton, III, 21.
[20] Burton, III, 34.

the English people.[21] This was the message that Hesilrige and the other commonwealthsmen came back to time and again, using ever more extreme language. Neville attacked the recognition of the Protector in these terms: 'when we are naturally free, why should we make ourselves slaves artificially';[22] Hesilrige accused the Protectorate of being 'a power without doors';[23] and, in a later debate on the Other House, he sighed, 'if this should pass, we shall next vote canvass breeches and wooden shoes [like those worn by French peasants] for the free people of England'.[24] This was a convenient stick with which to beat the Protectorate, but there are indications that the rights of the people were not in fact sacrosanct for the commonwealthsmen. On 9 February 1659, Major-General Packer stated, dismissively, that 'the people are like a flock of sheep', suitable to be led and flattered by others;[25] and on 14 February Hesilrige admitted that 'the people care not what government they live under, so as they may plough and go to market'.[26] Henry Neville, speaking on 12 March, was also less than flattering: 'the people are your children. You ought to take care of them.'[27]

The commonwealthsmen did not have a monopoly on the emotive language of 'representation'. The Presbyterians had their own tradition of upholding the people's rights, and in 1659, as they formed a closer alliance with the courtiers against the commonwealthsmen, they argued that such rights were defended by the Protectorate itself. Thus, John Trevor retorted to arguments that the Humble Petition was not the basis for the members' sitting by stating baldly that 'We sit here, it is true, by the people's choice, but upon the Petition and Advice.'[28] George Starkey agreed: 'the people ... have sent us hither to represent them, by his highness's call'.[29] Griffith Bodurda defended the Humble Petition itself as an act 'made as freely as any law since the beginning of the Long Parliament'.[30] Nathaniel Bacon went further, saying that 'the people of England have a right to the single person and two Houses of Parliament, and it cannot be taken away without their consent'.[31] This shift in the Presbyterian position, from hard-line support for a sovereign Parliament to allowing the Protector and the Humble Petition a place in the equation, shows how far they had been won over by the government position between 1656 and 1659. Some even questioned the absolute sovereignty of the people. Major Beake stated that there were 'fundamentals' that could not be altered by the people, and added 'it is disputable to me that all power is in the people'.[32] For Trevor, 'the peace of the people should be

---

[21] Burton, III, 88–102.   [22] Burton, III, 134.
[23] Burton, III, 141; for similar language later, see *ibid.*, IV, 25, 33, 35.
[24] Burton, IV, 79; see also Derbyshire RO, D258/10/9/2 (diary of Sir John Gell), fo. 10v.
[25] Burton, III, 161–2.   [26] Burton, III, 257.   [27] Burton, IV, 140.   [28] Burton, III, 72.
[29] Burton, III, 115.   [30] Burton, III, 135.   [31] Burton, III, 357.   [32] Burton, III, 114.

the main consideration of a Parliament' and that was dependent on uphold-ing the Protectoral government.[33] John Swinfen was also aware of limits, saying that 'unlimited liberty has been the source of all mischief ... I would not stir up that liberty that leaves you no liberty here [in Parliament].'[34] Unsurprisingly, the courtiers in the Commons agreed with the Presbyterian line, with the Protector's cousin, Robert Steward, defending the 1656 Parliament which passed the Humble Petition as a body that had upheld 'the interest of the nation'.[35] Nicholas Lechmere, Attorney of the Duchy of Lancaster, was also vigorous in his defence of the 1656 Parliament: 'they, in a fair way, did redeem the people's rights' and he asserted that the Humble Petition 'was a Petition of Right, and brought the heads of our liberties above the water'.[36] Secretary Thurloe was more succinct: the Protectorate was 'for the good of the people'.[37]

The theory of Parliament as having a unique place as the people's repre-sentative was not disputed by the different groups in the three Protectorate Parliaments, even if they differed as to how that should be interpreted. The commonwealthsmen and the courtiers had diametrically opposed views as to the nature of representation, and the extent to which an executive authority such as the Protector and his council could fit into a pattern of representative government. The Presbyterians, although inclined towards the common-wealth view in 1654, had shifted towards the court position by 1659. This was all on a rhetorical level, of course, and arguing about Parliament was a world away from trying to serve the people. So how far did members during these Parliaments actually represent the people of England?

THE REALITY OF REPRESENTATION

The short answer is that, if the *Journals* and diaries are to be believed, members of Parliament were not usually able, or even inclined, to live up to their professed ideals. There were three basic ways in which the general public could influence proceedings at Westminster: direct interference or intimidation, which was naturally resisted by a Parliament keen to assert its independence; petitioning, which at times could be tantamount to inter-ference; and finally private legislation, which was often initiated by petitions, but usually depended on the goodwill of constituency members, or others within Parliament. The way in which the three elements shade into one another highlights an additional problem: that the bounds of acceptability were often blurred, with one man's concern for the people's rights being

---

[33] Burton, III, 125.   [34] Burton, III, 290.   [35] Burton, III, 131.   [36] Burton, III, 556.
[37] Burton, IV, 69.

interpreted (often with good reason) by another as an attack on the privilege of Parliament or the integrity of the Protector and his council.

Interference in the workings of Parliament was encouraged by the wide dissemination of information about parliamentary proceedings through the printed word and written newsletters. This could not always be controlled by the government, or by Parliament, but there were constant attempts to prevent parliamentary proceedings from reaching a wider audience. On 22 September 1654, a committee was appointed to consider 'abuses in printing', with the power to 'put a stop, in the meantime, upon printing of diurnals, and newsbooks'.[38] As we have seen, major issues such as the kingship debates could not be kept out of the public sphere, despite attempts to hobble the press, and this free flowing of information involved minor matters as well. On 13 June 1657, for example, when 'a high breach of privilege, by talking what things pass in the House' was reported, one MP commented sardonically that: 'there is nothing done or said here, but is told abroad'.[39] Something similar was suggested by another MP in March 1659, who said that the debate on the Other House was already common knowledge across the country as 'the newsbooks have told the nation' what the Parliament had discussed.[40] The spread of news could be rapid. Later in the same month, a Scottish councillor warned that the protracted debate on the rights of Scottish members 'hears ill abroad. It is gone all England over, and by this night's post it will be in Scotland.'[41] Fears of those outside the Parliament turning against their representatives remained theoretical until April 1659, when the army – the greatest force 'without doors' – turned on its masters. As the storm clouds gathered, John Swinfen warned that 'the people rumour, as if they [the army] were a rod over your heads. Those are the people's apprehensions.'[42] On 21 April, the day before the dissolution of the 1659 Parliament, Lambert Godfrey conceded that they had lost control of the situation:

If all be true that is said, while you are debating it [the control of the militia], another without doors will get it. Strange pamphlets fly abroad directed to persons without . . . these are high and dangerous things, and these are printed without your allowance.[43]

Formal petitions were an accepted part of parliamentary business, and enshrined the rights of the people to ask Parliament to redress grievances; yet they were vulnerable to political manipulation by members, who promoted them, or opposed them, for their own reasons. When James Nayler's case was being debated in December 1656, petitions against Quakers were

---

[38] *CJ*, VII, 369.   [39] Burton, II, 237.   [40] Burton, IV, 9.   [41] Burton, IV, 147.
[42] Burton, IV, 454; see also remarks of Swinfen, *ibid.*, 451.   [43] Burton, IV, 480.

received from across England, from Northumberland to Cornwall.[44] These were presented, and probably solicited, by local MPs. On 18 December 1656, Thomas Bampfield, MP for Exeter and a leading Presbyterian, 'delivered the petition from the west'; and the courtier, Charles Howard, brought in another anti-Quaker petition from the north of England.[45] Others followed thick and fast, each presented by a local member; and even those without petitions refused to be left out: the Cumberland MP, William Briscoe, admitted to having no petition, 'but I am sure I have as much occasion to complain as any, for they are numerous in those parts', and Sir Christopher Packe could provide no petition from London, 'yet we are no less infested with them [Quakers]'.[46] When it came to the Quaker threat, popular opinion (whether through petitions or members' knowledge of local conditions) clearly had great force in the Commons. As we have seen, the kingship debates generated a similar level of petitioning from the localities, and in 1659, when 'addresses' came to the Parliament in support of the Protectorate, the commonwealthsmen were incensed: 'those addresses brought an evil measure to measure the people's affections by, not for his highness's service', while other members disagreed, saying that they considered them 'to contain the sense of the whole country'.[47]

   An outright refusal to accept petitions was relatively rare, but, once again, it was invariably prompted by politics within the Parliament. On 23 December 1656, a petition from the North Riding of Yorkshire calling for a reduction in assessments and excise, and for harsh measures against royalists, was 'excepted against' by other members 'as tending too much, at this time, to discourage assessments and to encourage others to petition for the taking off assessments', and it was laid aside.[48] But the bad feeling created was used for political ends, as it encouraged discontented members to admit a Quaker group to present its own petition later on the same day, using the right of petitioning as an excuse to introduce a controversial issue. As one of the northern members, Luke Robinson, put it, 'you ought not to discourage petitions by judging them before hearing', and Major Audley went further: 'it is the right of the people of England to petition this House'. As a result, the petition was admitted after a division carried by only one vote, although the debate on the petition itself (which asked for Nayler's punishment to be remitted) was rather strained.[49] On 9 February 1659, a petition from London, calling for the militia and the veto to be taken out of the Protector's hands, was initially refused on the grounds that it would interrupt important business, despite howls of protest from the commonwealthsmen who said that 'it was never denied to call in petitioners'.[50]

---

[44] *CJ*, VII, 470.   [45] Burton, I, 168.   [46] Burton, I, 169–71.   [47] Burton, III, 212.
[48] Burton, I, 208–9.   [49] Burton, I, 215–21.   [50] Burton, III, 153–5.

When it was pressed again, a few days later, the majority of members professed themselves reluctant to accept a petition from 'the commonwealth party in the city' being 'cautious . . . to prevent multitudes of petitions which might probably be offered of different and contrary strains'.[51] That this was political in motive is shown by the delay in receiving the petition and the majority of 202 to 110 against acknowledging the 'good affections' of the petitioners in the Commons' formal reply to them.[52] A Quaker petition presented in April 1659 was also given short shrift, with Arthur Annesley complaining that the 'petitioning [is grown] tumultuous. Unless you declare against the thing itself, you will be troubled next week with as many.' Hugh Boscawen warned those who encouraged such petitions that 'you will give them too great a reputation abroad'. They need not have worried. The Presbyterian and 'country gentry' majority in the House – many of whom served as justices in their counties – knew how to deal with Quakers: they were sent back to their homes, and told to submit to the law.[53]

Members of Parliament were very jealous of parliamentary time, and this prompted moves to prevent the 'private' business of constituents and others outside the Parliament from blocking 'public' bills. They were not always consistent in their efforts to prevent private business from taking over, however, and often the public and private concerns of members cut across each other. Injunctions against private business were observed rather patchily. On 22 November 1654, it was resolved 'that no private business be taken into consideration in this House for a month', but this self-denying measure lasted for little more than three weeks, and from 15 December private bills were creeping back in.[54] On 23 September 1656, the Commons again resolved that no private petitions would be allowed for a month and also stipulated that petitions were not to be printed until they had been presented to Parliament.[55] (This last comment is significant because it suggests that members were concerned that petitions would influence public opinion and thus put pressure on the Commons and its deliberations.) On 20 October, this prohibition on private petitions was extended for a further month, but this was soon being flouted and, when the Protector gave his assent to eleven acts on 27 November, six of them were 'bills of private concernment'.[56] The pressure for private business could be intense. On 22 December 1656, there was 'a great confusion for half an hour; five or six constantly up at a time to offer petitions' – a situation that led to rows between individual members in the chamber.[57] By 30 December, one member had had enough, complaining to the House that 'if you have nothing but private business, I wish we may go

---

[51] BL, Lansdowne MS 823, fos. 216–17; Burton, III, 288–9, 295.   [52] *CJ*, VII, 601, 604.
[53] Burton, IV, 444–5.   [54] *CJ*, VII, 387, 402–3.   [55] *CJ*, VII, 427.   [56] *CJ*, VII, 441, 460.
[57] Burton, I, 207.

home again. Let us do some public business. I dare say more private bills are brought in this Parliament than in all the Long Parliament.'[58]

One way of tackling the problem was to set aside particular days for public affairs, as in January 1657, when 'Tuesday, Wednesday, Thursday and Friday, in every week' was allocated to public bills, 'and no private business to be offered or admitted on those days'.[59] Even then there were complaints, with William Lenthall saying that 'private business should not be wholly laid aside. We must relieve those that cannot be relieved elsewhere.'[60] Even the kingship debates did not stop private business being discussed, and on 17 March 1657 the Commons ordered that all private business was to be put off for a week to allow members to devote all their time to the new constitution.[61] As the sitting wore on, and members became conscious of the amount of government legislation remaining to be passed, there were further calls for private bills to be suspended at the end of May. It was Lenthall, despite his earlier comments, who now led calls for a ban: 'I move that all private business may be laid aside ... I would have public business, as monies and the like, and the clamours for the public faith attended to.'[62] Samuel Disbrowe, a Scottish councillor, seconded him, commenting wryly that 'I am sorry that private business should be the only reason of the House coming together', and despite further pleas that 'poor people that cry unto you should be relieved', private business was banned for a fortnight.[63] This was extended in June, when all private committees were suspended for nine days (8–16 June) to allow the vital money bills to be discussed unhindered; and the ban was continued for a further week on 15 June.[64] There was an increasing danger that the suspension of private business would become routine, and there were some in the Commons (perhaps among the government managers) who no doubt welcomed such a move. But too much should not be read into this. It had, for example, become normal practice to prevent private affairs from impinging on the beginning of each parliamentary session or sitting. On 28 January 1658, shortly after the second Protectorate Parliament reconvened, a motion was passed forbidding private business to be discussed for a month – far longer than the Parliament would in fact survive.[65] And it is worth noting that this suspension was not moved by a government spokesman but by a critic, Thomas St Nicholas, who wanted to exclude private business to allow 'the business of settling the people's liberties'.[66]

---

[58] Burton, I, 269; Luke Robinson was the speaker.   [59] *CJ*, VII, 478; Burton, I, 291.
[60] Burton, I, 291.
[61] *CJ*, VII, 505; for private bills being discussed at this time, see *ibid.*, 498, 499, 501, 502, 503, 504.
[62] Burton, II, 124.   [63] Burton, II, 134.   [64] *CJ*, VII, 549, 558.   [65] *CJ*, VII, 589.
[66] Burton, II, 375.

The dichotomy between the rhetoric of representation and the limits placed on petitioning and private business in practice is problematic. The apparent reluctance of members to allow the consideration of private legislation certainly sits uneasily with the findings of Peter Gaunt and Ivan Roots: that, even during the upheavals of the Parliaments of 1654–5 and 1656–8, members 'spent much of their time trying to meet the needs of the nation and its people', and that 'many of the acts which passed in 1656–7 reflected local or private interests'.[67] Some of this business was sneaked through, using gaps in the 'order of the day',[68] or by flouting proscriptions against the consideration of private affairs, and there is no doubting the volume of private, as well as public, legislation passed in November 1656 and June 1657. At face value, the 1659 Parliament was, in contrast, barren terrain. Ronald Hutton's gloomy comment on the early weeks of 1659, when the Parliament became mired in constitutional debates, that those who 'suffered absolutely from the House's proceedings in its first two months were the local communities who had expected their representatives to further their interests, in the traditional manner, with private bills',[69] tends to affect our view of the whole of this parliamentary session. Yet, once the great constitutional debates had been resolved at the end of March, normality resumed. Matters of urgent public business were introduced, dealing with revenues, a public fast, and trade, and Irish and Scottish committees were set up, while the outstanding problem of the disputed elections was tackled. In this respect, April 1659 looks very similar (in the *Journals*, at least) to the first month of the 1656 Parliament. Moreover, whereas the second Protectorate Parliament had banned private business for a month from 23 September 1656, April 1659 witnessed a number of private petitions and bills, dealing with Lord Craven, Chief Baron Wylde, the Countess of Worcester, the company of parish clerks, and similar cases.[70]

---

[67] Peter Gaunt, 'Law-making in the First Protectorate Parliament', in Colin Jones, Malyn Newitt, and Stephen Roberts, eds., *Politics and People in Revolutionary England: Essays in Honour of Ivan Roots* (Oxford, 1986), pp. 164–5, 177–8; Gaunt, 'Oliver Cromwell and his Protectorate Parliaments: Co-operation, Conflict and control', in Ivan Roots, ed., *'Into another Mould': Aspects of the Interregnum* (2nd edn, Exeter, 1998), p. 77; Ivan Roots, 'Lawmaking in the Second Protectorate Parliament', in H. Hearder and H. R. Loyn, eds., *British Government and Administration: Essays presented to S. B. Chrimes* (Cardiff, 1974), pp. 132–43.
[68] See, for example, George Downing's ability to get a short bill changing the market day at Carlisle through the Commons before the main business began on 25 May 1657, and John Geldart's plea that a York bill 'no bigger than my thumb' be passed on 25 June 1657 (Burton, II, 120, 304).
[69] Ronald Hutton, *The Restoration: A Political and Religious History of England and Wales, 1658–1667* (Oxford, 1985), p. 32.
[70] See *CJ*, VII, 621–4; cf. *ibid.*, 423–38.

The initial conclusion of this survey might be that the Protectorate Parliaments, preoccupied by constitutional, political, and religious issues of national importance, were not the most conducive places for private business to flourish. To put it baldly, representing the 'interests' of the people of England did not necessarily include doing what they asked. Yet the volume of private business, and the levels of 'normality' achieved when matters of state allowed, suggests that there is another side to this – a side that is not readily apparent from the official sources, the diaries, or the surviving news-letters. These sources, by their very nature, focus on the public side of the equation. To get an accurate sense of the relationship between members and their constituents, it is necessary to turn to documents generated locally or privately, to flesh out the bones that can be picked from the dry records originating from Westminster. The next section will therefore consist of a case study of a 'typical' county and its members during the Protectorate.

CASE STUDY: REPRESENTING DORSET, 1654–9

Dorset was a medium-sized county, neither too close to nor impossibly remote from London, and politically unexceptional.[71] Between 1654 and 1658, Dorset was represented in Parliament by six county members, as well as four burgesses, one each from the county town of Dorchester and the ports of Poole, Lyme Regis, and Weymouth; in 1659 it reverted to the old fran-chise, having two knights of the shire, two burgesses apiece from seven boroughs (Poole, Shaftesbury, Wareham, Corfe Castle, Dorchester, Bridport, and Lyme Regis), and four from the curious double borough of Weymouth and Melcombe Regis. During the 1640s Dorset had been con-trolled by a county committee consisting of substantial landowners and merchants, and their conservative brand of Parliamentarianism continued to have an influence over the county in the 1650s. As a result, the members chosen for Dorset were a fairly closely knit group, linked either by family ties or by their experiences since 1640, and were prepared to work together at Westminster when local issues needed to be addressed. The letter-books of one of the county members, the moderate Presbyterian John Fitzjames, reveal the seriousness with which representation was taken during the 1654–5 Parliament. On 12 September 1654, Fitzjames wrote to Captain Chaffin at Sherborne, responding to a request to involve the whole county in the cost of maintaining local causeways. Fitzjames promised 'I shall wait all opportu-nities, either in that particular, or in any else, to do the country [= county] service', but he was forced to admit that 'as to the particular act (as you

---

[71] For an introduction, see James A. Casada, 'Dorset Politics in the Puritan Revolution', *Southern History*, 4 (1982), 107–22.

mention) ... 'tis not yet a time for that, neither will it be till the Parliament has dispatched their more public concernments'.[72] As a county member, Fitzjames did not just respond to specific requests from local gentlemen, he also solicited their views. On 14 October 1654, he wrote to one of the ministers of Dorchester, Stanley Gower, reporting on religious debates at Westminster, and adding 'let me desire that if you can impart anything to me, whereby you may fit and render me the more capable of public service, that you will be no niggard of your directions'.[73] This was not just the pious platitude of a remote member. The hunger for news from Westminster, the desire for local affairs to be addressed and national issues to have a satisfactory conclusion, was intense. Fitzjames was well aware of this. In November 1654, when he was making a brief visit to Dorset, he told his friend Robert Shapcote (member of Parliament for Tiverton in Devon) that 'the country gapes after news from above', and was so preoccupied with reports of business at Westminster 'that it affords none of itself'.[74]

Fitzjames's letters during the 1654–5 Parliament also show the extent of co-operation between the various Dorset members. The affairs of Lyme Regis, keen to regain its traditional jurisdiction over the neighbouring tithing of Colway, appear to have drawn in a wide range of support. On 10 October 1654 Fitzjames told one of the leading burgesses for Lyme, Anthony Ellesdon, that he had received a letter from the gentlemen of the county, and that 'tomorrow ... I shall wait on the Attorney-General [Edmund Prideaux, who sat for Lyme] and shall solicit your business to the best advantage I may', although he warned that 'I believe the doors will be for a time shut against business of that nature.'[75] The problem of public business blocking private bills was still apparent in December 1654, when Fitzjames wrote to another Lyme burgess, William Ellesdon, responding to 'the motion you desire', but he assured him that 'there shall be nothing wanting in me, or in others I hope', to make it a priority, and continued: 'you'll do well to let your cousin, Denis Bond [member for Weymouth], know, that I say he was very willing to oblige your town of Lyme'.[76] Fitzjames and the other Dorset members never gave up hope that the 1654–5 Parliament would bear fruit for their constituents, that the long debates on the constitution would eventually give way to the passing of local bills. And there are indications that, privately or in committee, the members were already preparing for that time. On 18 January 1655, four days before the dissolution of Parliament, Fitzjames

---

[72] Alnwick Castle, Northumberland MS 551, fo. 3r.
[73] Alnwick, Northumberland MS 551, fo. 5r; the strongest connection between Fitzjames and Gower was their shared Presbyterian beliefs: see David Underdown, *Fire from Heaven: Life in an English Town in the Seventeenth Century* (1993), p. 211.
[74] Alnwick, Northumberland MS 551, fo. 8v.   [75] Alnwick, Northumberland MS 551, fo. 4v.
[76] Alnwick, Northumberland MS 551, fo. 10v.

again wrote to William Ellesdon, this time with good news, saying that "'tis no small satisfaction unto me, that I have done anything acceptable to the town of Lyme', and hoping that a private bill would be introduced soon.[77] Although they were not successful in having the bill passed, it is significant that the burgesses of Lyme Regis were able to elicit support from one of the county members (Fitzjames) and a member for another borough (Bond) as well as from their own representative (Prideaux). This concern for the wider local community probably reflects the family relations between them (and certainly Bond was enlisted as one of William Ellesdon's cousins), but it also points to a sense of collegiality between the Dorset members, and the closeness of their relationship with their 'constituency' – in its broadest possible sense.

The willingness of the Dorset gentry to work together can be seen in the elections for the county seats in August 1656. Again, the letter-books of John Fitzjames are an important source for this. Fitzjames seems to have taken the preliminary discussions very seriously, and treated them almost as a benign conspiracy, telling Sir Anthony Ashley Cooper that "'tis of necessity, I acknowledge, that our meeting be speedy, and of no less consequence that it be private'. This cloak-and-dagger approach was necessary because Fitzjames and his friends intended to counterbalance attempts by the local major-general, John Disbrowe, to monopolise the list of candidates.[78] Fitzjames's cousin, John Trenchard, and another important gentleman, Sir Gerard Napper, were also in on these secret meetings, as was Major James Baker at Shaftesbury, Robert Coker, and Sir Walter Erle.[79] On 14 August Fitzjames reported the result of 'our meeting'. Six candidates had been decided upon, and 'all the Eastern parts are for the six, as I am assured, and some considerable number in the west likewise'.[80] Interestingly, the six candidates included the Protectoral councillor, and Disbrowe's ally, William Sydenham, and a councillor-turned-critic of the regime, Sir Anthony Ashley Cooper, as well as conservative Presbyterians such as Robert Coker and John Fitzjames himself. This does not seem to have been an attempt to provoke a confrontation with Disbrowe and the government, and the main intention may have been to return a wide range of members, who would represent the county rather than the government. With the election sewn up, and Fitzjames one of the chosen few, he wrote his acceptance letter to his 'neighbours' at Cerne Abbas the night before the election took place on 20 August: 'although

---

[77] Alnwick, Northumberland MS 551, fo. 16r.
[78] Alnwick, Northumberland MS 551, fos. 89v, 91; for Fitzjames's concern at 'the unparlia-mentary tickets that now fly abroad', see *ibid.*, fo. 93v.
[79] Alnwick, Northumberland MS 551, fos. 89v, 91, 94v.
[80] Alnwick, Northumberland MS 551, fo. 94v.

I am conscious enough of mine own inabilities for so great a trust, yet I hope never to want a heart to do my country the best service I can'.[81]

The letter-book covering the 1656–7 sitting of Parliament does not survive, but we can gauge the success of Fitzjames's machinations over the Dorset county elections, and the degree of truth behind his pompous promise 'to do my country ... service', by looking at the correspondence of borough members with their constituencies. Lyme Regis was once again privileged in having for its MP the attorney-general, Edmund Prideaux, and in 1656 – as in 1654 – there is evidence that he was more than willing to represent his constituents at Westminster. The borough archives include a letter from Prideaux to the mayor and burgesses, dated 8 November 1656, in which he recounts his attempts to help secure compensation promised to the town after its heroic resistance against royalist besiegers in 1644. Prideaux's advice was legal as well as political: 'I have considered of the deed of uses you sent me concerning the revenue settled upon you by the Parliament and do very well approve it ... and if any should be so vain as to question you for so doing, let the burden lie on me and the rest to answer it.' Whatever 'the rest' thought of the matter, Prideaux insisted that his own position towards the borough was unequivocal: 'I shall take care to serve you.'[82] The corporation minute-books for Dorchester indicate that the borough was in regular contact with its member, John Whiteway, and also used the good offices of other local members. On 3 November 1656, for example, 'Mr Bailiff [Henry?] Maber' was sent to London 'to confer with Mr [Denis] Bond, Mr Whiteway', and others about the need for an assistant minister at St Peter's church in the town.[83] Bond, although member for Weymouth in this Parliament, had longstanding links with Dorchester: he had been their representative during the Long Parliament, and was an obvious ally at Westminster thereafter.[84] On 7 April 1657 Whiteway wrote to the mayor about the possibility of restoring a former capital burgess, George Cole, to his position on the council, and relating his interview with Major-General Disbrowe on their behalf. The restitution of Cole a few days later suggests that Whiteway was successful.[85]

Similar lines of communication existed between Poole and its member, Edward Butler. The mayor's accounts for October 1656 include money spent on sending letters to Butler in London, and also for 'writing a copy of a letter sent to the Parliament'; in April 1657 there was a further sum paid 'for port of letters from Mr Butler'; and in June a messenger was paid for bringing

---

[81] Alnwick, Northumberland MS 551, fo. 95v.   [82] Dorset RO, DC/LR/D2/1, unfol.

[83] Dorset RO, B 2/16/4 (Dorchester corporation mins., 1637–56), p. 249.

[84] For Bond, see Underdown, *Fire from Heaven, passim.*

[85] Dorset RO, B 2/16/5 (Dorchester corporation mins., 1656–77), p. 30.

down the recently passed acts of Parliament.[86] Two letters from Butler to the mayor and corporation survive. The first, dated 21 October 1656, complains that no private business was being allowed at Westminster until the Spanish war had been debated, and adds that 'we are very tender generally of augmenting taxes on the country and hope shall so continue'.[87] The second, of 17 February 1657, also concerned the matter of raising money. He assured his constituents that although new taxes had been voted for the Spanish war 'no money [is to] be raised but by common consent in Parliament'. He also asked for more information to help him to fight Poole's corner over the customs revenues: 'though I doubt it will be very difficult to get any abatement at this time ... yet I shall try'.[88]

In this second letter, Butler appears to have been treading very carefully. The attitude of many members, who were amenable to raising money as long as it was taken by means of the customs and excise and not a land tax, was unlikely to be well received by the merchants of Poole. Butler was also careful to preface his remarks with good news: that he had been working with one of the county members, the councillor William Sydenham, to settle the town's interest in the rectory at Sherborne.[89] Weymouth was the only one of the Dorset boroughs to have left a mark on Burton's diary and the *Journals* for 1656–7, and these records show the determination of Dorset members to get individual cases a hearing in the Commons. The petition asking for compensation for Captain John Arthur, formerly vice-admiral for Dorset and a prominent alderman and merchant in Weymouth,[90] was presented to Parliament by the local member, Denis Bond, and Edward Butler (who sat for Poole) in December 1656, and was eventually read in March 1657, with a bill being drawn up in April. The committee formed after the second reading included Denis Bond and John Fitzjames, and it was Fitzjames who reported the committee's amendments on 30 May. The bill was given its third reading and sent for the Protector's consent on 2 June.[91] As with the other boroughs, Weymouth was able to gain support from a number of Dorset members and, indeed, from members from neighbouring counties, in order to secure a private act for one of its inhabitants.

The evidence for similar patterns of active representation is largely missing for Richard Cromwell's Parliament in 1659, and we have no way of knowing whether John Fitzjames's assurances on election to his new constituency of

---

[86] Poole Borough Archives, MS S105 (accounts, 1657–8), unfol.; *ibid.*, MS 29(7) (mayor's accounts, 1653–60), p. 27.
[87] Poole Borough Archives, MS L4.   [88] Poole Borough Archives, MS L5.
[89] Poole Borough Archives, MS L5.
[90] See M. Weinstock, ed., *Weymouth and Melcombe Regis Minute Books, 1625–1660* (Dorset Record Society, I, Dorchester, 1964), 96.
[91] Burton, I, 204; *CJ*, VII, 501, 510, 536, 542, 544.

Poole ('I shall wholly reserve myself to do you the best service I am able')[92] were fulfilled, although an entry in the borough accounts from the spring of 1659, referring to money paid to a Londoner 'for several letters under his cover to Colonel Fitzjames',[93] suggests that Poole was keeping him to his promises. From the surviving sources for the Parliaments of 1654–5 and 1656–8, however, it is possible to make some general points about the relationship between members and their constituents in Dorset during the Protectorate. First, there was clearly an expectation on both sides that the relationship would continue during the parliamentary sessions, as made clear by the comments of John Fitzjames and Edmund Prideaux to their constituents. There is evidence from the borough records that members were held to this, and regular correspondence was kept up between Dorset and Westminster. Sometimes this meant that members had to break bad news, as when Edward Butler had to announce new taxes and the continuance of high customs rates to his irate constituents at Poole, but mostly relations were cordial, and constituents valued members with national influence, most notably Attorney-General Prideaux, MP for Lyme. The second point is that boroughs were not narrowly dependent on their members, but were able to call on the support of others – as is especially obvious in the case of Lyme Regis in 1654–5. This was partly owing to the sense of obligation felt by many members towards Dorset as a whole; county members, such as Fitzjames, were keen to work for the interests of individual boroughs as well as interest groups. Others, such as William Sydenham, may have thought such activities were a natural part of their involvement in the national government. All the Dorset members we have looked at were conscious that the localities were well informed not just of events at Westminster but also of the activities of their individual members. The third point, which perhaps underlay the second, was the willingness of the Dorset gentry to work together on local issues, despite their disagreements on other matters. This is seen most obviously in the county elections in August 1656, and in the efforts of members to gain the support of their friends and relatives for causes particular to individual boroughs. Overall, Dorset appears to have been fairly well represented, and the major obstacle to the passage of legislation to further its local interests was not members pursuing their own interests or ignoring pleas from their constituents, but the steam-rollering effect of the big constitutional and political debates. In the Dorset context, there were specific complaints in 1654–5 that consideration of the government bill had led to the neglect of private bills; and in 1656 there were also concerns that the Spanish war had prevented the discussion of local

[92] Alnwick, Northumberland MS 552, fo. 68r.   [93] Poole Borough Archives, MS 29(7), p. 44.

issues. It is also likely that the kingship debates in the spring of 1657 and the constitutional rows for much of the 1659 Parliament hampered members in their attempts to fulfil the expectations of their constituents, in Dorset as elsewhere.

Thus, Dorset's experience of parliamentary representation seems to have had little to do with the theories touted by the rhetoricians at Westminster, and was positively retarded by the factionalism and concern with matters of state that characterised many members. This did not preclude the passage of private business, but the way that groups or individuals could get things done was through influence with those members they knew personally. It might be concluded, therefore, that, while the much-vaunted unity between Parliament and people was being eroded during this period, the ties between the localities and their individual MPs were as strong as ever.

TAXATION

The one issue expected to turn every member of Parliament into an eager representative of his county or borough was taxation – not least because every member had to pay his own share of what was agreed at Westminster. In the early Stuart period, taxation has been seen as the key factor encouraging a close relationship between members and their constituents, and, by 1640, 'aversion to the payment of money apparently provoked increasing local involvement in Parliamentary affairs, and increasing Parliamentary concern for public opinion'.[94] The vast increase in taxation through the Civil Wars and the Commonwealth period might be expected to have brought the centre and localities even closer together. The Protectorate saw a gradual decrease in direct taxation (the assessment) and a massive increase in indirect taxes, especially customs and excise and, in many respects, members seem to have lived up to expectations by policing the tax system generally.[95] This almost instinctive opposition to all forms of taxation can be seen in all three Parliaments. The arguments and assertions were not new. On 2 October 1654, when the Protector's power of making war and peace was discussed, members insisted 'that no tax can be made ... but by consent of Parliament'.[96] Initially the assessments on England were set at £60,000 a month (reduced from £90,000),[97] but in December 1654 the opponents of the Protectorate, led by the Presbyterian John Birch, proposed a new clause for the assessment bill, restricting 'the right of levying taxation to Parliament'

[94] Hirst, *The Representative of the People?*, pp. 166–76 (quotation at p. 173).
[95] For the background to this, see Michael Braddick, *The Nerves of State: Taxation and the Financing of the English State, 1558–1714* (Manchester, 1996).
[96] Burton, I, xlv.   [97] *CJ*, VII, 387.

(as allowed under the Instrument of Government) but omitting any provision safeguarding the money needed to run the government or pay the armed forces. The military, at least, were to be reduced considerably, under a general scheme of 'retrenchment'. The court interest, naturally enough, voted these proposals down.[98] On 5 January 1655 John Birch reported from the committee that the revenue should not include assessments further than for the next eighteen months, and even for that period suggested a reduced sum of £50,000 a month. This alarmed the government, with the treasury commissioner Edward Montagu complaining that this was based on a vast underestimate of current outgoings, but Birch's proposals received support in the Presbyterian-dominated Parliament, and were thrown out only after concerted efforts by the court interest, on 15 January 1655.[99]

During the 1656–8 Parliament, members seem to have been successful at keeping the government to a restricted budget – in some ways too successful. The government was aware of its financial difficulties, and keen to involve the Parliament in solving them. Cromwell admitted to members in September 1656 that 'the state is hugely in debt' and added that 'we shall not be an enemy to your inspection [of the revenues] but desire it . . . and we are not afraid to look the nation in the face upon this account'.[100] This invitation did not encourage members to grant new land taxes. In the next chapter we shall see the irritation created by members' reluctance to vote money for the Spanish war, despite their willingness to vote for war itself. The £400,000 raised in January 1657 was achieved only by careful management, and then only with guarantees that it would not be levied from property, and that Parliament's right to give consent would be honoured. When the Protector asked for a supplement to this sum it was refused.[101] The majority of members accepted the need for a fixed income for the government under the Humble Petition and Advice, but they were careful to ensure that 'no part thereof [was] to be raised by a land tax'. As Sir William Strickland said on 24 April 1657, 'the people would never have chosen us, if they had thought we would have ever moved that. Nothing is so like to blast your settlement as a land tax.'[102] He was followed by a number of members, notably high-profile Presbyterians such as Lambert Godfrey, Thomas Bampfield, Sir Richard Onslow, and Nathaniel Bacon – the leaders of the political interest that had supported the very constitution that had provided for a fixed income in the first place.[103]

Money, next to religion, was the issue most likely to drive the government and its Presbyterian allies apart during the spring of 1657. The result was an

---

[98] Gardiner, *Commonwealth and Protectorate*, III, 224.
[99] Gardiner, *Commonwealth and Protectorate*, III, 236–8, 243.   [100] Lomas–Carlyle, II, 542.
[101] See chapter 5.   [102] Burton, II, 24.   [103] Burton, II, 24–33.

uneasy compromise, with extra money being raised through indirect taxation; and, when Parliament reluctantly agreed to vote a further assessment, this was reduced to £50,000 *per mensem* across the three nations, with England footing a mere £35,000 of this. This left a shortfall calculated by some to amount to over £500,000 a year.[104] On 16 June 1657, as the money bills were prepared for engrossment, Secretary Thurloe complained that 'we shall want a good considerable sum' to make up the £1,300,000 promised under the Humble Petition and Advice; and he was not confident about finding the shortfall: 'where the residue must be had, will cost (I fear) a great debate in the House'.[105]

By the second sitting of this Parliament in January 1658, it was clear that the government was falling into ever more serious levels of debt, and that, even with increases in indirect taxation, the revenue was falling short by £200,000 per annum.[106] The failure of the sitting left the matter unresolved, and the situation had deteriorated further when Richard Cromwell's Parliament met in January 1659, although the full extent of the problem was not apparent until the committee on public revenue reported in early April: the government was by then £2.5 million in debt, with a yearly shortfall of £333,000 and, perhaps most worryingly, the army was owed £890,000 in arrears.[107] As Ronald Hutton has put it, the only sensible solution was 'a massive increase in direct taxation', but 'this was the most unpopular action that the country's representative could take', and instead the Parliament 'talked of retrenchment by the government, questioned the accuracy of the report and bullied the hapless excise farmers'.[108] Unsurprisingly, the commonwealthsmen also took the opportunity to question the legality of the Protectorate and its right to levy money from the people, and the discussion soon became bogged down,[109] despite Thurloe's insistence that much of the debt was inherited from the Rump and that measures were in place to tackle the financial crisis.[110] Nor was it just the government's opponents who caused trouble over the revenues. Although the Presbyterians were prepared to defend the excise bill against the criticisms of the commonwealthsmen on 1 April,[111] they were not eager to see it continued indefinitely. Thomas Gewen, speaking on 1 April, admitted that 'there's an invincible necessity at present to keep up the charge' but added 'it should be a gift and grant of this House and not imply that it's already done'.[112] On

---

[104] Firth, *Last Years*, I, 258–61.   [105] *TSP*, V, 352–3.   [106] Firth, *Last Years*, I, 261–2.
[107] Hutton, *The Restoration*, p. 35.   [108] Hutton, *The Restoration*, p. 36.
[109] Godfrey Davies, *The Restoration of Charles II, 1658–1660* (Oxford, 1955), p. 68.
[110] Derbyshire RO, D258/10/9/2, fo. 30r: 'the debt not so great, nor contracted since the death of the old Protector, but long before. There's not above 500 or 600,000 pounds since 1653'; see also Burton, IV, 365–7.
[111] Burton, IV, 320–4.   [112] Derbyshire RO, D258/10/9/2, fo. 12v.

9 April, John Birch, reporting from the committee on the revenue, called not only for a reduction in the army but also for a cut in salaried positions that 'eat out all your revenue', and an investigation into corruption.[113] Birch's call for reform was not very different from his demands in 1654–5, and indicates that the government and the Presbyterians still did not see eye to eye on financial matters. The royalist agent, John Barwick, was exaggerating only slightly when he reported on 9 April 1659 that 'the moderate party ... when they came to the matter of money ... fell from their former zeal, so that the Protector hath no great confidence in them'.[114] The Parliament was still in the midst of its debates on the revenues when it was brought to a sudden end on 22 April 1659, and that end was itself hastened by the army's concern to secure its pay arrears and avoid disbandment.[115]

But how far was this opposition to taxation prompted by a desire to relieve burdens on ordinary people, rather than by political manoeuvring? Again, the rhetoric of representation was there, and was used in debate by all sides. As one member pronounced on 21 November 1654, 'let us make what laws we please for the good and welfare of the people, yet if we did not ease them in their purses, we should never think to oblige them ever to us'.[116] Thurloe was aware of the pressures on members, reporting in October 1656 that he thought they would be happy to vote money for the Spanish war 'if anything can be done this way without taxing the people too high'.[117] When the £400,000 for this was eventually passed, the bill included a proviso 'asserting the rights of the people, that no money ought to be levied without common consent in Parliament'.[118] Other financial debates brought equally uncom-promising appeals to popular opinion. In December 1656, the Presbyterian Thomas Bampfield demanded the admission of the excluded members to ensure 'unanimity and general consent, especially when we come to tax the people',[119] and in January 1657 he opposed the new bill on excise and imposts saying that 'the people ... will curse us that sit here' and that such measures 'will make a Parliament stink in the nostrils of the nation'.[120] Similarly, moves to satisfy debts contracted on the 'public faith' were her-alded by William Sydenham as 'a work that will give you the greatest reputation that ever Parliament had'.[121] The same sort of language was used in the 1659 Parliament, when moves to produce an accurate general account were justified because 'the people [are] the purse of the nation',[122] and when Sir Henry Vane attacked the passing of money bills before grie-vances as a matter that 'will make the people that sent you think you came

[113] Burton, IV, 383–5.   [114] *TSP*, VII, 647.   [115] *Clarke Papers*, III, 190–2.
[116] Burton, I, lxxxv.   [117] *TSP*, V, 524.   [118] *CJ*, VII, 489.   [119] Burton, I, 194.
[120] Burton, I, 292–3.   [121] Burton, II, 240.
[122] Burton, III, 61; see also Derbyshire RO, D258/10/9/2, fo. 12r.

not to do their business but the business of the single person'.[123] For
Sir Arthur Hesilrige, the people were 'crying out' against the excise tax,
and he exhorted members, 'forget not the liberties of the people!'[124]

Perhaps the most significant feature of the various debates on taxation was
the way in which members tended to divide on county, regional, or national,
rather than party-political, lines. Thus Lord Eure, when he brought in a
petition from Yorkshire calling for 'the abating of assessments and the excise'
in December 1656, received support from a cross-section of northern members of Parliament, from army interest members such as Lambert, Robinson,
and Baynes to courtiers such as Downing, and they were opposed by MPs
from other regions, including the Dorset member (and stalwart of the army
interest) William Sydenham, and the Welsh Presbyterian Griffith
Bodurda.[125] In the debates that followed the second reading of the assessment bill in June 1657, members tended to demand special consideration for
their own localities. Sir Christopher Packe asked for London to be given
favourable treatment, and Robert West (MP for Cambridgeshire) immediately countered, saying that 'other parts have as much cause to complain as
the city'; Colonel Jones called for the Welsh counties to be treated more
leniently; and various members proved hostile to reductions in the assessments imposed on Ireland and Scotland, as (in West's words) 'it is not for the
House to make England the pack-horse, to bear what the others will not'.[126]
In the ensuing debate, Irish members of different political hues united against
the English; a Welsh member called for greater taxes to be imposed on
Scotland; and an Irish member suggested that the Scottish burden be quad-
rupled: an undignified game of pass the financial parcel.[127] The importance
of regional loyalties (and rivalries) is also suggested by Bampfield's proposal
that five members should be appointed to tax the east, west, north, south,
and midlands, 'except their own counties'.[128] These incidents are important.
They highlight the vulnerability of political groupings when challenged by
vested, local interests, and underline the difficulties facing parliamentary
managers desperate to deliver a majority in the Parliament to government
programmes. But they also demonstrate that, when it came to money matters, the language of representation used by members was not mere empty
rhetoric. Having said that, local representation was not necessarily at odds
with representing the 'people' in general, by delivering just legislation. As
Sir John Hobart asserted on 10 June 1657: 'it is true every man is bound to

[123] Burton, IV, 313.   [124] Derbyshire RO, D258/10/9/2, fo. 10v.
[125] Burton, I, 209.   [126] Burton, II, 208–9.
[127] Burton, II, 209–13; for a detailed discussion of Ireland and Scotland, see chapter 12.
[128] Burton, II, 234.

say for his country, but he is more bound to justice. The general concernment of justice is more our interest than in the county.'[129]

Like private bills, money bills were intrinsic to contemporary ideas of representation. In both cases, there were times when representation came to the fore, and even subverted the big 'party-political' issues that dominated these Parliaments, but the usual pattern was that private business was promoted by members when great matters of state, and the dictates of high politics, allowed. As a result, relations between members and their constituents were sometimes strained, but never to breaking point, and while the promise of 1640, that people would 'act in partnership with their representatives in the House',[130] had not come true, from the perspective of those being represented the Protectorate Parliaments were no worse than those of the early Stuart period, even if they were no better. And one of the things that made the Protectorate Parliaments distinctive was that 'representation' was deemed to cover not just England and Wales but also, as we shall see in chapter 12, Ireland and Scotland.

---

[129] Burton, II, 216–17.
[130] Hirst, *The Representative of the People?*, p. 187.

11

Parliament and foreign policy

When dealing with Protectoral foreign policy, historians have tended to overlook Parliament, and concentrate on Oliver Cromwell, or his council, instead.[1] Parliament's role is invariably reduced to that of a money-granting body, broadly reflective of public opinion, but essentially reacting to policies formulated, and promoted, by the Protectors and their councils.[2] According to one authority, 'Parliament served as a sounding-board for Cromwell to make long set-piece speeches extolling his views, achievements and intentions ... but its only involvement appears to have been a committee set up to coordinate European Protestant affairs in 1657 – at the initiative of some councillors sitting in the House, not back-benchers.'[3] Parliament's inactivity was not confined to decisions on policy, for the committee mentioned was (we are told) 'the only evidence of apparent Parliamentary interest in foreign policy'.[4] This chapter will suggest that such views are entirely fallacious. Parliament's right to become involved in foreign policy decisions was asserted in all three Parliaments, the members displayed a considerable interest in all aspects of foreign affairs, and they were also able to influence policy, both directly and indirectly.

Traditionally, Parliament's role in foreign policy was limited. When the Commons sought to advise James I on the Spanish match in 1621, the king forbade them to 'argue and debate publicly of the matters far above their reach and capacity', despite protests from members that debates on foreign

---

[1] For some historians, Cromwell is the main focus of interest: see C. P. Korr, *Cromwell and the New Model Foreign Policy: England's Policy toward France, 1649–1658* (Berkeley, Ca., 1975), pp. 77–8; Menna Prestwich, 'Diplomacy and Trade in the Protectorate', *Journal of Modern History*, 21 (1950), 103–21; and Steven Pincus, *Protestantism and Patriotism: Ideologies and the Making of English Foreign Policy, 1650–1668* (Cambridge, 1996), pp. 189–91. Others assert the role of the council: see Timothy Venning, *Cromwellian Foreign Policy* (1996), pp. 16–30.
[2] Korr, *Cromwell and the New Model Foreign Policy*, pp. 119, 184–5, 196–7; Prestwich, 'Diplomacy and Trade', 115.
[3] Venning, *Cromwellian Foreign Policy*, p. 19.
[4] Venning, *Cromwellian Foreign Policy*, p. 208.

policy were merely an extension of their duty to counsel the king on 'the arduous and urgent affairs concerning the king, state, and defence of the realm'.[5] James's pugnacious stance underlined the established convention that foreign policy decisions, and specifically the direction of the armed forces and the making of war and peace, were part of the royal prerogative; but he chose to ignore another, crucial matter: Parliament's right to give its consent to the taxation crucial to the funding of any royal war. Although the monarch had a monopoly on foreign policy, Parliament held a *de facto* veto that it could exercise by withholding money. In normal circumstances, the king's men of business – whether councillors or courtiers – would manage Parliament to ensure that financial measures were passed smoothly, usually by allowing the redress of grievances. But when royal policy went against popular opinion (at least as represented in the House of Commons), no deals could be struck, and deadlock ensued. James I was not the only Stuart monarch to discover this. The refusal of members to give generously to unpopular ventures hampered the wars against Spain and France conducted by Charles I in the later 1620s, and, in the 1670s, Charles II came under similar financial pressures to end the third Dutch war and (less successfully) to abandon his pro-French policy.[6] During the crisis and Civil Wars of the 1640s, this tense relationship collapsed altogether. Charles I continued to exercise his right to send ambassadors to foreign courts and to solicit support for his war effort, but Parliament was unable to do the same, and relied instead on informal mercantile networks to raise funds, especially from the Dutch.

With the execution of Charles I and the foundation of the republican commonwealth in 1649, the old forms were done away with. The new commonwealth assumed full prerogative powers for itself, justifying this through claims either 'that the new English regime's title to rule rested essentially on the right of conquest', or that the old royal powers had all along been 'derived' from the commonwealth, which now reclaimed them.[7] The Rump Parliament thus claimed to combine the prerogative and financial aspects of foreign policy, and was eager to force foreign representatives to acknowledge their status as 'the supreme authority of this nation'.[8] It was this combination that allowed an aggressive foreign policy to develop, notably during the first Dutch war, provoked in 1652. The creation of the

---

[5] Quoted in David L. Smith, *The Stuart Parliaments, 1603–1689* (1999), p. 45.
[6] Smith, *Stuart Parliaments*, pp. 47, 60.
[7] Richard Bonney, 'The European Reaction to the Trial and Execution of Charles I', in Jason Peacey, ed., *The Regicides and the Execution of Charles I* (Basingstoke, 2001), p. 253; Sean Kelsey, *Inventing a Republic: The Political Culture of the English Commonwealth, 1649–1653* (Manchester, 1997), p. 137.
[8] Kelsey, *Inventing a Republic*, pp. 133–4.

Protectorate in December 1653 changed the constitutional position once again. The functions of foreign policy, like those of the state in general, were again separated, with the Protector and council taking the prerogative powers, while the financial limitations were again part of Parliament's remit. Unlike the royal or republican situations, the Protectoral arrangement was set out clearly in article 5 of the Instrument of Government, which stated:

That the Lord Protector, by the advice aforesaid [i.e., that of the council], shall direct in all things concerning the keeping and holding of a good correspondency with foreign kings, princes, and states; and also, with the consent of the major part of the council, have the power to make war and peace.[9]

This appeared to be a return to the royal prerogative, exercised by the Protector and council as the joint holders of 'the chief magistracy'; but it was in fact weaker than that, for article 4 stipulated that, when Parliament was sitting, the ordering of the armed forces 'by sea and by land, for the peace and good of the three nations' must be 'by consent of Parliament'.[10] This concession of some parliamentary control over the army and navy, together with the continuation of the financial rights traditionally exercised by the Commons, promised to give Parliament a much greater role in foreign policy than it had enjoyed under the monarchy.

1654–5

Before the first Protectorate Parliament met in September 1654, the Protector and council could control foreign policy without any limitations, and one of the earliest acts of the new regime was to bring the costly Dutch war to an end. Indeed, throughout 1654, the thrust of Protectoral foreign policy was to secure peace.[11] With the Dutch problem solved, Cromwell encouraged the French and Spanish to bid against each other for an alliance with England, and he also concluded treaties with the Portuguese and the Swedes. Just before the Parliament convened, Cromwell decided to side with the French, and to open limited hostilities with Spain by fighting a naval war in the Caribbean, while maintaining cordial relations closer to home. This held out the chance of glory abroad, without the financial burdens of a war involving land forces and disrupting domestic trade. The Protector's speech at the opening of the Parliament, delivered on 4 September, played up these foreign policy achievements. 'You have peace with the Dutch: a peace unto which I shall say little, because it is so well known in the benefit and consequences of

---

[9] Gardiner, *Constitutional Documents*, p. 406.
[10] Gardiner, *Constitutional Documents*, p. 406.
[11] For the popularity of peace at this time, see Pincus, *Protestantism and Patriotism*, pp. 168–79.

it'; peace had been made with Portugal; and 'we are upon a treaty with France'. Cromwell also warned of the need to counter 'our enemies', who sought to divide them.[12] The nature of these enemies was not defined but, as the Dutch ambassador commented, 'he did not speak of Spain, but he did point at it'.[13] Interestingly, Cromwell invited Parliament to discuss foreign policy – 'I assure you it will not well be, without your counsel and advice' – and added that all the earlier decisions were now 'laid before you'.[14] These honeyed words came before the Parliament's challenge to Cromwell's authority, of course, and in a later speech he warned the members that their behaviour would cause 'the scorn and contempt' of foreign powers.[15] Even after this, however, Cromwell seems to have been sincere in his desire to include Parliament in his foreign policy deliberations – a concession that went far beyond the limits set by the Instrument of Government.

The relatively harmonious nature of foreign policy debates during the first Protectorate Parliament can be seen in the exchanges of 22 September 1654, when the fourth article of the Instrument was held up for scrutiny. The Commons resolved that the armed forces should be controlled by the Protector 'with the consent of Parliament'; in response, Cromwell sent a letter to the Speaker, 'wherein he did acquaint the House that there was an opportunity offered for the employment of some of the forces, especially by sea, for the advantage of the commonwealth, the design whereof was well known to some of our members (meaning those of the council), and if we were so pleased, it should be communicated to us'. The members reacted with similar courtesy, insisting that 'such designs, if they should be discovered, were more than half prevented' and resolving 'that the design should be wholly left to the management of the Lord Protector'.[16] Cromwell's gracious acceptance of the Parliament's right to give its consent to the use of the armed forces was matched by the Parliament's statement of trust in the Protector and (by extension) his advisory council. The exaggerated civility of this exchange contrasts with the rough handling accorded by both sides to the other political and religious matters. It also suggests that in foreign policy issues, at least, the councillors were performing their expected role in smoothing the passage of government business. As a result, the government was able to claim parliamentary approval for the ill-fated 'Western Design' against the Spanish West Indies.

The debate on 22 September 1654 should not suggest that this Parliament was entirely supine when it came to foreign affairs. As in other matters, the

---

[12] Lomas–Carlyle, II, 356–9.   [13] *TSP*, II, 588.
[14] Lomas–Carlyle, II, 358–9.   [15] Lomas–Carlyle, II, 387.
[16] Burton, I, xl–xli; for the original of Cromwell's letter to the speaker, see Bodl., MS Tanner 552, fo. 130r; see also *TSP*, III, 58.

government bill proposed an increase in Parliament's powers over foreign policy at the expense of the council. Accounts of the debates on these measures, in September and October, suggest that there were some members eager to push for parliamentary supremacy, as 'the power of making war is in itself an ancient right of the Parliament', and that 'his highness or his council ought not to have an absolute power for the taking up of arms'.[17] The final versions of the pertinent chapters, voted through on 6 December, were less aggressive.[18] In chapters 52, 53, and 54, it was laid down that the Protector and Parliament should have sole power of making war, and that peace would be decided the same way, except that in the intervals of Parliaments the Protector and council could make the decision, 'with such reservations and limitations as the Parliament shall approve'. The 'keeping and holding a good correspondence with foreign kings, princes, and states' was to be in the hands of the Protector and council, as before. Chapter 45, which gave control of the armed forces 'by land and sea' to the Protector and Parliament ('and not otherwise') also followed the Instrument of Government.[19] Overall, the changes between the Instrument and the proposed new 'government bill' were relatively few, and again this suggests that, in 1654–5 at least, foreign policy was not a controversial matter, with members being in broad agreement with the direction chosen by Cromwell and his councillors.

1656–7

The interval between the dissolution of the first Protectorate Parliament in January 1655 and the meeting of the second in September 1656 saw enormous changes in Cromwellian foreign policy. The peace treaty with France had been signed in 1655. The war against Spain had led to the disastrous attack on Hispaniola, and the disgrace of the commanders. There was also a heightened threat from the Stuarts, backed by Spain and (covertly) the Dutch States-General. The risks had been made abundantly clear by Penruddock's royalist rising in the spring of 1655, and a series of assassination plots against Cromwell himself. Security at home and abroad came at a price, and the financial crisis facing the Protectorate was the main reason for the calling of an 'extraordinary' Parliament before the agreed time limit of three years had expired. When the Parliament met, on 17 September, foreign policy was to become the driving force behind government business. This was to remain the case for the first four months of the Parliament – and its importance diminished only with the political and constitutional crisis that developed after the offer of the crown to Cromwell in February 1657.

[17] Burton, I, xliv–xlvi; *TSP*, II, 652–3.   [18] *CJ*, VII, 396.
[19] Gardiner, *Constitutional Documents*, pp. 444–5.

The importance of foreign policy in the government's agenda during the second Protectorate Parliament is apparent in Cromwell's speech on the opening of the first sitting, which was dominated by foreign affairs and, specifically, the war with Spain. The speech is full of his usual providential rhetoric: 'your great enemy is the Spaniard ... you could not have an honest or honourable peace with him ... he is naturally throughout an enemy; an enmity is put into him by God. "I will put an enmity between thy seed and her seed" ... And the Spaniard is not only your enemy accidentally, but he is providentially so.' Cromwell made explicit the link between Spain and Charles Stuart: 'Spain is that party that brings all your enemies before you ... for it is now, that Spain hath espoused that interest which you have all hitherto been conflicting with – Charles Stuart's interest', and he went on to call for a pan-Protestant alliance against 'the anti-Christian interest'.[20] As in 1654, Cromwell addressed the Parliament as a partner in the fight against Spain: 'so let you and me join in the prosecution of that war ... if you *can* come to prosecute it, prosecute it vigorously, or do not do it at all'.[21] At the end of this tirade, Cromwell suddenly came to the point. It was not partnership he needed most of all, but money. 'One may ask a very great question', he pondered, 'whence shall the means of it come? Our nation is overwhelmed with debts'; but then he sidestepped the question, and asserted the need to pull together, 'that we might join together to prosecute it vigorously', and returned to the matter of money only at the very end of the speech, promising to allow the Parliament leave to 'inspect the treasury' and investigate 'how moneys have been expended'.[22] It was a bravura performance, designed to win over sceptical MPs and open their pockets. As the French ambassador commented, 'the Lord Protector did very much enlarge himself against Spain, exaggerating all the enterprise, which that king had made formerly against England' and playing up the present threat. There were political as well as financial reasons for this. 'In regard there is very little advice conformable to this', he continued, 'many believe that it is invented and feigned to give an alarm, and to keep the army united at this present conjuncture.'[23]

Cromwell's dramatic call to arms was followed by a carefully organised campaign within the Parliament and without, managed by the secretary of state, John Thurloe, and important councillors. When the House 'entered upon the Spanish business' on 30 September,[24] the matter was first raised by John Lambert, who had consulted with the Protector, then taken up by Nathaniel Fiennes, who 'did open unto the House the grounds of this war';[25] he was followed, in turn, by other councillors.[26] On 1 October it

[20] Lomas–Carlyle, II, 511–19, 521, 524–5.   [21] Lomas–Carlyle, II, 533–4.
[22] Lomas–Carlyle, II, 534–5, 542.   [23] *TSP*, V, 427.   [24] *TSP*, V, 454.
[25] *CJ*, VII, 431.   [26] *Clarke Papers*, III, 75.

was resolved, *nemine contradicente*, 'that the Parliament doth declare the war against the Spaniard was undertaken upon just and necessary grounds, and for the good of the people of this commonwealth', and promises were made to 'assist his highness therein'. A committee was appointed 'to show the justice of this war, and the necessity of carrying it on', with three councillors, Lambert, Fiennes, and Sir Charles Wolseley, as well as Secretary Thurloe, Lord Commissioner Lisle, Lord Broghill, and Luke Robinson. Lambert was then sent back to the Protector with news of these developments.[27] The very next day, Thurloe released news of the victory by Robert Blake and Richard Stayner over the Spanish plate fleet, with the capture of part of its cargo of treasure. The Parliament responded by announcing a day of thanksgiving to be held on 8 October.[28] This was apparently a coincidence. Thurloe told the general-at-sea, Edward Montagu, that the Parliament passed their vote on 1 October 'before they heard one tittle of your success';[29] and according to his letter to Henry Cromwell, 'the vote passed in the morning … and in the afternoon came this news altogether unexpected and unlooked for, which is a great witness to the ingenuity and integrity of the Parliament in that vote'.[30] The Parliament had pre-empted news of the victory, but Thurloe was happy to use it to maintain the political momentum. The announcement was followed by a flurry of activity, which again demonstrated a high level of unity among the councillors. The committee appointed to attend the Protector with the vote for a day of thanksgiving included no less than eight councillors, Lambert reported on its activities, and Thurloe took charge of a committee to prepare a 'narrative' of the naval victory.[31] The day of thanksgiving on 8 October was marked not just by sermons but also by feasting, with many members of Parliament dining at Whitehall 'where the day occasioned great entertainment'.[32] Later in the month, Broghill, Lambert, and William Sydenham were prominent in sorting out the narrative, and arranging a further, general, day of thanksgiving, to be held on 5 November.[33]

Despite the enthusiasm among members, when it came to funding the war, they were reluctant to raise the money, especially through an increase in land taxes.[34] As the Venetian ambassador pointed out, 'the ease with which Parliament agreed to prosecute the war with Spain is matched by its slowness in discussing the means for waging it'.[35] Indeed, for some members the capture of the plate fleet, and the hope of similar successes to come, acted

---

[27] *CJ*, VII, 431.   [28] *CJ*, VII, 432.   [29] Bodl., MS Carte 73, fo. 41v.   [30] *TSP*, V, 472.
[31] *CJ*, VII, 432, 433, 434.   [32] *Clarke Papers*, III, 75.   [33] *CJ*, VII, 438, 440.
[34] Prestwich (in 'Diplomacy and Trade') overplays the 'unpopularity' of Cromwell's anti-Spanish policy; for a corrective, see Roger Crabtree, 'The Idea of a Protestant Foreign Policy', in Ivan Roots, ed., *Cromwell: A Profile* (1973), pp. 160–89.
[35] *CSPV*, 1655–6, 275.

as a disincentive to pay at all, as 'they thought that the booty would suffice for all the plans of the government, present and future'.[36] Thurloe was more optimistic. As he commented on 28 October, 'the House expresses a good readiness [to raise money]; only they are willing to try if any thing can be done this way without taxing the people too high'. Yet it was already clear that suggestions of increasing indirect taxation had borne 'little fruit', and Thurloe concluded that the only solution was 'to add something to the monthly tax'.[37] This proposal was met with polite obstinacy, but Thurloe already had another card up his sleeve. The date of the day of general thanksgiving had been set for 5 November ('being gunpowder treason day'),[38] and Thurloe deliberately heightened the mood of festivity by delaying the arrival of the Spanish treasure in London. Edward Montagu, who had returned with the fleet, was off Cornwall on 22 October, and arrived at Portsmouth shortly afterwards; Lieutenant-Colonel Francis White, who was in charge of the guard accompanying the plate, was at Petersfield in Hampshire on 31 October, and asked Thurloe if he should come to London directly, or await further instructions.[39] The reply does not survive, but can be surmised from what followed. The plate convoy reached the Tower only on 4 November, the same day that Montagu, 'being lately returned from sea with the Spanish prizes', was given the formal thanks of the Commons; on 5 November the day of celebration was duly held; and on 6 and 7 November, members were again asked to consider the financing of the war.[40] Thurloe tried to milk the victory one last time on 11 November, when Lieutenant-Colonel White presented members with a detailed report of the 200 chests of silver and other goods seized.[41]

Thurloe's theatrical efforts did not bring immediate rewards, however. It soon became apparent that the week of deliberation on how to raise money for the war, begun by the day of thanksgiving, had not brought the required result, and members remained 'loath, exceeding loath, to raise the tax', although, as Thurloe suspected, 'we shall be compelled to it at last'.[42] Even White's detailed inventory of the captured plate, attended by another motion 'that the monthly assessments might be increased', did not have the required effect, as the Commons resolved instead to set up 'a committee to consider how the customs and excise, or either of them, may be improved for the carrying on the said war'.[43] As the Venetian ambassador put it, 'after discussing it long, they [the Parliament] decided to put it aside, and keep it for some better opportunity'.[44] For the remainder of November and much of December, debate on the Spanish war became intermittent, and desultory.

[36] *CSPV*, 1655–6, 273.   [37] *TSP*, V, 524.   [38] *TSP*, V, 569.   [39] *TSP*, V, 509, 524, 542.
[40] *CJ*, VII, 450.   [41] *Clarke Papers*, III, 82.   [42] *TSP*, V, 584.
[43] *Clarke Papers*, III, 82–3.   [44] *CSPV*, 1656–7, 281.

The long-drawn-out dispute over the fate of the Quaker James Nayler during December created the most serious distraction, and Thurloe was left to opine that 'all our minds are set upon in Parliament is matter of religion', while the 'little debate' on raising money for the Spanish war 'came to nothing'.[45]

Thurloe was not alone in his irritation at the reluctance of members to vote money for war. In the first months of the Parliament, he had been ably supported by civilian courtiers, such as Lord Broghill, and members of the 'army interest', including Lambert and Sydenham. Despite their disagreements on other areas of policy, such men were prepared to unite in the common goal of ushering in a suitable foreign policy, and securing support for it in the Parliament. In the second half of December, the army interest, alarmed at reports that Charles Stuart was planning an invasion backed by Spanish troops, was united in its attitude to foreign affairs. On 20 December, William Sydenham pressed for more time to be given to government business, 'especially the business of the Spanish war', and suggested that two days a week be 'set apart for the business'. In this he gained support from a range of other members, including his fellow councillor, John Disbrowe, Monck's brother-in-law, Thomas Clarges, and the less reliable George Downing.[46] The debate left a bad taste in the army interest's mouth, and there were comments that it was 'very unreasonable to vote a war and leave it unprovided for', while 'the council and army men would not with any patience hear of such a motion: some said we could not take Spain nor Flanders with a bare vote'.[47] On 30 December, Lambert's ally, Adam Baynes, called for the Spanish war to be considered once again, according to 'the order of the day', and he was supported by Luke Robinson, with Denis Bond observing, darkly, that 'the Spaniard will not stay till you be provided for him'.[48] All these men were associated with the army interest at Whitehall. The army, like Cromwell in his 17 September speech, made a direct connection between the Spanish war and the royalist threat. On 25 December, immediately after the introduction of the militia bill (to perpetuate the rule of the major-generals in the localities), Robinson reminded members that 'the cavaliers are the cause of this war [with Spain], considering how near they are a kin to the Spaniard'.[49] A similar attitude can be seen in the comments of the hard-line major-general (and member of Parliament), William Boteler, to Edward Montagu on 9 January 1657, that 'we have not all this time raised one penny towards the Spanish war, nor are like to do after this rate we go till we hear of him upon our border I think, but instead of hastening that great concernment we have more mind to take away the militia and lessen our army, as though

---

[45] *TSP*, V, 727.   [46] Burton, I, 190–1.
[47] Bodl., MS Carte 228, fo. 81r (printed in *Clarke Papers*, III, 84n–85n).
[48] Burton, I, 267, 269–70.   [49] Burton, I, 230.

we had the greatest calm of peace that ever yet we saw'.[50] For Boteler and other officers, attacks on the militia bill were a threat not only to the major-generals but also to the fight against Spain.

The opponents of the major-generals also made the connection, but they drew the opposite conclusion. They argued that the failure to secure funding for the war in October and November could be overcome only if concessions were made at home and, specifically, if the army's grip on government locally and nationally was loosened, for only then would Presbyterian and country members be encouraged to vote the necessary money for the war. The result was a barely concealed bargain between civilian courtiers (including Thurloe) and leading Presbyterians. On 29 January this new alliance came together to defeat the militia bill; and on 30 January an overwhelming majority in the Commons 'resolved, that the sum of £400,000 shall be raised for carrying on the war with Spain'.[51] Thurloe's account shows how close the political connection was between these two votes: 'The next day [after the militia bill was voted down] the same persons who had stickled against the bill moved that the House would raise money for the carrying on the Spanish war', and members, jubilant at the fall of the major-generals, were happy to vote 'that they would raise £400,000 over and above what can be raised by the government for that purpose'.[52] There can be little doubt that the chief mover behind this deal was Thurloe himself, who had already proved himself skilled at manipulating the House. He may also have intended to influence the Protector to ditch military rule altogether, by demonstrating that the 'right' policies at home would reap immediate rewards abroad.[53] The political implications were obvious to the Irish member, Vincent Gookin, who reported that 'his highness took [the vote] exceeding kindly', but added that 'those that were for the decimation bill [i.e., the army interest], it was plainly perceived, were exceeding cold in the debate for raising money, and seemed to repine that the Parliament did so well'.[54]

Thurloe's ebullience at the result of the two votes masked important political realities. In the short term, the vote had alienated the army interest – a group that still had great influence at Whitehall; and in the longer term it would become apparent that many MPs gave their consent only grudgingly. The member of Parliament and diarist Thomas Burton saw signs of this as early as 4 February: 'you hear of the £400,000 which is voted to carry on the war – it was granted very willingly, the House choosing rather to give, than let necessity provide moneys, and some said they had rather give 40s in

---

[50] Bodl., MS Carte 73, fo. 18r (printed in *Clarke Papers*, III, 85n–86n).
[51] *CJ*, VII, 483.   [52] *TSP*, VI, 38.
[53] A point made in Barry Coward, *The Cromwellian Protectorate* (Manchester, 2002), p. 87.
[54] *TSP*, VI, 37.

Parliament than 20s to be taken without doors'.[55] When the grand committee met to discuss the raising of this money, with George Downing in the chair, the need for an assessment on land was agreed, but 'a very thin House' insisted on a proviso asserting 'that no money was to be levied but by consent of Parliament'. The low turnout prompted a motion to recall the House at a later date to reconsider this proviso, and, to Thurloe's dismay, 'it was opposed by several gentlemen, from whom that was not expected'. On 10 February, the clause was dropped, but there was no disguising the suspicion that some members felt towards the government.[56]

The decision to link the fate of the militia bill with that of the £400,000 had one further unintended consequence. During the bitter debate on the militia bill, the unity of the council, which had proved crucial for the management of foreign policy early in the Parliament, began to break down, as civilians and military men turned against one another. The defeat of the militia bill caused tremors within the council, and when the offer of the crown to Cromwell under the Remonstrance (later replaced by the Humble Petition and Advice) was made on 23 February, the council broke into two distinct factions. The effect of this split on foreign affairs was profound. Instead of representing the united policy of the government, the Spanish war now threatened to become partisan, associated only with the 'kinglings', led by Broghill, Thurloe, Whitelocke, and others, who had apparently gained the Protector's ear.[57] An early indication of a new direction in foreign policy can be detected in the terms of the treaty signed with France in March, which included the sending of 6,000 troops to fight the Spanish in Flanders. The deal was influenced by Thurloe, who submitted it to the Commons for approval on 7 March, and secured a resolution in favour on the same day;[58] it had been brokered by the ambassador in Paris – the Scottish courtier and supporter of kingship, Sir William Lockhart; and the troops were to be commanded by the prominent pro-kingship member, Sir John Reynolds. Reynolds was a close ally of Lord Broghill and, during the summer, would become Henry Cromwell's brother-in-law; and in early May Broghill would move the Commons to give Reynolds leave to go to France as general.[59] Later ambassadorial appointments underlined this shift: the prominent kingling, William Jephson, was sent to Sweden; another supporter of the kingship, George Downing, went to the Netherlands; and, with the death of Blake, command of the navy passed into the hands of another civilian courtier, Edward Montagu.

[55] Bodl., MS Carte 228, fo. 88r.   [56] *CJ*, VII, 487, 489; *TSP*, VI, 53; *Clarke Papers*, III, 88.
[57] The introduction of the Remonstrance, on the Monday after a Friday feast to celebrate Cromwell's survival of the Sindercombe plot (with its royalist and Spanish undertones), certainly looks like a classic piece of Thurloe's political choreography.
[58] *CJ*, VII, 499–500.   [59] *CJ*, VII, 530; Burton, II, 114–15.

Well might the poet, Edmund Waller, draw a connection between foreign policy and the offer of the crown, saying of Cromwell: 'With ermine clad, and purple, let him hold / A royal sceptre made of Spanish gold.'[60] The Parliament, amid the heady debates on the new constitution, at first welcomed the extension of the Spanish war. The Remonstrance, endorsed on 23 February 1657, echoed Cromwell's own grand vision of foreign policy, as laid out in his 17 September 1656 speech, proclaiming the people's support for the 'two years' war, so earnestly contended for', denouncing their 'common enemies', and lauding Cromwell as 'a deliverer to these nations'. In constitutional terms, this early version offered Cromwell 'the rights, privileges and prerogatives' belonging to the crown, and thus renounced Parliament's right to give its consent to war or peace or the control of the armed forces, and settled a permanent revenue on him, although extraordinary taxation could be levied only with parliamentary approval.[61] Thurloe boasted to Henry Cromwell on 10 March that 'they forthwith resolved, that his highness, with the advice of his council, might raise such further forces as shall be found necessary, whereby they showed their entire confidence in his highness'.[62] But the final version, the Humble Petition and Advice, passed on 25 March and presented to the Protector six days later, was more circumspect. The mention of 'prerogative' powers was dropped although, in the absence of other provision, the right to make war and peace presumably lay with the king's person; the 'constant revenue' was not to be raised as a land tax; and, in a return to the provisions of the Instrument of Government, the standing forces were to be deployed only with 'consent of both Houses' when Parliament was sitting.[63]

Cromwell's delay in accepting the monarchical Humble Petition seriously weakened the political position of the kinglings from the end of March, and worse was to come on 21 April. On that date, Cromwell sent a number of queries to the Commons, including the demand that the amount agreed to fund the Spanish war be increased to a more realistic level, and that the Parliament declare 'what farther sum they will raise for the carrying on of the same, and for what time'.[64] This met with open hostility from the majority of members, who had already voted £400,000 for the war in January. They now questioned the need for these additional taxes. During the debate on 24 April, the leading Presbyterian Lambert Godfrey condemned 'this additional sum, upon a bare proposal from without doors'.[65] Despite Thurloe's efforts to placate members by tabling a motion asserting that the £400,000 was guaranteed, and merely promising that 'what is further necessary' would be

[60] Quoted in Burton, II, 141n. [61] See appendix 2. [62] *TSP*, VI, 107.
[63] Gardiner, *Constitutional Documents*, pp. 448, 452–3.
[64] lomas–carlyle, III, 122; see also BL, Lansdowne MS 822, fo. 51r. [65] Burton, II, 25.

raised later, Godfrey, Sir Richard Onslow, and other Presbyterians rejected such a hostage to fortune, and the resolution, as passed, made no reference to additional sums.[66] It was the first snub that Cromwell had received over foreign policy. Complete collapse was narrowly averted by yet another deft piece of parliamentary management by Thurloe. On 28 May 1657, he released news of Admiral Blake's victory against the Spanish plate fleet at Santa Cruz in Tenerife. The plate itself was not taken, but the entire fleet was destroyed or captured, and, as Thurloe put it, 'though we received no benefit by it; yet certainly the enemy never had a greater loss. It is the Lord's doing, and the glory be His.'[67] The councillor, Walter Strickland, then proposed a day of thanksgiving, and the motion was supported by two other councillors, Francis Rous and Philip Jones.[68] There was no opposition to this, or to the rewards promised to Blake, or to the other measures of celebration ordered by the Commons. Unity on foreign policy had been restored, at least on the surface – although it was ominous that the committee appointed to attend Cromwell to ask for his consent to the day of thanksgiving contained no army officers, and only two councillors.[69] In the next few days, the 'Spanish war' assessment bills for Ireland and Scotland were guided through the Commons, and the third reading of the English assessment bill was passed on 4 June. All three received the Protector's consent on 9 June.[70] Even an order asking Cromwell to promote a 'pan-Protestant' union across Europe, passed at the very end of the sitting, seems to have been a council initiative designed to promote a veneer of unity, not an indication that all was well between Protector and Parliament.[71] By the time of the adjournment on 26 June, the government had got what it wanted; but popular enthusiasm for war, stirred up by Cromwell in September 1656, and evident in the Parliament as late as January 1657, had collapsed.

1658

The foreign situation changed markedly in the autumn and winter of 1657. The Cromwellian commitment to an Anglo-French war in Flanders was complicated by growing suspicions that the Dutch were in league with the Spanish. The outbreak of war between Denmark and Sweden threatened trade with the Baltic. There were also important changes at home. When the second Protectorate Parliament reconvened in January 1658, there were two important differences in its constitution, as a result of the passing of the Humble Petition and Advice the previous June: many of Cromwell's closest

---

[66] Burton, II, 32–3; *CJ*, VII, 523.   [67] Burton, II, 143.   [68] Burton, II, 143.
[69] *CJ*, VII, 541.   [70] *CJ*, VII, 542–3, 545, 550–3.
[71] *CJ*, VII, 578; Venning, *Cromwellian Foreign Policy*, p. 208.

advisers (including most of his councillors) were now in the Other House and, for the time being at least, isolated from the day-to-day management of the Commons; and the Commons, under the new rules governing qualifications to sit, had been swelled by members of Parliament excluded in September 1656, including a number of commonwealthsmen – veterans of the Rump Parliament, and ardent critics of the Protector and his government.

Despite these obvious weaknesses, the Parliament was treated to two lengthy speeches in the old style, dominated by foreign affairs. The first, by the civilian councillor, Nathaniel Fiennes, on 20 January, once again warned of 'the conjunction of our late in-bred enemy [the Stuarts] with that old enemy of our nation and religion [Spain]' and played up the risk that Charles Stuart would be 'brought in upon the wings of that double-headed black eagle, or rather vulture', the Habsburgs. After such flourishes, Fiennes came to the point: 'I must acquaint you that the supplies granted have fallen short of the commonwealth's necessities, because they have indeed fallen short of the Parliament's expectations', and that more money was needed to ensure security.[72] This was a familiar tale, and Fiennes's efforts were ridiculed by one newsletter-writer, who sent 'the prologue of a new tragicomedy, Fiennes His Speech', to a correspondent abroad, commenting acidly that the government now claimed that the constant revenue, the assessment for the Spanish war, and other extraordinary measures agreed in 1657 'are not sufficient to maintain that Holy War which they have adopted against Spain'.[73] The second speech, a rambling affair delivered by Oliver on 25 January, was (in Thurloe's words) 'especially to set forth the state of the Protestant cause abroad and the necessity of finding money at home', and Cromwell afterwards promised to provide a wary Commons with 'a state of the revenue, that they might provide better'.[74] Cromwell's words were typically lurid, warning of the threat to 'the Protestant cause', and the intention of the 'House of Austria ... to destroy the whole Protestant interest'. The gallant Swedes held out against them alone, while the perfidious Dutch worked with the Catholic powers. France provided a 'balance' and must be supported. Although he insisted that 'I never did, I hope I never shall, use any artifice with you', there was little doubt where all this was leading, and the Protector ended with an appeal for more money.[75] It is doubtful that the majority of members of the Commons, however loyal to the Protectorate, would welcome such demands for money if they led to an increase in land taxes. But the chance to debate foreign affairs never came. The short, and bitter, sitting was brought to end, and the Parliament dissolved, by Cromwell on 4 February, leaving the war unprovided for.

---

[72] *CJ*, VII, 586–7. [73] Bodl., MS Tanner 52, fo. 218r (misdated 5 January 1658).
[74] BL, Add. MS 22919, fo. 11r. [75] Lomas–Carlyle, III, 163–72.

1659

Between the dissolution of the second Protectorate Parliament in February 1658 and the opening of the third in January 1659, the nature of foreign affairs changed still further. The last months of Oliver's Protectorate had seen remarkable victories by the English forces in Flanders, including the capture of Dunkirk (June 1658), which was ceded by the French, to become a permanent British enclave on the continent. Such victories seemed to justify the controversial land war begun in 1657. Cromwell's reputation abroad was also enhanced by the success of Philip Meadowe in negotiating the Treaty of Roskilde in February 1658, which brought the war between Sweden and Denmark to an end. The death of Oliver did not affect the general thrust of Protectoral foreign policy, but changes abroad would soon complicate matters, as the French became increasingly keen to end their ruinously expensive war with Spain, and as Karl X Gustav of Sweden broke the Roskilde agreement to launch a sudden, devastating attack on Denmark, defeating the Danish forces, besieging Copenhagen, and provoking an alliance against him that incorporated not just the Danes but the Dutch, and Catholic powers such as Poland and (ominously) the House of Austria itself.

When the third Protectorate Parliament met in January 1659, a decision on the direction of foreign affairs was long overdue. The French ambassador was impatient with Richard Cromwell, whom he considered a weak ruler, preoccupied by the need to prevent divisions at home. Without strong support from the council, the ambassador concluded, Richard was 'unable to determine on any specific course before the meeting of Parliament', and there was a risk that, 'although the Protector cannot avoid an accommodation with Spain', he might be persuaded otherwise, as 'a war with Spain might serve as a pretext for obtaining money from the people of England', who now had 'hopes of conquest in Flanders'.[76] The French, determined to effect a 'general peace' with Spain, continued to hope that Richard Cromwell was pursuing an anti-Spanish policy only in order to raise money at home, but Thurloe's evasiveness in meetings soon raised doubts that this was in fact the case.[77] Moreover, although the French were keen for English ships to enforce mediation between Sweden and Denmark in the Baltic, there were suspicions that 'the inclination here is to favour the designs of the King of Sweden', even if that meant war with the Dutch.[78]

---

[76] Guizot, *Richard Cromwell*, I, 278, 282–3.
[77] Guizot, *Richard Cromwell*, I, 290–2, 294, 297, 318, 331, 353.
[78] Guizot, *Richard Cromwell*, I, 340, 351.

French concerns were not calmed by Richard Cromwell's speech at the opening of the third Protectorate Parliament on 27 January 1659. In style and content, the speech was a diluted version of those made by his father to earlier Parliaments: Spain was 'an old enemy, and a potent one, and therefore it will be necessary, both for the honour and safety of these nations, that that war be vigorously prosecuted'; the situation in the Baltic was not just a matter of trade, but a religious struggle involving 'the Roman Emperor with other Popish states'; and, overall, 'the Protestant cause abroad … seems at this time to be in some danger, having great and powerful enemies, and very few friends; and I hope and believe that the old English zeal for that cause is still among us'.[79] Richard avoided mentioning money directly (in contrast with speeches by his father in earlier Parliaments), but his intentions were plain. The Spanish war was to continue; and in the Baltic the Protectorate would support Sweden against Denmark and its 'Popish' allies. His equation of Sweden with 'the Protestant cause abroad' is significant, as such words echoed Oliver's private views; reflected a general British reverence for the heroic reputation of Gustav II Adolf; and chimed in with the pro-Swedish bias of a wide range of courtiers, including not only the former ambassador to Sweden, Bulstrode Whitelocke, and other civilians, but also Charles Fleetwood and some members of the army interest.[80] By emphasising the war with Spain and intervention on behalf of Sweden, Richard may have intended to unite the factions in the Parliament and at court, even at the risk of antagonising his French allies. His speech certainly went down well with the rank and file. As one observer reported, 'he was much applauded, and encouraged them much, for carrying on the war with Spain and relieving of the Swede'.[81]

The only members of Parliament not to share Richard's basic foreign policy aims were the commonwealthsmen, who remained wedded to the anti-Dutch agenda promoted by the Rump. Their hostility emerged in the early weeks of the 1659 Parliament. On 7 February, Sir Arthur Hesilrige delivered his critique of the Protectorate, dredging up the disastrous Western Design of 1655, and claiming that, more recently, the 'trade and the glory of the nation are much diminished'. Hesilrige was seconded by Thomas Scott, who attacked the peace made with the Netherlands in 1654, and asked if the Protector was 'fain to fight Holland over again'. The courtier-lawyer, John Maynard, in response to these long speeches, remarked, sarcastically, that 'if

[79] Burton, III, 9–10; Guizot, *Richard Cromwell*, I, 297.
[80] For attitudes to Sweden, see the introduction to Michael Roberts, ed., *Swedish Diplomats at Cromwell's Court, 1655–6* (Camden Society, 4th series, 36, 1988); also M. Roberts, 'Cromwell and the Baltic', in Michael Roberts, *Essays in Swedish History* (1967), pp. 157–70.
[81] Bodl., MS Clarendon 60, fo. 41r.

you go on at this rate, to have a speech a day, the Dutch will give you £2,000 a day to do so'.[82] As the debates on the recognition of the government dragged on, other members expressed similar impatience, saying that the setting out of the navy (to the Baltic) was delayed as a result, and 'the King of Spain, once on his knees, is now on horseback'. The commonwealthsmen, in return, suggested that 'these threatenings from the Dutch are but tricks', designed to 'settle things in a hurry'.[83] The mood of the House was against them, however. On 17 February, the Protector asked the Parliament 'to take speedy measures to provide the necessary funds for the maintenance of the fleet' to be sent to the Sound, and 'in spite of the opposition of the Republicans' a committee was appointed to that end.[84] Henry Neville's speech, arguing in favour of peace with Spain and citing 'one thousand particular decays of trade by war', fell on deaf ears, and, despite Vane's attempts to return to the recognition debate first, the Commons resolved to consider foreign affairs on 21 February, 'and no other affairs to intervene'.[85]

The debate on foreign policy began on 21 February in the familiar way, with a long speech by Secretary Thurloe, who said that he had been sent 'by order of his highness, ready to give that account'. Thurloe rehearsed the history of the war in the Baltic, and emphasised that 'Sweden is alone' against a host of enemies. Oliver Cromwell had acted as an 'arbitrator' at the Treaty of Roskilde, but the new war was much more threatening to British interests, not least because of Austrian designs 'to command the Baltic', to join the war in Flanders, and to overthrow the 'Protestant interest, in general'.[86] Despite the openly pro-Swedish bias of such comments, Thurloe insisted that the sending of a powerful fleet was 'to make a peace' between the warring parties, and to prevent the Dutch from imposing their own settlement on the region.[87] The Protector had already begun to prepare such a fleet, Thurloe continued, but 'he thought it fit and necessary that this House should be acquainted with it, that we, knowing of it, may advise as we shall think fit in this case'. It was a clear and forceful speech, and was greeted with '*altum silentium* for a good while'.[88] Thurloe had in fact raised two distinct issues. The first was the probity of intervention in the Baltic without provocation – and, by extension, the rightness of the Protectoral policy in general; and, secondly, by asking Parliament's 'advice' on foreign policy, while tacitly confirming the Protector's own right to make peace and war and to control the armed forces (as Oliver Cromwell had done in 1654), the

---

[82] Burton, III, 102, 111–12, 117.   [83] Burton, III, 121, 122, 128, 164, 304.
[84] Guizot, *Richard Cromwell*, I, 308.
[85] Burton, III, 314–16; *CJ*, VII, 605; royalist reports that MPs were 'highly offended' at the Protector's letter may be wishful thinking (see Bodl., MS Clarendon 60, fo. 135r).
[86] Burton, III, 376–8, 382.   [87] Burton, III, 383–4; see also *CSPV*, 1657–9, 295–6.
[88] Burton, III, 384.

constitutional relationship between Protector, council, and Parliament had been raised in a provocative way. This was probably unintentional; but it is possible that Thurloe wanted to divert attention from the 'recognition' of the government towards a more popular subject, and to gain an early parliamentary victory before the more difficult debates on the nature of the Protectorate were tackled. If so, it was a very risky strategy.

The debate initially followed the paths set out by Thurloe. The rights and wrongs of the war were disputed. Sir Henry Vane, in the first speech following the 'silence' after Thurloe's account, sought to remind the Commons that Sweden had been the aggressor in the war, leaving the secretary to reply, rather lamely, that the Protector intended 'not to espouse either interest in the quarrel' but to protect 'the good of this nation and of our trade'.[89] Henry Neville responded by saying that the Baltic situation was not a religious war, that there was no good reason to trust the Swedes more than the Danes, and that the war with Spain should be brought to an end. This riled the Presbyterian, John Birch, who argued that 'the Protestant cause is deeply concerned in this business', and followed Thurloe in stating that the Austrians wanted control of the Baltic, that the Swedes deserved support, and that the fleet would allow them to make peace 'with sword in hand'.[90] Neville and Birch's speeches are typical of the debates that followed. Members either asserted that the Dutch (allied to the Danes) were enemies, and had to be dealt with, or portrayed the Swedes as the greater threat; the war was either a religious duty, or not a religious war at all; trade would be advanced, or retarded, by war.[91] This was the basic division on 23 February, when the Welsh Presbyterian Griffith Bodurda made a further connection between the Dutch, the Danes, and the Stuarts, who, he said, stood to benefit from any delay in deciding foreign policy.[92] There was little movement on either side at this stage of the debate. Despite the arguments of the commonwealthsmen, the majority of members accepted that an expeditionary force was necessary, and a general vote approving the sending of the fleet to sea 'for the safety of this commonwealth and the preservation of the trade and commerce thereof' was passed *nemine contradicente* on 23 February.[93] But by then the central question was no longer the morality of intervention, but how far Parliament had a right to determine foreign policy.

The commonwealthsmen had already identified the question of Parliament's rights as their best chance to defeat the government. In doing so, they exploited the general feeling that the Humble Petition was in need of major revision – and asserted that until the Parliament perfected it (and 'recognised' the government) the constitution remained undecided. On

[89] Burton, III, 385.   [90] Burton, III, 387–9, 392.   [91] Burton, III, 395, 397, 400, 402–3.
[92] Burton, III, 444.   [93] *CJ*, VII, 606.

21 February Thomas Scott taunted those members who supported the government as poor dupes, saying, 'you should be made somewhat more than purse-bearers, and to tell the Protector "if you will make the war, we will find the purses"'. If there were to be a war, Scott continued, it had to be 'by your direction', so that Parliament would be 'the great disposer of peace and war. This will otherwise determine the dispute of the militia.'[94] This was a shrewd blow. By appealing to Parliament's rights over money, war, and the armed forces, Scott and his friends could perhaps encourage some of the less committed members to oppose the Protectorate. It was also a difficult point for any Parliamentarian to argue against. Richard Knightley tried hard, but could only point out (as some members had done in 1654) that the Protector and council should consider the matter of war 'because of secrecy'; John Bulkeley said that this expedition to the Baltic did not amount to a 'war' in any case; but both conceded that a proviso 'not to prejudice us in the great business of the militia' would have to be added to any motion.[95] Others supported intervention, but were cautious about giving up any of Parliament's rights. This uncertainty opened the way for Lambert and Vane to raise the question of control of the militia once more, and the debate was adjourned.[96]

On 23 February, as those who favoured intervention continued to argue for the inclusion of a proviso, commonwealthsmen such as Vane and Hesilrige were busy weaving ever more complicated webs around the issue. They suggested that to refer the matter to the Protector and council would in effect 'recognise' the council and 'confirm them in a lump', and it might even, by default, confirm the power of the Protector himself.[97] Defenders of the government denied that any such trick was intended. As John Trevor said, 'his highness does not seem to demand it [the militia] of you, by his submitting this to you. He that asks authority, assents that he of whom it is demanded, hath it.'[98] This was an important point, and one that may have been crucial in securing the vote allowing the fleet to be sent out. Afterwards, the commonwealthsmen seem to have become increasingly wild in their arguments, proposing a new committee to discuss the matter (and thereby delay its conclusion); when the solicitor-general, William Ellis, pointed out that the Other House might need to be included in any further consultations, Vane revealed his intention of wrecking the debate altogether by retorting that 'the question will inevitably involve you in the business of the militia, and negative voice, and the Other House'.[99] The debate was again adjourned, until 24 February, when the controversies of the common-wealthsmen provoked a more sustained defence from the Presbyterian MPs

---

[94] Burton, III, 393.   [95] Burton, III, 395–6.   [96] Burton, III, 397, 399, 400–3.
[97] Burton, III, 441–2.   [98] Burton, III, 442.   [99] Burton, III, 447.

who supported the Protectorate. Sir Richard Onslow called for a plain, open question to resolve the matter of how the fleet should be 'disposed', and Thomas Bampfield rebuffed attempts to 'creep into the other debates', telling members that 'till you come to your constitution, I see you are gravelled in every debate. Whatever you propound, the constitution will, inevitably, come in upon you.'[100] The mood of the House was turning against the commonwealthsmen, and even a senior army officer like Thomas Kelsey was impatient for action, and inclined to trust the Protector, that 'he will do nothing without your advice'. Hesilrige's response ('I rise with a sad heart to see worthy gentlemen that have been with us from the beginning, so differ from us in this business') was an admission of the failure of the commonwealthsmen to win the argument, as well as the backing of the majority.[101] They did not admit it until the end of 'a long debate, till almost eleven' on the night of 24 February, and the passing of a motion, by 176 votes to 98, to put the main question. The question itself was conceded, and instead of another vote it was simply resolved that the sending of the fleet would be 'referred' to the Protector, 'saving the interest of this House in the militia and in making of peace and war'.[102] As the French ambassador pointed out, even with the proviso (which went beyond the terms of the Humble Petition), this was a victory for Richard Cromwell, 'as it maintains him in possession of the forces' and had the effect of 'recognising his authority' over the state.[103] It also had the effect, as one royalist noted, of admitting that Richard's real intention was to send 'assistance to the Swede'.[104]

The management of foreign policy during the debates in the spring of 1659 deserves close attention. As we have seen, Thurloe introduced the business on the Protector's behalf, and replied to Vane's first attack on the probity of the war on 21 February; but he then seems to have left matters to the Parliament. Presbyterians, such as John Trevor, began by moving that the whole question of policy, and the disposal of the fleet, be referred to the Protector.[105] In these initial exchanges, the commonwealthsmen set the pace, and Scott successfully introduced an element of doubt in members' minds by warning them of the implications of a vote for the rights of Parliament over the militia, and the making of peace and war. Vane furthered this by raising suspicions 'of some court design' behind the motion, and it was largely through the efforts of the commonwealthsmen that the first day's debate ended in an adjournment.[106] The debate on 23 February was successfully subverted by

---

[100] Burton, III, 451–2.   [101] Burton, III, 456–7; Schilling, pp. 108–10.
[102] *CJ*, VII, 607; Burton, III, 493; *Clarke Papers*, III, 183; BL, Lansdowne MS 823, fo. 235r.
[103] Guizot, *Richard Cromwell*, I, 323; the council were specifically excluded from this: see *TSP*, VII, 626.
[104] Bodl., MS Clarendon 60, fo. 156v.   [105] Burton, III, 385–6.   [106] Burton, III, 393, 401.

the commonwealthsmen, although Trevor was effective in debate against them, and Onslow was able to move the vote agreeing, in principle, that a fleet should be sent out. The turning point came on the morning of 24 February, when a group of Presbyterian-courtiers, led by John Maynard, seized the initiative. Maynard's point was similar to that made by Bampfield earlier in the day: 'the right of the militia, in this discourse, looked rather like a diversion, and seemed very wide of the matter'; the Dutch could not be trusted, and there was no time to lose; 'a committee will but clog the business'; and a proviso could be added to any motion.[107] Maynard was supported by a phalanx made up of Sir Richard Onslow, John Swinfen, Charles Lloyd, and Major Robert Beake, the latter urging 'that there is a necessity to do something with all speed'.[108] On the afternoon of 24 February, other Presbyterians took up the same line, leaving the commonwealthsmen on the back foot.[109] It was only then that Thurloe rejoined the fray, once again denying that there was an 'engagement' with the Swedes, or that war was intended, and asserting that intervention was 'to secure the interest of England'.[110] Vane tried to turn the tables once again, with a direct accusation that there was indeed 'an underhand, secret treaty' with Sweden, and that 'our counsels have been mingled with France, and taken from the cardinal'; but, apart from provoking Bulkeley into a 'very hot' reply, he could not prevent the final vote from being passed by a large majority.[111]

The government's performance during the foreign policy debate in 1659, with its strong start, the loss of initiative to the commonwealthsmen, and the eventual counterattack by pro-government members on the third day of debate, shows its essential inability to manage the Commons.[112] Yet, there is another side to this coin: despite the chaotic mismanagement of the Commons, the government managed to get a firm vote in its favour in three days flat. Furthermore, the winning of this vote on foreign policy was a huge political success, badly needed amid the difficult constitutional debates of February 1659. It also signalled the firm support that the regime could expect from the Presbyterians and moderates in the House, and it thus marks a revival of the general unity over foreign policy that had been apparent before the spring of 1657. No further money had been promised at this stage, but, with the Parliament's blessing, Richard Cromwell duly sent a fleet under Edward Montagu to the Sound.[113] This was a remarkable

---

[107] Burton, III, 461–3.   [108] Burton, III, 463–5, 471–2; Schilling, pp. 114–15.
[109] Burton, III, 472–80; Schilling, pp. 118–19; [Slingsby Bethel,] *A True and Impartial Narrative* (1659), p. 8, refers to the debate being 'carried with a strong hand by the court party'.
[110] Burton, III, 481–8.
[111] Burton, III, 489–90, 492, 493; Guizot, *Richard Cromwell*, I, 330–1.
[112] See chapter 5.   [113] TSP, VII, 636.

achievement, but it could not be sustained. New debates on the funding of the war and Montagu's efforts to mediate between Sweden and Denmark were both cut short by the dissolution of the Parliament and the resignation of Richard as Protector. Under the restored Rump, English foreign policy veered sharply, supporting not Sweden but the Danes and Dutch, in the prolonged peace negotiations that followed. Furthermore, the new commonwealth, although continuing the Spanish war and the French alliance, made no secret of its lack of commitment to both. The days of vigour and victory in foreign affairs had passed.[114]

CONCLUSION

The Protectorate marked a unique phase in the history of Parliament's involvement in foreign policy. The constitutional provisions made in the Instrument of Government and the Humble Petition and Advice allowed Parliament not only control of the financial aspects of war, but also the right to give consent to the deployment of the armed forces. This was a huge advance from the situation in the early seventeenth century, when kings jealously guarded their prerogative rights; but it was also a very different situation from the commonwealth of 1649–53, which claimed sovereign powers over foreign affairs. The result was an uneasy compromise, as foreign policy became drawn into domestic agendas, especially of those who sought to give more powers (even kingly powers) to the Protector, and those (like the commonwealthsmen) who wanted a return to parliamentary dominance. In other respects, however, the Protectorate Parliaments behaved in a very traditional way. War – especially war with Spain – was popular, and in each Parliament there were unanimous votes to engage in conflict, whether in the West Indies (in 1654), against Spain at sea (in 1656) and on land (in 1657), or in an intervention in the Baltic (in 1659) which was likely to end in war with the Dutch. MPs were far less enthusiastic when it came to raising money for such wars. In 1654 and 1659 the matter was not tackled head-on, as the Parliaments died prematurely; but in 1656–7 the government's managers faced an uphill struggle, securing the £400,000 assessment only on the back of the defeat of the major-generals scheme, and then being refused the additional money requested in April 1657, despite the direct intervention of Oliver Cromwell.

Faced with these constitutional tensions, and the members' reluctance to pay up, the government made strenuous efforts to manage each Parliament to ensure the passage of legislation. Indeed, it was in the area of foreign policy

---

[114] For the Rump's foreign policy, see Ruth Mayers, *1659: The Crisis of the Commonwealth* (Woodbridge, 2004), pp. 113–48.

that the government managers proved most industrious, and most successful. A central figure in this was John Thurloe, who used his positions as secretary of state and head of the intelligence service to good effect, especially in 1656–7 and 1659. It was Thurloe who timed the arrival of the captured Spanish plate in London with the day of thanksgiving on 5 November 1656 and the demand for money that followed; in January 1657 he secured the passing of the £400,000 assessment for the war, despite strong opposition among MPs to a 'land tax'; and in 1659 he opened the debate on the Baltic situation, and set the agenda for the discussion that followed. Thurloe was a constant presence, but his associates changed dramatically over the course of the last two Parliaments: the unity of the council broke down in the winter of 1656–7, the civilian courtiers became more prominent in the spring and summer of 1657, and, finally, the Presbyterians came through as the main supporters of the Protectorate in 1659. These changes in the managers echoed political changes at Whitehall, and again demonstrated how closely foreign policy was related to domestic politics. By playing down the role of Parliament in foreign policy, historians have missed not only the influence that Westminster could have on decisions made at Whitehall (and vice versa), but also the strong links that existed between events abroad and constitutional and political upheavals at home.

12

Irish and Scottish affairs

When considering Ireland and Scotland during the Protectorate Parliaments, historians have tended to concentrate on two areas. First, they have emphasised the role of Irish and Scottish members of Parliament as supporters of the Protectorate in the kingship debates of 1657 and the union debates of 1659.[1] While there is much truth in this approach, it is also problematic, as it tends to emphasise their importance as a 'bloc' of votes, to be manipulated by English interests, when it is by no means clear that Irish and Scottish members formed a single body. Secondly, historians have examined the three sets of elections, which are seen as a test of how representative the members were, and thus how successfully 'union' had been imposed – or embraced – in the localities.[2] This approach can also be misleading, as it encourages an analysis of returns purely on an ethnic basis, in other words, whether members were 'English' or 'Irish/Scottish' in their backgrounds. This obsession with ethnicity ignores any divisions within Irish or Scottish society, which may undermine a sense of an agreed 'national interest' to which local members would subscribe;[3] it also glosses over the possibility that Englishmen may have been as effective at representing constituents' concerns as natives, and, because of their greater influence in England, they might even have been more attractive

---

[1] See, for example, C. H. Firth, 'Cromwell and the Crown', *EHR*, 17 (1902), 429–42, and 18 (1903), 52–80; Hugh Trevor-Roper, 'Oliver Cromwell and his Parliaments', in Trevor-Roper, *Religion, the Reformation and Social Change* (3rd edn, 1984), pp. 345–91; Patrick Little, *Lord Broghill and the Cromwellian Union with Ireland and Scotland* (Woodbridge, 2004), chapter 5.

[2] Paul J. Pinckney, 'The Scottish Representation in the Cromwellian Parliament of 1656', *Scottish Historical Review*, 46 (1967), 95–114; James A. Casada, 'The Scottish Representatives in Richard Cromwell's Parliament', *Scottish Historical Review*, 51 (1972), 124–47; T. C. Barnard, 'Lord Broghill, Vincent Gookin and the Cork Election of 1659', *EHR*, 88 (1973), 352–65; Frances Dow, *Cromwellian Scotland, 1651–1660* (Edinburgh, 1979), pp. 148–53, 185–7, 237–40; Patrick Little, 'Irish Representation in the Protectorate Parliaments', *Parl. Hist.*, 23 (2004), 336–56.

[3] Historians of Scotland are particularly prone to this: see Pinckney, 'Scottish Representation', 105, 113; Dow, *Cromwellian Scotland*, pp. 150–1, 238–9.

as representatives.[4] In this chapter, the primary focus will not be on elections or great matters of state: rather on the conduct of day-to-day Irish and Scottish business within the Parliaments. What was this business and how was it managed? Did Irish and Scottish matters provoke hostility or indifference among the English members? Finally, to what extent can Irish and Scottish affairs at Westminster be treated as a single entity? It is only once these questions have been addressed that the Irish and Scottish elections can be understood, and the big debates put into their proper 'British' context.

1654-5

At first sight, the Parliament of 1654–5 seems to have been nothing but a disappointment for the Irish and Scots. Interminable debates on the Instrument of Government, which the Presbyterians in the Commons wished to rewrite completely, led to open conflict with the Protector and his supporters, and the sudden dissolution of the session in January 1655. In the face of the constitutional debate, Irish and Scottish business was apparently forgotten. In the traditional account, Scotland was particularly hard hit. Scottish involvement in this Parliament was hampered by incomplete elections, as many areas were unable to return members, either because of the insurgency led by the royalist Earl of Glencairn in the highlands or a lack of suitably qualified electors. Only twenty-two of the thirty possible members were returned, and, of these, nine were Englishmen connected with the government or the army. In the circumstances, we are told, it was hardly surprising that Scottish affairs were sidelined at Westminster.[5] As Paul Pinckney put it, 'there was not much room for Scottish affairs in the 1654 Parliament'.[6] According to Frances Dow, 'the response of the Scots to this opportunity for political activity was one of overwhelming apathy', and, partly as a result, 'the first Protectoral Parliament rarely comprehended Scottish affairs'.[7] Yet a thorough investigation of Scottish activity within the 1654 Parliament suggests that, while weak in numbers and unable to compete against the constitutional debates in the Commons, Scottish business was in fact flourishing.

The chief vehicle was the committee of Scottish affairs, appointed on 29 September 1654, which included 'all the gentlemen that serve for Scotland' and a smattering of English councillors, including General George Monck's main ally at Whitehall, John Lambert. The committee was designed as a way

---

[4] A point conceded in Pinckney, 'Scottish Representation', 105–6; and Dow, *Cromwellian Scotland*, pp. 151, 186.
[5] Dow, *Cromwellian Scotland*, pp. 148–53. [6] Pinckney, 'Scottish Representation', 96–7.
[7] Dow, *Cromwellian Scotland*, pp. 149, 151.

of managing government business outside the Commons' chamber, and from
the outset it was ordered to 'take into consideration the ordinances which
have passed touching Scotland', including crucial measures such as the union
ordinance, and those dealing with creditors, debtors, and taxation.[8] The
government seized the opportunity. On 30 September Monck's agent in the
Commons, George Downing, told him of the committee's appointment, and
asked for 'your directions what you think fit for the committee to consider of
for Scotland'.[9] In the next few months, business before the committee
included a bill for taking away the tenure of wards and knight service in
Scotland, and detailed consideration of the chapter in the revised parliamentary constitution concerning the qualifications for Scottish voters.[10] The
most pressing matters put before it were the settlement of the assessment
tax and the ratification of the ordinance of union as an act of Parliament.

The Scottish assessment bill was referred to the committee of Scottish
affairs on 5 December.[11] By this time it was abundantly clear that, in matters
of taxation at least, the Scottish government was in tune with the people.
At the very beginning of the session, Monck instructed senior army officers
(including some members) to lobby at Whitehall for new ways to support the
burden of the army in Scotland,[12] and at regular intervals throughout the
session he wrote to Cromwell and Lambert, complaining that the £10,000 a
month levied from Scotland was unsustainable, warning that 'not above
£7,300 can be received ... though many through poverty are unable to pay
it'.[13] Monck's protestations coincided with a representation from 'the gentlemen that serve in Parliament for Scotland', which also argued that £10,000
per month was unfair, basing their requests on the union ordinance of April
1654 which had promised proportionate taxation. They pointed out that
England's rate had been reduced unfairly, and promised that a similar
reduction in Scotland would ensure 'a sweet and cordial compliance with
your highness's government'.[14] English members were not unsympathetic to
such requests, but there was disagreement as to the merits of proportionate
rating. When the assessments were debated on 21 November 1654, the
diarist Guybon Goddard recorded that when the English bill (reducing the
tax there to £60,000 per month) was proposed

the Scots and Irish moved that those nations might be involved in the same bill of
charge with England, and not be rated by themselves; but that was not yielded unto, in
regard their nations were not at present in such a condition of peace and improvement
as ours was, and therefore could not be laid at a full proportion. But they moved it

[8] *CJ*, VII, 371. [9] BL, Egerton MS 2618, fo. 46r. [10] *CJ*, VII, 407, 414.
[11] *CJ*, VII, 395. [12] Worcester College, Oxford, Clarke MS 3/9, unfol.: 6 September 1654.
[13] Clarke MS 3/2, fos. 74r, 81v, 84v, 85.
[14] NLS, MS 7032, fo. 116r: representation, no date [1654–5].

upon another account; for they did fear that £60,000 would be so low a charge as would nothing near satisfy, and therefore they were jealous that all the rest that fell short would be laid upon them.[15]

When the Scottish assessments were debated again, on 5 December, a compromise was reached 'after a long debate', with assessments being reduced to £8,000 for three months, 'and afterwards to raise them to a due proportion'.[16] Once again, there was no meeting of minds between the English and Scottish members. Goddard, like other members from the south, seems to have assumed that 'proportionate' taxation would be higher than the current rate, while the Scottish members petitioning Cromwell clearly thought that it would reduce their burden still further.

One reason for the Scots' insistence on proportionate taxation was that it was part and parcel of the concessions allowed to the nation under the 1654 union ordinance. Apart from the fair apportionment of tax, the ordinance promised the Scots thirty seats in Parliament, reform of their legal system, and free trade. These measures were not set in stone, however. The ordinance awaited confirmation through an act of Parliament and, as the instructions for the committee of Scottish affairs had indicated, it could be reshaped, or added to, in the meantime. The union bill was under consideration in the committee of Scottish affairs by 18 December, and received its first reading on 22 December.[17] This was business of the highest importance for the government, but this did not indicate that English officials took a cold, dispassionate view of the new bill. In his interventions, the partiality of Monck's promotion of 'Scottish interests' is apparent. He was happy to support the shire members, but his attitude towards the burghs was hostile. This can best be seen in letters he wrote on consecutive days in January 1655. On 18 January, thinking that 'the act for union will shortly be considered of and passed', he urged Cromwell that the new legislation should not confirm the rights of Edinburgh to the detriment of the merchants (including Englishmen) of the neighbouring 'unfree' (non-royal) burgh of Leith.[18] On 19 January, by contrast, he sent Downing a 'paper of desires of some gentlemen of 15 shires of Scotland who lately met at Edinburgh', asking that their concerns would be passed on to Lambert, unless the Parliament had already decided the business.[19]

Monck's preferences are significant, as they marked his willingness to become involved in a rift that had existed in Scottish politics since the 1640s, and which re-emerged in the committee of Scottish affairs in 1654. A letter from the member for the 'Haddington burghs' and town clerk of Edinburgh, William Thomsone, dated 29 December, reveals that tensions

---

[15] Burton, I, lxxxviii–lxxxix.   [16] Burton, I, cvii.   [17] *CJ*, VII, 403, 407.
[18] Clarke MS 3/2, fo. 92v; cf. *TSP*, V, 754.   [19] Clarke MS 3/9, unfol.: 19 January 1655.

between the burgh and shire members were running high.[20] According to Thomsone, the chosen ground for their dispute was the committee of Scottish affairs itself. Of the eight members returned for Scottish burghs in 1654, four were Scots and four Englishmen, but they had all been issued with detailed instructions by the convention of royal burghs, which sought free trade, restrictions on English merchants setting up in unfree burghs, and the protection of creditors against the claims of landowners, as well as making a common call for a reduction of assessments. Instead of dividing on ethnic lines, the burgh members seem to have worked closely together on behalf of their constituents, especially during the union debates in the committee, when they moved to 'have passed an addition and clause for the liberties and privileges of burghs'. This clause was included in the draft bill presented to the Commons on 22 December, despite 'opposition' – not least from General Monck and those shire members who had vested interests in the unfree burghs. A further cause of problems between shire and burgh members was the discussion of the ordinance for distribution of Scottish seats, as 'the gentlemen representing the shires did overvote us in committee and labour to have 22 of the 30 for the shires and leave eight only for the burghs' – prompting protests, and then a walk-out, by the burgh members in the committee. The assessment bill also caused problems. Although there was agreement that the rate should be reduced, the burgh members were eager to overturn the current system of collecting the tax, which placed them under the power of commissioners chosen by the shires. Overall, Thomsone's letter shows that the committee of Scottish affairs was a forum for a great deal of business, and a hotbed of factionalism. It also suggests that the factional lines were drawn not by ethnicity but by vested interests. This involved not only the Scottish members, but also government officials such as George Monck.

The constant jockeying for position within the committee was to no purpose, however. The dissolution of the Parliament in January meant that the Scots lost the new union bill, and the reversion to the old union ordinance of April 1654 marked a defeat for the burghs and probably for the shires as well. Other ordinances remained as they were. Despite Monck's support for a reduction in the assessments, in February 1655 the English council announced a return to the previous level of £10,000 per month.[21] Nor had the army of occupation, the greatest expense charged on the country, been reduced. When the Scottish members took their leave of the Protector after the dissolution, they raised the issue with him. In reply, Cromwell blamed the heavy military presence north of the border on 'the ministry, [who] preach up

---

[20] The following paragraph is based on Patrick Little, 'Scottish Affairs at Westminster: A Letter from the Union Parliament of 1654–5', *Scottish Historical Review*, 84 (2005), 247–56.

[21] *A & O*, II, 1029.

the interest of Charles Stuart and did much inveigh against the present authority, so that there was a necessity of their continuance'. He added that, if they could find a way to reduce the troops without jeopardising security, 'he was willing to answer their desires thereon'. Interestingly, the response of the Scottish members was not to distance themselves from the regime, but to seek to draw closer, and it was reported that, after their interview with Cromwell, 'the said members are now considering of an expedient' to satisfy him.[22]

Irish members displayed a similar degree of engagement in the 1654 Parliament, but there is no evidence of the divisions and infighting that had marred Scottish affairs. This was not only because the Irish Protestant community was smaller and more homogeneous than the Scots, but also because they were united in their hatred of the governor of Ireland, Charles Fleetwood. This hostility was reciprocated. In the summer of 1654, Fleetwood had argued in favour of nominating members, rather than allowing the Protestant community to elect their own members, only to be overruled by the Protector and his council in England. As the returns came in, Fleetwood's fears were justified, as nearly two-thirds of the seats were taken by Irish Protestants or their allies. This not only reflected 'grass-roots involvement in politics' in Ireland, it also had an effect on affairs at Westminster, where Irish affairs were much less prone to government influence than those of Scotland.[23] Once in Parliament, the Irish members found that the redrafting of the Instrument of Government put much of their business on hold. By 12 November there were complaints that 'no private business is likely to be heard' in the House, and on 8 January 1655 it was thought that 'if the Protector and Parliament agree, something will be done for the good of Ireland', but it was beginning to look doubtful.[24] Delay did not mean inactivity, however. As with Scotland, much of the business specific to Ireland was being prepared in its own committee. The committee of Irish affairs, appointed on 29 September 1654, was charged with considering 'such acts, orders and ordinances as have been made touching the same' and, although detailed evidence of its deliberations is lacking, it probably had a wide-ranging competence similar to that of its Scottish counterpart. It is also likely that the Irish members, who were all named to the committee, were among its most regular members,[25] although it is unlikely that the (probably vexatious) proposal in early October 'that Ireland should be hereafter called West England' originated from the Irish contingent.[26]

The activity of Irish Protestant members can also be seen in the trade and customs committee during October 1654. Two leading Irish Protestants,

[22] Clarke MS 1/15, fo. 44.   [23] Little, 'Irish Representation', 338–44.
[24] HMC *Egmont*, I (1905), 561, 564.   [25] *CJ*, VII, 371.   [26] *Clarke Papers*, V, 216.

Lord Broghill and Arthur Hill, were especially added to its membership on 12 October, and later in the month Broghill was teller in favour of easing restrictions on the transport of corn and butter – two of the most lucrative Irish exports.[27] Discussion of the assessments in November prompted the Irish members to join the Scots in requesting, unsuccessfully, that 'those nations might be involved in the same bill of charge with England' to avoid shouldering the burden of any shortfall.[28] This was particularly important for Ireland, as under a council ordinance of 2 June 1654 the assessment rate was set to rise year on year, soon reaching extortionate levels.[29] In December 1654 there was a victory of sorts: Parliament agreed that the Irish assessment rate would be reduced from £10,000 to £8,000 a month, although calls for further abatement were not accepted, and the matter was referred back to the committee of Irish affairs.[30] Trade concessions and equal treatment over taxation formed important parts of the Irish union bill, which had its first reading on 15 January 1655. This bill seems to have been modelled on the Scottish ordinance of April 1654, offering free trade, law reform, a guarantee of parliamentary representation, and proportionate taxation, but in this case there is little doubt that it was an initiative that came from the Irish Protestant community, rather than the government. Indeed, Fleetwood had opposed the resurrection of the traditional law courts, just as he had questioned the desirability of free elections, and, when it came to free trade, this was demanded not by the Dublin government but by the Dublin merchants.[31] Instead of managing Irish business, Fleetwood sniped from the sidelines, making dark comments to Thurloe that 'there are some, who relate to Ireland (not of the soldiers) who do ill offices in England', and who must be opposed at all costs.[32] The Parliament was dissolved before the union bill had had its second reading, and the constitutional status of Ireland remained uncertain. The closure of the Parliament also destroyed the bill to reduce Irish assessments, which reverted to the incremental scale imposed by the English council in June 1654.[33] Fleetwood may have been pleased,[34] but the Irish, like the Scots, were painfully aware that they had nothing to show for their diligence.

When looking back at the 1654 Parliament, the Scottish minister Robert Baillie was downbeat. 'They went from Scotland thirty, and from Ireland also thirty. Ours and their choices were men who, for peace, were resolved to do or say anything they found tolerable to their large mind, and, I think, were

[27] Patrick Little, 'The First Unionists? Irish Protestant Attitudes to Union with England, 1653–1659', *Irish Historical Studies*, 32 (2000), 47–8.
[28] Burton, I, lxxxvi–lxxxix. [29] *CSPI*, 1647–60, 801. [30] Burton, I, cvii; *CJ*, VII, 395.
[31] Little, 'First Unionists?', 46–9. [32] *TSP*, III, 23.
[33] *A & O*, II, 1029; *CSPI*, 1647–60, 809. [34] *TSP*, III, 136.

all complying with the Protector as he would have wished.'[35] Yet Baillie's gloomy comments, made nearly a year after the Parliament was dissolved, must not be taken at face value. In particular, the surviving evidence suggests that the members, far from 'complying' for the sake of 'peace', were actively engaged with parliamentary business, especially through the committees of Irish and Scottish affairs. Such bodies offered the opportunity for members to haggle (or even fight) over business before it was presented to the Commons, and gave them a chance to change unpalatable measures imposed by the government. The Irish and Scottish members had also gained valuable political experience in the chamber itself. English members were not necessarily hostile to Ireland and Scotland but, as the assessment debate showed, they were often ignorant or uninterested. Whether or not the Irish and Scottish members worked together on issues of common concern is uncertain. The business of the two nations often ran in parallel: the committees of Irish and Scottish affairs were named on the same day;[36] the assessment bills were considered together in November and early December;[37] and the Irish union bill was influenced by that for Scotland; but, as yet, this probably reflected the procedural concerns of English parliamentary officials, rather than a sense of fraternity between the Irish and the Scots themselves.

SCOTLAND, 1656–7

It would be difficult to overemphasise the importance for the Cromwellian union of the appointment of Lord Broghill as president of the Scottish council in April 1655.[38] In parallel with the Protector's younger son, Henry Cromwell, who replaced Fleetwood as effective ruler of Ireland in the summer, Broghill spearheaded a new style of government, which sought to reduce the influence of the army and the religious radicals associated with them, encouraging instead civilian, moderate rule, which brought the native Protestant population into the local administration and (increasingly) into positions of national importance. For Broghill, in particular, such reforms were made with half an eye on the situation in England, where the army and its allies dominated the council. In the 1656–7 sitting of the second Protectorate Parliament, Broghill and his allies at court were able to muster a considerable majority by harnessing the Presbyterian majority in England, successfully despatching the major-generals, and then, in February 1657, introducing a new, monarchical constitution, based on the ancient

[35] D. Laing, ed., *The Letters and Journals of Robert Baillie* (3 vols., Bannatyne Club, Edinburgh, 1841–2), III, 289.
[36] *CJ*, VII, 371.   [37] *CJ*, VII, 387, 388, 390, 394, 395.
[38] See Little, *Broghill, passim*, esp. pp. 121–3.

constitution of king and two Houses of Parliament. Broghill, as an Irish Protestant and president of the Scottish council, could easily marshal a coherent party of Irish and Scottish MPs behind his reformist policies. This group was identified by contemporaries, and its influence was soon apparent in the Commons. In February 1657 the Irish member Vincent Gookin commented that 'the major-generals are much offended at the Irish and Scottish members, who being much united do sway exceedingly with their votes'.[39] In the kingship debates that followed, the Scots and particularly the Irish were noted as being strongly in favour, and twenty-nine (fourteen Scots, fifteen Irish) were listed among the 'kinglings' who voted in favour of the offer of the crown.[40] It was entirely appropriate that Broghill's ally on the Scottish council, Charles Howard, partnered Henry Cromwell's agent, Sir John Reynolds, as teller in the crucial vote on the new constitution, passed on 25 March.[41]

The close involvement of Irish and Scottish members of Parliament in decisions that determined the very nature of the Cromwellian state marked a radical departure from their peripheral position earlier in the Protectorate. There were immediate advantages to being in such an influential position. The Humble Petition and Advice was drafted with the three nations in mind; and from March 1657 a number of financial bills were drafted or amended to include all three nations, not just England, covering measures such as wine prices, customs and excise, the postal system, the inspection of treasuries, the grant of tonnage and poundage, and the general assessment.[42] It was now accepted that Ireland and Scotland would be included in English money bills or trade arrangements, and, in theory at least, the basic principle of union had been conceded. But there were also considerable disadvantages in all this, for the priorities of an ambitious courtier such as Lord Broghill were not necessarily those of the ordinary Irish and Scottish members. In following him, they were in danger of sacrificing their own interests on the altar of his grand three-nations design. There are signs that the members soon realised that they had struck a Faustian pact. During the kingship debates, it was reported that 'many of our Irish members grow weary of their seats and talk resolutely of their return',[43] while one Scottish commentator, writing at almost the same time, complained that 'our Scots business is at a stand'.[44] Worse still, a close identification with the Protectorate made the Irish and Scots vulnerable to attacks by malcontents hoping to weaken the government

[39] *TSP*, VI, 37.
[40] *A Narrative of the Late Parliament* (1657), p. 23; Little, *Broghill*, pp. 151–2.
[41] *CJ*, VII, 511.   [42] Little, 'First Unionists?', 51–2; *CJ*, VII, 541, 543; Burton, I, 325.
[43] BL, Lansdowne MS 821, fo. 326v.
[44] James D. Ogilvie, ed., *Diary of Sir Archibald Johnston of Wariston*, vol. III, *1655–1660* (Scottish History Society, 3rd series, 34, Edinburgh, 1940), p. 72.

or discredit Broghill and his friends. The underlying tension between unionist and domestic agendas, and the internal stresses within the 'unionist' camp, become apparent only when the ordinary business of Ireland and Scotland is considered separately from the big issues that dominated this Parliament.

Broghill's presidency of the Scottish council gave him a central role in the government's management of the parliamentary elections there, but he chose to use his influence sparingly, with government intervention taking place only if completely unacceptable candidates were proposed.[45] Of the thirty members returned, sixteen were English and fourteen Scottish, but once again the ethnic divisions are not always a helpful guide to attitudes or loyalties. Two of the councillors elected, John Swinton and Sir William Lockhart, were native Scots, and others had happily served in the local and central administration. George Downing, the scoutmaster-general, was an Englishman closely connected with the regime, but he was also chosen as the agent for the convention of royal burghs in 1657;[46] Colonel Stephen Winthrop was an army colonel, but he received detailed instructions from his Aberdeen constituency, and acted upon them in the Parliament.[47] As in 1654, there were issues in the 1656–7 sitting of Parliament that were as important to the government as to the Scots themselves, and key business was arranged through the committee of Scottish affairs. The committee was appointed on 23 September, with a mixture of English and Scots, including six members of the Scottish council.[48]

The most pressing business before the committee of Scottish affairs was the Scottish union bill. Its first reading was given on 25 October 1656 and the second on 4 November,[49] and thereafter the Scottish councillors argued for the bill to be passed without delay.[50] During November, the debate turned on the Scottish legal system, and the use of the word 'incorporate' in the first clause. This 'took up two hours debate, many interpreting that it could not be properly said to be incorporated with one commonwealth with England, except all their laws were first altered, and be as the laws of England are'. The point was 'well answered', however, and incorporation was accepted without the need for a common legal system.[51] The clause allowing free trade also 'admitted to much debate', especially as the importing of cheap Scottish salt threatened the trade from Newcastle, but it was also passed.[52] The only debate to be recorded in full by the diarist Thomas Burton was that on

---

[45] Pinckney, 'Scottish Representation', 98–9, 102.
[46] Pinckney, 'Scottish Representation', 105; Dow, *Cromwellian Scotland*, pp. 185–7.
[47] L. B. Taylor, ed., *Aberdeen Council Letters, III: 1645–1660* (Oxford, 1952), pp. 270–4.
[48] *CJ*, VII, 426.
[49] *CJ*, VII, 445, 450; the grand committee met on 8, 15, 17, and 21 November, but there is no record of debates: *CJ*, VII, 452–7.
[50] Burton, I, 6, 12, 95, 215.   [51] *Clarke Papers*, III, 80–1.   [52] *Clarke Papers*, III, 81–2.

4 December, which saw councillors such as Samuel Disbrowe pressing for the inclusion of a clause 'for confirmation of privileges of corporations in Scotland' which was very similar to that discussed in 1654.[53] On this occasion, burgh rights were championed by agents of the Scottish council, including Disbrowe, Downing, and Judge George Smyth, and they were opposed by a mixture of English officer-MPs and Scottish landowners, including Lord Cochrane, who had a vested interest as lord of the unfree burgh of Paisley. The treasury commissioner and common lawyer, Bulstrode Whitelocke, also questioned the clause, saying that it would predetermine any legal case in favour of the burghs and, after a fairly amicable debate, the matter was recommitted.[54] Oddly, renewed consideration of the bill on 14 January 1657 did not bring a repeat of the divisions of a month before, even though Monck again weighed in against the burgh interest, writing to Thurloe on 4 January that the new union bill must include an 'exception', preventing Edinburgh from claiming jurisdiction over Leith, 'without which the English, who are in Leith, will be much discouraged'. Instead, Leith (and, by implication, other unfree burghs?) should have 'equal liberty' with the royal burghs.[55] When it came to it, the burgh privileges clause – like those on legal union and free trade – was passed 'upon long debate', while the sticking point was another clause, stipulating that the Scots would have to pay only those taxes imposed by consent of Parliament. As Thomas Burton recorded, 'the objection against it was that it put the people of Scotland into a better condition than those of England', and, despite the best efforts of Downing and Howard, the discussion broke down, and 'we rose in confusion'.[56] Later attempts to resuscitate the union bill met with no success, and as a stopgap measure, on 28 April the Parliament ratified the existing union ordinance of April 1654 instead.[57] All the discussion and argument about modifying and expanding the terms of the union had been wasted.

Attempts by the committee of Scottish affairs to settle matters between Scottish debtors and their creditors were more successful. This was a historic problem, arising from the wars of the 1640s and early 1650s, which had left many nobles and lairds deeply indebted, the main creditors being wealthy merchants from the burghs – especially Edinburgh – and the situation had been further complicated by the forfeiture of many leading Scottish landowners by the English after 1652, as confirmed by the act of pardon and grace in 1654. English policy towards the two sides had initially favoured the creditors of forfeited estates, but in April 1656 a new order was passed allowing

---

[53] Burton, I, 12.   [54] Burton, I, 12–19.
[55] *TSP*, V, 754; for an undated paper of objections to union, perhaps drawn up for Monck, see *Clarke Papers*, V, 258–9.
[56] Burton, I, 346–8.   [57] *CJ*, VII, 524.

the indebted landowners to sell their estates to pay their debts, as part of a wider plan to reconcile former royalists to the new regime. The terms of the new measure made it disadvantageous to the merchants, who stood to recoup only a fraction of their original investment. The English council was eager to gain parliamentary approval for the new order, but the creditors introduced their own bill demanding the payment of interest on the debts before creditors could take advantage of the other provisions.[58] This bill excited great interest in Scotland. In February the convention of royal burghs noted that the business 'is yet lying before ... the committee of Scottish affairs, and nothing as yet concluded therein',[59] while Scottish landowners affected by the proposed legislation were alarmed at this 'act for forfalters', which they considered a 'hotch potch'.[60] On 28 April 1657, Broghill and Samuel Disbrowe were among the MPs appointed to consider the original ordinance of 1654, and Disbrowe reported on it the next day, when three interested parties, Lambert, Swinton, and Lord Cochrane, were added to the committee and the matter was recommitted.[61] Disbrowe's final report, delivered later that day, recommended allowing further time for forfeited landowners and their trustees to lodge claims, but stipulated that those with 'donatives' were to be compensated first. The committee also blocked the Countess of Lauderdale's claim to jointure payments until she had relinquished her claim to her jointure lands.[62] As a result of this report, the Commons agreed a compromise, voting to continue the April 1656 order, but adding the committee's provisos on behalf of the holders of donatives.[63]

The decision on the Scottish land settlement had been swayed by vested interests at the highest level. 'Donative' lands from forfeited estates had been granted to a number of English officers earlier in the 1650s, including John Lambert, who had received part of the Lauderdale lands, and George Monck, whose donative was the Duchess of Hamilton's barony of Kinneil. Monck's position was awkward, because he had sold on his interest to others, but remained liable for their secure title. Other recipients of donatives included two Scottish councillors: John Swinton, who had been granted a slice of the Lauderdale estate which was supposed to form the countess's jointure lands; and, at second hand, Sir William Lockhart, who had purchased a donative over the Hamilton lands on the duchess's behalf, and now advised her in her attempts to recover the whole inheritance.[64] Interestingly, although they did not agree on political matters, Lockhart was eager to

---

[58] David Menarry, 'The Irish and Scottish Landed Elites from Regicide to Restoration' (Ph.D thesis, University of Aberdeen, 2001), pp. 332–3.
[59] NAS, B9/12/11 (Burntisland council mins., 1655–60), fo. 94v.
[60] BL, Add. MS 23112, fo. 48r.   [61] *CJ*, VII, 526, 527; Burton, II, 66.
[62] NRAS, no. 332, Lennoxlove, Hamilton MS L.1/189/15.   [63] Hamilton MS L.1/189/15.
[64] Hamilton MS F.1.197, 208; NAS, GD 406/2/M.1/202.

preserve Swinton's donative rights, which he recommended to Thurloe on 7 January 1657.[65] Broghill was also more than willing to work with his political opponents when it came to the land issue, supporting Lambert and others in pressing for Monck's bill to be decided swiftly.[66] A similar partnership of unlikely people can be seen in the donative bill. Immediately after Samuel Disbrowe's report on 29 April had confirmed the lands of Swinton and Lambert, Swinton moved that the claims of Monck and others would also be protected – a proposal that Broghill seconded. Swinton then proposed that the pardons of the Earl of Callander and Lord Cranston, which had been promoted by the Scottish council in 1656, should be confirmed. This was generally agreed, and Broghill, with Lambert, Swinton, Charles Howard, and the Earl of Tweeddale, was ordered to bring in the bill.[67] A surviving report of the committee's activities suggests further deals were being struck. On 17 June there were eight MPs present, including John Lockhart (brother and political agent of William), Sir James MacDowall, the Earl of Tweeddale (who was a trustee, and financially liable, for Callander's estates), and two MPs closely connected with the Scottish council, Samuel Disbrowe and George Downing. The business was referred to Tweeddale, Lockhart, and MacDowall, who reported back to the committee the next day, with the recommendation that earlier orders from the Scottish council were to be upheld. Tweeddale then presented the committee's findings to the Commons. Everyone seemed to gain from this smooth process.[68] The Scottish council's decisions had been respected, and the Earl of Tweeddale had secured his financial interests. But whether any of these arrangements truly reflected 'Scottish interests' is another matter.

Scottish religious matters also became entangled with English concerns. Broghill was a staunch supporter of the majority Resolutioner party, which he thought 'will prove the honester of the two',[69] and they could also rely on supporters in the English council and the court.[70] By contrast, Monck was a partisan for the Protester (or Remonstrant) ministers, who he thought 'better to be trusted than the other party which are called the general resolution men'.[71] He was seconded by Lambert, Fleetwood, Pickering, and Strickland, who were described by the Resolutioner agent, James Sharp, as 'the Parliament party of the council which appeareth for the Remonstrators'.[72] Broghill's patronage can be seen clearly in September and October 1656, when he went out of his way to persuade the Resolutioners to accept the fast called by the Parliament. Despite assurances of their fidelity to the regime,

[65] *TSP*, V, 769. [66] Burton, I, 227; Little, *Broghill*, p. 131.
[67] Burton, II, 75–7; *CJ*, VII, 527. [68] NLS, MS 7032, fo. 97r–v. [69] *TSP*, V, 656.
[70] Stephen, II, 42. [71] Clarke MS 3/3, fo. 1v.
[72] NLS, Wodrow Folio MS 26, fo. 158r; Stephen, II, 20, 30.

the Resolutioners refused to accept such an order from the civil authorities, and that was that.[73] This was followed by a much more serious dispute about the approval and maintenance of ministers, which was at first discussed in the English council, but then spilled over into the Commons in March 1657 when the qualifications for Scottish voters in article 4 of the Humble Petition and Advice were debated. In the early summer of 1657, when the Additional Petition was considered, the row resurfaced. In May, the Protester ministers submitted a paper urging that all supporters of the Duke of Hamilton's engagement in 1648 should be 'excluded from trust' in the Humble Petition, 'because if these be not excluded, the members of Parliament shall be only of the malignant stamp'.[74] The debate in June was bad-tempered. The Protesters' demand for greater restrictions (and the effective exclusion of their political rivals) was taken up by Lambert, Fleetwood, and other senior army officers, while those associated with the Scottish council, including Monck's brother-in-law, Thomas Clarges, and Samuel Disbrowe, counter-attacked, trying to force through a proviso that would except all those employed by the Scottish council, and thus making the issue one of confidence in the council itself. The supporters of the proviso could make little headway, however. The absence of Lord Broghill, who was ill from gout for the whole debate, was seen as the crucial factor in this. As the leading Protester, Sir Archibald Johnston of Wariston, put it on 17 June, 'blessed be God that has laid aside these three weeks Broghill by the gout, or else he had stopped both our public and private business'.[75] There was another important consideration, however. Even with the heavyweight politicians engaged on both sides, ordinary English back-benchers remained indifferent to Scottish issues. Wariston had thought that the qualification issue was being discussed in such detail because it was part of the Humble Petition, 'which is more than in an act about [Scottish] magistrates, which will not readily win in this Parliament'.[76] But when the vote was forced through, James Sharp blamed his disappointment on the English members, for those who backed the Scottish councillors' proviso had gone out to vote, and 'many looked upon themselves as too unconcerned in the business (Scots concernments do not much take with Englishmen) that they thought it not worth the pains of going to the door'.[77]

This was not the first time that English disinclinations had hampered Scottish business. On 3 December 1656, Sir Thomas Wroth successfully

---

[73] Patrick Little, 'The Political Career of Roger Boyle, Lord Broghill, 1636–1660' (Ph.D thesis, University of London, 2000), pp. 230–1.
[74] Stephen, II, 39–41.
[75] *Wariston Diary*, III, 81–2, 84, 86; Stephen, II, 42–4; Burton, II, 249–53.
[76] *Wariston Diary*, III, 82.　　[77] Stephen, II, 43–4.

moved that a bill on recusants should take precedence over the Scottish union bill.[78] Subsequent delays to the union bill were caused by the English preoccupation with the Nayler case, and its eventual collapse was no doubt caused, at least in part, by English reluctance to give it parliamentary time. One objection to the bill was that the English members did not understand Scottish laws, causing Samuel Disbrowe to exclaim: 'this is a judicature of the three nations, so I wonder why ignorance of their laws should excuse'.[79] In April 1657 Wroth was again showing his prejudices against the Scots, when he attacked the confirmation of former ordinances 'by the lump' as being 'like the way of Scotland', where the lords of the articles prepared legislation before the session.[80] Some English members ridiculed Scottish matters. English officials who had 'gone native' by supporting Scottish interests were a favourite target. In December 1656 Lambert called Judge George Smyth 'another St George risen up for Scotland', and in January 1657 Thomas Bampfield made similarly snide comments about Judge William Lawrence.[81] English members were not always unsympathetic, especially where their own interests were concerned. Vested interests smoothed the passage of legislation on Scottish donatives, as we have seen, and on 18 December Thomas Burton found that a group of members from northern England had gathered in a pub with a number of 'Scotchmen' to discuss the borders bill, which concerned them all equally.[82] But when it came to trade, and to customs in particular, English members opposed moves led by the provost of Edinburgh and supported by the Scottish councillors to reduce the payments due on Scottish coal.[83]

In the second Protectorate Parliament, Scottish money bills were apparently less controversial than they had been in 1654–5. The first Scottish assessment bill, to raise £15,000 in three years, was introduced on 28 May, and referred to the committee of Scottish affairs two days later.[84] It was reported to the Commons by Sir James MacDowall on 8 June.[85] The second bill, which formed part of the general assessment levied across the three nations, was drawn up by three Scottish members: MacDowall, Tweeddale, and Smyth. On 10 June it was moved by Downing that the Scottish rate would go 'hand-in-hand with that for England' and, despite efforts by some members to reduce it further, on the same day it was agreed that the Scots would pay £6,000 *per mensem*.[86] Both bills duly became acts on 26 June. As in 1654–5, George Monck was supportive of the Scots position. On 4 June 1657 he asked Thurloe that when the general assessment bill was brought in 'you will consider this poor country', and urged

---

[78] Burton, I, 6.   [79] Burton, I, 18.   [80] Burton, II, 47.   [81] Burton, I, 18, 330.
[82] Burton, I, 175.   [83] Burton, II, 273.   [84] *CJ*, VII, 541–2.   [85] *CJ*, VII, 550.
[86] *CJ*, VII, 554; Burton, II, 207, 213–14.

proportionate taxation: 'unless there be some course taken, that they may come in equality with England, it will go hard with this people ... since we have united them into one commonwealth, I think it will be most equal to bring them into an equality'.[87] Monck's plea came too late, however, and on 16 June he told Thurloe that the final arrangement was not ideal, 'for truly, though the Scotch gentlemen above are well satisfied with it, the Scotch gentlemen here [in Scotland] think it very much'.[88] Monck's hint that the Scottish members at Westminster were becoming detached from public opinion at home is interesting. It suggests that the interplay of vested interests, of high politics and matters of constitutional importance, had taken over Scottish affairs in the Parliament; and, after more than nine months away from home, even the 'native' members were in danger of becoming divorced from what those north of the border considered to be 'Scottish interests'.

IRELAND, 1656–7

The Irish elections in 1656 were held in a very different climate from those in 1654. With the generally popular Henry Cromwell in charge as acting governor, the Irish Protestants were happy to co-operate with the return of government candidates, many of whom were provided with seats in 'safe' constituencies, while the radical army officers were reduced to a handful of seats in Ulster and the south-east. Of the thirty members of Parliament returned, nineteen were Irish Protestants (eleven of whom had sat in 1654–5), eight were moderate 'Cromwellians', and only three were army radicals.[89] Management of business at Westminster was again conducted through the committee of Irish affairs, which was appointed on 23 September 1656. The initial roll-call of the committee included Broghill and ten other Irish members.[90] Lord Broghill did not manage business in the House, instead acting behind the scenes, intervening on specific issues at moments of crisis, and advising Henry Cromwell on the overall strategy that would best advance Irish legislation in the Parliament and the English council.[91] Instead, the most important figures were Henry Cromwell's agents, all of whom held Irish seats: Anthony Morgan, William Aston, Sir John Reynolds, and (to a lesser extent) John Bridges. They also received occasional support (and more frequent obstruction) from Charles Fleetwood, who continued as lord deputy and therefore had overall responsibility for Irish affairs.[92] Henry's agents had charge of the four bills that formed the core of

[87] TSP, VI, 330.   [88] TSP, VI, 351–2.   [89] Little, 'Irish Representation', 344–7.
[90] CJ, VII, 427.   [91] Little, Broghill, pp. 135–6.   [92] Burton, I, 215, 337.

the Irish government's legislative programme: those for union, attainder of Irish rebels, the land settlement, and assessments.

The Irish union bill, which had its first reading on 15 November 1656, was read for the second time and committed on the nineteenth of that month, and thereafter ran in parallel with the bill for Scotland.[93] Aston and Reynolds pushed for the Irish bill to be considered during December, although the concentration of the Commons on the Nayler case meant it was put off time and again.[94] When a grand committee eventually debated the union on 17 January 1657, there was a long debate about 'that clause about quitting that nation of custom', which was described by Thomas Burton as 'the main of all'.[95] The prospect of Irish merchants gaining free trade was undoubtedly unpopular with their English counterparts, and the issue had to be referred to a sub-committee,[96] where the bill apparently stalled. Before it could be revived the kingship debates began, starving the union bill of parliamentary time, and eventually killing it off completely.[97] Other Irish bills looked like sharing the same fate. In February and March 1657 there were repeated complaints by managers that the Irish members were disillusioned with the slow rate of progress. On 3 March Reynolds told Henry Cromwell that he was particularly annoyed that 'the new model of government ... takes up the whole time, and no room for Ireland in the thoughts of any until this be despatched'.[98] On 17 March he reported that 'I am not yet enabled to present unto your Lordship a full account of the public settlement, and therefore Ireland is still in arrear with its four bills.'[99] A week later he was a little more hopeful, considering that Irish support for kingship might pay dividends for domestic legislation: 'I hope one or two bills will be the guerdon [= reward] of your servants here, whose diligence is taken notice of, and also unanimity: except two persons, all those of Ireland are of one mind.'[100] Reynolds's optimism was not well founded. While the Irish attainder bill finally received a second reading on 30 March (over two months after its first), progress thereafter was slow; and the bill for settling lands, which had been ordered on 6 February, did not receive its first reading until 11 May.[101] It is telling that on 29 April the Commons ordered that the committee of Irish affairs itself should be 'revived', apparently after it had given up meeting for lack of business.[102] On 26 May Morgan and Aston tried to cajole the House into making Irish business more of a priority, pointing out that

---

[93] *CJ*, VII, 454, 455.   [94] Burton, I, 95, 127, 215; *CJ*, VII, 464, 466–7, 468.
[95] Burton, I, 352.
[96] T. C. Barnard, 'Planters and Policies in Cromwellian Ireland', *Past and Present*, 61 (1973), 62–3.
[97] Little, 'First Unionists?', 51–2.
[98] BL, Lansdowne MS 821, fo. 316r; see also *ibid.*, fo. 296r.
[99] BL, Lansdowne MS 821, fo. 356r; for Bridges's comments, see *ibid.*, fo. 326v.
[100] BL, Lansdowne MS 822, fo. 3.   [101] *CJ*, VII, 481, 486, 515, 532.   [102] *CJ*, VII, 526.

it was 'of great consideration, otherwise all the expense of blood and treasure spent there will be lost'.[103] In the end, important Irish business had to be squeezed into the dying hours of the first sitting. The land settlement bill was passed on 8 June, after nearly five months under consideration.[104] On 23 June Morgan apologised for the brevity of his report to Henry Cromwell, as 'I have been so close tied to the House, lest I should lose an opportunity I wait for to pass the bill of attainder (which is engrossed), that I have scarce time left to write.'[105] The bill was read for the third time, and passed after various amendments, on 25 June – one day before the end of the sitting.[106]

While government legislation was delayed by more important matters, the progress of other Irish business was hampered by English vested interests in the land settlement there. In March 1657, the surveyor Benjamin Worsley warned of divisions between the adventurers (who had invested in the reconquest of Ireland in the early 1640s) and the soldiers (who were owed Irish lands in lieu of pay arrears). When it came to the land settlement, Worsley 'saw several acts were prepared, and actually given in the House in order to it', but he found 'little union between the adventurers and the soldiers in this business, and not much agreement even among the adventurers themselves – the interest of those who were got into their land being one thing, and the interest of such who were deficient being another'.[107] Private bills to recompense individual Irish Protestants had to compete with English claims over the rapidly diminishing stocks of Irish land. The claims of the City of Gloucester were particularly worrying for the Irish members, as there were other English towns and cities waiting to see if their test case was successful. Anthony Morgan told Henry Cromwell that he feared that 'the Gloucester bill ... will engage all the land and Houses in Ireland', with nothing left for the Irish Protestants;[108] but when the bill was passed the danger had been headed off, as a new proviso preserved the claims of those soldiers who had served Parliament in Ireland before 1649.[109] This proviso was a victory for Morgan and his friends, especially Lord Broghill, who went on to press for further compensation for the pre-1649 officers in early June. Yet Broghill's illness during June threatened to scupper the business. He wrote frantic letters to Whitelocke, who agreed to introduce a letter that Broghill had drafted, and to support it in the House,[110] and it received the approval of the Parliament only at the very last moment, on 26 June – the first day that Broghill had struggled back to Parliament to take his seat.[111]

---

[103] Burton, II, 124.   [104] *CJ*, VII, 550.   [105] BL, Lansdowne MS 822, fo. 112r.
[106] *CJ*, VII, 559, 561, 571, 573, 574.   [107] BL, Lansdowne MS 821, fo. 352r–v.
[108] BL, Lansdowne MS 822, fo. 45r.   [109] *CJ*, VII, 530.
[110] Longleat, Whitelocke Papers 18, fo. 64r–v; Whitelocke, *Diary*, pp. 468–9.
[111] *CJ*, VII, 576.

Unlike the cordial gentleman's agreement over the fate of Scottish estates, the Irish land question was acrimonious. Two cases, in particular, caused a revival of the political faction-fighting that characterised this Parliament. A bill confirming an earlier grant of £1,000 per annum in Irish lands to Lord Broghill was read for the first time in April, and swiftly passed through its second reading and the committee stage, with the report being delivered by the Scottish agent George Downing. Yet at the final reading, on 5 June, Broghill's enemies among the army interest turned up in force and, led by Lambert, opposed a proviso increasing the land grant by 2,000 acres to make up for mistakes in the land survey. The vote was eventually passed, but Lambert, Fleetwood, Sydenham, and John Disbrowe withdrew immediately beforehand, in a calculated insult.[112] The second row was intimately connected with the first. A motion on 8 June to grant Fleetwood £1,500 per annum in Irish lands, to reward his services there in earlier years, proved highly controversial, with Fleetwood's allies in the army ending up speaking and voting against it. This was not a straightforward reward, rather an attempt by the more moderate courtiers to mollify Fleetwood, whom they soon expected to be replaced as Lord Deputy by Henry Cromwell. As Lambert said, 'I know it will not please him. I wish it had not been mentioned.'[113] Anthony Morgan, who, with William Aston, had first suggested rewarding Fleetwood, was appalled at the resulting spat: 'I am sorry I moved it, since it occasioned so much stir, but I thought it reasonable that at parting we should show kindness.'[114] The vote was narrowly passed, but Fleetwood declined to accept the grant.[115]

The debate over the Irish assessments also caused great ill feeling. This was partly because the army interest, indignant at Irish support for Broghill and the kingship, tried to increase the rate. Adam Baynes moved on 10 June 1657 that the Irish assessments should comply with the 1654 order, which increased them at regular intervals, even though the English burden had been steadily falling in the meantime. This led to protests from Irish members, who pointed out the poverty of their constituencies. Another hostile speaker, William Sydenham, then provoked them further by saying that Ireland was only a colony and a conquered nation, which should pay its own way. Morgan riposted, saying that even colonies should not be ruined, for 'it is not in your interest to flay, but to clip, your sheep, if you hope for another fleece', but he was countered by Lambert, who called, once again, for an incremental scale, 'for they grow better and better'. When it came to a division, the rate of £10,000 was imposed by 71 to 51 votes.[116] But this was

[112] Little, 'Political Career of Lord Broghill', p. 159.   [113] *CJ*, VII, 550; Burton, II, 198.
[114] BL, Lansdowne MS 822, fo. 84r.   [115] Burton, II, 198n, 200.
[116] Burton, II, 209–13; *CJ*, VII, 554.

not the end of the matter. On 12 June Fleetwood presented a paper 'from some members that serve for Ireland' asking for a reduction to £7,000. This caused a furore, as English members were concerned that it went against the orders of the House, and, 'the example of it being disliked generally', the paper was withdrawn. When on the next day it was proposed to reduce the tax to £8,000, the motion was rejected by five votes, and the rate was eventually settled at £9,000 a month.[117] This ended the argument, but bad feeling continued, and 'it was moved that the members serving for Ireland might be sent to the Tower for their contest about the proportioning the assessment twixt England and Ireland'.[118]

The inequalities of the assessment tax underlined the precarious state of Ireland without a formal union bill. A paper of complaints, probably dating from the summer of 1657, highlighted the unfairness of Ireland paying £9,000 a month while England had to find only £35,000. This, along with the heavy taxes which continued to be levied on all exports and imports, made the Irish Protestants feel like 'foreigners to our own country'.[119] Worse still, when the sitting ended on 26 June, the loose ends of the Humble Petition had not been tied up; and the most glaring omission was the failure to stipulate the number of members to be returned from Ireland in future Parliaments. In the absence of legislation on this and other aspects of the union, the Scots could fall back on the 1654 ordinance (which had passed, as it stood, as an act of Parliament in June 1657); the Irish were left with no such guarantees. The failure of the union bill cast a shadow over the 1656–7 sitting; but the Irish managers could be proud of their endeavours in other areas. Three of the four government bills had been passed, and numerous private grants had also gone through. More significantly, the Irish had remained united in their support of the reforming legislation, and had played an important role in bringing down the major-generals and in setting up the Humble Petition and Advice.

The great debates in 1656–7 had seen a high degree of co-operation between the Irish and Scottish members, but this reflected their common allegiance to Broghill, rather than a sense of fellow feeling that bridged the North Channel. When it came to domestic affairs, there were occasional moments of interaction. In June 1657, the attempt to broaden the Scottish franchise was supported by 'all the Irish commissioners [MPs] at my Lord Broghill's desire'.[120] In the previous March, there were reports that Henry Cromwell's enemy, the Irish colonel Jerome Sankey, was intimate with the leading Scottish Protester, James Guthrie.[121] There are also signs that the Irish and Scottish union bills were designed to run together, at least once they

---

[117] Burton, II, 224–6, 245–7; *CJ*, VII, 555, 557.   [118] BL, Lansdowne MS 822, fo. 92r.
[119] *CSPI, 1647–60*, 699.   [120] Stephen, II, 42.   [121] Stephen, II, 30.

reached their respective grand committees. But even in the union legislation relations between the Scots and the Irish remained fragile. On 4 December 1656 there was 'a great dispute' among interested members whether the Scottish or Irish union bill should proceed to debate first, with the Irish agent, William Aston, eventually giving way.[122] Aston was also at the centre of a row over Irish and Scottish assessments in June 1657. The Irish members were understandably unhappy at being left with a rate of £9,000 while Scotland had £6,000, but there was nothing but malice in Aston's suggestion that Scotland should instead bear £20,000 a month, 'or at least £12,000', as a 'richer nation' by far than Ireland.[123] It is perhaps significant that both incidents took place during Broghill's absence from the Commons due to gout. He had created this artificial union of the two nations, and it seems that it could not survive without his leadership.

1658 AND 1659

The brief second sitting of the Parliament in January and February 1658 achieved nothing in terms of Irish and Scottish affairs. Fleetwood had promised to consult Broghill and other allies of Henry Cromwell over the Irish revenues on 19 January,[124] but the Parliament was dissolved before any progress was made. This was more than merely a temporary setback. The Humble Petition had been passed in a provisional form, with various matters set aside for later legislation, including the distribution of Irish and Scottish seats. The chaotic collapse of the sitting brought the second Protectorate Parliament to a close without the passage of any further bills, and left Irish and Scottish rights of representation undecided. Perhaps as a reaction to the uncertain legitimacy of Irish and Scottish representation, the management of elections for the third Protectorate Parliament in the winter of 1658–9 was much more heavy-handed than in earlier years. The relatively free elections, conducted with the minimum of governmental interference, witnessed in 1654 and 1656 now gave way to stringent measures, co-ordinated not in Dublin or Edinburgh but at Whitehall. Thurloe sent up lists of approved candidates to take safe seats, and Monck's brother-in-law, Thomas Clarges, advised on both Scottish and Irish elections, promising to provide a phalanx of supporters for the Protectoral regime. The results were mixed. In Ireland the collaboration between Henry Cromwell and the Irish Protestants continued, with twenty Protestants and seven Cromwellians being returned, while the army interest could manage only three members. But the quality of the members was doubtful – only five of the twenty Irish Protestants had

---

[122] Burton, I, 12.   [123] Burton, II, 213.   [124] BL, Add. MS 43724, fo. 23.

sat in previous Parliaments – and there were signs of tension within the Irish Protestant community during the elections, as exemplified in the row between Broghill and his former ally, Vincent Gookin, over the Cork seats.[125]

In the Scottish elections, twenty-eight members were returned, with seventeen Englishmen and only eleven Scots. Six of these English members were carpet-baggers, including three with personal or family connections with the House of Cromwell (Lawrence Oxburgh, Edward Sedgewick, and William Stane) and Monck's Cornish cousin, Sir Peter Killigrew. As Frances Dow has pointed out, this imbalance marked not so much a triumph for 'the English interest' as 'a result of the efforts of the Protectoral party in England to capture as many "safe" seats as possible'.[126] Yet the details of the native Scottish members suggest that Scotland had become increasingly divided along religious lines. The minority Protester faction still looked to the army interest (now among the opponents of the regime) in England for political allies, but unlike in 1656–7 this brought them into conflict with George Monck, who had begun to favour the rival, Resolutioner party. In particular, Monck had turned against the leading Scottish ally of the Protesters, the Marquess of Argyll, and tried, unsuccessfully, to block his election in 1659. At least four other Protesters were returned alongside Argyll to the Commons; the election of others was only narrowly avoided;[127] and in Parliament they were assisted by Johnston of Wariston, who sat in the Other House.[128] Overall, the Irish and Scottish elections in 1659 saw a deterioration in the quality of representation in both nations. A significant minority of the Englishmen returned for Scotland lacked a direct connection with their constituents, and the native Scottish members were deeply divided among themselves. The Irish members, although mostly loyal to the Protectorate, included many new and inexperienced men, and key parliamentary managers were no longer in the Commons: Bridges had retired; Reynolds had drowned; and Lord Broghill, as a member of the Other House, could only be a spectator of debates in the Commons.[129]

As in 1654 and 1656–7, Irish and Scottish business in the 1659 Parliament was dominated by the great debates on the constitution. The importance

---

[125] Little, 'Irish Representation', 348–52.

[126] Dow, *Cromwellian Scotland*, p. 238; see also Casada, 'Scottish Representatives', 125 and *passim*.

[127] In the Perthshire election, the Scottish councillor, Sir Edward Rodes, was challenged by John Campbell, Fiar of Glenorchy, and only narrowly won the seat: see NAS, GD 112/39/104/1 (Henry Christie to Glenorchy, 29 January 1659). Monck's comment that Argyll and his friends tried to get 'all Scotchmen' chosen (*TSP*, VII, 583–4) no doubt refers to incidents like this.

[128] NRAS 217, Stuart Earls of Moray MSS, box 6, no. 140.

[129] Little, 'Irish Representation', 348–50.

attached to the bill of recognition of the Protector, acceptance of the Humble Petition, and the problem of transacting with the Other House provoked a clash between the Protectoral 'court' party, now allied with the Presbyterian interest, and the republican commonwealthsmen, increasingly in conjunction with the disaffected army officers. Yet, instead of sidelining Irish and Scottish affairs, in this Parliament the row over the future of the Protectorate sucked them in. As early as January 1659 doubts were voiced about rights to sit, with reports that 'there will be a considerable party for the Scots members to sit, but not for the Irish'.[130] Other comments and murmurs of discontent followed,[131] but in early March the issue exploded. The immediate trigger was the debate on the Other House, during which it became clear that 'most of the members of Ireland and Scotland [had] voted for it', prompting the opposition to 'set on foot the debate about the illegality of their sitting'.[132] As the Commons argued backwards and forwards over the course of nearly two weeks, the Scottish union was the more favoured of the two, not only because the Scottish members could claim a right to sit through the act of union, but also because critics of the government were happy to see 'my Lord Argyll's presence with some other his countrymen', whereas the Irish were considered government stooges to a man.[133] When the Scottish right was put to the vote on 21 March, it passed by 211 to 120 – a majority of 91 – while the Irish members' right was confirmed two days later by a much thinner House, by 156 votes to 106 – giving a smaller majority of 50.[134]

The union debates did not mark an upsurge of interest in Irish and Scottish affairs among English members, a sudden acceptance of the importance of their place within the union. Rather, it revealed the downside of Irish and Scottish successes as a voting bloc in the kingship debates two years before, for they were now perceived not as representatives of the other two nations but as the staunchest supporters of the Protectorate in the Commons. This was accepted as a truism by both sides in the debate, and the union was strongly supported by other Cromwellians and bitterly derided by the commonwealthsmen and their allies. According to Thomas Skipwith, 'they chose such as never saw Scotland. They are nominated, but how [were they] chosen?';[135] for Slingsby Bethel, these 'usurpers in making laws for England' were 'chosen by the pretender's [i.e., Protector's] interest'.[136] Hesilrige raised the matter of the past form of the Irish and Scots in 1656–7, reminding members that 'They overthrew the Instrument of Government and made the Petition and Advice.'[137] In debate, the issue was

---

[130] *Clarke Papers*, III, 176.   [131] *TSP*, VII, 605; BL, Lansdowne MS 823, fo. 204r.
[132] BL, Lansdowne MS 823, fo. 239r.   [133] Bodl., MS Clarendon 60, fo. 224r.
[134] *CJ*, VII, 616, 619.   [135] Schilling, pp. 209–10.
[136] [Slingsby Bethel,] *A True and Impartial Narrative* (1659), pp. 5, 7.   [137] Schilling, p. 247.

not Ireland and Scotland at all, but the fate of the Protectorate itself. The few Irish and Scottish members who took part in the debate also tended to treat union as a political football. There was little of the personal experience, the pleading for local concessions that had appeared when assessments were discussed in 1657. Instead, the arguments were broad, constitutional, over-arching, and increasingly divorced from the reality of the constituencies the Irish and Scottish members supposedly represented.[138] This can also be seen in the impingement of party politics on national interests. Arthur Annesley, as a crypto-royalist, was happy to go against the views of most Irish Protestants by calling for an end to the union and return to an Irish Parliament at Dublin.[139] Even more striking were the comments of another Irish member, Dudley Loftus, who opposed the withdrawal of Scottish members from the House, saying 'to withdraw will not stand with our trust, nor discharge our duty to him that called us, and his father that redeemed us'.[140] Such emotive language may account for the reluctance of some Scottish members to become too involved in the debate. As James Sharp reported, when the Solemn League and Covenant was used by some Presbyterians to justify union with Scotland, 'none of our own countrymen had the courage or honesty once to mention it, or plead anything upon that score in any of their studied speeches'.[141]

Even though the debates on the union had little to do with Ireland and Scotland, their result – the passing of a vote allowing the nations' members to continue sitting in the Commons – was of great importance to both. It was only after their legitimacy had been decided that Irish and Scottish bills could be considered. Accordingly, support for union among Irish and Scottish members was unanimous.[142] On 1 April, a committee of Scottish affairs was appointed, which initially included thirteen Scottish members (but, apparently deliberately, excluded Argyll) and was later expanded to encompass all of them.[143] The Scots were still divided among themselves over religious issues, and allied with rival groups in the English council to further their ends. The Protesters were favoured by a group of officers around the disaffected Independent divine, Dr John Owen, which included Fleetwood and Disbrowe, and there were reportedly tensions between the government and Wariston, who was judged to be 'Argyll's man'.[144] The Resolutioners again looked to Broghill and sympathetic English councillors such as Thurloe and Philip Jones,[145] and they could now add Monck to that number.

---

[138] See Burton, IV, 137–8, 169, 187, 241–2, and *passim*.   [139] Little, 'First Unionists?', 55–6.
[140] Schilling, p. 231.   [141] Stephen, II, 160.
[142] Derbyshire Record Office, D258/10/9/2 (Sir John Gell's diary), fo. 6r.
[143] CJ, VII, 623, 636; Hesilrige moved for Argyll's addition on 7 April (Burton, IV, 364).
[144] Stephen, II, 158, 160.   [145] Stephen, II, 148–9.

Religious issues came to a head in late March and early April, when a fast day was declared by the Commons. Previous fasts (notably that in October 1656) had been rejected by the Resolutioners, as coming from the civil power, and the Protesters now threatened to use the matter to embarrass their rivals. On 31 March it was reported that Argyll was a member of the fast committee, although 'friends' of the Resolutioners such as the Presbyterians Lambert Godfrey and Thomas Grove were also included. In debate a few days later, Argyll caused a stir by saying that Scottish ministers should not be required to observe the fast, but it was suspected that this was a ploy, as his speech was followed by those of Sir Henry Vane and other commonwealthsmen, who proceeded to attack the Scottish church.[146] In the face of such criticism, the threat was defused in a new way. In mid-April, the Resolutioners were persuaded to conform, using the convenient fiction (as apparently suggested by Monck and Broghill) that the synods and presbyteries were to hold fasts on their own initiative to coincide with the national day.[147] The reason for this may not have been purely political, for in the same period there were hopes that the Presbyterian members would push through 'the Confession of Faith agreed upon by the late Assembly of Westminster', with minor modifications concerning church discipline, and it seems that many Resolutioner ministers were satisfied with this compromise.[148] Proposals for further union legislation were also marked by political and religious differences among the Scots. The matter had been raised during the March debates, when the commonwealthsmen proposed that, if the Scots were ejected from the Commons, 'a bill [was] to be prepared to confirm the union, and give them power to send members hither'.[149] After the Scottish members were confirmed, the union was again debated, this time in the context of a new union bill to replace the ordinance-turned-act of 1657, which had proved unsatisfactory in 1654 and 1656–7. In mid-April 1659, Argyll reportedly moved 'in the bill for union for Scotland and England that security to our church judicatures and disciplines as it was in the year 1650 may be put in as one of the clauses' – causing consternation among the supporters of the Resolutioners, who realised that this would exclude them entirely, as 'it gives the Protesters their will in all the differences betwixt us and them'.[150] There is no evidence that burgh rights had resurfaced as an issue in this latest round of union debates; but, even if it had been contentious, there is no doubt that the most serious rift between Scottish members was now religious and political.

---

[146] Stephen, II, 161–2, 164, 165–6; Burton, IV, 330–2.
[147] NLS, Wodrow Folio MS 26, fos. 77, 163r, 169r; Stephen, II, 172–3.
[148] Stephen, II, 164, 168, 171. [149] BL, Lansdowne MS 823, fo. 261r.
[150] Stephen, II, 172–4.

In the last weeks of the Parliament, the Commons became the arena for a battle between Fleetwood's client, Jerome Sankey, and Henry Cromwell's ally, Dr William Petty. On 24 March 1659, Sankey submitted articles against Petty,[151] accusing him of taking bribes and embezzling lands when administering the settlement in Ireland. Petty, who was still in Ireland, hastened to Westminster to refute the charges, which he suspected of being politically motivated – a thinly veiled attack on Henry Cromwell's government – and made a vigorous speech in his defence on 21 April, the day before the Parliament was dissolved.[152] The progress of other Irish matters was less dramatic. The committee of Irish affairs was appointed on 1 April (with Annesley conspicuous by his absence),[153] and by the middle of the month a programme of Irish legislation had been drawn up. As Dudley Loftus told Henry Cromwell, 'several bills are prepared for Ireland: an act for settlement of the ministry of Ireland upon legal title . . . an act for union, [and] an act for probate of wills' as well as measures to strengthen Henry's government, drafted by Loftus himself.[154] The Irish members, at least, seem to have emerged from the union debates with a renewed sense of purpose. On 12 April, Sir Maurice Fenton told his patron, the Earl of Cork, that things were returning to normal: 'the occasion of my so long silence is because Parliament did nothing concerning Ireland until 3 or 4 days since, when they named a committee for Irish affairs, which are to offer things for the benefit of the country'. He went on to request that his constituents (in County Cork) send their grievances to him 'for the encouraging the plantation of English in Ireland' as well as their suggestions on 'how our tax be eased', and asked for any private instructions from the earl himself. Fenton's letter ended with an expression of faithfulness rare even among English members in the 1650s: 'It is, my lord, my very great study and ambition really to contribute some advantage for the country that elected me, I can promise them I shall with industry and fidelity serve them in what they shall command me.'[155]

CONCLUSION

The tendency of historians to concentrate on elections and great debates distorts the nature of Irish and Scottish affairs at Westminster. Ethnic labels are often misleading: Scots were drawn up against Scots over the extension of burgh rights in 1654 and 1656, and over church government in 1657 and

---

[151] *CJ*, VII, 619.
[152] *TSP*, VII, 651; T. A. Larcom, ed., *The History of the Survey of Ireland Commonly Known as the Down Survey by Dr William Petty* (Dublin, 1851), pp. 292–300.
[153] *CJ*, VII, 623; Annesley was added on Hesilrige's motion on 7 April (Burton, IV, 364).
[154] BL, Lansdowne MS 823, fo. 297r–v.   [155] NLI, Lismore MS 13228, unfol.

1659. At the same time, there is plenty of evidence that Englishmen in the Scottish government or at Whitehall were more than happy to become involved in traditional Scottish disputes. The Irish were less divided among themselves, but they still experienced a blurring of ethnic divisions, as their interests were championed as readily by Cromwellian officials as by members of Parliament from the Irish Protestant community. This integration between the English and the other two nations (at least in political terms) explains the strong degree of uniformity which emerged between the Irish and Scots during the militia bill and the kingship debates in 1657, and in defence of the Protectorate in 1659; but it should not disguise the real differences between the nations on domestic affairs. There were surprisingly few instances in which Scots and Irish collaborated to their own advantage, and these occurred mostly in 1656–7 when they were being encouraged to do so by the strong political lead given by Lord Broghill. Domestic legislation tended to push Ireland and Scotland apart, even when matters such as the union bills were considered in parallel. Indeed, when it came to assessment bills, Ireland and Scotland often found themselves in direct competition, with predictable results. This mixture of indifference and rivalry between the Irish and Scots matched that of the English members when dealing with either of them. For many Englishmen, the presence of the other two nations was baffling, unwelcome, and (especially in 1659) illegal.

Despite the many problems facing the Irish and Scottish members during these Parliaments, they never lost their appetite for pursuing domestic legislation. The 1654 Parliament demonstrated that both nations had a desire for Westminster solutions to their problems. This desire can also be seen among the distractions of the 1656–7 sitting, and was redoubled once their right to sit had been confirmed at the end of March 1659. Such an urge to legislate suggests that, by 1659, little distinguished the Irish and Scots from their English counterparts, despite the posturing and name-calling that attended the union debates. Ireland and Scotland were treated as a source for electoral patronage no different from Cornwall or Wiltshire; Irish and Scottish affairs had become an accepted part of parliamentary business; and the Irish and Scots were happy to see Westminster as the centre of their political world. This was perhaps a sign that, despite the difficulties, the Cromwellian Union was in reasonable working order. In the words of one native Scot, speaking in the Commons in March 1659, 'I think myself at home when I am here.'[156]

---

[156] William Ross of Drumgarland, MP for Dumfriesshire (Burton, IV, 138).

13

Conclusion

The apparent failure of the Protectorate Parliaments is usually seen as contributing to, and being symptomatic of, the deep-seated problems that afflicted the Cromwellian regime. There is an element of truth in this. All three Parliaments were at times crippled by factionalism; two of the three were 'addled', producing no legislation; and of the four sittings all but one ended with a premature dissolution by the Protector. But the traditional account goes beyond these obvious shortcomings to damn the Parliaments and the regime entirely. The failure of most of these Parliaments to fulfil the expectations of the Protectors appears to underline not only the weakness of the regime as a whole, but also the shortcomings of the Protectors as politicians. Thus, Oliver Cromwell is sometimes characterised as a distant, rather other-worldly figure, unwilling to interfere in parliamentary business, and passive in the face of mounting difficulties at Westminster; and Richard comes across as an inept ruler, whose inexperience and weak character meant that his Parliament, like his Protectorate, was bound to fail. Such assumptions are not supported by this present study. Instead of portraying the Parliaments as an unremittingly negative feature of the Protectorate, the picture that emerges from this book is more mixed, and often surprisingly positive. While deadlock and division certainly existed, and fundamental disagreements over religion and reform were indeed major obstacles to the Protectorate government, the attitude of members of Parliament was often very constructive, and there was a considerable appetite for Westminster solutions to local and regional problems. The government, too, was not inflexible, and there was a growing desire to secure a long-term settlement, and to meet its critics halfway. In this, the Protectors seem to have been surprisingly successful. This positive element can be seen in all the chapters above.

The written constitutions that underpinned the Protectorate, and that contributed so much to the distinctive character of the period, were never seen as immutable. Indeed, there were many different attempts to modify or overthrow the existing arrangements, and these provide an important

294

indicator of how the government was shifting politically during the Protectorate. The Instrument of Government of December 1653 was seen as the army's constitution, and as such attracted considerable hostility from the Presbyterians and their allies in the 1654–5 Parliament, much to Oliver Cromwell's disgust. The Presbyterian agenda was to reduce the power of the council (where the army had its seat of power) and to elevate that of Parliament, so that Parliament had a far greater say in the executive as well as the legislative functions of government. Another important factional interest opposed to the Instrument was the group known as the 'civilian courtiers', who proposed the Remonstrance in February 1657, offering the crown to Oliver, and asking for a return to the 'ancient constitution'. This document would have given King Oliver the sort of prerogative powers and governmental freedoms enjoyed by King Charles before the Civil War, and, unsurprisingly, the Presbyterians supported it only after drastic modifications. In order to get the new civilian constitution through the Parliament, compromises had to be made, especially over the powers of Parliament and the limitation of religious toleration, and with Oliver's refusal of the crown other changes were brought in to ensure that the new arrangement was acceptable both to him and to the army. The changing constitutions and the debates surrounding them reveal more than the details of government, however: what was happening, especially in 1657, was a dramatic shift away from the army rule and towards civilian forms of government, and this was to have massive political consequences for the last years of the Protectorate.

The third and fourth chapters, dealing with elections and exclusions, emphasise that the 1654–5 Parliament, so often criticised for its factionalism and sterility, was not born of controversy and opposition. The 'traditional country gentlemen' were keen to be elected, and very few were formally excluded by the council, while the withdrawal of perhaps fifty or eighty members who refused to sign the 'recognition' of the government on 12 September caused less controversy than one might have expected. The elections in 1656 were much more divisive, as the major-generals were keen to have their own men returned locally, and in some places their plans were overturned by massive resistance, especially from the 'old Parliamentarians', the traditional supporters of Parliament during the 1640s, in the south and east of England. In return, a large number of these members were then excluded. The fact that the disputed elections and subsequent exclusions occurred in the old Parliamentarian strongholds is significant. The opponents of the regime, led by the 'Presbyterians', were not engaged in plots to overthrow Oliver Cromwell and usher in the Stuarts; they were intent on changing the Protectorate from the inside, by securing seats in Parliament. They were also confident that the major-generals could now be challenged without weakening the Protectorate generally. Other regions, with more mixed or even pro-royalist traditions in the 1640s, were remarkably quiescent during the 1656 elections, and proportionately fewer members from these areas were excluded. Put together, the evidence from elections and exclusions suggests that the regime was in fact relatively stable, and that dissent was channelled into Parliament, where it could be won over, or at least contained, rather than being forced into conspiracy and revolt. The return to the old franchise and distribution of seats (except in Ireland and Scotland) in 1659 may have increased the desire for ordinary gentlemen to sit in Parliament – it certainly led to more disputes, and to greater efforts by the government to manage the elections. The removal of the council's power to exclude members, effected under the Humble Petition and Advice, meant that the government could not ban troublemakers, and this resulted in the return of men openly hostile to the regime. This was a cause of weakness, of course, but it also helped to reconcile those very Presbyterians and 'old Parliamentarians' who had opposed the Protectorate in 1656 and who found Protector Richard a much more acceptable ruler than his father.

An analysis of the rival factions demonstrates that the political, as well as the constitutional, landscape was changed greatly during the Protectorate. In 1654–5 the opposition, led by the Presbyterians and the country gentry, was successfully countered by a united council, but already there were distinctions being made between the army officers and the 'civilians' led by men such as John Thurloe and Lord Broghill. During the 1656–7 sitting, this led to a rift in the council, which severely affected its ability to manage affairs at Westminster. The civilian courtiers who brought in the Remonstrance were now in open opposition to the army interest, and made common cause with the Presbyterians, who were slowly turning from opposition to co-operation with the Protectorate regime. It was this alliance between courtiers and Presbyterians that brought down the major-generals in January 1657 and ensured that the Remonstrance gained a hearing; efforts to keep the Presbyterians on board explain the transformation of the Remonstrance into the Humble Petition and Advice during the spring. By 1659, and the opening of Richard Cromwell's Parliament, key Presbyterians were supporting the Protectorate, and they played an important role as government managers in the Parliament. There were risks in this, as the army was forced into opposition instead, and sought allies among the disaffected former Rumpers, the commonwealthsmen, but the winning over of the Presbyterians and the traditional Parliamentarian gentry marked an important shift in the Protectorate, towards a stable, broad-based government.

When the constitutions, elections and exclusions, and factionalism are looked at in detail, a pattern starts to form. The Protectorate Parliaments were not intrinsically flawed. Ordinary 'country' gentlemen, as well as committed Presbyterians, had a great appetite to engage with the regime, to sit in Parliament, to support certain initiatives, to oppose others, and always to seek to change the nature of the government *from within*. In collusion with the civilian courtiers, such changes were possible, with Parliament being the obvious vehicle for reform. This pushed the army – which had always been Oliver Cromwell's chief support – into opposition, and created difficulties for the Protector himself. In chapter 6, we turned to Oliver's own attitudes to Parliament, and it is here that the mixed success of the Protectorate Parliaments is highlighted most vividly. Oliver Cromwell was guided by the hope that he could reconcile the nation (as represented in Parliament) with the 'godly people' (most obviously fronted by the army). This was a common theme that emerged during the later 1640s and early 1650s. Although a supporter of Parliament in principle, Oliver was aware of the distance between the intolerance of most members of Parliament and his own (and the army's) concerns for liberty of conscience. The two goals were fundamentally irreconcilable, but Oliver's intransigence on this point per-haps explains the uneasiness of the last years of his reign, as the Presbyterians and courtiers seem to have taken charge of government policy, while the army interest still had a hold over the Protector. It was this tension that caused Oliver to accept the Humble Petition but not the crown, and that made the last months of his life so unsatisfactory, personally and politically. Richard Cromwell was not a man of his father's stamp. Without a strong belief in liberty of conscience and without close links with the army, he was free to take the obvious step – to secure a broad-based settlement by embra-cing the Presbyterians. This was a very dangerous tactic, but it very nearly worked. By the end of March 1659, the constitutional arguments in Parliament had largely been won. The new Protector's government had been 'recognised', the Other House was established, and the rights of Irish and Scottish members to sit had been accepted. But Richard had under-estimated the army's willingness to make yet another direct intervention in political affairs. The Parliament was dissolved and, after a few weeks of uncertainty, Richard resigned as Protector. Richard Cromwell may have been a very different ruler from Oliver, but the two men faced the same fundamental problem: how to reconcile the army and Parliament. It was this problem, rather than the intrinsic unpopularity of the Protectorate, that caused the downfall of the regime in May 1659.

The basic pattern established by the earlier chapters, that the Protectorate Parliaments were essentially constructive institutions, despite the enormity of the problems they faced, can also be seen in the areas of law reform and the judicature and religion. The legal system was ripe for reform, and previous initiatives under the Rump Parliament and Barebone's had not borne fruit. The programme of legal reform promoted in 1654–5 and 1656–7 was ambitious, involving changes to the law courts and the legal process, and it inevitably attracted opposition from lawyers who benefited from the existing arrangements. But the failure of the programme was the result of other factors: the pressures on parliamentary time created by the big constitutional and political debates, and the inability of an increasingly divided council to manage business in the Commons. The only time when the legal system did make headway was to prove divisive, as the case of the Quaker, James Nayler, raised questions about the Commons' ability to act as a court of law and prompted equally controversial efforts to erect a new upper chamber, the 'Other House'. Religion was perhaps the most difficult issue faced by these Parliaments, and it underlay the factional alignments discussed above. The army interest, like Oliver Cromwell, saw liberty of conscience as being at the heart of the matter, but this was incompatible with what the majority of members wanted, which was a national church with strict measures against heresy and blasphemy. The Presbyterian interest was again at the forefront of efforts to restrict liberty of conscience, and their activities can be seen in 1654–5 and 1656–7, especially within the debates on the Parliamentary Constitution, the Nayler case, and the modifications introduced in the Humble Petition and Advice. The advance of the Presbyterians was restricted by Oliver Cromwell's insistence on toleration, and it was only in Richard's Parliament that a new drive was begun, basing the national church on a slightly modified form of the Westminster Confession of 1647. This was an important cause of the breach with the army in April 1659, and again demonstrates how far the Protectorate had changed since its inception five and half years before.

The final three chapters explore further the theme that the Protectorate Parliaments helped to promote a greater degree of political stability than has often been recognised. The question of representation bulked large in parliamentary debate, and was a common rhetorical device, usually being used to argue that the government was trampling on the rights of 'the people' and of Parliament as their representatives. The reality was not quite so impressive, as often petitions and private bills were restricted or refused. But when the local position is studied in greater detail, the picture is not as gloomy. Members of Parliament were still representing their constituents, and working together for local concerns, even if their success was often hampered (like that of the proponents of legal reform) by the demands of the bigger issues that took up the majority of parliamentary time. When it came to the issue of taxation, English and Welsh members were vigorous in defence of their constituents' interests, even to the extent of dividing on regional rather than party lines, and ignoring political gains that could be made at the expense of their constituents. Such a local perspective underlines the normality of much of parliamentary business during this period, and again suggests that political stability was much better established than has been recognised.

This can also be seen in the case of foreign policy. Even in 1654–5, an aggressive, anti-Spanish policy was popular among members, and this continued in 1656–7. The stumbling block, as usual, was money, and Secretary Thurloe, in particular, went to great lengths to persuade members to increase direct and indirect taxation. The vote of £400,000 for the war in January 1657 was a major achievement and was probably the result of political horse-trading behind the scenes, with the government's abandonment of the major-generals as part of the deal. Richard Cromwell's pro-Swedish policy in the Baltic was also popular, and again provides evidence that the Presbyterians were managing business in the Commons at this time, much to the disgust of the army interest and the commonwealthsmen.

Such a view is reinforced by the chapter on Irish and Scottish affairs, which emphasises that business was often conducted in committees, and thus beneath the radar screens of historians working with the official sources. From 1654–5 onwards, many Irish and Scots were eager to engage with the regime and to seek solutions to their problems at Westminster. The major problem they faced was the dominance of the great debates in Parliament, and these often delayed business or prevented necessary bills from being passed. The importance of the Irish and Scots as supporters of the regime was especially apparent in 1657 and 1659, and created a further distraction, as some English members moved from treating them with indifference to outright hostility. Most striking, perhaps, is the continued sense of purpose among Irish and Scottish members after the bruising union debates of March 1659. In April, with new committees established, Irish and Scottish affairs were again promoted. This suggests that the Protectoral union was in a healthy state right to the end, and again points to a stability across the three nations that is not always apparent from the bitter disputes that dominated affairs at Westminster.

Three important themes can be extracted from this survey. The first is the rise of the Presbyterians and country gentry and the decline of the army interest. In 1654–5 the Presbyterians constituted the core of the parliamentary opposition, and leading figures were duly excluded in 1656; but events in the spring of 1657 brought them into a prominent position, from which they were able to influence the Humble Petition and Advice and to exert pressure on the Protectoral government. The result was a new Protectorate, which was not only civilian in ethos but also decidedly Presbyterian in outlook, notably when it came to religion. This shades into the second theme: a reappraisal of the careers of both Oliver and Richard Cromwell. Protector Oliver can no longer be seen as a remote figure, but his intransigence over religion, in particular, was responsible for throwing the Protectorate out of gear after 1657, when the regime was changing but its head was apparently unwilling to confront uncomfortable new political realities. No wonder the civilian courtiers were confused by the Protector's refusal to sideline his military advisers, or that the army suffered a serious loss of trust in a ruler who had drawn back from betraying them only at the last minute. Richard Cromwell was less scrupulous than his father, but he may have been the shrewder politician. By embracing civilian government and encouraging the Presbyterians, Richard took a risk, but it was a calculated one, as the long-term survival of the Protectorate would depend on completing the task of removing the army from politics. This brings us to the third theme: the extraordinary degree of 'engagement' between the Protectorate Parliaments and the people of the three nations. Despite the abstruse nature of much of the constitutional and religious debate at Westminster, and the sometimes cynical use of the language of 'representation', there is no doubt that local issues were dealt with and that members of Parliament were keen to serve their constituents. In return, people in the localities were eager to be involved in elections and to have their private business dealt with in the Commons, and they were apparently happy to trust Parliament to defend their interests generally, notably when it came to taxation. The nature of Parliament might have changed radically since the sixteenth and early seventeenth centuries, but in the 1650s it still operated as a 'point of contact' between the government and the people. This engagement was a sign of political stability, as people had recourse to Parliament rather than joining conspiracies or rebellions, and critics of the regime were encouraged to seek seats and fight their corner in the House of Commons. This can be added to other indications of growing political stability through the period: the royalist uprising of 1655 and the various plots later in the Protectorate received very little support across the country; formerly royalist areas proved the most ready to co-operate with the government in the elections of 1656; the army did not mutiny, despite being sorely provoked, until April 1659. As a result of this stability, the Protectorate regime had considerable political leeway in Parliament. The rows and divisions at Westminster were serious enough, but they did not destabilise the three nations. And when the political machinations and endless debates ceased, the private bills, petitions, and letters began to arrive and members busied themselves with legislation on matters of less moment, but of more importance locally. Nowhere is this more obvious than in April 1659. The government had by this time seen off the major constitutional and political challenges of the commonwealthsmen and their allies, and members happily settled down to transact business as usual. The Irish and Scottish committees put forward new legislation; private bills were debated and given their first readings; a new, far-reaching religious settlement was being prepared; and, at long last, the financial problems of the government were being addressed. There were few signs of impending catastrophe – far from it. In mid-April 1659, Richard Cromwell's Protectorate looked strong, and his Parliament was confident. It may have been the Parliament's confidence which prompted its members to take on the army; and it may have been the strength of the regime, rather than any weakness, that provoked the senior officers to make their own, pre-emptive, strike against it.

APPENDIX 1
MEMBERS EXCLUDED FROM THE
SECOND PROTECTORATE PARLIAMENT

The table below is based on the five surviving contemporary lists of those who were excluded from the second Protectorate Parliament before it assembled. The columns indicate which members are listed as having been excluded in each of these sources as follows:

A = TNA, SP 18/130/29
B = Bodl., MS Rawlinson A 73, fo. 317r
C = Bodl., MS Tanner 52, fo. 156r
D = CJ, VII, 425
E = BL, Stowe MS 361, fo. 103 (printed in Whitelocke, *Memorials*, IV, 280)

The number of members listed in each of these sources is 96, 95, 98, 79, and 95, respectively.

The least full source is D, and the least reliable one (for the reasons discussed in the main text) is E. That leaves A–C – which are the three surviving contemporary manuscript lists – as the fullest and most reliable sources.

Ninety-three names appear in all three of A–C. A further three names (Allanson, Gewen, and Peyto) appear in two of them. Five names (Beresford, Bisse, John Davies, Sir Paul Davies, and Tighe) can also be reliably established of Irish members who were excluded (see chapter 4): they have therefore been included here even though they do not appear on any of these five contemporary lists. This gives a total of 101 members who can pretty safely be regarded as having been excluded.

In addition, there are four individuals (Fenwick, Hobart, Holt, and Raymond) who appear in C, but not A or B: they may well have been excluded also, but this conclusion is slightly less secure than for the first 101. Including them would take the total to 105.

Finally, there are a further ten names that appear in none of A–C: three appear in both D and E; one appears only in D; and six appear only in E. Given that D, though less full, is a more reliable source than E, there is a stronger possibility that the four who appear in D (Clavering, Hinton,

Thurbane, and Wyren) were excluded than is the case for the six who appear only in E (Bentley, Thomas Birch, Lloyd, Radcliffe, Tooker, and Worth).

This might take the final total to 109 or even, at the absolute maximum, to 115. However, it seems highly improbable that all ten of the members in the last category could have been excluded without this fact showing up in any of lists A–C. It is therefore likely that the number of those excluded was at least 101 but not as high as 115, and an overall total in the region of 105 is probably the most plausible figure that can be arrived at on the basis of the surviving evidence.

Name	A	B	C	D	E
Adams, Thomas	*	*	*		*
Allanson, Francis	*	*			
Arthington, Henry	*	*	*	*	*
Ashley Cooper, Sir Anthony	*	*	*	*	*
Aston, John	*	*	*		*
Barker, Abel	*	*	*	*	*
Beale, Richard	*	*	*	*	*
Bentley, Jeremy					*
Beresford, Tristram (Ireland)					
Biddulph, Theophilus	*	*	*		*
Birch, John	*	*	*	*	*
Birch, Thomas					*
Bisse, John (Ireland)					
Bloys, William	*	*	*	*	*
Bowes, Sir Thomas	*	*	*	*	*
Bowyer, John	*	*	*		*
Boys, John	*	*	*	*	*
Brown, Richard	*	*	*		*
Buckland, John	*	*	*	*	*
Bulkeley, John	*	*	*	*	*
Buxton, John	*	*	*	*	*
Chute, Chaloner	*	*	*		*
Clavering, James				*	*
Courthop, George	*	*	*		*
Darley, Henry	*	*	*	*	*
Darley, Richard	*	*	*	*	*
Davies, John (Ireland)					
Davies, Sir Paul (Ireland)					
Doddridge, John	*	*	*	*	*
D'Oiley, Sir William	*	*	*	*	*
Drury, William	*	*	*		
Fagge, Sir John	*	*	*		*
Fenwick, George			*	*	*
Fisher, William	*	*	*		*

Name	A	B	C	D	E
Gell, John	*	*	*		*
Gewen, Thomas	*		*	*	
Gibbs, William	*	*	*	*	*
Godfrey, Lambert	*	*	*	*	
Goodwin, John	*	*	*	*	*
Gore, Sir John	*	*	*	*	*
Gott, Samuel	*	*	*		*
Grenville, Richard	*	*	*	*	
Grimston, Sir Harbottle	*	*	*	*	*
Hale, John	*	*	*	*	*
Hall, Charles	*	*	*	*	*
Hare, Sir Ralph	*	*	*	*	*
Harley, Edward	*	*	*	*	*
Harvey, Edmund	*	*	*	*	*
Hesilrige, Sir Arthur	*	*	*	*	*
Hide, William	*	*	*	*	
Hinton, Richard				*	
Hobart, John			*	*	*
Holt, Thomas			*		
Hooper, Edward	*	*	*	*	*
Hungerford, Henry	*	*	*	*	*
Hussey, Charles	*	*	*	*	*
Irby, Sir Anthony	*	*	*	*	*
James, William	*	*	*	*	*
Jones, John	*	*	*		*
Jones, Samuel	*	*	*	*	*
Le Neve, Edward	*	*	*	*	
Lister, Thomas	*	*	*	*	*
Litton, Rowland	*	*	*	*	*
Lloyd, Andrew	*	*	*	*	*
Lloyd, Charles					*
Long, Robert	*	*	*	*	*
Lucy, Sir Richard	*	*	*	*	*
Matthews, Joachim	*	*	*	*	
Maynard, John	*	*	*	*	
Mildmay, Henry	*	*	*	*	*
Minors, Thomas	*	*	*		*
Moore, Samuel	*	*	*	*	*
Morley, Herbert	*	*	*	*	
Morrice, William	*	*	*	*	*
Moyle, Walter	*	*	*	*	*
Nanson, John	*	*	*		*
Norris, Sir Francis	*	*	*		
North, Henry	*	*	*	*	
Northcote, Sir John	*	*	*	*	*

Name	A	B	C	D	E
Peckham, Henry	*	*	*		*
Peyto, Edward	*	*			
Popham, Sir Alexander	*	*	*	*	*
Radcliffe, Richard			*	*	*
Raymond, Oliver					*
Rivers, Sir Thomas	*	*	*		
Salisbury, William, Earl of	*	*	*	*	*
Saunders, Thomas	*	*	*	*	*
Savile, William	*	*	*	*	*
Scott, Thomas	*	*	*	*	*
Selliard, John	*	*	*	*	*
Shetterden, Daniel	*	*	*	*	*
Sicklemore, John	*	*	*	*	*
Sotherton, Thomas	*	*	*	*	*
Southby, John	*	*	*		*
St Nicholas, Thomas	*	*	*	*	*
Stanhope, John	*	*	*	*	*
Styles, Sir Thomas	*	*	*	*	*
Tempest, Henry	*	*	*	*	*
Thorpe, Francis	*	*	*		*
Throckmorton, Clement				*	*
Thurbane, James					
Tighe, Richard (Ireland)					*
Tooker, Edward					*
Turner, Edward	*	*	*	*	*
Vincent, Walter	*	*	*		*
Wall, Daniel	*	*	*	*	*
Weaver, John	*	*	*	*	*
Welby, William	*	*	*		*
Whalley, Peniston	*	*	*	*	*
Wittewrong, Sir John	*	*	*	*	*
Woodhouse, Philip	*	*	*	*	*
Woolley, William					*
Worth, Henry				*	*
Wyren, Richard					
Young, Sir John	*	*	*	*	*

APPENDIX 2
THE REMONSTRANCE OF
23 FEBRUARY 1657

To his highness the Lord Protector of the commonwealth of England, Scotland and Ireland.[1]

The humble[2] Remonstrance of the knights, citizens and burgesses now assembled in the Parliament of this commonwealth.

We, the knights, citizens and burgesses in this present Parliament assembled, taking into our most serious consideration the present estate[3] of these three nations, joined and united under your highness's protection, cannot but in the first place with all thankfulness acknowledge the wonderful mercy of Almighty God in delivering us from that tyranny and bondage, both in our spiritual and civil concernments, which the late king and his party designed[4] to bring us under, and pursued the effecting thereof by a long and bloody war, and also it hath pleased the same gracious God to preserve your person in many battles, to make you an instrument for preserving our peace, although environed with enemies abroad and filled with turbulent, restless and unquiet spirits in our own bowels. And we have great cause to hope that as the Lord hath used[5] you so eminently in treading down our enemies and restoring us to peace and tranquillity, so also that he will further use you in the settling and securing our liberties, both as we are men and Christians, which are those innate[6] and glorious ends which the good[7] people of these nations have so freely, with the hazard of their lives and estates in a two years' war, so earnestly contended for. We are[8] far from complaining to your highness of those various distempers, which have not only assaulted but almost overwhelmed the liberty of these nations during and since the wars, much less do we intend to impute the same to you, or those worthies of the

---

The version of the Remonstrance published here is that held at the Bodleian Library in Oxford (MS Clarendon 54, fos. 118r–119v), but rendered into modern English. Variations found in the versions at Worcester College, Oxford (Clarke Papers 1/17, fos. 10v–11r, 12v–14r, 16v–17r, 19v–20r, 21v–22r), and the National Library of Scotland (Wodrow Folio MS 30, fos. 126r–7r) are included in the notes, and described as 'Clarke' and 'Wodrow' respectively.
[1] Clarke inserts 'and the dominions thereunto belonging'.
[2] Clarke inserts 'address and'.   [3] Clarke: 'state'.   [4] Clarke: 'endeavoured'.
[5] Clarke: 'raised'.   [6] Clarke: 'great'.   [7] Omitted in Clarke.   [8] Clarke inserts 'very'.

army who have been led under your most successful conduct through many dangers and hazards of their lives in several battles fought with our common enemies, but do attribute those things to the necessity of the times, well knowing what difficulties your highness and the army (whose love and faithfulness to the common cause we and all good men will ever acknowledge and put a just value upon) have been always put to contest with, both from the late king's party, and several other discontented people, in so much that your highness hath been constrained both before and since your access to the protection of these nations, to labour rather to preserve our being than that you have time to consider our rights or well being.

We beseech you likewise give us leave to reflect upon that which lies much upon our hearts, which is the continual danger[9] your life is in from the bloody practices both of the malignants and discontented party (one whereof, through the goodness of God, you have been lately delivered from), it being a received principle amongst them that (no person being declared to succeed you in the government) nothing is wanting to bring us into blood and confusion and them to their desired ends but the destruction of your person, and therefore they leave nothing unattempted to effect it, and in case things should thus remain at your death, we are not able to express what calamities would in all human probability ensue thereupon, sedition and civil war must needs break forth, and therein these nations be exposed to be made a prey to foreigners, which we trust your highness (as well as we) do hold yourself obliged to provide against, and not to leave a people whose common peace and interest you are entrusted with in such a condition as may hazard both, especially in this conjuncture, where there seems to be opportunments[10] of coming to a settlement upon just and equal foundations, and that you have had some experience of the love and affections which this people and their representatives bear unto you, and the entire confidence they have in your highness's affection towards them and their liberties, upon this consideration they have judged it a duty incumbent upon them with all earnestness to express and remonstrate these their most just and necessary desires to your highness.

Whereas it hath been found by long experience, that the ancient constitution of this nation, consisting of a king and two Houses of Parliament, is most agreeable to the temper and inclination of this people, and conform to their laws, and the best means to preserve[11] our nation and fundamental rights and privileges, which have made this nation above all[12] others, under what form of government soever, for many ages, famous and happy even to a great degree of envy.

---

[9] Clarke inserts 'which'.   [10] Clarke reads 'an opportunity'.
[11] Omitted in Clarke (in error?).   [12] Omitted in Clarke (in error?).

And seeing Charles Stuart son of the late king, and all other his sons[13] and posterity and all other person or persons claiming under him or them, are most justly excluded and barred from holding the crowns of England, Scotland and Ireland or any of them or[14] enjoy the power, government or supreme magistracy of this commonwealth or any part thereof, we the knights, citizens and burgesses now assembled in Parliament do most earnestly desire and pray,[15] that your highness will be pleased to assume the name, style, title, dignity and office of king of England, Scotland and Ireland[16] and the respective dominions and territories thereunto belonging, and the exercise thereof, to hold and enjoy the same, with the rights, privileges and prerogatives justly, legally and rightly thereunto belonging.

God who puts down one[17] and sets up another, and giveth the kingdoms of the world to whomsoever he pleaseth, having by a series[18] of providences raised you to be a deliverer to these nations, and made you more able to govern us in peace and prosperity,[19] than any other whatsoever, so long as God shall continue to us the blessing of your life and government, and for the[20] preventing such confusions and inconveniences that otherwise may ensue upon your death.

1. First,[21] That your highness will be pleased in your life time to appoint and declare the person who shall immediately after your death succeed you[22] in the government of these nations, and we shall esteem your highness' acceptance of our unfeigned desires herein as a further testimony of your care and good affection to us and this commonwealth, and do faithfully oblige our selves to adhere to you, with the expense of our lives and estates.

2. That your highness will for the future be pleased to call Parliaments, consisting of two Houses, once in three years at the furthest, or oftener as the affairs of the nation[23] shall require, that being your great council, and in whose affection and advice yourself and this people will be most safe and happy.

3. That the ancient and undoubted liberties and privileges of Parliament (which are the birthright and inheritance of the people, and wherein every man is interested), be preserved and maintained, and that you will not break nor[24] interrupt the same, nor suffer them to be broken or interrupted; and particularly, that those persons who are legally chosen by a free election of

[13] Clarke inserts 'issue'. [14] Clarke inserts 'to'.
[15] Clarke inserts '1', making this the start of the first article. Wodrow starts here, omitting the whole preamble.
[16] Wodrow changes order to 'Scotland, England and Ireland'.
[17] Omitted in Clarke (in error?). [18] Blank in Wodrow. [19] Wodrow omits 'and prosperity'.
[20] Omitted in Clarke. [21] Omitted in Clarke. [22] Omitted in Wodrow.
[23] Wodrow reads 'these nations'. [24] Clarke reads 'or'.

the people to serve in Parliament may not be excluded from sitting in Parliament to do their duty but by judgement and consent of that House whereof they are members.

4. That those who have advised, assisted, or abetted the rebellion of Ireland, and those that[25] do or shall profess the popish religion, be disabled and made incapable forever to be elected or give any vote in the election of any member to sit or serve in Parliament; as also every person or persons who have aided, advised or[26] assisted in any war against the Parliament,[27] since the first day of January 1641[/2]. Under such penalties, as shall be thought fit, unless[28] they have been since in the service of the Parliament, or of your highness and have given signal testimonies[29] of their good affections,[30] and that the persons who shall be elected to serve in Parliament be such and no other than such as are persons of known integrity, fearing God, and of good conversation, and that these qualifications may be observed, and yet the privileges[31] of Parliament maintained, we desire that it may by your highness' consent be ordained that a committee of the House of Commons of every preceding Parliament consisting of [blank] in number, may with the privy council from time to time examine whether the persons so elected and returned be either disabled or not qualified as aforesaid to sit or[32] serve in Parliament, then such persons may not presume to come into the House, until their case with the proceedings thereupon be brought before the House (which shall be at their first meeting) and then[33] determined; and that the number of persons to be elected and chosen to sit and serve in Parliament for England, Scotland and Ireland[34] and the distribution of persons so chosen within the counties, cities and boroughs of them respectively, may be according to such proportion as shall be agreed and declared in this present Parliament.

5. That your highness will consent that none may be called to sit and vote in the Other House, but such as are not disabled, but qualified as aforesaid, and that they exceed not seventy in number nor be under the number of forty, and that as any of them do die or be legally removed, no new one[35] be admitted to sit or vote in their rooms,[36] but by consent of the House itself.

6. That in all other particulars which concern the calling and holding of Parliaments your highness will be pleased that the laws of the land be observed and kept, and that no laws be altered, suspended, abrogated and[37] repealed, or new ones made, but by act of Parliament.

---

[25] Clarke reads 'who'.   [26] Wodrow omits 'advised or'.
[27] Wodrow omits 'against the Parliament'.   [28] Wodrow reads 'except'.
[29] Clarke reads 'testimony'.   [30] Clarke reads 'affection'.
[31] Clarke reads 'privilege'.   [32] Clarke reads 'and'.   [33] Clarke reads 'there'.
[34] Order changed in Wodrow to read 'Scotland, England and Ireland'.
[35] Clarke reads 'ones'.   [36] Clarke reads 'room'.   [37] Clarke reads 'or'.

7. That to the end your highness may have a constant revenue for support of the government, and to be enabled to provide for the safety and defence of the nations by sea and land, we declare our willingness to settle forth a revenue of [blank] not to be diminished but by the consent of the three estates in Parliament, and to grant such other temporary supplies, according as the necessity of the nations do or shall require, and do pray your highness that it may be ordained that no person be compelled to contribute to[38] tax, tallage,[39] aid or other like charge[40] without common consent by act of Parliament, which is a freedom the people of this nation ought by the laws to inherit.

8. That none may be admitted or added[41] to the privy council of your highness or successors, but such as are of known piety and undoubted affections[42] to the rights of these nations, and a just Christian liberty in matters of religion, nor[43] without consent of the council, to be afterwards approved[44] by both Houses of Parliament, as also, that after your highness's death, the commander in chief under your successors of such army or armies, as shall be necessary to be kept in England, Scotland or Ireland,[45] as also such field-officers at land[46] or general by sea (which often time shall be newly made and constituted by your successors)[47] be by the consent of the council and not otherwise.

9. Whereas your highness out of your zeal to the glory of God and the propagation of the Gospel of our Lord Jesus Christ hath been pleased to encourage a godly ministry[48] in this nation, be earnestly desired that such as[49] openly revile them or disturb their assemblies to the dishonour of God, scandal of good men and breach of the peace, may be punished according to law, and where the laws are defective, that your highness will give your consent to such laws as shall be made in that behalf.

10. That the true Protestant reformed[50] religion, and no other,[51] be asserted and recommended for the public profession of these nations, and in case there be any who profess faith in God by Jesus Christ his eternal son and true God blessed for ever, that shall differ in doctrine, discipline or worship from the public profession held forth, endeavours shall be used to convince them by sound doctrine and the example of a good conversation, but that they may not be compelled thereto by penalties, nor restrained from their profession but protected therein, while they abuse not this liberty to the

---

[38] Clarke inserts 'any'.   [39] Omitted in Wodrow.
[40] Wodrow replaces 'like charge' with 'assistance'.
[41] Both Clarke and Wodrow read 'added or admitted'.   [42] Clarke reads 'affection'.
[43] Clarke reads 'not'.   [44] Omitted in Wodrow (in error?).
[45] Wodrow changes order to 'Scotland, England or Ireland'.
[46] Wodrow omits 'at land'.   [47] Clarke omits the parentheses.
[48] Wodrow omits 'godly ministry', having what looks like 'excellency' instead.
[49] Clarke inserts 'do'.   [50] Omitted in Wodrow.   [51] Wodrow omits 'and no other'.

civil injuries of others, or the disturbance of the public peace, so that this liberty be not extended to popery or prelacy, nor to the countenancing of[52] such who publish horrible blasphemies or practice or hold forth licentiousness or profaneness under the profession of Christ. And that your highness will give your consent that all laws, statutes, ordinances[53] or[54] clauses in any law, statute or ordinance to the contrary of the aforesaid liberty be repealed.

11. That the acts and ordinances of Parliaments[55] made for the sale or other disposition of the lands, rents and hereditaments of the late king, queen[56] and prince; of archbishops, bishops, deans and chapters, the lands of delinquents, forest lands, or any of them, or any lands, tenements, rents[57] or hereditaments, lately belonging to the commonwealth, shall, nor may be impeached, but that they may remain good and firm, and that the security given by act, order, ordinance[58] of Parliament for any sum or sums of money[59] by any of the said lands, the excise, or by any[60] public revenue,[61] may remain firm and good and not be made void by any pretence whatsoever.

12. That they who have aided, assisted or abetted in any war against the Parliament since the first day of January 1641[/2], unless they have been since in the service of the Parliament, or your highness, or otherwise given signal testimony of their good affection, and all those who have any ways aided, assisted, or abetted in any of the late insurrections, be made incapable forever of holding or enjoying any office or place of trust in these nations, unless they be restored thereunto by act of Parliament, and that they be enjoined to take an oath, the form of which to be agreed on[62] in Parliament, for abjuring and renouncing the pretended title of Charles Stuart, James Stuart, Henry Stuart, or any of[63] the children or[64] posterity of the late king, or any other claiming under him, them, or any of them to the government of these nations, within [blank] months upon pain of forfeiting [blank] part[65] of their estates for the public use and banishment of their persons, and the like law for papists.

And these our desires being granted by your highness, we shall hope through the rich mercies[66] and goodness of God that it will prove some remedy to these dangers, distractions and disturbances, which these nations are now in, and be an effectual means to remove those jealousies and fears which remain in the minds of many men concerning the government of this

---

[52] Omitted in Clarke.   [53] Wodrow changes order to read 'ordinances, statutes'.
[54] Clarke reads 'and'.   [55] Clarke reads 'Parliament'.
[56] Omitted in Wodrow.   [57] Omitted in Wodrow.   [58] Clarke reads 'acts and ordinances'.
[59] Clarke inserts open parenthesis.   [60] Clarke inserts 'other'.
[61] Clarke inserts close parenthesis.   [62] Clarke reads 'upon'.
[63] Clarke omits 'of' and inserts 'other'.   [64] Clarke reads 'and'.
[65] Wodrow omits '[blank] part' and reads 'the proportion' instead.
[66] Wodrow reads 'right merit' instead of 'rich mercies'.

commonwealth, and thereby we shall be enabled and encouraged with all cheerfulness in the settling of such things as shall be further necessary for the good of these kingdoms, and be most ready to join with you in promoting the work of reformation happily begun by your highness, the regulating of courts of justice, and abridging both the delays and charges of lawsuits, and apply ourselves to such other courses and counsels as may be most like to heal our breaches and divisions, and restore these poor nations to a union and consistency among themselves, and to lay foundation of further confidence between your highness and them to the rejoicing of the hearts of our friends and terror of our enemies.

BIBLIOGRAPHY

This bibliography contains full details of all the sources cited in the footnotes of this book. It is divided into three main sections: manuscript sources, printed primary sources and secondary sources. The place of publication of printed primary sources and secondary sources is London unless otherwise indicated.

MANUSCRIPT SOURCES

England

Bodleian Library, Oxford

MSS Carte 73, 74, 80, 228 (Ormond papers)
MSS Clarendon 52, 54, 55, 59, 60 (Clarendon State Papers)
MS Nalson 16 (letters and papers)
MSS Rawlinson A 9–64, 73, 328 (Thurloe State Papers)
MS Tanner 52 (letters and papers)

British Library

Add. MSS 4156–8 (Thomas Birch collection: Thurloe papers)
Add. MS 5138 (diary of Guybon Goddard)
Add. MSS 15859–64 (diary of Thomas Burton)
Add. MS 17677 U (transcripts from the archives of the United Provinces)
Add. MS 21425 (Baynes correspondence)
Add. MS 22919 (Sir George Downing correspondence)
Add. MS 23112 (registers of Secretaries of State for Scotland)
Add. MS 43724 (Henry Cromwell correspondence)
Egerton MS 2618 (Clarke correspondence)
Harleian MS 6848 (Whitelocke papers)
Lansdowne MSS 821–3 (Henry Cromwell correspondence)

Stowe MS 322 (Revenue papers)
Stowe MS 361 (speeches in Parliament)

Microfilm of Alnwick Castle, Northumberland MSS 551–2 (letter-books of John Fitzjames, V–VI)

Coventry City Archives

BA/H/Q/A79/302 (Robert Beake to Leonard Piddock, 28 March 1657)

Derbyshire Record Office, Matlock

MS D258/10/9/2 (diary of Sir John Gell)

Dorset Record Office, Dorchester

DC/LR/D2/1 (correspondence of the town clerk of Lyme Regis, 1570–1696)
B 2/16/4 (Dorchester corporation minutes, 1637–56)
B 2/16/5 (Dorchester corporation minutes, 1656–77)

Poole Borough Archives (now at the Dorset Record Office)

MS 29(7) (mayor's accounts, 1653–60)
MSS L4–5 (letters to the mayor and corporation)
MS S105 (accounts, 1657–8)

Longleat House, Warminster, Wiltshire

Whitelocke Papers 18

The National Archives (Public Record Office), Kew

PRO 31/3/95–103 (Baschet's transcripts)
PRO 31/17/33 (miscellaneous transcripts)
SP 18 (State Papers Domestic, Interregnum)
SP 25 (Council papers, Interregnum)
SP 78 (State Papers, France)

Surrey History Centre, Woking

Loseley MS LM/1331/56

Worcester College, Oxford

Clarke MSS 1/15–17, 3/2–3, 3/9

Ireland

National Library of Ireland

Lismore MS 13228

Scotland

Edinburgh University Library

Special Collections, D.K.3.29 (correspondence relating to James Sharp)

National Archives of Scotland

B9/12/11 (Burntisland council minutes, 1655–60)
GD 112/39/104/1 (Breadalbane papers)
GD 406/2/M.1/202 (Hamilton papers)

National Library of Scotland

MS 7032 (Yester papers)
Wodrow Folio MS 26
Wodrow Folio MS 30

National Register of Archives for Scotland

NRAS 217, Stuart Earls of Moray MSS, box 6, no. 140
NRAS 332, Lennoxlove, Hamilton MSS L.1/189/15, F.1.197, 208

PRINTED PRIMARY SOURCES

Sources published before 1700

An Apology for the Ministers of the County of Wilts, in their Actings at the election of Members for the approaching Parliament ([12 August] 1654)
An Appeale from the Court to the Country, made by a Member of Parliament lawfully chosen, but secluded illegally by my L[ord] Protector (1656)
Baker, Richard, *A Chronicle of the Kings of England* (1670)
[Bethel, Slingsby,] *A True and Impartial Narrative* (1659)
A brief relation of the proceedings before his Highness Councel concerning the petitioners of the Isle of Ely, against George Glapthorne Esquire; to take away the false report that is made touching the same, and that the truth may plainly appear ([4 November] 1654)
The Copy of a Letter sent out of Wiltshire, to a Gentleman in London ([13 July] 1654)
[Cromwell, Richard,] *The Speech of His Highness the Lord Protector, made to both Houses of Parliament at their first meeting on Thursday the 27th of January 1658[/9]* (1658[/9])
A Declaration of the Lord Protector and both Houses of Parliament (1659)
Englands Remembrancers. or, A word in season to all English men about their elections of the members for the approaching Parliament (1656)
[Fiennes, Nathaniel,] *The speech of the right honourable Nathaniel Lord Fiennes, one of the Lord Keepers of the Great Seale of England, made before his Highnesse, and both Houses of Parliament on Thursday the 27th of January, 1658[/9]* (1658[/9])
[Frewen, Henry,] *An Admirable Speech made by the Maior of Reading, upon the occasion of the late choice of a burgess for that Town, June 28, 1654* (1654)

Keeble, N. H., and Nuttall, Geoffrey F., eds., *Calendar of the Correspondence of Richard Baxter* (2 vols., Oxford, 1991)
Mercurius Politicus, no. 222 (7–14 September 1654)
  no. 223 (14–21 September 1654)
  no. 225 (28 September–5 October 1654)
  no. 226 (5–12 October 1654)
  no. 227 (12–19 October 1654)
  no. 232 (16–23 November 1654)
  no. 233 (23–30 November 1654)
  no. 235 (7–14 December 1654)
  no. 236 (14–21 December 1654)
  no. 237 (21–28 December 1654)
  no. 238 (28 December 1654–4 January 1654[/5])
  no. 350 (19–26 February 1656[/7])
  no. 372 (16–23 July 1657)
  no. 561 (31 March–7 April 1659)
A Narrative of the Late Parliament (1657)
[Newcomen, Matthew,] *Irenicum; or, An essay towards a brotherly peace & union* (1659)
Owen, John, *God's Word in Founding Zion, and His Peoples Duty thereupon. A Sermon Preached in the Abby Church at Westminster, ... Septemb[er] 17th 1656* (Oxford, 1656)
A Perfect Account of the Daily Intelligence from the Armies in England, Scotland and Ireland, and the Navy at Sea (1–8 November 1654)
Prynne, William, *A Plea for the Lords, and House of Peers* (1658)
  A summary collection of the principal fundamental rights, liberties, proprieties of all English freemen (1656)
The Publick Intelligencer, no. 61 (8–15 December 1656)
  no. 72 (23 February–2 March 1656[/7])
Severall proceedings in Parliament, no. 265 (19–26 October 1654)
  no. 275 (28 December 1654–5 January 1654[/5])
  no. 277 (11–18 January 1654[/5])
Severall Proceedings of State Affairs, no. 255 (10–17 August 1654)
  no. 261 (21–28 September 1654)
Sheppard, William, *Englands Balme* (1656)
To all the worthy gentlemen who are duely chosen for the Parliament, which intended to meet at Westminster the 17 of September 1656. And to all the good people of the Common-wealth of England. The humble remonstrance, protection, and appeale of severall knights and gentlemen duly chosen to serve their countrey in Parliament; who attended at Westminster for that purpose, but were violently kept out of the Parliament-house by armed men hired by the Lord Protector ([7 October] 1656)
To His Highness the Lord Protector, etc. and our General: The Humble Petition of Several Colonels of the army (1654)
To the High Court of Parliament of the Common-wealth of England, &c. The humble petition of John Wagstaff, gent. Inhabitant of the county of Warwick (1655)
A true catalogue, or, An account of the several places and most eminent persons in the three nations, and elsewhere, where, and by whom Richard Cromwell was proclaimed Lord Protector of the Commonwealth of England, Scotland, and

*Ireland. As also a collection of the most material passages in the several blas-
phemous, lying, flattering addresses, ... which were sent to the aforesaid* (1659)
[Wharton, Sir George,] *A Second Narrative of the late Parliament (so called)*
(1658)

Sources published since 1700

Abbott, W. C., ed., *Writings and Speeches of Oliver Cromwell* (4 vols., Cambridge,
Mass., 1937–47)
Birch, Thomas, ed., *A Collection of the State Papers of John Thurloe, Esq.* (7 vols.,
1742)
Calendar of State Papers Domestic
Calendar of State Papers Ireland
Calendar of State Papers Venetian
Clarendon, Edward, Earl of, *The History of the Rebellion and Civil Wars in England*,
ed. W. Dunn Macray (6 vols., Oxford, 1888)
[Clarendon, Edward, Earl of,] *State Papers collected by Edward, Earl of Clarendon*
(3 vols., Oxford, 1757)
Firth, C. H., ed., 'A Letter from Lord Saye and Sele to Lord Wharton, 29 December
1657', *EHR*, 10 (1895), 106–7
   ed., *The Memoirs of Edmund Ludlow* (2 vols., Oxford, 1894)
   'A Speech by Richard Cromwell, 14 October 1658', *EHR*, 23 (1908), 734–6
Firth, C. H., and Henderson, Frances, eds., *The Clarke Papers* (5 vols., Camden
Society, 2nd series, 49, 1891; 54, 1894; 61 [*recte* 60], 1899; 62, 1901; 5th series,
27, 2005)
Firth, C. H., and Rait, R. S., eds., *Acts and Ordinances of the Interregnum,
1642–1660* (3 vols., 1911)
Gardiner, S. R., ed., *Constitutional Documents of the Puritan Revolution,
1625–1660* (3rd edn, Oxford, 1906)
Guizot, F. G. P., *History of Oliver Cromwell and the English Commonwealth*, trans.
A. R. Scoble (2 vols., 1854)
   History of Richard Cromwell and the Restoration of Charles II, trans. A. R. Scoble
(2 vols., 1856)
HMC, *Sixth Report* (1877–8)
   Egmont, I (1905)
   The Manuscripts of the House of Lords, 1699–1702 (1908)
Hutchinson, Lucy, *Memoirs of the Life of Colonel Hutchinson*, ed. Julius Hutchinson
(1968)
Journals of the House of Commons (1803–13)
Journals of the House of Lords (1846)
Kenyon, J. P., *The Stuart Constitution, 1603–1688: Documents and Commentary*
(Cambridge, 1966); 2nd edn (Cambridge, 1986)
Laing, D., ed., *The Letters and Journals of Robert Baillie* (3 vols., Bannatyne Club,
Edinburgh, 1841–2)
Lambert, Sheila, ed., *Printing for Parliament, 1641–1700* (List and Index Society,
special series, 20, 1984)
Larcom, T. A., ed., *The History of the Survey of Ireland Commonly Known as the
Down Survey by Dr William Petty* (Dublin, 1851)
Lomas, S. C., ed., *The Letters and Speeches of Oliver Cromwell, with Elucidations by
Thomas Carlyle* (3 vols., 1904)

'The Memoirs of Sir George Courthop, 1616–1685', *Camden Miscellany XI* (Camden Society, 3rd series, 13, 1907), pp. 93–157

Ludlow, Edmund, *A Voyce from the Watch Tower, Part Five: 1660–1662*, intro. by Blair Worden (Camden Society, 4th series, 21, 1978)

MacFarlane, Alan, ed., *The Diary of Ralph Josselin, 1616–1683* (British Academy, Records of Social and Economic History, new series, 3, Oxford, 1976)

Nelson, Carolyn, and Seccombe, Matthew, eds., *British Newspapers and Periodicals, 1641–1700: A Short-Title Catalogue of Serials Printed in England, Scotland, Ireland and British America* (New York, 1987)

Ogilvie, James D., ed., *The Diary of Sir Archibald Johnston of Wariston, vol. III, 1655–1660* (Scottish History Society, 3rd series, 34, Edinburgh, 1940)

[Various editors,] *The Parliamentary or Constitutional History of England* (24 vols., 1751–61)

Return of Members of Parliaments of England, 1213–1702 (2 vols., 1878)

Roberts, Michael, ed., *Swedish Diplomats at Cromwell's Court, 1655–6* (Camden Society, 4th series, 36, 1988)

Roots, Ivan, ed., *Speeches of Oliver Cromwell* (1989)

Rutt, J. T., ed., *Diary of Thomas Burton, Esq.* (4 vols., 1828); reprinted with intro. by Ivan Roots (New York, 1974)

Schilling, W. A. H., 'The Parliamentary Diary of Sir John Gell, 5 February–21 March 1659 (MA thesis, Vanderbilt University, 1961)

Spalding, Ruth, ed., *The Diary of Bulstrode Whitelocke, 1605–1675* (British Academy, Records of Social and Economic History, new series, 13, Oxford, 1990)

Stephen, William, ed., *Register of the Consultations of the Ministers of Edinburgh and Some Other Brethren of the Ministry* (2 vols., Scottish History Society, 3rd series, 1, 1921; 16, 1930)

Stainer, Charles L., ed., *Speeches of Oliver Cromwell, 1644–1658* (1901)

Taylor, L. B., ed., *Aberdeen Council Letters, III: 1645–1660* (Oxford, 1952)

Underdown, David, ed., 'The Parliamentary Diary of John Boys', *Bulletin of the Institute of Historical Research*, 39 (1966), 141–64

Vaughan, Robert, ed., *The Protectorate of Oliver Cromwell and the State of Europe during the Early Part of the Reign of Louis XIV* (2 vols., 1839)

Warner, G. F., ed., *The Nicholas Papers* (4 vols., Camden Society, 2nd series, 40, 1886; 50, 1893; 57, 1897; 3rd series, 31, 1920)

Weinstock, M., ed., *Weymouth and Melcombe Regis Minute Books, 1625–1660* (Dorset Record Society, I, Dorchester, 1964)

Whitelocke, Bulstrode, *Memorials of the English Affairs* (4 vols., Oxford, 1853)

Wolfe, Don M., ed., *Leveller Manifestoes of the Puritan Revolution* (1944)

SECONDARY SOURCES

Adamson, J. S. A., 'Oliver Cromwell and the Long Parliament', in John Morrill, ed., *Oliver Cromwell and the English Revolution* (Harlow, 1990), pp. 49–92

Aylmer, G. E., 'The Last Years of Purveyance, 1610–1660', *Economic History Review*, new series, 10 (1957), 81–93

Barnard, T. C., 'Lord Broghill, Vincent Gookin and the Cork Elections of 1659', *EHR*, 88 (1973), 352–65

'Planters and Policies in Cromwellian Ireland', *Past and Present*, 61 (1973), 31–68

Black, Stephen F., '*Coram Protectore*: The Judges of Westminster Hall under the Protectorate of Oliver Cromwell', *American Journal of Legal History*, 20 (1976), 32–64

Bonney, Richard, 'The European Reaction to the Trial and Execution of Charles I', in Peacey, *The Regicides and the Execution of Charles I*, pp. 247–79

Braddick, Michael, *The Nerves of State: Taxation and the Financing of the English State, 1558–1714* (Manchester, 1996)

Butler, A., *A Biography of Richard Cromwell, 1626–1712, the Second Protector* (Lampeter, 1994)

Cannon, John, *Parliamentary Reform, 1640–1832* (Cambridge, 1973)

Casada, James A., 'Dorset Politics in the Puritan Revolution', *Southern History*, 4 (1982), 107–22

'The Scottish Representatives in Richard Cromwell's Parliament', *Scottish Historical Review*, 51 (1972), 124–47

Catterall, Ralph C. H., 'A Suspicious Document in Whitelock's "Memorials"', *EHR*, 16 (1901), 737–9

Cliffe, J. T., *The Puritan Gentry Besieged* (1993)

Coleby, Andrew M., *Central Government and the Localities: Hampshire, 1649–1689* (Cambridge, 1987)

Collins, Jeffrey R., 'The Church Settlement of Oliver Cromwell', *History*, 87 (2002), 18–40

Collinson, Patrick, 'England and International Calvinism, 1558–1640', in Menna Prestwich, ed., *International Calvinism, 1541–1715* (Oxford, 1985), pp. 197–223

Cotterell, Mary, 'Interregnum Law Reform: The Hale Commission of 1652', *EHR*, 83 (1968), 689–704

Coward, Barry, *The Cromwellian Protectorate* (Manchester, 2002)

Oliver Cromwell (1991)

Crabtree, Roger, 'The Idea of a Protestant Foreign Policy', in Ivan Roots, ed., *Cromwell: A Profile* (1973), pp. 160–89

Cromartie, Alan, *Sir Matthew Hale, 1609–1676: Law, Religion and Natural Philosophy* (Cambridge, 1995)

Damrosch, Leo, *The Sorrows of the Quaker Jesus: James Nayler and the Puritan Crackdown on the Free Spirit* (Cambridge, Mass. 1996)

Davies, Godfrey, 'The Election of Richard Cromwell's Parliament, 1658–9', *EHR*, 63 (1948), 488–501

The Restoration of Charles II, 1658–1660 (Oxford, 1955)

Davis, J. C., 'Cromwell's Religion', in John Morrill, ed., *Oliver Cromwell and the English Revolution* (Harlow, 1990), pp. 181–208

Dean, David, *Law-Making and Society in Late Elizabethan England: The Parliament of England, 1584–1601* (Cambridge, 1996)

Douglas Southall Freeman Historical Review (Richmond, Va.; spring 1999)

Dow, Frances, *Cromwellian Scotland, 1651–1660* (Edinburgh, 1979)

Duke, Alastair, 'The Ambivalent Face of Calvinism in the Netherlands, 1561–1618', in Menna Prestwich, ed., *International Calvinism, 1541–1715* (Oxford, 1985), pp. 109–34

Durston, Christopher, *Cromwell's Major-Generals: Godly Government during the English Revolution* (Manchester, 2001)

'Policing the Cromwellian Church: The Activities of the County Ejection Committees, 1654–1659', in Little, *Cromwellian Protectorate*, pp. 189–205

Egloff, Carol S., 'John Hobart of Norwich and the Politics of the Cromwellian Protectorate', *Norfolk Archaeology*, 42 (1994), 38–56
  'Robert Beake and a Letter Concerning the Humble Petition and Advice', *HR*, 68 (1995), 233–9
  'The Search for a Cromwellian Settlement: Exclusions from the Second Protectorate Parliament', *Parl. Hist.*, 17 (1998), 178–97, 301–21
  'Settlement and Kingship: The Army, the Gentry, and the Offer of the Crown to Oliver Cromwell' (Ph.D thesis, Yale University, 1990)
Elton, G. R., *F. W. Maitland* (1985)
  The Parliament of England, 1559–1581 (Cambridge, 1986)
  Studies in Tudor and Stuart Politics and Government (4 vols., Cambridge, 1974–92)
Farr, David, *John Lambert, Parliamentary Soldier and Cromwellian Major-General, 1619–1684* (Woodbridge, 2003)
Firth, C. H., 'Cromwell and the Crown', *EHR*, 17 (1902), 429–42, and 18 (1903), 52–80
  The Last Years of the Protectorate, 1656–1658 (2 vols., 1909)
Fletcher, Anthony, *Sussex, 1600–1660: A County Community in Peace and War* (1975)
Foster, E. R., *The House of Lords, 1603–1649: Structure, Procedure and the Nature of its Business* (Chapel Hill, 1983)
Gardiner, S. R., *History of the Commonwealth and Protectorate, 1649–1656* (4 vols., 1903; reprinted 1989)
Gaunt, Peter, 'The Councils of the Protectorate, from December 1653 to September 1658' (Ph.D thesis, University of Exeter, 1983)
  'Cromwell's Purge? Exclusions and the First Protectorate Parliament', *Parl. Hist.*, 6 (1987), 1–22
  'Law-making in the First Protectorate Parliament', in Colin Jones, Malyn Newitt, and Stephen Roberts, eds., *Politics and People in Revolutionary England: Essays in Honour of Ivan Roots* (Oxford, 1986), pp. 163–86
  Oliver Cromwell (Oxford, 1996)
  'Oliver Cromwell and his Protectorate Parliaments: Co-operation, Conflict and Control', in Roots, *'Into another Mould'*, pp. 70–100
  '"The Single Person's Confidants and Dependents"? Oliver Cromwell and his Protectoral Councillors', *HJ*, 32 (1989), 537–60
  ' "To create a little world out of chaos": The Protectoral Ordinances of 1653–1654 Reconsidered', in Little, *Cromwellian Protectorate*, pp. 105–26
Goldwater, Ellen D., 'The Scottish Franchise: Lobbying during the Cromwellian Protectorate', *HJ*, 21 (1978), 27–42
Graves, Michael A. R., *Elizabethan Parliaments, 1559–1601* (2nd edn, Harlow, 1996)
Groenhuis, G., 'Calvinism and the National Consciousness: The Dutch Republic as the New Israel', in A. Duke and C. Tamse, eds., *Church and State since the Reformation* (The Hague, 1981), pp. 118–33
Hammer, J. R., *Protector: A Life History of Richard Cromwell, Protector of the United Kingdom, 1658–1659/60* (New York, 1997)
Hart, James S., *Justice upon Petition: The House of Lords and the Reformation of Justice, 1621–1675* (1991)
  The Rule of Law, 1603–1660: Crown, Courts and Judges (Harlow, 2003)
Hartley, T. E., *Elizabeth's Parliaments: Queen, Lords and Commons, 1559–1601* (Manchester, 1992)

Hause, E. M., *Tumble-Down Dick: The Fall of the House of Cromwell* (New York, 1972)

Heath, G. D., 'Making the Instrument of Government', *Journal of British Studies*, 6 (1967), 15–34

Hessayon, Ariel, '"Gold Tried in the Fire": The Prophet Theauraujohn Tany and the Puritan Revolution' (Ph.D thesis, University of Cambridge, 1996)

Hexter, J. H., 'Parliament under the Lens', *British Studies Monitor*, 3 (1972–3), 4–15

'Quoting the Commons, 1604–1642', in DeLoyd J. Guth and John W. McKenna, eds., *Tudor Rule and Revolution* (Cambridge, 1982), pp. 369–91

Hirst, Derek, 'Concord and Discord in Richard Cromwell's House of Commons', *EHR*, 103 (1988), 339–58

England in Conflict, 1603–1660: Kingdom, Community, Commonwealth (1999)

'The Failure of Godly Rule in the English Republic', *Past and Present*, 132 (1991), 33–66

The Representative of the People? Voters and Voting in England under the Early Stuarts (Cambridge, 1975)

Holmes, Clive, 'John Lisle, Lord Commissioner of the Great Seal, and the Last Months of the Cromwellian Protectorate', *EHR*, 122 (forthcoming, 2007)

Seventeenth-Century Lincolnshire (Lincoln, 1980)

Why Was Charles I Executed? (2006)

Howell, Roger, 'Cromwell and his Parliaments', in R. C. Richardson, ed., *Images of Oliver Cromwell: Essays by and for Roger Howell, Jr* (Manchester, 1993)

Hughes, Ann, 'The Frustrations of the Godly', in John Morrill, ed., *Revolution and Restoration: England in the 1650s* (1992), pp. 70–90

Politics, Society and Civil War in Warwickshire, 1620–1660 (Cambridge, 1987)

Hutton, Ronald, *The Restoration: A Political and Religious History of England and Wales, 1658–1667* (Oxford, 1985)

Jansson, Maija, 'Dues Paid', *Parl. Hist.*, 15 (1996), 215–20

Jenkins, Geraint H., *The Foundations of Modern Wales: Wales, 1642–1780* (Oxford, 1987)

Jones, Sarah E., 'The Composition and Activity of the Protectorate Parliaments' (Ph.D thesis, University of Exeter, 1988)

Keeler, Mary Frear, *The Long Parliament, 1640–1641: A Biographical Study of its Members* (Memoirs of the American Philosophical Society, 36, Philadelphia, 1954)

Kelsey, Sean, *Inventing a Republic: The Political Culture of the English Commonwealth, 1649–1653* (Manchester, 1997)

Kendall, R. T., *Calvin and English Calvinism to 1649* (Oxford, 1979)

Kishlansky, Mark A., *Parliamentary Selection: Social and Political Choice in Early Modern England* (Cambridge, 1986)

Korr, C. P., *Cromwell and the New Model Foreign Policy: England's Policy toward France, 1649–1658* (Berkeley, Ca., 1975)

Little, Patrick, ed., *The Cromwellian Protectorate* (Woodbridge, 2007)

'The First Unionists? Irish Protestant Attitudes to Union with England, 1653–1659', *Irish Historical Studies*, 32 (2000), 44–58

'An Irish Governor of Scotland: Lord Broghill, 1655–1656', in A. MacKillop and Steve Murdoch, eds., *Military Governors and Imperial Frontiers, c. 1600–1800: A Study of Scotland and Empires* (Leiden and Boston, 2003), pp. 79–97

'Irish Representation in the Protectorate Parliaments', *Parl. Hist.*, 23 (2004), 336–56

Lord Broghill and the Cromwellian Union with Ireland and Scotland (Woodbridge, 2004)

'Monarchy to Protectorate: Re-drafting the Humble Petition and Advice, March–June 1657', *HR*, 79 (2006), 144–9

'The Political Career of Roger Boyle, Lord Broghill, 1636–1660' (Ph.D thesis, University of London, 2000)

'Scottish Affairs at Westminster: A Letter from the Union Parliament of 1654–5', *Scottish Historical Review*, 84 (2005), 247–56

'Year of Crisis or Turning Point? 1655 in its British Context', *Cromwelliana*, new series, 3 (2006), 28–43

Matthews, Nancy L., *William Sheppard, Cromwell's Law Reformer* (Cambridge, 1984)

Mayers, Ruth, *1659: The Crisis of the Commonwealth* (Woodbridge, 2004)

Menarry, David, 'The Irish and Scottish Landed Elites from Regicide to Restoration' (Ph.D thesis, University of Aberdeen, 2001)

Miller, Leo, ed., *John Milton and the Oldenburg Safeguard* (New York, 1985)

Morrill, John, *Cheshire, 1630–1660: County Government and Society during the English Revolution* (Oxford, 1974)

'Getting Over D'Ewes', *Parl. Hist.*, 15 (1996), 221–30

The Nature of the English Revolution (Harlow, 1993)

'Parliamentary Representation, 1543–1974', in B. E. Harris, ed., *Victoria History of the County of Chester, Volume II* (Oxford, 1979), pp. 98–166

'Paying One's D'Ewes', *Parl. Hist.*, 14 (1995), 179–86

'Reconstructing the History of Early Stuart Parliaments', *Archives*, 21 (1994), 67–72

Revolt in the Provinces: The People of England and the Tragedies of War, 1630–1648 (2nd edn, Harlow, 1999)

'Textualizing and Contextualizing Cromwell', *HJ*, 33 (1990), 629–39

'Through a Venetian Glass, Darkly', *Parl. Hist.*, 17 (1998), 244–7

Morrill, John, and Baker, Philip, 'Oliver Cromwell, the Regicide and the Sons of Zeruiah', in Peacey, *The Regicides and the Execution of Charles I*, pp. 14–35

Nourse, G. B., 'Law Reform under the Commonwealth and Protectorate', *Law Quarterly Review*, 75 (1959), 512–29

'The Nomination of Richard Cromwell', *Cromwelliana* (1979), 25–31

'Richard Cromwell's House of Commons', *Bulletin of the John Rylands Library*, 60 (1977), 95–113

Nuttall, W. L. F., 'Hezekiah Haynes: Oliver Cromwell's Major-General for the Eastern Counties', *Transactions of the Essex Archaeological Society*, 1, part 3 (1964), 196–209

Oxford Dictionary of National Biography (Oxford, 2004)

Pares, Richard, and Taylor, Alan J. P., eds., *Essays Presented to Sir Lewis Namier* (1956)

Peacey, Jason, 'The Protector Humbled: Richard Cromwell and the Constitution', in Little, *Cromwellian Protectorate*, pp. 32–52

ed., *The Regicides and the Execution of Charles I* (Basingstoke, 2001)

Peters, Kate, *Print Culture and the Early Quakers* (Cambridge, 2005)

Pinckney, Paul J., 'Bradshaw and Cromwell in 1656', *Huntington Library Quarterly*, 30 (1966–7), 233–40

'The Cheshire Election of 1656', *Bulletin of the John Rylands Library*, 49 (1966–7), 387–426

'A Cromwellian Parliament: The Elections and Personnel of 1656' (Ph.D thesis, Vanderbilt University, 1962)

'The Scottish Representation in the Cromwellian Parliament of 1656', *Scottish Historical Review*, 46 (1967), 95–114

'The Suffolk Elections to the Protectorate Parliaments', in Colin Jones, Malyn Newitt, and Stephen Roberts, eds., *Politics and People in Revolutionary England: Essays in Honour of Ivan Roots* (Oxford and New York, 1986), pp. 205–24

Pincus, Steven, *Protestantism and Patriotism: Ideologies and the Making of English Foreign Policy, 1650–1668* (Cambridge, 1996)

Prall, Stuart E., *The Agitation for Law Reform during the Puritan Revolution, 1640–1660* (The Hague, 1966)

Prestwich, Menna, 'Diplomacy and Trade in the Protectorate', *Journal of Modern History*, 21 (1950), 103–21

Ramsey, R. W., *Richard Cromwell* (1935)

Richardson, R. C., ed., *Images of Oliver Cromwell: Essays for and by Roger Howell, Jr* (Manchester, 1993)

Roberts, Michael, 'Cromwell and the Baltic', in Michael Roberts, *Essays in Swedish History* (1967), pp. 157–70

Roberts, Stephen K., 'The 1656 Election, Polling and Public Opinion: A Warwickshire Case Study', *Parl. Hist.*, 23 (2004), 357–74

Recovery and Restoration in an English County: Devon Local Administration, 1646–1670 (Exeter, 1985)

Roots, Ivan, 'The Debate on "the Other House" in Richard Cromwell's Parliament', in Richard Ollard and Pamela Tudor-Craig, eds., *For Veronica Wedgwood these Studies in Seventeenth-Century History* (1986), pp. 188–203

ed., *'Into another Mould': Aspects of the Interregnum* (2nd edn, Exeter, 1998)

'Introduction to the Revised Edition', in Roots, *'Into another Mould'*, pp. xi–xix

'Lawmaking in the Second Protectorate Parliament', in H. Hearder and H. R. Loyn, eds., *British Government and Administration: Essays presented to S. B. Chrimes* (Cardiff, 1974), pp. 132–43

Russell, Conrad, *Parliaments and English Politics, 1621–1629* (Oxford, 1979)

Unrevolutionary England, 1603–1642 (1990)

Seddon, P. R., 'The Nottingham Elections to the Protectorate Parliaments of 1654 and 1656', *Transactions of the Thoroton Society of Nottinghamshire*, 102 (1998), 93–8

Smith, David L., ed., *Cromwell and the Interregnum* (Oxford, 2003)

'Oliver Cromwell and the Protectorate Parliaments', in Little, *Cromwellian Protectorate*, pp. 14–31

'Oliver Cromwell, the First Protectorate Parliament and Religious Reform', *Parl. Hist.*, 19 (2000), 38–48

'Reconstructing the Opening Session of the Long Parliament', *HJ* (forthcoming)

The Stuart Parliaments, 1603–1689 (Oxford, 1999)

Smuts, R. Malcolm, and Kinney, Arthur F., eds., *Responses to Regicide* (Amherst, 2001)

Snow, Vernon F., 'Parliamentary Reapportionment Proposals in the Puritan Revolution', *EHR*, 74 (1959), 409–42

Sutton, John, 'Cromwell's Commissioners for Preserving the Peace of the Commonwealth: A Staffordshire Case Study', in Ian Gentles, John Morrill, and Blair Worden, eds., *Soldiers, Writers and Statesmen of the English Revolution* (Cambridge, 1998), pp. 151–82

Taft, Barbara, 'The Humble Petition of Several Colonels of the army: Causes, Character, and Results of Military Opposition to Cromwell's Protectorate', *Huntington Library Quarterly*, 42 (1978–9), 15–41

Thomas, Keith, 'The Levellers and the Franchise', in G. E. Aylmer, ed., *The Interregnum: The Quest for Settlement, 1646–1660* (1972), pp. 57–78

Trevor-Roper, Hugh, 'Oliver Cromwell and his Parliaments', in Trevor-Roper, *Religion, the Reformation and Social Change* (3rd edn, 1984), pp. 345–91

Underdown, David, *Fire from Heaven: Life in an English Town in the Seventeenth Century* (1993)

Pride's Purge: Politics in the Puritan Revolution (Oxford, 1971)

Somerset in the Civil War and Interregnum (Newton Abbot, 1973)

Veall, Donald, *The Popular Movement for Law Reform, 1640–1660* (Oxford, 1970)

Venning, Timothy, *Cromwellian Foreign Policy* (1996)

Warmington, A. R., *Civil War, Interregnum and Restoration in Gloucestershire, 1640–1672* (Woodbridge, 1997)

Williams, A. R., 'John Desborough: Gloucestershire's Major-General', *Transactions of the Bristol and Gloucestershire Archaeological Society*, 89 (1970), 123–9

Wilson, Theodore A., and Merli, Frank J., 'Nayler's Case and the Dilemma of the Protectorate', *University of Birmingham Historical Journal*, 10 (1965–6), 44–59

Woolrych, Austin, *Britain in Revolution, 1625–1660* (Oxford, 2002)

Commonwealth to Protectorate (Oxford, 1982)

'Historical Introduction', in R. W. Ayers, ed., *The Complete Prose Works of John Milton*, vol. VII (New Haven and London, 1980), pp. 1–228

'Last Quests for a Settlement, 1657–1660', in G. E. Aylmer, ed., *The Interregnum: The Quest for Settlement, 1646–1660* (1972), pp. 183–204

'Milton and Cromwell', in Michael Lieb and John T. Shawcross, eds., *Achievements of the Left Hand: Essays on the Prose of John Milton* (Amherst, 1974), pp. 185–218

Worden, Blair, 'The "Diary" of Bulstrode Whitelocke', *EHR*, 108 (1993), 122–34

'Oliver Cromwell and his Council', in Little, *Cromwellian Protectorate*, pp. 82–104

'Oliver Cromwell and the Sin of Achan', in Derek Beales and Geoffrey Best, eds., *History, Society and the Churches: Essays in Honour of Owen Chadwick* (Cambridge, 1985), pp. 125–45

Roundhead Reputations: The English Civil Wars and the Passions of Posterity (2001)

The Rump Parliament, 1648–1653 (Cambridge, 1974)

'Toleration and the Cromwellian Protectorate', in W. J. Sheils, ed., *Persecution and Toleration* (Studies in Church History, 21, Oxford, 1984), pp. 199–233

'Whig History and Puritan Politics: The *Memoirs of Edmund Ludlow* Revisited', *HR*, 75 (2002), 209–37

INDEX

Titles in the series

*Sir Matthew Hale, 1609–1676: Law, Religion and Natural Philosophy**
ALAN CROMARTIE

*Henry Parker and the English Civil War: The Political Thought of the Public's 'Privado'**
MICHAEL MENDLE

*Protestantism and Patriotism: Ideologies and the Making of English Foreign Policy, 1650–1668**
STEVEN C. A. PINCUS

*Gender in Mystical and Occult Thought: Behmenism and its Development in England**
B. J. GIBBONS

*William III and the Godly Revolution**
TONY CLAYDON

*Law-Making and Society in Late Elizabethan England: The Parliament of England, 1584–1601**
DAVID DEAN

*The House of Lords in the Reign of Charles II**
ANDREW SWATLAND

Conversion, Politics and Religion in England, 1580–1625
MICHAEL C. QUESTIER

*Politics, Religion and the British Revolutions: The Mind of Samuel Rutherford**
JOHN COFFEY

*King James VI and I and the Reunion of Christendom**
W. B. PATTERSON

*The English Reformation and the Laity: Gloucestershire, 1540–1580**
CAROLINE LITZENBERGER

*Godly Clergy in Early Stuart England: The Caroline Puritan Movement, c. 1620–1643**
TOM WEBSTER

*Prayer Book and People in Elizabethan and Early Stuart England**
JUDITH MALTBY

Sermons at Court, 1559–1629: Religion and Politics in Elizabethan and Jacobean Preaching
PETER E. MCCULLOUGH

*Dismembering the Body Politic: Partisan Politics in England's Towns, 1650–1730**
PAUL D. HALLIDAY

Women Waging Law in Elizabethan England
TIMOTHY STRETTON

*Also published as a paperback